HOW DRUGS INFLUENCE BEHAVIOR

A Neuro-Behavioral Approach

Jaime Diaz

Department of Psychology
Interdisciplinary Program in Behavioral Neuroscience
University of Washington

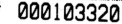

Prentice Hall, Upper Saddle River, New Jersey 07458

Library of Congress Cataloging-in-Publication Data

Diaz, Jaime.
    How drugs influence behavior : a neuro behavioral approach / Jaime Diaz.
        p   cm.
    Includes bibliographical references and index.
    ISBN 0-02-328764-0
    1. Neuropsychopharmacology.   I. Title.
    [DNLM: 1. Behavior—drug effects.   2. Central Nervous System Agents—
    pharmacology.   3. Behavior—drug effects—examination
    questions.   QV   77   D542h   1997]
    RM315.D496   1997
    615'.78—dc20
    DNLM/DLC
    for Library of Congress   96-35333
                                                                        CIP

Editor in chief: *Pete Janzow*
Assistant editor: *Nicole Signoretti*
Director of production and manufacturing: *Barbara Kittle*
Managing editor: *Bonnie Biller/Fran Russello*
Editorial/production supervision: *Publisher Studio*
Manufacturing manager: *Nick Sklitsis*
Buyer: *Tricia Kenny*
Cover director: *Jayne Conte*
Illustrator: *Publisher Studio*
Copy editor: *Publisher Studio*
Marketing manager: *Michael Alread*

This book was set in 10/12 Times Roman by NK Graphics
and was printed and bound by Courier Companies, Inc.
The cover was printed by Phoenix Color Corp.

© 1997 by Prentice-Hall, Inc.
Simon & Schuster/A Viacom Company
Upper Saddle River, New Jersey 07458

Printed in the United States of America
10   9   8   7   6   5   4   3   2   1

ISBN   0-02-328764-0

Prentice-Hall International (UK) Limited, *London*
Prentice-Hall of Australia Pty. Limited, *Sydney*
Prentice-Hall of Canada Inc., *Toronto*
Prentice-Hall Hispanoamericana, S.A., *Mexico*
Prentice-Hall of India Private Limited, *New Delhi*
Prentice-Hall of Japan, Inc., *Tokyo*
Simon & Schuster Asia Pte. Ltd., *Singapore*
Editora Prentice-Hall do Brasil, Ltda., *Rio de Janeiro*

Dedicated to My Parents

CONTENTS

2 BASIC NEUROPHYSIOLOGY: HOW THE BRAIN MEDIATES BEHAVIOR   24

8   STIMULANTS: DRUGS THAT ENERGIZE   154

9   DRUGS USED TO TREAT MENTAL DISORDERS   190

11   DRUG INTAKE DURING PREGNANCY   245

PREFACE

Drugs, in one form or another, have always been an important part of most cultures. The profound effect certain drugs have on behavior has ignited popular curiosity and prompted a scientific search for the brain mechanisms that might be altered with drugs. I have always been fascinated by how the brain works to mediate our behavior. Early in my career, I directed my research and academic pursuits to learning how drugs alter brain functioning and thereby alter a person's behavior. As an active neuroscientist, I am fortunate to be able to directly participate in the discipline of behavioral neuroscience. In the last few decades, there have been some amazing findings that have forged a better understanding about how drugs may be altering normal brain functioning. It is from this enthusiasm that I developed an undergraduate curriculum to examine these issues. Subsequently, my efforts led to this book.

I have found there are two principal challenges when teaching about the behavioral consequences of drugs. The first concerns the audience; the second regards one's outlook or mind-set when addressing these issues.

The main challenge I have found in teaching about how drugs alter behavior relates to the surprisingly large number of students interested in drugs and behavior who were not in premedical, biology, or physiology programs. Traditionally, any course of study about drugs has required students to have extensive prior training in chemistry and physiology. However, there are many people who lack this specific intensive training but who want to learn about the behavioral consequences of drugs.

Nevertheless, an understanding of the fundamental concepts of pharmacology and neurophysiology is essential in the study of drugs and behavior. The challenge, then, is to teach the basic principles of pharmacology and neurophysiology in a way that the person who is motivated to learn will be able not only to understand them but also to apply them to the issues surrounding drugs and behavior. This is one of the prime objectives of this book. Moreover, the number of individuals who are motivated to learn about drugs and behavior is far greater than the number of individuals who may actually be enrolled in colleges or universities. These people might include an attorney who seeks preliminary information for a case, a social worker who wants to better understand his or her client's behavior, or a concerned parent who wants to keep abreast of the latest developments in this vital field. My book will help all of these individuals learn the behavioral consequences of drugs.

Another challenge concerns the approach to how drugs alter behavior. One can examine these issues from a variety of viewpoints, each significant in its own right. However, when one considers that the single most important organ for the expression of behavior is the brain, understanding certain behavioral concepts becomes imperative. One of the most important of these concepts is set and setting. The expectation of the user and the immediate environment in which a drug is taken are two critical factors in behavioral expression following ingestion of a drug. While the pharmacology of a drug and the physiological changes that particular drug induces are important considerations, one must also consider learning and the resultant expectations of a user when considering behavior. It is this concept of set and setting that will endure throughout the specific drug topics in this book. There are numerous examples of how higher-order brain processing, typically in the cerebral cortex, can alter brain functioning, and it is imperative to remember this principle when examining the ways in which drugs alter behavior.

For the classroom professor, I have presented the chapters in this text in the order that I teach them in my classes. The logic of this presentation has evolved over a decade of experimentation, as I attempted to fashion a curriculum that would maximize the learning experience of undergraduates who were not biology majors. Each chapter attempts to illustrate specific principles about behavioral neuropharmacology in a sequence that seems to facilitate students' understanding of the salient issues. One of the outcomes I have observed is the cumulative building of students' confidence and sophistication concerning drugs and behavior. This, in turn, provides students with enough confidence to read original literature. Because the field is constantly expanding, I encourage students to refer to journal articles whenever possible. Of course, I would never presume to impose a specific curriculum on any teacher; I simply offer this particular sequence of topics as a suggestion for consideration, because it has worked for the student populations I have taught. I eagerly await teachers' comments about how this book has served them, and I welcome suggestions about how this curriculum might be altered.

To the students—whether or not you are formally enrolled in a college or university—I congratulate you for your interest in this vital topic. For students who are enrolled in a class: You probably did not have to take this course; you decided to take it as an elective. This alone distinguishes you from many other students. By enrolling in a course about drugs and behavior, you have demonstrated that you wish to learn about these issues in a formal classroom setting. For those motivated readers who are not enrolled in a college or university, you have shown that you are curious enough about drugs and behavior to take the time to learn about these issues. To all students, feed and encourage your curiosity and sense of purpose. The field of behavioral pharmacology is an exciting and important field. As you read this book and become more aware of the issues surrounding drugs and behavior, you will see that many of these issues are constantly in the news media. Indeed, for many, the principles you learn will be useful on a day-to-day basis. Do not be intimidated by the medical jargon and physiological principles. You can and will learn what you need to understand about how drugs alter behavior. Remain logical. Always question and seek resolution to those issues that may be confusing at first. Realize that one of the most significant outcomes of a course like this is that you can delve deeper into these issues and continue to keep yourself informed. As new findings appear, you will read more, ask more questions, and be able to keep up with information about drugs.

At the beginning of each chapter, I have outlined the general issues that will be addressed, so you will have an idea of what will be discussed in that particular chapter. Likewise, at the end of each chapter, there is a practice review exam so you can test yourself and gain a better sense of how well you have learned the issues in that chapter. Make use of these tools. Even though they may take some effort and time, they will help you in the long run.

There are many people I must thank for their contributions in making this book a reality. I thank Drs. Alan Marlatt, Bill George, and Alan Unis for the time they spent reading this manuscript and the suggestions they provided. I also thank the editing staff at Prentice Hall for their incredible patience. In particular, I would like to thank Nicole Signoretti for leading me through the unfamiliar corridors of this process. I also appreciate the extensive manuscript reading by and suggestions of outside reviewers. Their comments and suggestions kept me focused. Finally and foremost, I would like to thank my family, especially my wife Marie, for her support and incisive editing. She could always improve my copy and was an essential asset during this entire project. I also would like to thank my children for their patience and for accommodating my writing schedule as well as they did.

Jaime Diaz, Ph.D.
November 1995

CHAPTER ONE
BASIC PHARMACOLOGY:
How Drugs Enter, Navigate Through, and Exit the Body

GENERAL ISSUES ADDRESSED IN THIS CHAPTER

- Definition of a "drug"
- How a drug can be introduced into the body
- Once inside the body, how a drug is distributed throughout the body and eventually excreted
- Dynamics and impact on the behavior of drug molecules that interact with certain receptors

INTRODUCTION

We must begin with the fundamental question: What is a "drug"? The definition of a substance that should be considered a drug is not without some controversy. For our purposes, the following rather large-scope definition seems appropriate. A drug is any exogenous substance or compound. By exogenous, I mean originating outside of the body. Notice that this particular definition would include food stuffs as drugs. Often the distinction between food and drugs is not clear. Consider that for some, sliced mushrooms can enhance a salad or steak—for others, certain mushrooms would enhance a music concert by inducing hallucinations. Clearly, there is an active component in the hallucinogenic mushroom that is not found in the garden-variety mushroom. However, the presence of an active component that may cause physiological changes does not always resolve the issue of whether or not a substance should be considered a drug. Take, for example, the case of a drug that has perhaps the longest history of use—alcohol. Despite the powerful physiological effects alcohol has, especially on the brain, many still consider it a food. In fact, our laws deal quite differently with alcohol than they do with other drugs. Thus, we will use the broader definition of drug, stated above.

Ingesting a drug leads to a logical series of dynamic events that can be outlined as follows:

1. A drug is introduced into the body;
2. The drug is distributed throughout the body;
3. The drug is often but not always distributed to certain body compartments that will biotransform it, which means the molecular structure of the drug is changed;
4. The drug is excreted from the body as soon as it comes into contact with the body compartments that are involved in excretion;
5. As soon as the drug is introduced into the system and for its duration inside the body (even while it is being excreted), the drug molecule population interacts with whatever structures recognize it. These structures are called receptors.

In summary, then, a drugs enters the body, it is distributed throughout the body, it is excreted either in a changed or an unchanged form, and the entire time it is in the body it is interacting with receptors.

Now, for there to be a particular outcome, behavioral or otherwise, following the ingestion of a drug, the drug must be present in sufficiently high concentrations at certain receptors. Drugs that influence behavior typically will interact with receptors in the brain, thus the discussions in the following chapters will focus on those classes of drugs that act on brain receptors.

Let us examine more closely each of the events outlined above.

ROUTES OF ADMINISTRATION: HOW DRUGS ENTER THE SYSTEM

The digestive system is a wonderfully efficient system for the intake of nutrients and for the expulsion of waste products. It is the digestive system that is critical in distinguishing the two main routes of drug administration: enteral and parenteral.

Enteral Routes

Enteral routes of drug administration are those routes that use the alimentary canal ("enteron" is the Greek word for "gut"). One should not consider enteral synonymous with oral. There are two principal enteral routes of administration:

1. Oral—The easiest, most ancient route of drug administration—namely, swallowing it. While clearly one of the most convenient methods of drug intake, it has some major limitations. First, oral drug administration is dependent upon a person being willing and able to swallow. An unconscious or uncooperative person makes this route a difficult choice. Second, if a person has an irritable stomach and is vomiting, he or she will be unable to keep a drug dose down. Third, depending on the contents in the stomach, the absorption from an oral route will be variable. Finally, the stomach is a rather hostile acid environment that may interfere with the absorption of certain types of drugs.

2. Rectal—One can use the other side of the alimentary canal for an enteral drug administration with the use of special suppositories. For example, a young infant, for whom vomiting is a common occurrence, may have a drugs administered via a suppository. The main limitation of this route is the tremendous variability of absorption, depending on the presence of materials at the administration site as well as the speed of intestinal movement.

Parenteral Routes

Parenteral routes of drug administration are all of those routes that do not make use of the alimentary canal. There are several types of parenteral administration:

1. Injection Route—The invention of the hypodermic syringe revolutionized drug administration. There are several types of injection routes:
   a. Intravenous (IV) means directly putting a drug into the blood system. This is one of the fastest ways to get drugs into the brain. The main advantage of this route is the accuracy of the drug dosage and its speed. However, this is a dangerous route of drug administration. With enteral oral administration there is often the possibility of inducing the person to vomit, or to pump out the contents of a person's stomach in the event of a toxic or an allergic reaction to a drug. However, with the parenteral IV administration, once a drug is administered, it cannot be retrieved. So, in the case of an allergic or toxic reaction, the person could quickly be put into a

life-threatening situation. In addition, IV administrations have a high risk of infection if sterile procedures are not followed. In some populations of drug users there is the risk of contracting the Acquired Immunodeficiency Syndrome (AIDS) virus.

b. Intramuscular (IM) means the injection of a drug into a muscle mass, usually the arm or buttocks. The absorption of a dose is slower than an IV but often that is desirable in certain medicating situations.

c. Subcutaneous (SQ) means "under the skin." A drug dose literally is put under the skin, usually by injection. However, there are "implants," drugs in solid form, that are placed without a needle, under the skin, to dissolve slowly. An example of this is the Norplant® contraceptive "spikes," inserted under the skin in a woman's arm to deliver months of contraceptive medication.

d. Central nervous system administration, where in certain situations in pain management drugs are injected directly into the central nervous system, usually into the spinal cord. In these cases, the medical procedures are called epidural or spinal anesthetics. An epidural is the injection of an analgesic drug just outside the protective layers surrounding the spinal cord. A spinal is the injection of an analgesic directly onto the spinal cord. Both of these types of injections are designed to keep the drug dose confined to a relatively small area. The common analagous situation in the peripheral nervous system is when a dentist injects Novocaine or a similar agent directly onto certain nerves to anesthetize a tooth for a procedure such as filling a cavity.

2. Pulmonary Route—Inhaling a drug and utilizing the lungs is another parenteral route. Of course, the drug has to be in a form suitable for inhalation. A typical drug that uses this route is the gaseous anesthetic called ether. Free base (or crack) cocaine use and glue sniffing are other examples of pulmonary routes of administration. In both of these examples, absorption of the drug is quite rapid.

Tobacco smoking is a peculiar route of drug administration. Initially, it is a true pulmonary route of administration, however, the situation may change with repeated dosing. Chronic inhalation of smoke actually coats the lining of the lungs with tar as well as various other substances. Over time, this would essentially create an artificial barrier and may make smoking a topical route, which will be discussed next.

3. Topical Route—This route involves physically laying a drug onto a body surface, usually but not always a mucous membrane of some sort. There are several topical routes.

a. Sublingual means placing a drug under the tongue. Heart patients who take nitroglycerin capsules for angina are using this topical route. Although this is a topical route, some of it may be swallowed, making it a partial enteral route. Chewing tobacco (or smokeless tobacco) is another example of a sublingual route, where the tobacco is typically held in the side of the mouth or under the lower lip, not usually under the tongue.

b. Intranasal involves an intense inhalation of a drug, usually in powdered form, directly under a nostril. Taken this way, the drug does not reach the lungs but rather comes to lay on the olfactory mucousal membranes of the nose. Cocaine snorting is an example of this route.

c. On the skin, means drugs that can be absorbed directly from skin contact. Certain pesticides can be absorbed from skin contact. Another substance called dimethyl sulfoxide (DMSO), an incredibly efficient solvent, can be readily absorbed through the skin. Drugs can be dissolved in DMSO, making this substance a unique vehicle. Other examples of a topical route on the skin are the various drug patches used clinically to treat a variety of conditions. Specifically, there are drug patches that contain seasick medication, nicotine patches for people who are trying to break a smoking habit, and patches with painkillers for chronic pain patients.

TABLE 1.1   Summary of the Routes of Administration

ENTERAL ROUTES	PARENTERAL ROUTES
Oral	Injection Routes
Rectal	Intravenous (IV)
	Intramuscular (IM)
	Subcutaneous (SQ)
	Central nervous system
	Pulmonary
	Topical
	Sublingual
	Intranasal
	On the skin

DRUG DISTRIBUTION: HOW DRUGS NAVIGATE THROUGH THE BODY

Now that we have reviewed the various ways in which drugs can be introduced into the body, we should consider how drugs spread throughout the body.

It is important to remember that the term *drug* refers to a substance that is composed of molecules that have a characteristic shape. The dynamics of how a particular drug is distributed throughout the body, however, focus on the movement and fate of the actual number of drug molecules that have been introduced into the body. The difference between a low dose and a high dose of a drug is the difference in the number of drug molecules. The principal force that underlies the distribution of drug molecules is concentration gradient force.

Concentration Gradient Force

Let us conduct a simple experiment, illustrated in Figure 1–1. If there was a chamber with a divider down the middle and one side was filled with marbles, what do you suppose would happen if that divider was removed? The marbles would run into the empty side until both sides were somewhat even. This is an example of concentration gradient force. The marbles were running "down" their concentration gradient. For some, opening the door to a stuffed closet often illustrates this principle as well. The same forces operate on particles in a solution. Figure 1–2 shows a similar experiment as Figure 1–1, except the chamber is full of water and the barrier that divides it into two compartments will allow water to pass and has holes big enough to allow the particles to also pass through the barrier. In this case, when a solution full of these particles is poured into one compartment, initially that compartment will contain all of the particles (Figure 1–2A). The particles will eventually distribute themselves fairly evenly in both sides of the chamber (Figures 1–2B and 1–2C). The particles had a concentration gradient force that promoted their movement from an area of high density to areas of less density.

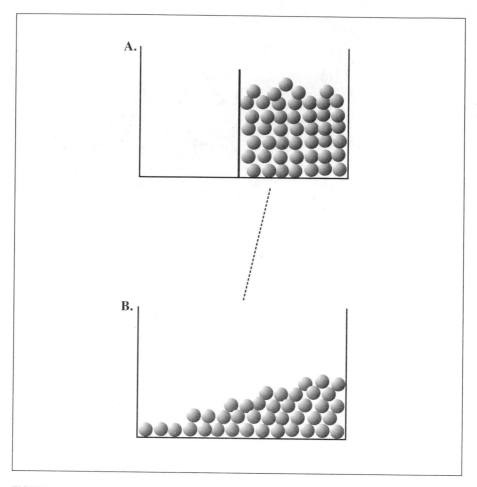

FIGURE 1–1   A Simple Demonstration of Concentration Gradient Force

Figure 1–2 is a metaphor for the forces involved in drug distribution throughout the body. A solution containing drug molecules is first introduced into one compartment, creating a high-concentration gradient. The drug molecules will then move (or distribute) down its concentration gradient to the compartment adjacent to it, until there is a balance between the two compartments.

Body Compartments

Figure 1–2 may illustrate concentration gradient force, but it does not adequately model drug distribution because the body is not simply two compartments in contact with one another (Figure 1–3A). The body is made up of many compartments (Figure 1–3B). Each organ can be considered a discrete compartment. In addition, there are two other tissue compartments that are especially important: fat and blood.

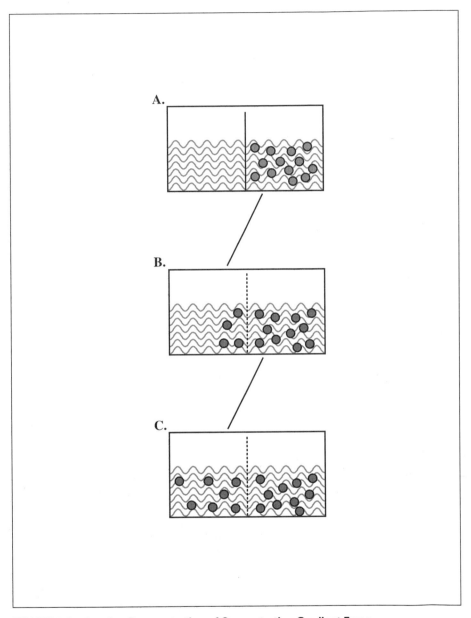

FIGURE 1–2 Another Demonstration of Concentration Gradient Force
A. A water chamber is divided with a permeable membrane that would allow water to pass but not large particles. If large particles are dissolved on one side they will remain on that side.
B. If that permeable membrane is removed, the particles will tend to diffuse to the other side.
C. The particles in the solution will distribute themselves fairly equally throughout the chamber.

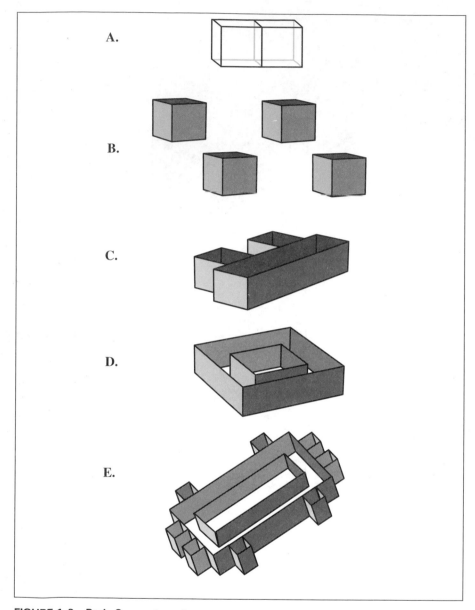

FIGURE 1–3   Body Compartments

A. The two-compartment model, seen in Figure 1–2

B. The body is composed of various separate discrete compartments, which can be illustrated by "boxes."

C. The compartment of blood or circulation is the one body compartment that touched all other body compartments.

D. The blood or circulation compartment can be better illustrated as a circular trough with all of the other body compartments attached.

There are well-described depots of fat cells throughout the body that collectively can be considered one compartment. As we shall see in later chapters, this compartment of total body fat plays an important role in the dynamics of drugs that specifically affect the brain.

The other notable compartment is blood—the circulatory system. One can consider the blood compartment as a continually flowing stream in a closed loop. Blood functions not only to circulate nutrients and oxygen to all of the cells of the body, but also to carry waste products away from the cells to other compartments that will filter and expel these waste products from the body. Let us follow the blood for one cycle. From the heart, the blood supply is carried by large vessels that have elastic and connective tissues surrounding them. These relatively large "organic pipes" split up into more and more branches that are increasingly smaller in diameter until they become only one cell thick and are now called capillaries. The capillaries form a dense network called capillary beds in the individual tissue compartments. It is at the capillary that exchanges between cells and blood of oxygen and carbon dioxide, nutrients, and cellular waste products are made. The capillaries then begin to collect, and the vessels, now termed veins, become larger and larger as they return to the heart for a pass through the lungs to dump their carbon dioxide and pick up more oxygen. Returning to the heart from the lungs, the blood supply is pumped for the next loop through the body.

Whether a discrete organ, or a tissue mass like bone or fat, each body compartment is made up of cells. Every cell must have nutrients and a way to expel waste products. Thus, all of the compartments in our body have one feature in common: They all must make contact and interact with the blood compartment. This is a key concept for drug distribution, because regardless of the route of administration, a drug that has been introduced into the body will find its way into the blood compartment. In Figure 1–3C, the blood compartment is illustrated as a long trough that has all of the other body compartments attached to it. However, since the blood compartment is actually a loop of continually flowing liquid, the closed loop in Figure 1–3D with various compartments attached at different sites is a better model. Looking at this preceding model, we arrive at Figure 1–4.

Absorption. The time from the administration of a drug to the time that population of drug molecules enters the blood is called absorption. The speed with which absorption occurs depends a great deal on the route of administration. Absorption is immediate with an IV dose, because the drug is administered directly into the blood compartment. The absorption following inhalation of certain drugs can be almost as rapid as IV administration, due to the natural efficiency of the respiratory system. All other routes of administration, parenteral as well as enteral, go through a significantly longer period of absorption. For example, a drug that is taken orally will spend some time in the stomach and perhaps in the intestines as it is being absorbed into the circulatory system. Another example would be a parenteral administration in which the drug is given as an injection in the muscle. That particular population of drug molecules will rely on blood flow through that muscle tissue for its entry into

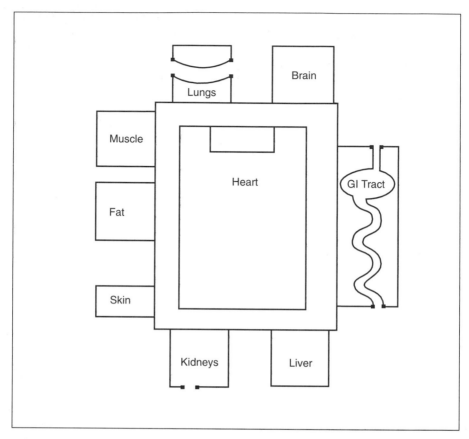

FIGURE 1–4   A Complex Body Compartment Model
Looking at the model proposed in Figure 1–3 from the top, one might see this complex of contiguous compartments.

the circulation. However, regardless of the route of administration, once in the circulation, a population of drug molecules has access to virtually every compartment of the body. Let us now examine the actual entry point into body compartments—the capillary.

Capillaries.   Capillaries are not solid tubes. Like any other part of our bodies, capillaries are made up of cells (Figure 1–5A). Even though they are tightly packed to form thin "pipes," there are gaps between the cells (Figures 1–5B and 1–5C). Usually there is ample room between the cells that form the capillaries to allow small things like nutrients and drug molecules to move out of the blood. To be sure, large things like blood cells and proteins are too large to fit through these gaps and thus remain in the blood (Figures 1–6A and 1–6B). In the circulation, there will be a portion of a given population of drug molecules that will attach, that is, "bind," to large proteins in the blood, typically albumin. These drug molecules are said to be "bound," as opposed to "free." Only the free drug molecules are able to leave the circulation. Because the proteins to which the bound drug molecules are attached are too large to leave the capillaries, the bound drug molecules are essentially trapped in the blood compartment. The ratio of bound-to-free drug molecules is constant and is maintained dynamically, which means that as free drug molecules move out of the

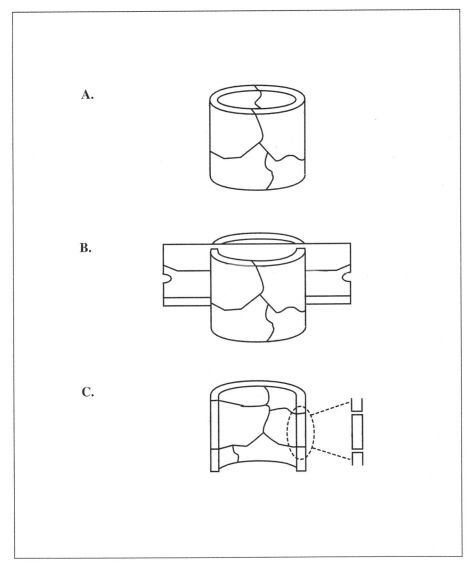

FIGURE 1–5 Capillaries
A. In a small section of a capillary a "tube" is formed by cells.
B. When this "tube" is cut in half, a close examination of the "walls" of the capillary reveals that there are gaps between these cells.

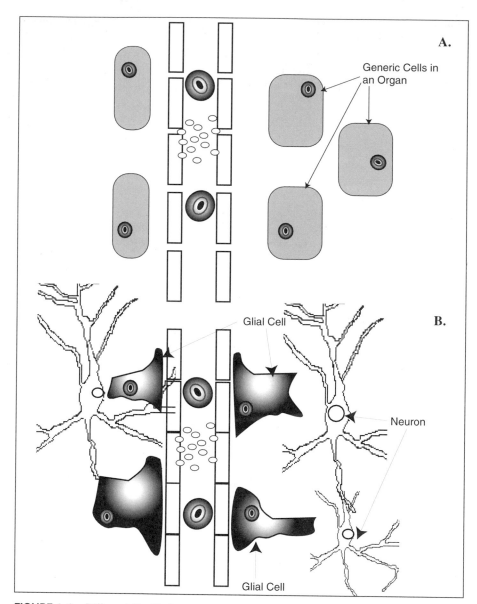

FIGURE 1–6   Different Capillaries

A. Capillaries in areas outside of the brain have rather large gaps between the cells that make up the capillary, so most molecules can move fairly easily from the blood and into the extracellular fluid around the cells.

B. Inside the brain, the gaps between the cells that make up the capillary are so tight that molecules cannot exit the circulation through the gap. In addition, there are specialized cells, called glial cells, that cover a great deal of the capillary surface. Neurons do not usually have direct access to brain capillaries. So, for a molecule to leave the circulation and enter the brain, it must literally go through the cells that make up the brain capillaries and through the glial cells.

circulation, some bound drug molecules detach from the protein and become free drug molecules. In the following chapters, the discussions about drug molecules will concern only free drug molecules.

Cell membrane. When there is a population of drug molecules in the circulation, there is a concentration gradient that is very similar to the one illustrated in Figure 1–2. The drug molecule population in the circulation will move out wherever it can into all the compartments in its path. Once outside the circulation, the drug molecules are in the fluid surrounding the cells of that particular compartment. These drug molecules can then interact with any drug receptors that are on the surface of the cells in that compartment. However, if the drug molecules are to enter that cell, they must cross through that cell's membrane, which poses a significant problem.

Cells are made up of a double layer of lipids—fats. Figure 1–7 shows how this is arranged. These membranes have holes called pores. The normally existing pores in cell membranes are too small to allow typically sized drug molecules to pass. Therefore, unless there is a specific transport mechanism for that drug molecule in the membrane, to enter a cell that drug molecule has to go through the membrane, which means it has to go through a double layer of fat. Only drug molecules that can dissolve in fat can accomplish crossing a cell membrane. Thus, an important characteristic of drug molecules is their ability to dissolve in fat, which is called "lipid solubility." It is a drug's lipid solubility that will determine its ability to cross cell membranes. The greater its ability to dissolve in fat, the easier it is for that drug molecule to cross the double layer of fat in the cell membrane.

Since drugs that influence behavior typically alter brain functioning in some fashion, we should direct our attention to those drugs that have the ability to enter the brain compartment. However, due to a unique protective system, it is much more difficult to enter the brain compartment than any other body compartment.

BLOOD-BRAIN BARRIER

The adult brain in any mammal has a fixed number of neurons. In fact, there are no new neurons formed in the brain after late adolescence. So, in adult animals, a neuron that dies is not replaced with a new neuron. Therefore, the brain must protect its fixed number of neurons from any influence, toxic or otherwise. However, the brain also has a demanding need for nutrients and oxygen, so blood flow through the brain is quite high, which increases the risk of some toxic agent entering the brain. To solve this dilemma between protecting the brain and still satisfying a high need for nutrients, nature evolved a "blood-brain barrier."

Components to the Blood-Brain Barrier

There are two components to the blood-brain barrier: 1. the capillary beds that feed the brain are specialized; and 2. the presence of a special type of cell—the glial cell.

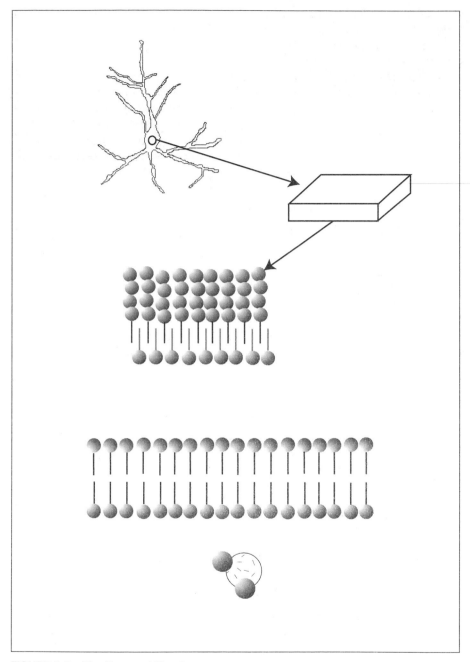

FIGURE 1–7   The Neuronal Membrane
If one were to take a section of the neuron's membrane, one would find that it is made up
of a phospholipid bilayer. The "balls" represent phosphates and the "tails" represent
lipids. This is the barrier that a drug molecule must cross to enter a neuron.

The cells that form the brain capillaries have virtually no gaps between them. These cells are so tightly packed that drug molecules cannot pass between them. In fact, the space between these cells is smaller than the pores in a membrane. The result of these tight gaps is that a molecule must go through the membrane of the capillary cells to get out of circulation and into the brain compartment. In addition, neurons rarely make direct contact with capillaries. The brain capillaries are wrapped by glial cells that then make contact with neurons. Thus, for a molecule to enter the brain compartment, it must: 1. go through the cell that forms the capillary, which means it must cross two membranes (one to enter and one to exit the capillary cell); and 2. go through the glial cell, which means it must cross two additional membranes (one to enter and one to exit the glial cell). (See Figure 1–6). Since cell membranes are made up of a double layer of fat, only molecules that are highly lipid-soluble can enter the brain compartment. In fact, the drugs we will be examining in this course are all highly lipid-soluble.

DRUG BIOTRANSFORMATION AND EXCRETION

Functions of the Kidneys and Liver

The kidneys filter out waste in the blood and collect it in the bladder as urine for eventual excretion. This process is the main mechanism for removing drug molecules from the blood. However, there is a problem with drugs that are able to cross to the brain compartment. Since these drugs are so highly lipid-soluble, it is difficult for the kidneys to hold onto them long enough to excrete them. After they are collected, these molecules simply cross back into the circulation before excretion can occur. The function of the liver thus becomes a major factor in the excretion of these highly lipid-soluble drug molecules.

The liver has several critical functions, two of which are mobilizing newly ingested nutrients and protecting the body from toxic substances in the blood. So important are these two processes that the blood supply from the gastrointestinal (GI) tract is uniquely routed to the liver. The capillaries in the GI tract collect into larger vessels, but instead of returning to the heart, they form another capillary bed in the liver to gain access to the liver cells that have the enzyme systems which can detoxify harmful substances.

With regard to drug molecules in the blood, the liver performs the critical function of transforming highly lipid-soluble drugs into a form the kidneys can excrete. The enzymatic biotransformation that occurs in the liver usually results in a drug molecule that has been changed from a highly lipid-soluble molecule to a less lipid-soluble (more water-soluble) molecule the kidneys can contain and excrete. However, there are some instances when the liver transformation results in a changed molecule that is still highly lipid-soluble and able to exert effects on the brain. These molecules are called "active metabolites."

Thus, the primary process of excreting a dose of drug molecules that are psychoactive involves two steps: 1. the biotransformation of molecules by liver enzymes into a less lipid-soluble (more water-soluble) form; and 2. the filtering from the blood and collection into the urine for subsequent excretion from the body.

There are occasional instances where some drug molecules can be kept in the urine long enough to be excreted. These drug molecules are said to pass unchanged in the urine. Usually this does not account for a significant amount of a drug dose. One of the more interesting exceptions to this is the hallucinogenic agent in *Amanita muscaria,* a mushroom indigenous to the Siberian area. The amount of psychoactive substance in the urine of a person who has eaten this mushroom is so high that, according to legend, tribal members would drink the urine of the person experiencing hallucinations after eating the mushroom, and would then themselves hallucinate (see chapter 10).

The kidneys are not the only avenue for drug excretion. The lungs provide another mechanism that is typical for the gaseous anesthetics, like ether and halothale, which are inhaled (i.e., parenterally administered, via a pulmonary route). These particular drugs are so lipid-soluble that they are not only absorbed from the lungs but also can be excreted in relatively large amounts with each expired breath. Thus, this "blowing off" via the lungs is a principal method of excretion. Some of the drug molecules are excreted via the liver and kidney systems as well. It should be noted here that alcohol also can be consistently detected in expired breath, which is the basis for Breathalyzer® examinations in the field, performed by police officers to estimate the blood alcohol level of a person suspected of intoxication. The amounts are exceedingly small, therefore this is not a main mechanism of excretion for alcohol, as we will see in chapter 5.

There are two other mechanisms in which drug molecules leave the body. Liver cells secrete about a quart of bile each day, which is then released into the gut. In the process of biotransformation in the liver cells, some drug molecules may accumulate in the bile to be later released in the intestines. While there may be detectable levels of a drug in the feces as a result of this process, this is not a principal method of drug excretion. One notable exception to this is the extremely high levels of marijuana metabolites found in feces (see chapter 6). Likewise, in the course of distribution throughout the body, drug molecules will find their way into fluid compartments like sweat and mother's milk. As is the case with bile excretion, this is not a primary method of excretion as much as it is a distribution of drug molecules to those particular fluid compartments.

HALF-LIFE AND CLEARANCE

In trying to understand how a drug will influence behavior, it is critical to monitor two parameters: 1. the amount of the drug in the body following a dose; and 2. how quickly the body is excreting the drug. In other words, how long is the population of drug molecules going to remain in the body? To answer these questions, the blood compartment is typically monitored by taking time samples of blood to describe the changing concentrations of the drug in the blood. This data is usually expressed as the half-life of the drug. In general, the half-life of a drug is the time it takes to clear half of an initial dose from the blood. It takes approximately four and one-half half-lifes to clear about 94 percent of a given dose. This is important to know, because if dosing occurs before the body has had the opportunity to clear a drug, then the body will necessarily accumulate drug molecules. The four and one-half half-life rule of thumb suggests that if one doses before four and one-half half-lifes, the drug will accumulate in the body. As we will see in subsequent chapters, this has important implications in predicting behavior.

RECEPTORS

As soon as a drug is administered and for however long it remains in the body, those drug molecules will interact with whatever drug receptors are available. Once a drug does gets into the circulation and has access to all body compartments, that population of drug molecules also will have access to any and all drug receptors. What exactly are drug receptors? There are two fundamental criteria for calling a structure a drug receptor. First, the drug molecule must be able to attach or bind to this structure. Second, the presence of the bound drug molecule on this structure will alter some normally occurring physiological event. Remember that drug molecules may bind to blood proteins (i.e., bound drug). This binding does not lead to any alteration in any physiological event, so these proteins are not considered drug receptors per se. Typically drug receptors are proteins, and there are at least three distinctive types of drug receptors.

Types of Drug Receptors

1. Receptors for Neurotransmitters—Nerve cells, whether inside the brain or not, communicate by releasing a substance onto its targets. This substance is called a neurotransmitter, and the target surface has specialized proteins that bind neurotransmitters (see chapter 2). Drug molecules also can bind to these proteins and change the normal interactions that result when the neurotransmitter is bound to these receptors.
2. Enzymes—Certain enzymes can bind drug molecules and have their activity changed as a result. In some cases, the normal activity of the enzyme is blocked.
3. Membrane Transport Mechanisms—Some cells have specialized proteins in their membranes that have the function of transporting specific items across the cell membrane. Certain drugs can bind to these proteins and prevent this cellular movement.

"Main Effect" and "Side Effect"

It is important to note that the various types of drug receptors exist throughout the entire body. A population of drug molecules in the circulation will bind to as many receptors as its concentration gradients and absolute numbers will allow and, thus, will exert a variety of different effects. A drug never has a single effect, but rather multiple effects. The terms "main effect" and "side effect" are often used to designate a particular outcome to the administration of a drug, compared to the other outcomes. Understand that while main effect may refer to the most apparent or most intense outcome of a drug, this term usually reflects the outcome that is of interest to the author—one person's main effect is another person's side effect. For example, one effect of antihistamines is relief of some cold symptoms, and another effect is drowsiness. Two medications, each with antihistamines, will have different literature concerning main and side effects. In the case of a cold medication, the relief of a runny nose is a main effect and the user is cautioned about the side effect of drowsiness. However, in a sleep aid medication like Sominex® or Nytol®, the main effect is considered drowsiness. Be cautious of these terms.

Let us reexamine the statement in the beginning of this chapter, with drug receptors in mind:

> . . . for there to be a particular outcome, behavioral or otherwise, following the ingestion of a drug, the drug must be present in sufficiently high concentrations at certain receptors.

The distinct effect a drug will have is the result of various groups of drug receptors in various areas in the body detecting drug molecules and changing the normal functioning of that particular system. Furthermore, the greater the number of drug molecules administered (i.e., the higher the dose) the greater the number of receptors that are affected and the greater the overall drug effect. Thus, the dose of a drug can often be correlated to the intensity of any given effect. This relationship is described in the dose response curve, and it can be expressed in several ways.

DOSE RESPONSE CURVES

Intensity

One way to express dose response relationships is to examine the actually intensity of a given response to a drug. If one sees a particular response to a certain drug dose, then would that response increase in intensity if one were to give more of that drug? For example, if a certain amount of amphetamine produces a certain level of arousal, then a larger dose should produce an even greater level of arousal (Figure 1–8A illustrates this type of dose curve).

Frequency Distribution

Another way to express dose response relationships is to examine the frequency distribution of a certain response to various drug doses. In this method, one looks at the population of subjects and determines the occurrence of a certain response at different dose levels. Figure 1–8C shows that expressing a dose response curve as a frequency distribution will take the shape of a bell curve. Just how wide this curve will be will vary between drugs, but some fundamental principles illustrated by this type of curve will be consistent across various drugs. There will be a

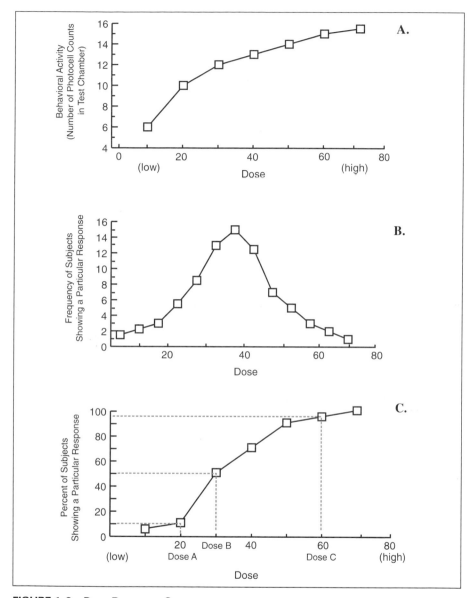

FIGURE 1–8   Dose Response Curves

A. This is a simple illustration of behavior increasing in intensity as the drug dose is increased.

B. If one selects a particular behavior, one can plot the frequency of subjects in a particular sample that illustrate this behavior at different drug doses.

C. A common dose response curve involves selecting one behavior and then plotting the cumulative frequency of the occurrence of that selected behavior as the dose is increased. This type of dose response curve helps determine the effective dose of a drug to elicit a behavior for a given percentage of a population of subjects.

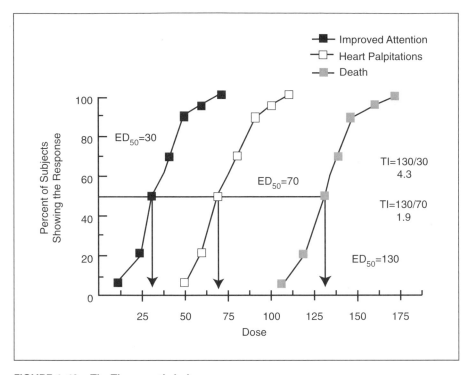

FIGURE 1–10   The Therapeutic Index
From the family of dose response curves seen in Figure 1–9, one can determine the ED_{50} values for the two behaviors and the LD_{50} for the drug. The Therapeutic Index (TI) for each of the two behaviors is calculated by dividing the LD_{50} value by the ED_{50} of the behavior in question. Notice that the larger the TI, the further away that behavioral response curve is from the lethal dose curve.

5.   Name the three classes of parenteral routes of drug administration.
6.   What is the significance of a drug entering into circulation?
7.   What are the structural components of the cell membrane?
8.   Define absorption.
9.   What is the difference between bound and free drug molecules?
10.   What is lipid solubility?
11.   What is the blood-brain barrier and how does it impact upon how drugs influence behavior?
12.   What are the two steps in getting a drug out of the body?
13.   What is the half-life of a drug and what is the significance of this value?
14.   Name the different types of drug receptors.
15.   What are the various ways to express dose response curves?
16.   What is the ED_{50} of a drug?
17.   What is the LD_{50} of a drug?
18.   What is the Therapeutic Index (TI)?

REFERENCES

The classic resource for fundamental pharmacology is:

GOODMAN, L., & GILMAN, A. (1990). *The Pharmacological Basis of Therapeutics* (8th ed.). New York: Macmillan Publishing Co.
Note: A variety of introductory pharmacology textbooks, which can provide additional information on the topics discussed in this chapter, also are available. However, these pharmacology textbooks frequently assume some prior coursework in biochemistry and physiology and may be of limited use to the novice reader.

CHAPTER TWO
BASIC NEUROPHYSIOLOGY:
How the Brain Mediates Behavior

GENERAL ISSUES ADDRESSED IN THIS CHAPTER

- Various components of the central nervous system and the peripheral nervous system
- Basic anatomy of the brain
- How certain brain areas form functional systems
- How neurons communicate
- Understanding the various dimensions of drug tolerance
- Appreciating the role of central nervous system activity, especially in learning, tolerance and withdrawal, and the mediation of behavior following drug administration.

INTRODUCTION

The single most important organ in the mediation of behavior is the brain. Every thought, emotion, pain, and pleasure we experience, everything that makes us what we are, is the result of the processing in our brain. Trying to answer the fundamental question: "What are the primary functions of the brain?" becomes rather involved. One could argue that on the most fundamental level, the brain is designed to maximize the condition of the individual, or the role of the brain is to make sure we secure and maintain the proper amounts of those items necessary for survival, that is, food, water, warmth. Certainly our bodies have robust homeostatic responses that are critical for survival. If we need food, we experience hunger, and our behavior is directed to finding food. Likewise, if we are cold, we may first activate heat-conserving behavior, like muscle shivering. If that is not enough, we then may engage in more overt behavior, like finding a warmer spot or putting on more clothes. Thus, one of the primary functions of the brain is to monitor (or sense) the external and internal environment of an individual, then respond on an unconscious and/or conscious level.

However, our behavior is much richer and more complex than maintaining survival. Humans regularly engage in many behaviors that do not seem directly related to survival, but rather to hedonics (pleasure) or secondary motivators like money or approval (i.e., doing well in school to please one's parents). Consider your behavior right now, namely reading this book. In fact, some behaviors that are altruistic not only will not satisfy any biological need but in some extreme cases will actually compromise survival. It is not within the scope of this text to resolve the question of what the motivators of human behavior are, except to recognize the staggering complexity of human behavior.

We have learned from the previous chapter the fundamental dynamics of how drugs enter, are distributed throughout the body, and are excreted. Those drugs that cause behavioral changes typically will alter basic brain functioning. If we wish to understand how drugs influence behavior, we first should consider how the brain normally operates. I urge the reader to pursue additional coursework and/or additional readings in the neurosciences to gain a more thorough understanding of the neural basis of behavior. The following is intended to be an overview of the fundamental concepts of how the central nervous system mediates behavior.

THE NERVOUS SYSTEM

The brain does not operate independently, but rather is one of several interacting systems that collectively make up the nervous system. The nervous system can be divided into two main divisions:

Central Nervous System (CNS)

The central nervous system (CNS) consists of the brain and spinal cord. This is where all sensory input terminates, where motor commands to contract muscles originate, and where final decisions concerning behavioral strategies are formulated. Subsequently, associations are made, and memories are formed and stored. This represents the highest level of information processing.

Peripheral Nervous System (PNS)

The peripheral nervous system contains those neurons outside the CNS that link the CNS to the real world in two ways: by 1. bringing information into the CNS; and 2. by carrying commands to the muscles. The PNS is made up of two subdivisions:

1. Somatic Nervous System. Certain information about the internal environment and information about the external world are conveyed to the CNS by the somatic division of the PNS. In addition, all commands from the CNS to skeletal muscle groups are also conveyed by the somatic division of the PNS.

2. Autonomic Nervous System (ANS). The ANS conveys sensory information from the body's internal organs (called the viscera) and carries output commands of the CNS to the visceral organs and smooth muscle (like the muscles that regulate the diameter of blood vessels). It is termed autonomic because most of its functioning occurs below a conscious level. For instance, we do not have to remember to increase our breathing or heart rate during exercise. The autonomic nervous system consists of:

   a. The sympathetic division which, when activated, will mediate the so-called flight or fight response that prepares a person to either fight or run in response to a sudden stressor. Heart rate goes up, the pupils dilate, and blood is shunted toward skeletal muscles and away from the muscles of digestion. This is a critical system for survival.

   b. The parasympathetic division which, when activated, will mediate the so-called rest and digest response, generally mediates the opposite of a sympathetic response, namely activation of those processes that are involved in digestion and repair.

Note that certain drugs will stimulate the sympathetic division of the ANS, in addition to any effects it may have on the CNS, and some drugs will stimulate certain aspects of the ANS and not be able to cross the blood-brain barrier to have any direct effects on the CNS. Remember that the brain monitors the internal environment of the individual as well as the external environment. If a drug elicits a sympathetic response even though it may not cross the blood-brain barrier, it will produce changes in bodily functions (like increased heart rate and respiration) the brain will detect. The brain will essentially try to make sense of the sympathetic response in the context of the events and circumstances surrounding the individual. Thus, this drug may indirectly alter brain functioning by altering the PNS.

Later in this chapter we will examine a study that directly addresses this issue. But first let us examine the basic anatomy of the brain.

BASIC NEUROANATOMY: THE ESSENTIAL GEOGRAPHY OF THE BRAIN

The brain is divided into five divisions from top to bottom. The top of the CNS is called the rostral end and the bottom is called the caudal end. The top of the box in Figure 2–1 shows the lateral (side) view of the brain. Note how the cerebral cortex covers up much of the brain. If one were to use a gigantic razor blade to slice the brain in half, right down the middle, one would be able to clearly see the five main CNS divisions. The following brief review of the major structures of the CNS will begin at the caudal (bottom) end and proceed rostrally.

Myelencephalon

The most caudal division of the brain and the division of the brain that is continuous with the spinal cord is called the myelencephalon (Figure 2–1A). Referred to as the medulla (or the medulla oblongata), this division contains a host of nuclei which sustain basic life-supporting functions. (Note that a collection or aggregate of neurons which share a common function is called a nucleus; nuclei is the plural.) There are two nuclei of particular importance to behavior in the myelencephalon: the area postrema and the nucleus of the solitary tract. The area postrema is one of the few structures in the brain that has a very weak blood-brain barrier, which allows this area to sample the blood more accurately than most of the brain. The area postrema appears to be important in the mediation of vomiting, the emetic response. The nucleus of the solitary tract is a vital link between the brain and visceral organs. It is the brain area that mediates direct parasympathetic activity in the visceral organs. In addition, the nucleus of the solitary tract receives sensory information originating in the visceral organs.

Metencephalon

The next rostral brain division is the metencephalon (Figure 2–1B) in which the pons are found on the ventral (front) side of the brain and the cerebellum is found on the dorsal (back) side of the brain. Within this brain division is a nucleus called the locus coeruleus, which is extremely important to behavior. The locus coeruleus projects to virtually every brain area and is involved with the mediation of arousal and also perhaps with the mediation of pleasure or reinforcement. The cerebellum (or "little brain") is essential for smooth and coordinated motor behavior.

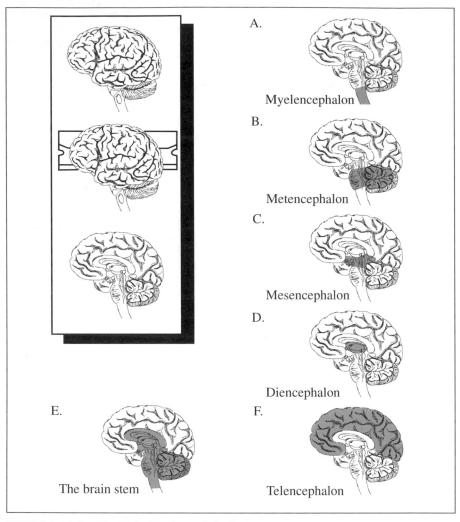

FIGURE 2–1A–F   The Main Divisions of the Brain
The five main divisions of the brain cannot be seen from a lateral view of the brain (top).
The brain must be cut in half along the midline to see these divisions (middle). From this
midline view (bottom) one can follow the major brain divisions from the spinal cord to the
top of the brain.
A. The Myelencephalon. This is the "lowest" (i.e., most caudal) brain division that is con-
tinuous with the spinal cord.
B. The Metencephalon. The next brain division "up" (i.e., rostral) consists of the pons on
the front side and the cerebellum on the back side.
C. The Mesencephalon. The next brain division is often referred to as the mid-brain.
D. The Diencephalon. The next brain division consists of the hypothalamus and thalamus.
E. Collectively, these four brain divisions make up the brain stem.
F. The Telencephalon. This is the "highest" (i.e., most rostral) brain division and consists
of the cerebral cortex and a variety of structures that are under the cortex.

Mesencephalon

The next rostral brain division is the mesencephalon (Figure 2–1C) or midbrain, in which the following nuclei reside: 1. the substantia nigra; 2. the central gray (or periaqueductal gray); and 3. the raphe nuclei. The substantia nigra is another nucleus that is critical for smooth and coordinated motor behavior. The central gray is a nucleus that is involved in the mediation of pain. The raphe nuclei are a collection of nuclei that lie along the midline of the mesencephalon and have an extensive projection pattern like the locus coeruleus. The raphe nuclei are involved with the mediation of arousal, more specifically with sleep, and with the mediation of pain.

Diencephalon

The next rostral brain division is the diencephalon (Figure 2–1D), which consists of the hypothalamus and thalamus. The thalamus is primarily involved with sensory signals and is the last stop for almost all sensory input on the way to the cerebral cortex. The thalamus is also involved in the mediation of pain and emotion in general. Virtually every motivated behavior emitted by an animal relies on the hypothalamus. The hypothalamus has been implicated in the mediation of feeding, thirst, sex, emotion, sleep, memory and learning, aggression, and so on. The hypothalamus has receptors for a variety of critical body parameters like oxygen, carbon dioxide, glucose, blood temperature, the amount of water in the cells, and blood insulin, as well as receptors for virtually every neurotransmitter in the brain. Thus, the hypothalamus directly monitors body functions and can detect what is needed. Thereby, it appears to be involved in the mediation of all functions needed for survival. Furthermore, the hypothalamus interacts with the pituitary gland to control the hormones that are secreted. It plays a major role in maintaining the appropriate hormonal environment of an animal.

Collectively, the aforementioned four divisions form the "brain stem" (Figure 2–1E) on which the remaining brain division grew and elaborated.

Telencephalon

The telencephalon (Figure 2–1F) is the most rostral division of the brain. The major structures in this division are the cerebral cortex, which is the outer surface, and several nuclei, which lie beneath the surface of the cortex. Some of the nuclei are the basal ganglia, amygdala, and hippocampus. The basal ganglia works together with other nuclei and the cerebral cortex to coordinate motor behavior. The amygdala has dense reciprocal connections with the hypothalamus and, among many other functions, is involved in the mediation of aggressive behavior. The hippocampus is a critical nucleus in the formation of memories. Finally, there is the cerebral cortex, the highest CNS structure which is involved with the most complex processing. It is here that language is processed, as is planning and such high functions as reason, logic, creativity, imagination, and certainly, learning.

FUNCTIONAL NEUROANATOMY: BRAIN SYSTEMS

In general, brain functioning can be categorized as: 1. sensory—the processing of input coming into the CNS; 2. motor—the processing and coordination of motor activity; and 3. motivational—in other words, the reason for engaging in or initiating a behavior. An important component of this motivational system is a subsystem which mediates emotion. Underlying all of these functions is a method of storing and retrieving information, that is, learning.

Specific structures throughout the CNS are anatomically connected to one another and form systems that mediate certain brain functions. There are numerous systems which are involved in the individual sensory modalities like vision, hearing, and smell, and in some of the more mechanical aspects of motor processing. For each of these systems, information is processed in certain nuclei in the brain and is conveyed to other nuclei, which in turn will process the information further and pass it along to the next nucleus, in addition to feeding back to its sources. A sensory system like vision can illustrate this process. Light is transduced in the retina and ultimately causes retinal ganglion cells to fire. The recipient of this firing is a nucleus in the thalamus called the lateral geniculate. The cells of the lateral geniculate will then project to a specific area in the cerebral cortex, which will project to at least two other areas of the cerebral cortex—thus, the perception of vision is achieved. Certainly there are other brain nuclei that receive information from the retina and lateral geniculate that are involved in other behaviors beside the perception of vision. The important point is that the various nuclei in the brain are literally interconnected into functional systems.

The collection of interconnected structures that play a significant role in the mediation of emotion is called the limbic system. These structures span the brain and include particular areas of the cerebral cortex, the hypothalamus, specific areas of the thalamus, amygdala, hippocampus, and certain mesencephalic nuclei. These structures are interconnected in an extremely complex network to produce the various aspects of what is termed "emotion." The limbic system is a critical factor in the expression of behavior.

The following are just a few examples of other specific systems that impact on behavioral processing:

Nigrostriatal System

Cells in the substantia nigra of the mesencephalon project to the basal ganglia of the telencephalon to help coordinate motor behavior. Damage to the cells in the substantia nigra is the causal pathology in Parkinson's disease.

Medial Forebrain Bundle

Specific cells in the metencephalon and mesencephalon project to certain areas virtually throughout the rest of the brain to form a system that mediates reinforcement, or pleasure. This system also seems to regulate arousal levels. One particular portion of this system, which consists of cells originating in the mesencephlon (specifically, the ventral tegmental area) and projecting to the telencephalon (specifically, the nucleus accumbens), seems to be especially important in mediating the positive effects of certain drugs like cocaine and opiates (see chapters 7 and 8 for more information).

Mesolimbic/Mesocortical System(s)

Cells in the mesencephalon project to either specific limbic structures (the mesolimbic system) like the hippocampus, amygdala, and certain cerebral cortical areas, or to particular cerebral neocortical and prefrontal areas (the mesocortical system). This system seems to be malfunctioning in people who have severe mental disorders.

Regardless of the specific functional system, there are two principles involving the functional organization of the CNS that may be helpful in understanding how drugs influence behavior. First, the further rostral in the CNS, that is closer to the top, the more complex the processing. For example, reflexive behavior may be mediated exclusively from the spinal cord. So, if you sit on a tack the processing that occurs in the spinal cord is sufficient to activate the necessary muscles to sit up. Further rostral (up) in the CNS, the brain stem contains several areas that are critical in maintaining vital life functions like respiration and heart rate. These functions do not operate like reflexes in the spinal cord, but rather are more involved in the information that is coming in and the response that is coming out of these nuclei. Further rostral in the CNS in the diencephalon is the hypothalamus, which is a critical area for the expression of behavior. It receives information from numerous sources, projects to a host of nuclei in the brain and spinal cord, and interacts with the pituitary. Finally, there is the cerebral cortex, the most rostral part of the CNS. It is here that such complex behaviors as language and thought and social rules and planning are primarily mediated.

The second critical principle of CNS organization is that processing does not occur in a linear fashion, that is, Area A projects to Area B and then to Area C, but rather that processing occurs in a parallel fashion. Parallel processing refers to the fact that many areas feed back to one another, so adjustments can be made at every level. Even at the level of the spinal cord, parallel processing is taking place. Consider the thumb-tack reflex we mentioned earlier. This reflex does not occur without awareness, nor is this reflex free from control from higher CNS areas, including the cerebral cortex.

NEURONS: THE BASIC UNITS

The neuron is the fundamental unit of the CNS. Figure 2–2 shows a typical neuron in the mammalian cerebral cortex. All CNS functioning relies on how this cell and other neurons operate. In many ways, the neuron is a metaphor for overall brain functioning. An individual neuron will receive a vast number of inputs, some inhibitory and

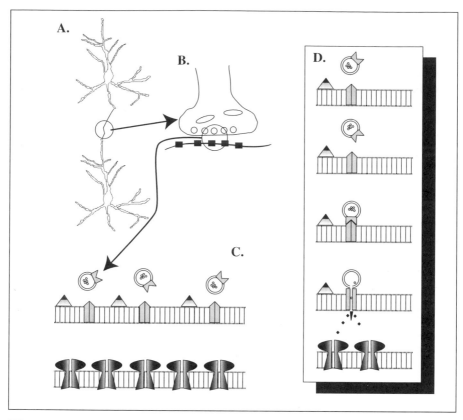

FIGURE 2–3A–D   The Synapse
The point where communication between neurons occurs is called the synapse.
A. This shows the axon of a cortical pyramidal neuron forming a synapse on the receptive surface of one of its targets; in this case, the target is another neuron.
B. A closer examination of this synapse reveals that the synapse consists of a presynaptic side, which is the axon ending of the neuron that has fired, and the postsynaptic
   side, which is the receptive surface of the target neuron. Notice there is no direct contact between these neurons. The space between the presynaptic and postsynaptic
   sides is called the synaptic cleft. Also notice that the presynaptic side contains structures called vesicles which store neurotransmitter molecules.
C. An even closer examination of this synapse reveals two other important structures.
   First, the vesicles seem to congregate around a structure on the presynaptic membrane called the dense bar. Second, there are specialized structures on the postsynaptic surface called receptors, onto which the neurotransmitter molecules bind.
D. This illustrates how a neuron releases neurotransmitter molecules when it fires. When
   the action potential reaches the axon terminal, it initiates a series of events that will
   cause the vesicle to attach to and move down the dense bar to make contact with the
   membrane. The pore on the vesicle aligns with the pore on the membrane and forms
   one complete pore. That pore will dilate and the neurotransmitter molecules inside the
   vesicle are then released into the synaptic cleft. These molecules will then bind to the
   receptor structures on the postsynaptic surface. It is the presence of these neurotransmitter molecules on these receptors that will stimulate or inhibit the target neuron.

all three monoamines (dopamine, norepinephrine, and serotonin), the restoration process of the axon terminal is accomplished by literally pulling the neurotransmitter molecules away from the postsynaptic receptors. There is a powerful membrane transport mechanism in the presynaptic membrane that draws back the neurotransmitter molecules by a process called reuptake. During this process an axon terminal draws neurotransmitter molecules that have just been released back into itself. Thus, the terminal releases neurotransmitter molecules and instantly pulls them back into the terminal, allowing only a brief period for the molecules to stimulate the postsynaptic receptors.

In addition to reuptake, the postsynaptic surface also has a powerful membrane transport mechanism that will remove neurotransmitter molecules from the synaptic cleft and off of the receptors. This process is called uptake. Since the actual binding sites on the postsynaptic receptors for the neurotransmitter molecules are on the side of the receptor that is outside of the cell, facing into the synaptic cleft, neurotransmitter molecules inside of the postsynaptic surface are unable to stimulate the receptor. For some neurotransmitter molecules, like gamma-aminobutyric acid (GABA), the neighboring glial cells also have uptake mechanisms to clear the synaptic cleft of neurotransmitter molecules (Figure 2–4).

This is the essence of CNS processing. Drugs that will affect behavior will somehow alter some aspect of this neuronal process of communication. Some drugs

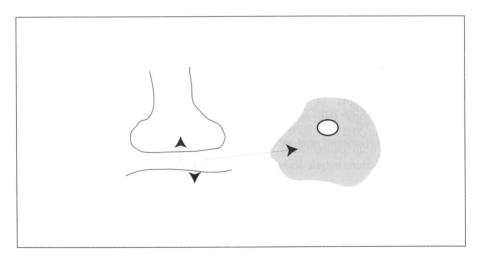

FIGURE 2–4   Reuptake
For many cells in the brain, one way of terminating the action of neurotransmitter molecules on the postsynaptic receptors is to draw those molecules back into the presynaptic side. There are specialized proteins in the membrane that act as a transport mechanism. These proteins will draw these neurotransmitter molecules away from the receptors and bind them, then move them across the membrane depositing them into the presynaptic side. This process is called reuptake. In some synapses, there is a similar membrane transport mechanism on the postsynaptic membrane and also on neighboring glial cells. In these cases, the neurotransmitter molecules are pulled out of the synapse and into either the postsynaptic cell or glial cell.

and release acetylcholine as a neurotransmitter. The neurons of the second nucleus in the striatum use GABA as a neurotransmitter and send its axons back to the substantia nigra. Thus, the different nuclei of the nigrostriatal system each use a different neurotransmitter.

Another example of how the cells of a nucleus all use one neurotransmitter is in the mesolimbic system. The neurons of the mesolimbic system release dopamine molecules when they fire. As we shall see, the mesolimbic system is the target of antipsychotic medications.

The medial forebrain bundle offers still another example in that each of the various nuclei that contribute axons to the medial forebrain bundle use one of the monoamines as neurotransmitter molecules. Thus, the medial forebrain bundle contains three types of axons, and depending on the particular nucleus of origin the terminals of each of those types of neurons release one of the monoamine molecules when they fire.

In addition to these nuclei which are discrete components of functional systems, there are general types of neurons which use specific neurotransmitter molecules. For example, in the cerebral cortex there is a class of small neurons which inhibit other cells from firing. These small inhibitory neurons use GABA as their neurotransmitter. So the normal inhibition of cerebral cortical activity relies on neurons which release GABA molecules when they fire.

In summary, brain functioning is the result of millions and millions of neurons in all of the different functional systems, synthesizing their neurotransmitter molecules, releasing them when they fire, and feverishly getting ready for the next firing.

Let us now turn our attention to some basic issues of behavior.

Behavior

Behavior is the outcome of a great deal of brain processing. The complexity of the factors which involve the mediation of behavior is reflected in the many and varied scientific disciplines that have been studying specific aspects of behavior.

A partial listing of the principal factors involved in the mediation of behavior would include: the physiological state of the brain, the intensity of the particular drive state of the person, the perceived hedonics involved in the situation, and the learning history and expectations of the individual, to name just a few. Because of the many factors included in the mediation of behavior, changing any one part is not likely to produce an invariant behavioral outcome. More specifically, changing the physiology of the brain with a drug will not produce the identical behavioral outcome from person to person and may not even be consistent within the same person. Since a given drug will have the same mechanism of action in altering CNS functioning from one person to the next, the drug will influence behavior in a predictable fashion. In subsequent chapters, we will examine the nature of how specific drugs influence the expression of behavior.

However, there are some behavioral concepts that are common across the various drug classes we will discuss. These concepts include tolerance, dependency and withdrawal, and the overwhelming role of cerebral cortical processing.

Tolerance

Tolerance is the process whereby a particular drug effect diminishes with repeated doses. In other words, repeated administrations of a drug require progressively higher doses to maintain the initial intensity of a particular effect. Traditionally, two mechanisms have been thought to account for the mediation of tolerance. One is called metabolic tolerance (or drug dispositional or pharmacokinetic tolerance). Basically, those systems involved in the biotransformation and/or the excretion of a population of drug molecules operate more efficiently with repeated doses. In most cases, but certainly not all, it is the enzyme system in liver cells that increases efficiency to biotransform drugs. The process whereby the liver increases this function is called hepatic induction. The net result of increasing the liver's functioning is that there are more molecules of a drug which are able to be filtered. Thus, repeated administration of a drug may actually lead to more drug molecules excreted faster, leaving fewer drug molecules circulating and interacting with receptors.

However, enhanced biotransformation and excretion of drug molecules as a result of repeated administrations cannot solely account for the occurrence of tolerance. For one thing, not all of the various effects of a drug will develop tolerance at the same rate. Furthermore, some drug effects may not develop tolerance at all with repeated doses, while others may. Something else must be operating.

The other traditional mechanism of tolerance is called physiological tolerance (or cellular or pharmacodynamic tolerance). Essentially, this concept holds that even if a population of drug molecules remains constant with repeated doses, the body adjusts to the changes induced by a drug. In particular, the brain will actually counter the effects. If one of the effects of a drug is a decrease in body temperature, the brain will cause an increase in body temperature once the drug is in the system. We are powerfully driven by homeostasis—an intense need for stability. If that stability is disrupted in any way, not just by drugs, the nervous system will try to counter the induced perturbations. One striking example of a nondrug disruption involves an early experiment in which subjects were fitted with glasses that had prisms which inverted the visual field. These subjects literally had their world turned upside down. Within a week, their nervous systems had responded so that they now were perceiving the world right side up again. The changes in perceptions induced by drugs will likewise result in CNS compensatory responses. The actual knowledge of the nature of the specific brain counter responses to chronic drug administration varies. In some cases, researchers have documented populations of specific brain receptors changing with repeated administrations of a given drug. In other cases, only global descriptions of whole physiological systems have been described. Ongoing research efforts will better articulate specific compensatory responses to specific drugs.

It must be mentioned that even though certain drug effects diminish with repeated doses, it is not accurate to think of physiological tolerance as the brain somehow becoming less sensitive to the drug/receptor interactions. Rather, it is better to consider physiological tolerance as the neuronal adjustment to repeated exposures of a population of drug molecules.

However, metabolic tolerance, together with physiological tolerance, still cannot solely explain the occurrence of tolerance. In order to formulate a more complete understanding of tolerance, one must take into account higher-order complex central nervous system processing. Two concepts that address this issue are behavioral tolerance and learned tolerance. The following experiment illustrates behavioral tolerance.

Behavioral tolerance.   One study[1] demonstrated: 1. the effects of ethanol on the ability of animals to walk on a treadmill; and 2. the development of tolerance to the impaired treadmill walking. Among all of the groups in this particular experiment, three were of particular interest: each day, two groups of animals received 2.2 g/kg of ethanol given intraperitoneally (IP), and one group of animals received saline (IP). All of the groups were trained to walk on a treadmill device and were tested each day. The two groups of animals that received ethanol differed only in that one group was given the ethanol one hour before the treadmill testing and the other group was given the ethanol after the testing, then placed in their home cage.

Let us first consider the results of the animals that were injected before the testing, namely the animals that walked on the treadmill under the influence of ethanol. At first, the animals were intoxicated and made many errors. However, with repeated doses, the animals did progressively better in their performance, so after approximately twenty days of daily injections they were performing as well as the animals that were receiving saline injections. The animals receiving ethanol developed tolerance to the repeated administration. Through this equipment the animals that were given ethanol after the testing had as much practice on the treadmill as did the other groups, and they received the same amount of ethanol as did the other ethanol group. However, they never walked on the treadmill under the influence of ethanol. After twenty-four days, when tolerance had developed in the "ethanol before the testing" group, both ethanol groups and the saline group were given the ethanol one hour before being tested on the treadmill. This was the saline group's first exposure to ethanol. As you would have predicted, these animals performed as poorly as the "ethanol before the testing" group did on their first exposure to ethanol. However, the results of the "ethanol after the testing" group were somewhat surprising. Since the "ethanol after the testing" group received the same amount of ethanol as the other ethanol group, the development of metabolic and physiological tolerance should have been the same for both groups. In fact, blood tests were done on the two ethanol groups after the testing. The tests revealed that the blood levels of ethanol for the two groups were the same. However, the animals that were not accustomed to receiving ethanol prior to the treadmill testing, even though they had been receiving ethanol daily, performed as poorly as animals receiving ethanol for the first time. Thus, the mechanisms of metabolic and physiological tolerance cannot explain the differences between the two ethanol groups.

The tolerance demonstrated by the animals that were tested after the ethanol doses is termed behavioral tolerance. Behavioral tolerance is the development of alternate strategies to minimize the behavioral impairments induced by repeated administrations of a drug.

Learning how to compensate for changes in CNS processing induced by a particular drug can play a critical role in the behavioral outcome following the ingestion of certain drugs. This is not unlike the situation we discussed earlier, in which the effect of inverting the world by prisms was "corrected" by CNS processing. In the case of drug-induced changes in CNS processing, the CNS learns how to compensate and counter the drug effects.

This is a particular example of physiological tolerance, in that the CNS has changed its processing in response to the actions of a drug, so the behavioral effects of that drug diminish with repeated doses. Remember that the animals that experienced repeated doses of a drug, but did not have the opportunity to "practice" while under the influence of the drug, did not demonstrate tolerance in their behavior. Thus, behavioral tolerance is truly a reflection of a change in the way the CNS mediates a particular behavior.

Learned tolerance.   Incorporating higher CNS processing into an understanding of the phenomenon of tolerance must involve learning per se. Learning, which is basically the formation of associations between relevant events, is a critical function for survival. Animals that have the simplest nervous systems have the ability to form associations and learn that what were previously insignificant environmental cues can have dire consequences in certain circumstances. Learned tolerance can be defined as the situation in which, following repeated administrations, the compensatory responses to a particular drug are initiated by the environmental cues associated with the ingestion of that drug.

That physiological processes can be altered or triggered by previously ineffective environmental cues has been an accepted and well-documented principle since the pioneering studies of Pavlov regarding classical conditioning in the 1920s. Following the appropriate pairings with food, the sound of a bell, for example, which ordinarily for most dogs will not be terribly significant, can trigger the physiological response of salivating. Pavlov himself recognized that the effects induced by drugs could also be subject to the rigors of classical conditioning.

Numerous investigators have shown that conditioning to environmental cues is involved in the tolerance that develops to repeated drug dosing.[2, 3] Typical demonstrations of these principles can be evidenced in studies done by Shepard Siegel regarding the development tolerance to the various effects of morphine. An example follows.

In this particular study,[4] rats were injected with either morphine (40 mg/kg, subcutaneously) or saline daily for nine days, at which time all of the animals, both the saline and morphine groups, were administered morphine for another five days to test for their tolerance. For the first nine days, the animals were always injected in one of two distinctly different environments—in this case, either the animal's colony room or a laboratory room with a distinct noise. In this study, half of the morphine animals were always injected with morphine in the colony room and the other half were always injected in the laboratory room. The sedating effects of this chronic relatively high dose of morphine was assessed daily throughout the experiment. What makes this particular study notable is that during the five days of tolerance testing half of the animals were given the morphine in the usual morphine room, but half were given the morphine in the room that was not previously used for drug administration. There were two striking results.

First, the animals that were given morphine in the same room that was used for the previous nine administrations were more tolerant to the sedating effects of morphine than were the animals that were given morphine in the different room. Thus, even though their drug history was identical, the animals that received morphine without the environmental cues that had been associated with morphine administration showed behavior that was similar to the animals that were given morphine for the first time (the saline animals).

Second, just prior to the actual morphine administration, the animals that were given chronic morphine and tested in the usual morphine room exhibited a pronounced hyperexcitability that was not present in the animals that were given chronic morphine but tested in the room that was not associated with morphine administration. Thus, the detection of the environmental cues associated with the administration of morphine was enough to trigger a behavior that would counter the sedating effects of the drug.

Tolerance can be considered a compensatory response of the whole system to the changes in its normal physiological functioning, induced by a certain drug. This compensatory response can be so robust and rapid, depending on the body system or systems that are affected, that it is termed acute tolerance. Acute tolerance is the development of a compensatory response to the first or initial doses of a particular drug. However, most drug effects do not show acute tolerance but rather develop compensatory responses more slowly with repeated administrations. Usually, repetitive drug administrations fall into a routine. Many of the particular environmental cues surrounding drug administration become associated with the resulting effects of the drug. In a sense, the CNS "learns" that certain environmental cues signal the presence of a particular drug in the system, and those cues will be sufficient to trigger an anticipatory compensatory response to the drug effects before the actual presence of the drug.

One should not think that the concepts of learned tolerance, or even behavioral tolerance in any way challenge the validity of metabolic or physiological tolerance. The occurrence of metabolic and physiological tolerance has been rigorously demonstrated and is not in question. However, in many behavioral instances, these concepts alone cannot explain the data. The involvement of learning in the process called tolerance seems to expand our understanding of the methods involved.

Learned tolerance is not restricted to controlled laboratory situations, but rather is a reflection of learning and memory systems that occur in real-life situations. As we shall see in chapter 7, the principles of learned tolerance have direct relevance to the fatal heroin overdose. Learned tolerance has significant implications, not only for the way one considers withdrawal, but also for the formation of strategies for clinical treatment of addiction.

Withdrawal and dependency.   When a drug is given repeatedly, a sudden halt of drug administration may precipitate a condition called withdrawal. Withdrawal is the expression of a compensatory response to the effects of a drug that has been administered chronically, after drug administration has been terminated. Sometimes also referred to as the abstinence syndrome, withdrawal can be characterized as a constellation of responses that are the opposite of the effects induced by the drug.

The concept of dependency is tightly aligned with withdrawal. Let us now turn our attention to the concepts of physical and psychological dependency. The term physical dependency is essentially a retrospective observation. A person is said to be physically dependent if an abstinence syndrome is precipitated by an abrupt halt of the usual drug administration. The term psychological dependency is an ill-defined term used to refer to the intense drug-seeking behavior a person may exhibit, which ostensibly reflects a keen desire or craving for that particular drug. The use of these terms can be dangerously misleading.

First, these terms imply that while physical dependence has a neurological and physiological basis, psychological dependence does not. This is not true. Every thought, desire, emotion, craving, everything that is concocted, has a physiological basis and is mediated by neurons in the brain, firing in whatever pattern is necessary to achieve that particular outcome. Second, these terms imply that physical dependence is an invariant consequence to chronic drug use, which is not always the case. Because of the profound pitfalls of using the terms physical and psychological to distinguish different levels of dependency, one might consider dependency as being a unitary phenomenon with varying levels of severity. It may be more prudent to leave the discussions concerning the distinctions between physical and psychological dependency for philosophy courses.[5] Unfortunately, as we shall see in the next chapter, these terms have been woven into the current laws that deal with drug classification and drug regulation.

Set and setting.   In addition to the CNS processing involved in learning (forming associations), perceiving environmental cues, and experiencing reinforcement, the CNS processing that formulates a person's expectation is another significant factor in the mediation of behavior following the ingestion of a drug. This is different from the compensatory responses of tolerance that are classically conditioned to certain environmental cues. A person may have an expectation prior to the first drug administration. What a person expects to happen in a particular situation, including the outcome of a drug administration, has a powerful influence on the resulting perceptions and interpretations of what actually occurs. The classical experiment described next illustrates this well.

In one study,[6] subjects were administered adrenaline and told it was an experimental "vitamin." The purpose of the study was to measure the effects of this "vitamin." The subjects were then divided into three groups. Only one group was actually told about the effects of the drug it would be experiencing in the next twenty to thirty minutes. Thus, two groups of subjects would experience the heart-pounding, face-flushing, hand-shaking effects of a sympathetic arousal without any context. The subjects would not have a good reason why they should be feeling this way. For these subjects nondrugged confederates would feign either euphoria or anger in order to provide the context for subjects who were given adrenaline. Sure enough, the subjects who received adrenaline and were in the room with the "euphoric" confederate reported experiencing euphoria. Those subjects who received adrenaline and were in the room with the "angry" confederate reported experiencing anger. The sympathetic response elicited by the drug was the same for all of the subjects, but the various expectations formed by each led to different group experiences. Thus, a person's expectations about taking a drug can be a factor in determining whether or not the experience of the drug's effects are pleasurable.

As we have said before, there are many factors involved in the mediation of behavior, some having to do with the dynamic processes of homeostatic responses by the nervous system. To achieve a balanced and more accurate model of how drugs alter behavior, one has to appreciate a great many issues, not the least of which are issues concerned with the cerebral cortical processes, in particular, learning. It would be foolish to think that changes just in the physiology of brain functioning induced by a drug would always lead to invariant behavioral consequences. This is not to respect the role of cerebral cortical processing in the mediation of behavior. Among the major determinants of behavior following drug administration is set and setting—the expectations of the user and the immediate environment in which the drug is administered. We shall see in subsequent chapters just how robust these factors are.

REVIEW EXAM

1. What is the difference between the central nervous system and the peripheral nervous system?
2. What are the two divisions of the autonomic nervous system?
3. What does the sympathetic division of the autonomic nervous system do?
4. What are the five basic neuroanatomical divisions of the brain?
5. Name a structure for each of the five divisions in question four.
6. What is the limbic system?
7. Describe one specific functional system.
8. What are the components of the synapse?
9. What is a vesicle?
10. How does exocytosis occur?
11. What are the ways in which a neuron recovers from exocytosis?
12. What are the various classes of neurotransmitters?
13. Define tolerance.
14. Define metabolic tolerance.
15. Define physiological tolerance.
16. Define behavioral tolerance.
17. Define learned tolerance.

18. What is the abstinence syndrome?
19. What is the difference between physical and psychological dependency?
20. Define the factors set and setting.

REFERENCES

1. WENGER, J., TIFFANY, T., BOMBARDIU, C., NICHOLLS, K., & WOODS, S. (1981). Ethanol tolerance in the rat is learned, *Science,* 213, 575–577.
2. EIKELBOOM, R., & STEWART, J. (1982). Conditioning of drug-induced physiological responses. *Psychological Review,* 89, 507–528.
3. SIEGEL, S., & MACRAE, J. (1984). Environmental specificity of tolerance. *Trends in Neuroscience,* 7(5), 140–143.
4. HINSON, R., & SIEGEL, S. (1983). Anticipatory hyperexcitability and tolerance to the narcotizing effect of morphine in the rat. *Behavioral Neuroscience,* 97, 759–767.
5. GRANT, K., HOFFMAN, P., & TABAKOFF, B. (1990). Neurobiological and behavioral approaches to tolerance and dependence. In G. Edwards & M. Lader (Eds.) *The Nature of Drug Dependence* (pp. 135–169). Oxford: Oxford University Press.
6. SCHACHTER, S. & SINGER, J. (1962). Cognitive, social, and physiological determinants of emotional state. *Psychological Review,* 69, 379–399.

CHAPTER THREE
DRUG CLASSIFICATION

GENERAL ISSUES ADDRESSED IN THIS CHAPTER

- Criteria for grouping the different classes of drugs
- Various categories of a behaviorally based drug classification scheme
- Categories of the legal classification of drugs

INTRODUCTION

A comprehensive list of all drugs is a formidable task, however, this task is success-fully accomplished in certain books like Goodman and Gilman's *The Pharmacolog-ical Basis of Therapeutics.*[1] As we have discussed in chapter 1, it is difficult for a drug molecule to cross the blood-brain barrier and enter the brain. Most drugs will not be able to cross the barrier, thus most drugs do not exert a direct influence on brain func-tioning. Some drugs, however, may directly affect the peripheral nervous system, specifically the sympathetic and/or the parasympathetic arousal system and, by so doing, will indirectly influence the central nervous system. We will focus our atten-tion on the drugs that have a significant impact on behavior, which then presents the problem of organizing those drugs into common groups.

CATEGORIZATION OF DRUGS THAT AFFECT THE CENTRAL NERVOUS SYSTEM

One can create a drug category system based on the specific actions of a class of drugs on specific brain functioning. This sounds logical except that the mechanism of action of many drugs has not been well-described nor understood (for example, in al-cohol and marijuana). Thus, at this time in drug research, there is no sufficient data base to categorize all drugs by their direct effects on brain functioning.

One can create a scheme based on the behavior elicited by a class of drugs. One major problem with this criterion, as we shall see in our discussion of sedatives in chapter 6, is that one drug can elicit a variety of different behaviors, depending on the dose and on the tolerance of the user.

Another way of classifying drugs is by the medical use of a particular class of drug. There are medical situations for which certain drugs have been found to be most useful. The *Physicians' Desk Reference* (PDR)[2] is a compendium of drugs for which physicians and other professionals with prescription-writing privileges can use in medical treatment. A casual examination of the PDR reveals a unique classifi-cation of these medicinal agents, which focuses on the presentation of symptoms of particular disorders. This type of categorization is useful to the medical practitioner who is seeking information concerning a specific drug, but it is not useful to the stu-dent who wishes to determine how drugs influence the brain's mediation of behavior. Moreover, there are drugs that are not legitimately prescribed for medical treatment that need to be categorized because of their effects on behavior. Thus, this single cri-terion is also lacking.

The drug categorization we will use does not depend exclusively on any one of these criteria, but enforces the criteria as is appropriate for the specific drug in question.

Sedatives and Hypnotics—CNS Depressants

These drugs are grouped together because of their similar effects on depressing behavior. Even though these drugs share the common ability to cause intoxication, the way they alter brain functioning is not the same. Each drug has its own unique mechanism of action on the brain. The different subclasses of the sedatives/hypnotics include:

a. Barbiturates (phenobarbital, secobarbital, etc.)
b. Benzodiazepines (Valium®, Librium®, triazolam, alprazolam, etc.)
c. Other non-barbiturate sedatives (methaqualone, meprobamate, etc.)
d. Newer non-benzodiazepines (buspirone hydrochloride, alpidem, etc.)
e. Ethanol (alcohol)
f. Cannabis (marijuana, hashish)
g. Antihistamines

Chapter 4 will deal with the principles of the sedatives/hypnotics. However, since alcohol is such a pervasive drug in Western culture, there will be a separate treatment in chapter 5 of those issues surrounding it. Likewise, the seemingly permanent controversy that surrounds cannabis (marijuana) will be treated separately in chapter 6.

Opiates—Drugs That Alter the Brain's Pain Processing

The drugs in this category share the common property of acting on a specific class of brain receptors.

a. Natural opiates (morphine, codeine, etc.)
b. Synthetic opiates
   1. similar in structure to the opiates (heroin, Percodan®, etc.)
   2. not similar in structure to the opiates (methadone, Demerol®, etc.)
c. Opiate antagonists (naloxone, naltrexone, etc.)

The special issues concerning these drugs will be discussed in chapter 7.

Stimulants—Drugs That Produce Behavioral Arousal

The principal criterion for grouping these particular drugs is their common outcome of behavioral arousal. The specific mechanism of action varies for each of the different types of stimulants.

a. Amphetamine (including methamphetamine)
b. Cocaine (including synthetic cocaines)
c. Methylxanthines (caffeine, theophylline, and theobromine)
d. Drugs used to treat hyperactivity (Ritalin®, pemoline)

e. Over-the-counter appetite suppressants (phenylpropanolamine hydrochloride)
f. Khat—a naturally occurring stimulant, similar to amphetamine

These drugs will be discussed in chapter 8.

Drugs Used to Treat Mental Disorders

The drugs included in this category have proven useful in the treatment of specific mental disorders. There are two main classes of these particular drugs:

a. Drugs used to treat affective disorders, such as depression and/or mania. (There are several classes within this one subclass):
   1. Tricyclic antidepressants (imipramine, amitriptyline, desipramine hydrochloride, etc.)
   2. The newer "heterocyclic" antidepressants (fluoxetine—Prozac®, sectraline-zoloft)
   3. Monoamine oxidase inhibitors (tranylcypromine sulfate—Parnate®)
b. Drugs used to treat psychosis (for example, schizophrenia):
   1. Phenothiazines (chlorpromazine—Thorazine®, thioridazine—Mellaril®, etc.)
   2. Butyrophenones (haloperidol—Haldol®)

Not only are there special issues involved in this type of drug administration, but also these drugs have provided a wealth of information about the nature of neural communication. They will be discussed in chapter 9.

Hallucinogens

The drugs in this category share the unusual behavioral outcome of inducing hallucinations. They can be further divided into the following classes:

a. Agents that have a molecular structure similar to serotonin (lysergic acid diethylamide (LSD), psilocin, etc.)
b. Agents that have a molecular structure similar to norepinephrine (mescaline, 3,4 methylenedioxymethamphetamine—"ecstasy")
c. Agents that do not fall into the first two subclasses (ibotenic acid, phencyclidine hydrochloride—"angel dust")

These drugs are surrounded by controversy and create a great deal of concern. The special issues of hallucinogens will be discussed in chapter 10.

Drugs Used for Anesthesia

There is a class of drugs that alter brain functioning and have proven to be quite effective in producing an anesthetic state for surgical procedures. Anesthesia is a reversible loss of sensation that is usually but not always accompanied by a loss of consciousness. Anesthetics fall into several subclasses:

a. Gaseous anesthetics (nitrous oxide)
b. Volatile anesthetics (agents that are liquids at room temperature, such as ether and halothane)
c. Parenterally administered anesthetics (barbiturates, ketamine hydrochloride)

TABLE 3.1   Drug Classification

SEDATIVE AND HYPNOTICS— CNS DEPRESSANTS	OPIATES	STIMULANTS	DRUGS USED TO TREAT MENTAL DISORDERS
Barbiturates (phenobarbital, secobarbital, etc.) Benzodiazepines (Valium®, Librium®, triazolam, alprazolam, etc.) Other nonbarbiturate sedatives (methaqualone, meprobamate, etc.) Ethanol (alcohol) Cannabis (marijuana, hashish) Antihistamines	Natural opiates (morphine, codeine, etc.) Synthetic opiates (heroin, methadone, Demerol®)	Amphetamines (including methamphetamine) Cocaine (including synthetic cocaines) Methylxanthines (caffeine, theophylline, and theobromine) Drugs used to treat hyperactivity (Ritalin®, pemoline) Over-the-counter appetite suppressants (phenyl-propanolamine hydrochloride)	Tricyclic antidepressants (imipramine, amitriptyline hydrochloride, desipramine hydrochloride, etc.) The newer "heterocyclic" antidepressants (fluoxetine—Prozac®, trazodone hydrochloride) Monoamine oxidase inhibitors (tranylcypromine sulfate—Parnate®) Phenothiazines (chlorpromazine—Thorazine®, thioridazine—Mellaril®, etc.) Butyrophenones (haloperidol—Haldol®)
HALLUCINOGENS	DRUGS USED FOR ANESTHESIA	DRUGS USED TO TREAT EPILEPSY	
Structurally similar to serotonin (LSD, psilocin, etc.) Structurally similar to norepinephrine (mescaline, MDMA—"ecstasy") Other agents (ibotenic acid, phencyclidine hydrochloride—"angel dust")	Gaseous anesthetics (nitrous oxide) Volatile anesthetics (ether, halothane) Parenterally administered anesthetics (barbiturates, ketamine hydrochloride)	Hydantoins (diphenylhydantoin—Dilantin®) Barbiturates (phenobarbital) Carbamazepine Valproic acid	

The development of anesthetic agents is a colorful and engaging story, and the reader is urged to pursue this history in further readings. Because these drugs are so specifically used, this class will not be discussed in the text.

Drugs Used to Treat Epilepsy

One of the most common neurological disorders successfully managed with medication is epilepsy. The drugs that have proven effective in altering brain functioning to offer relief from this disorder can be divided into the following classes:

a. Hydantoins (diphenylhydantoin—Dilantin®)
b. Barbiturates (phenobarbital)
c. Carbamazepine
d. Valproic acid

The use of these drugs is restricted to the therapeutic situation of seizure control, which will not be discussed in this text. Although easily available, these drugs are rarely abused, with the exception perhaps of the barbiturates, which will be discussed in chapter 6.

LEGAL SCHEME

There is another drug classification that merits attention. In an attempt to limit the availability of potentially dangerous drugs to the public, laws have evolved that impose a structure to the distribution of drugs, as well as penalties for not complying with this scheme.

The particular evolution of our current drug control legislation is fascinating. As a fledgling nation, drug control was nonexistent, and the importation of all drugs was uncontrolled and unrestricted. By the late 1800s, for example, the use of opiates in a host of "tonics" and other medicinal products lead the United States, as a nation, to develop an intense consumption of opiates. The unrestricted use of cocaine at this time also grew, both in legitimate medical treatment, with endorsements from high-profile professionals, and also recreationally, in levels that were drawing concern. Legislators both locally and nationally, motivated to protect the public from the perceived harm of chronic intoxication from these drugs, responded by drafting specific drug legislation. Thus began an evolution of laws to deal with the problems of drug importation, distribution, and availability in general. The dynamics involved in this particular part of American history are covered in depth by David Musto in *The American Disease—Origins of Narcotic Control*[3].

The present federal legislation that deals with the control of drugs is the Comprehensive Drug Abuse Prevention and Control Act, passed in 1970. This law divides drugs into five categories or "schedules," according to the perceived risk of developing a dependency on that drug. As with any legislation, there are a great many factors involved in the conception and actual wording of a law. One of the main motivating factors in any legislation is the pressure exerted by the constituency of an elected legislator. In other words, the impressions of the public are at times more influential in drafting legislation than the actual facts surrounding an issue. In the case of drug legislation, the public perception (including the perceptions of a legislator) of the dangers of a substance are often shaped not by scientific data but rather by newspaper and television accounts of drug issues. Thus, there are some peculiarities to the schedule system, which hopefully will be adjusted by subsequent legislation. However, it is important to remember that regardless of any scientific pharmacological data that may argue the specific merits of a particular drug, this is the law. While some may choose to work for modifications, the public is still subject to its regulations and penalties.

The following is the drug categorization, according to the Comprehensive Drug Abuse Prevention and Control Act of 1970:

Schedule I

The drugs in this category have the highest risk for the development of drug dependency and are drugs that have no accepted medical use in treatment. Drugs in this schedule include:

1. Heroin, LSD, mescaline, peyote, psilocybin
2. Certain morphine preparations—benzylmorphine, dihydromorphinone hydrochloride, morphine methylsulfonate
3. Marijuana

The drugs in this schedule are the "forbidden" drugs and cannot be obtained by prescription. These drugs can be obtained for scientific research following the submission and approval of a research grant.

Schedule II

The drugs in this category also have the highest risk for the development of drug dependency, however these drugs are accepted by the medical community for treatment. Drugs in this schedule include:

1. The opiates—opium, morphine, codeine, methadone, meperidine hydrochloride (Demerol®), oxycodone hydrochloride (Percodan®)
2. The stimulants—amphetamines, methamphetamines, methylphenidate hydrochloride (Ritalin®)
3. Certain barbiturates—pentobarbital (Nembutal®), secobarbital (Seconal®), and amobarbital (Amytal®)

These drugs can be obtained legally only by prescription.

Schedule III

The drugs in this category have a risk for the development of moderate physical drug dependency or a high psychological dependency. Drugs in this schedule include:

1. Preparations that contain limited quantities of opiates (i.e., morphine, codeine)
2. Phencyclidine (also known as "angel dust")
3. The barbiturates not classified in schedules II or IV

Schedule IV

The drugs in this category have only a slight risk for the development of mild physical or psychological drug dependency. Drugs in this schedule include:

1. The barbiturates—phenobarbital and methylphenobarbital
2. Meprobamate
3. The benzodiazepines—diazepam (Valium®) and chlordiazepoxide (Librium®)

Schedule V

The drugs in this category have even less risk for the development of mild physical or psychological drug dependency than do the drugs in Schedule IV. Drugs in this schedule include the barbiturates—phenobarbital and methylphenobarbital.

As you can see, this particular categorization of drugs is based on the potential of a drug to be "abused" and not based on behavior per se. Thus, this breakdown of drugs will not be useful in examining the issues of drugs and behavior.

The exclusion of alcohol or tobacco in our current schedule system, which is based on the "abuse" potential of drugs, merits a comment. Alcohol is such a part of Western culture and tobacco is such a part of American culture that many individuals do not consider either a "drug." In fact, the federal government deals with ethanol and tobacco in the same way our founding fathers did in the late 1700s. The legislation relating to alcohol and tobacco concerns the collection of taxes and falls under the jurisdiction of an agency called the Alcohol, Firearms, and Tobacco (AFT), a division of the U.S. Department of Treasury.

In the following chapters, we will examine the various drug classes and specific drugs as they relate to the alteration of brain functioning and subsequent changes in behavior. There are general issues that are illustrated clearly by some classes of drugs, and there are some unique topics concerning specific drugs.

REVIEW EXAM

1. How are drugs categorized in the Physicians' Desk Reference (PDR)?
2. Name the five types of sedatives/hypnotics.
3. Give at least one example of each of the five types of sedatives/hypnotics.
4. Give one example of a naturally occurring opiate.
5. What is the difference between the two types of synthetic opiates?
6. Give at least one example of the two types of synthetic opiates.
7. Name five types of stimulants.
8. List specific examples of three of these stimulant types.
9. List the two main classes of drugs used to treat mental disorders.

10. Name two subtypes of each of the main classes of drugs used to treat mental disorders.
11. Give one specific example for each subtype of each of the main classes of drugs used to treat mental disorders.
12. What are the differences between the types of hallucinogens?
13. List specific examples of each type of hallucinogen.
14. Name the types of drugs used for anesthesia.
15. Name the types of drugs used for treating epilepsy.
16. What are the criteria for a drug to be classified as Schedule I?
17. What are the criteria for a drug to be classified as Schedule II?
18. List specific examples of drugs in Schedules I and II.
19. What is the difference in the criteria between Schedule III and IV?

REFERENCES

1. GOODMAN, L., & GILMAN, A. (1990). *The Pharmacological Basis of Therapeutics* (8th ed.). New York: Macmillan Publishing Co.
2. BARNHART, E. (ED.). (1993). *Physicians' Desk Reference.* New Jersey: Medical Economics Co. Inc.
3. MUSTO, D. (1987). *The American Disease—Origins of Narcotic Control.* New York: Oxford University Press.

CHAPTER FOUR
SEDATIVES AND HYPNOTICS:
Drugs That Calm

HISTORY

Excluding ethanol and marijuana, the history of the use of sedative/hypnotic drugs is relatively recent, less than 100 years old. It can be divided according to the appearance of the barbiturates, and later, the benzodiazepines.

Pre-barbiturates

The mid 1800s was an exciting period in the history of medicine. This era saw the first demonstrations of anesthetic agents, which dramatically changed the way surgery was performed. No longer would patients have to experience the once-excruciating pain and physical restraints of surgical procedures, now that they could be rendered unconscious in a controlled manner. In addition, several drugs were developed that would induce sedation for nonsurgical situations, for example, chloral hydrate, the bromides, and paraldehyde. Chloral hydrate (Somnos®), the oldest of these agents, was developed in 1832 and is still an effective sedative. Sometimes referred to as "knockout drops" or a "Mickey Finn," chloral hydrate acquired the reputation of being quite potent, especially when added to an ethanol drink. Thus, the scenario of a person being rendered unconscious, "knocked out," from consuming a drink that had chloral hydrate added to it, is not uncommon in many plots, both literary and real-life. Chloral hydrate's reputation as a potent knockout drop has not been upheld in subsequent studies.[2] Chronic use of this sedative can lead to dependency and to similar problems that are seen with chronic ethanol use. The pronounced adverse effects of nausea and gastrointestinal upset, as well as its unpleasant taste, has played a role in restricting the widespread use of this drug.

The bromides were introduced in 1857. Plagued with a long half-life, approximately twelve days, and a host of adverse side effects like rashes, gastrointestinal disturbances, and excessive drowsiness, the bromides were not a pleasant choice for a sedative.

Paradehyde (Paraly) was introduced in 1882. Although an effective sedative, it also had major adverse side effects which limited its popularity and use, including a distinctly obnoxious taste and odor. In addition, exposure to light and air would cause the drug to break down to acetaldehyde and acetic acid—both quite toxic, thus, careless handling could lead to accidental poisoning.

The medical community was ready for the development of a better sedative. Enter the barbiturates.

Barbiturates

The barbiturates were first synthesized in 1864. However, it was not until 1903 that the first barbiturate, barbital (Veronal®), was introduced into medical practice. Phenobarbital (Luminal®) was introduced shortly thereafter, in 1912. Literally thousands of forms of barbiturates have been synthesized since the turn of the century. Many, like phenobarbital, are still used today. The medical community finally had a sedative/hypnotic drug with a wide range of effects that could be used in a variety of medical situations, including the treatment of anxiety and insomnia. For nearly fifty years, the barbiturates were the sedative/hypnotic drugs of choice. The particulars of barbiturate use are discussed following.

Pre-benzodiazepine Non-barbiturates

Two other drugs of note were introduced around this time as well—Meprobamate (Miltown®) and Methaqualone (Quaalude®).

Meprobamate was introduced in 1951 and is an effective sedative with a moderately short half-life of about ten hours, however the risk of dependency is serious and withdrawal is rather difficult.

Methaqualone was introduced in the 1950s and was distinctive in that this drug seems to have an even wider spectrum of effects than the barbiturates. In addition to sedation, methaqualone had antitussive (i.e., cough-suppressing) as well as antihistamine properties. It also became a popular illicit sedative. The seemingly high risk of dependency and the relatively low safety index far outweighed the usefulness of methaqualone as a sedative. There now are safer drugs which can treat any condition the methaqualones could. Without a market, the legal manufacturing of methaqualones has ceased in the United States.

Benzodiazepines

The benzodiazepines were actually first synthesized in the early 1930s, but it was not until the 1960s that they were introduced as a medication to treat anxiety. Despite their extraordinarily short history, the benzodiazepines have become the most frequently prescribed medication in our culture. The principal reason for this overwhelming success is due to the safety of the benzodiazepines, as compared to the barbiturates. Lethal overdose following extremely high doses of the benzodiazepines is quite rare, thus establishing this medication's place as the sedative/hypnotic drug of choice for most medicating situations. Although initially advertised as nonaddictive, the risk of dependency following treatment with the benzodiazepines is well-documented. In addition, the lethal consequences of mixing the benzodiazepines with other sedatives/hypnotics has tempered the general impression of its safety. The newer benzodiazepines have much shorter half-lives, shorter durations of action, and fewer if any active metabolites. The specific aspects of benzodiazepine use will be discussed following.

The Newer Non-benzodiazepines

Within the last ten years, a new generation of sedative/hypnotic drugs has been introduced that have the potential to replace the benzodiazepines as the medication of choice for the treatment of anxiety and insomnia. One family of these newer drugs, the azopirones, represents a different approach to sedation than do the barbiturates and benzodiazepines, as these drugs alter brain functioning in a different way. Instead of acting on brain GABA systems, these drugs act on brain serotonin systems. New additions to the sedative/hypnotic list of drugs are discussed later in this chapter.

ABSORPTION AND DISTRIBUTION

The most common method of administration for the sedatives/hypnotics is an oral (enteral) route (Figure 4–1). All of the various sedative/hypnotic drugs can be absorbed from the GI tract. However, there are certain medical situations that would require faster absorption, and thus parenteral injection routes are used usually for the barbiturates and the benzodiazepines. The need for immediate calming or sedation, as in the case of a person who is about to undergo surgery, or a person who is totally out of control and may harm themselves or others, are examples of situations that would call for parenteral administration of a sedative/hypnotic drug.

The distribution of the barbiturates and benzodiazepines is peculiar because of their high lipid solubility, which means these drugs can be easily dissolved in fat. There are two significant consequences to this high-lipid solubility: 1. These drugs will be able to cross cell membranes easily, and will be able to cross into the brain compartment; and 2. These drugs will be able to dissolve in body fat and will tend to accumulate in fat stores throughout the body. The process whereby a drug accumu-

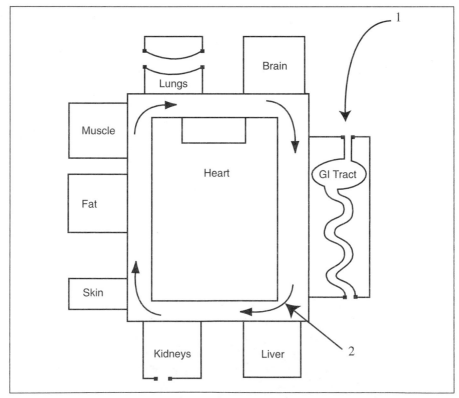

FIGURE 4–1   Typical Routes of Administration for the Sedatives/Hypnotics
There are two typical routes of administration for the sedatives/hypnotics. These drugs are swallowed (enteral—oral) or injected (parenteral—injection) either IV or IM.

lates in a body compartment, usually in fat, and later goes back into the blood is called redistribution. Redistribution plays a significant role in the clearance of barbiturates and benzodiazepines from the circulatory system.

The duration of action of a drug typically depends on how long the population of drug molecules remains high enough in the blood to maintain a steep enough concentration gradient that would allow more of the drug molecules to enter the brain. For the barbiturates and benzodiazepines, the number of drug molecules in the blood, that is, the blood level, depends primarily on two factors: the metabolic transformation of the drug molecules by the liver; and redistribution. Sampling blood at various times after drug administration, measuring the levels of the drug at this time, and plotting these results generates a clearance curve for that drug at that dose for that person. Figure 4–2A illustrates the clearance curve for a benzodiazepine following an enteral route of administration. Notice the delay in reaching the highest level in the blood, which is due to absorption from the GI tract. The time of absorption

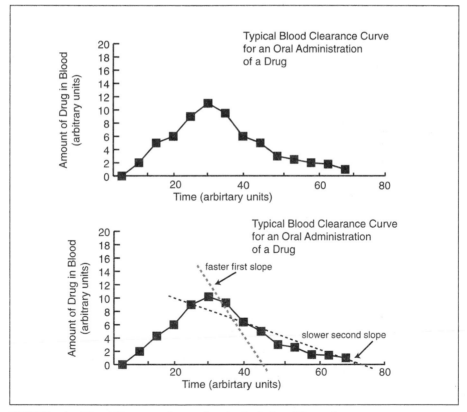

FIGURE 4–2 Blood Clearance Curves for the Sedatives/Hypnotics
A. Following an enteral—oral—dose, notice the slight delay for blood levels to peak. This is due to the delay of absorption from the GI tract. Also notice the biphasic clearance: very rapid at first, followed by a slower phase.

following a parenteral IV administration is virtually zero, since the drug is being injected directly into the circulation. This is illustrated in Figure 4–2B, which shows the clearance curve for an IV dose of thiopenthal, a fast-acting barbiturate. Regardless of the route, the clearance curves for these drugs typically have two phases. This "biphasic" clearance is initially very fast, then is much slower. The fast phase cannot be attributed to liver and kidney activity and is due to redistribution. At first, the drug molecules are rapidly accumulating in fat depots throughout the body. The second slower phase is due to liver transformation and kidney filtration and excretion from the body. The implication of redistribution is discussed later in this chapter.

Both the barbiturates and benzodiazepines have considerable variability in the half-lifes of their particular types. Table 4–1 shows some of the half-life values. The barbiturates can be subclassified by their half-lifes into long, short, and ultra-short

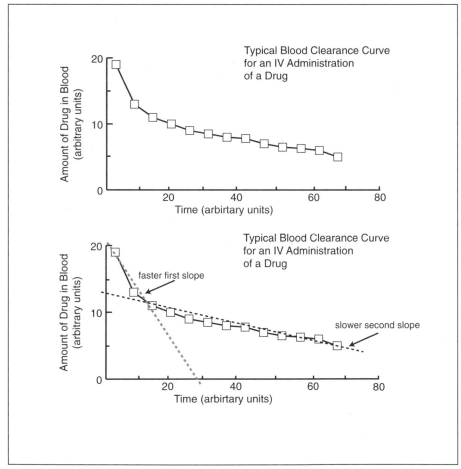

FIGURE 4–2 (Continued) B. Following a parenteral injection dose, there is virtually no absorption delay, but the biphasic clearance is still apparent.

TABLE 4-1   Half-lifes for the Barbiturates and Benzodiazepines

LONG-DURATION BARBITURATES	SHORT-DURATION BARBITURATES	ULTRA-SHORT DURATION BARBITURATES	BENZODIAZEPINES
Phenobarbital (Luminal®)—up to 140 hrs. (>5 days)	Pentobarbital (Nembutal®)—up to 48 hrs. (2 days)	Thiopental (Pentothal®)— 3–8 hrs.	Chlordiazepoxide (Librium®)—up to 28 hrs. (1 day)
	Secobarbital (Seconal®)—up to 34 hrs. (1.5 days)	Methohexital (Brevital®)— 3–6 hrs.	Diazepam (Valium®)—up to 90 hrs. (>3 days)
	Amobarbital (Amytal®)—up to 48 hrs. (2 days)		Flurazepam (Dalmane®)—up to 100 hrs. (4 days)
			Oxazepam (Serax®)—up to 21 hrs. (1 day)
			Alprazolam (Xanax®)—up to 20 hrs. (<1 day)
			Triazolam (Halcion®)—up to 4 hrs.

duration agents. The ultra-short-acting thiopental has a half-life of only three hours compared to the long-lasting phenobarbital (Luminal®) which has a half-life of three days. The newer benzodiazepines have much shorter half-lifes than the traditional ones. Alprazolam (Xanax®) and triazolam (Halcion®) have half-lifes of six to twenty hours and two to three hours respectively, while diazepam (Valium®) has a half-life of forty-eight hours.

BIOTRANSFORMATION

Both the barbiturates and benzodiazepines are biotransformed by enzymes in liver cells, which renders the transformed drug molecules less lipid-soluble and enables filtration and excretion by the kidneys. In addition, these transformed drugs are not psychoactive, which means they no longer exert an influence on brain activity.

The additional work that the liver has to perform to biotransform these populations of drug molecules will usually result in the increased efficiency of the liver enzyme systems, as well as in a physically larger liver. Thus, one would suspect that metabolic tolerance would be a significant factor in the effects observed after ingesting these drugs.

The benzodiazepines in particular illustrate an additional pharmacological principle—that of active metabolites. The first liver biotransformation of many of the benzodiazepines yields a metabolite that is also psychoactive. These "new" molecules exert an effect on the brain as well as the "parent" molecules. In the case of diazepam (Valium®), the active metabolite is a substance called desmethyl-diazepam. Not only is this substance psychoactive, but it has a much longer half-life than does diazepam. This means there will be a population of molecules that will continue to exert its effects on the brain long after the diazepam is cleared. The outcome of accumulating psychoactive drug molecules becomes a matter of vital concern when benzodiazepines are used frequently, such as every day or at least before all of the last dose has been cleared out of the body. For example, the original benzodiazepine used to induce sleep was flurazepam (Dalmane®), which has a half-life of seventy-two hours. Remember that it takes approximately four and one-half half-lifes to clear about 96 percent of an initial dose. For flurazepam, this means that if a person doses more often than once every two weeks, then that person will accumulate the drug. Considering that people who are seeking relief from insomnia will tend to dose every night, and considering the much longer half-lifes of the active metabolites, then accumulation of psychoactive drug molecules becomes a problem because it may interfere with the person's activity during the day. The concept of sleep induction will be discussed in the behavioral section that follows.

BEHAVIORAL OUTCOMES

One of the striking characteristics of the barbiturates is the exceedingly wide range of behaviors that can be elicited with increasing dosages (Figure 4–3). At low dosages, decreased anxiety may be experienced. As the dose is increased, the fol-

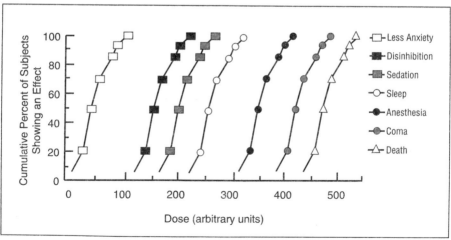

FIGURE 4–3   The Family of Dose Response Curves for the Sedatives/Hypnotics
As the dose of sedatives/hypnotics increases, one can see the wide range of behaviors that result.

lowing other behaviors are typically observed: disinhibition, leading to sedation, sleep a state of general anesthesia, coma, and finally, death.

The benzodiazepines have a similar range as do the barbiturates, however, only on the lower end of this spectrum. Benzodiazepines will relieve anxiety and treat insomnia, but higher doses will not lead to anesthesia, coma, or death. Furthermore, the newer anxiolytic drugs alleviate anxiety, without the sedation produced by higher doses. The following addresses these behaviors.

Disinhibition

Disinhibition is the release from inhibition, so a drug that is a depressant, like a barbiturate, may at the right dose, usually a low dose, lead to an actual increase in behavior. This may be due to the drug's depressing those CNS circuits which inhibit behavior. The result would be the expression of a behavior that is normally suppressed, for example, the improved dancing and socializing skills a person experiences after a low-dose depressant (usually alcohol). Of course, it is impossible to determine if the decrease in anxiety and subsequent disinhibition is totally pharmacologically induced or due in part to the expectation of anxiety relief. We will discuss the particular issue of expectation in more detail in chapter 5. Another example of disinhibition is that a person given the right dose of a barbiturate will be unable to keep from disclosing secret information. Sodium pentobarbital has been known as a "truth serum" because of its use in interrogations.

Treating Insomnia

Sleep is a complex behavior which involves a variety of brain structures working in synchrony. There is no such thing as pharmacologically induced sleep. The sedative hypnotics that are used to induce "sleep" will alter and rearrange the normal phases of sleep. One can render a person unconscious with a high enough dose of a sedative. Unconsciousness is not the same as sleep. If a person is struck on the head hard enough to render him or her unconscious, one would hardly think of that person as being asleep. The same is true about pharmacologically induced sleep. Sedative hypnotics can render a person unconscious, but that is not sleep. One of the most important phases of normal sleep is a period called "REM" or "rapid eye movement," when dreaming usually occurs. REM sleep may play a role in the memory's consolidation of the day's events. We have a biological need for REM sleep. The barbiturates will actually decrease the amount of time the user spends in REM sleep. A popular benzodiazepine for inducing sleep was, and in some circles still is, flurazepam (Dalmane®), which alters normal sleep by decreasing the amount of time in stage four sleep, sometimes referred to as slow wave sleep or deep sleep.[3] In general, benzodiazepines used as hypnotics will not only reduce stage four sleep but will also reduce stages one and three and REM sleep, while increasing stage two.[4]

What is the usefulness then of sedatives/hypnotics in the treatment of insomnia? Appreciate that being unable to fall asleep may be anxiety-provoking in and of itself. For these individuals, sedation will offer some relief from this particular anxiety and by so doing may help the person sleep, even though the medication does not actually produce sleep. The role of the benzodiazepines used to help insomniacs, including the newer shorter-acting ones, is that of a short-term aid to help the person stay asleep in the earlier phases of sleep. These medications were never intended to be used on a regular basis. In fact, a recent report indicates that medicating for sleep problems has declined by 10 percent in the last few years, and there was an even sharper decline in the use of benzodiazepines for insomnia.[5] The use of behavioral strategies has proven to be quite useful in these cases.

Adverse Behavioral Effects

There are behavioral outcomes to benzodiazepine use that are considered aversive or unwelcome. Three are common, one is uncommon and controversial. The three common effects are unwanted sedation, motor impairment during the day, and impairment of memory. The sedation is usually experienced as fatigue and tiredness during the day. Tolerance develops to this behavioral outcome, so with chronic use this effect should abate within a week or two. The incoordination and ataxia commonly observed with benzodiazepine use is more than a reflection of the unwanted sedation just discussed. These impairments have been reported independent of sedation,[6] suggesting that perhaps those brain areas which are involved with fine motor behavior, like the cerebellum, may be responsible for this effect separate from those brain areas, like the cerebral cortex, that may be more involved with the anxiolytic effects of the benzodiazepines. The impairment of motor behavior is not merely a laboratory phenomenon and has been shown to include impaired driving skills as well.[7]

The benzodiazepines will induce a mild-to-moderate anterograde amnesia,[8,9] which means established memories remain intact, but the formation of new memories is impaired. This impairment of memory is a reliable effect following either chronic use or even a single dose of a benzodiazepine, seen with the longer and shorter half-life benzodiazepines. In fact, the short half-life benzodiazepines, triazolam (Halcion®) and alprazolam (Xanax®), are more likely to precipitate memory deficits following a single dose.[10] Although reliable, this impairment of memory is not a large effect in that one has to use precise testing devices to illustrate the anterograde amnesia. It is unlikely that, at normal clinical doses, this level of memory impairment is enough to cause difficulties in normal everyday activities. However, the extent to which this small drug-induced memory deficit can worsen an existing memory problem, for example, in elderly patients, remains to be determined.

These three common effects of the benzodiazepines are more intense in elderly patients. This poses a major problem in a population that may already be experiencing difficulty in motor behavior and memory.

There is an uncommon behavioral reaction to the benzodiazepines that is the center of some controversy. Several investigators have reported what some call paradoxical aggression, as a result of benzodiazepine medications. These reports conclude that benzodiazepines will precipitate feelings of hostility and overt aggression in a small portion of the population.[11] Even though there has been some research confirming of these findings, not all investigators have been able to demonstrate this effect. In fact, some report benzodiazepine-induced decreases in aggression.[12] There simply is not enough data to state that the aggression seen following benzodiazepine medication can be attributed solely to the drug.

The Controversy Surrounding Triazolam (Halcion®)

A great deal of negative publicity has been generated concerning triazolam (Halcion®). It has been suggested that there are major behavioral problems that are precipitated with triazolam use. However, when one thoroughly examines the results of controlled studies, there is meager evidence at best that the adverse behaviors and reactions seen after triazolam administration are any different than those associated with other benzodiazepines.[13]

EFFECTS ON BRAIN FUNCTIONING

The brain system which has been the focus of attention concerning the possible mechanism of action for the more traditional sedatives/hypnotics is the GABA system. There are neurons in the CNS that use the amino acid gamma-aminobutyric acid (GABA) as a neurotransmitter. This means that when these neurons fire, they secrete GABA into their synapses. When GABA receptors are stimulated by the presence of GABA they typically inhibit the post-synaptic neuron from firing. Thus, the result of driving those neurons that use GABA as a neurotransmitter is a decrease in neuronal activity. Most small inhibitory neurons throughout the CNS use GABA in their synapses. In the cerebral cortex, the normal mediation of inhibition is accomplished by these GABA neurons.

The mechanism of action for the benzodiazepines has been well-described.[14] There is a class of receptors in the CNS that detects the presence of GABA. There are actually two subtypes of GABA receptors—$GABA_A$ and $GABA_B$. When $GABA_A$ binds to this receptor, it allows the flow of chloride ions through a special channel in the membrane. This flow causes inhibition of the neuron's firing. In addition to a site for GABA, the $GABA_A$ receptor has a site for the benzodiazepine molecule. When benzodiazepines are present on the $GABA_A$ receptor, they increase the efficiency of GABA to bind to the receptor. In the absence of GABA molecules, the benzodiazepine molecule itself does not cause the flow of chloride ions, nor does it in any way induce inhibition. It is by enhancing the normal interaction of GABA with the $GABA_A$ receptor that benzodiazepines decrease brain activity.

The discovery of a benzodiazepine site on the $GABA_A$ receptor begs the question, "Why should the CNS have a detector of an exogenous substance?" One answer is that the brain must have its own natural substance that normally binds to these sites. The situation is similar to the discovery of opiate receptors in the brain and the ensuing search for the endogenous opiates. As we will see in chapter 7, the endogenous opiates were found and are now well-characterized. The search for the endogenous benzodiazepines is in its early stages and has only preliminary results.[15]

The mechanism of action for the barbiturates is less clearly understood. There are two possible mechanisms by which the barbiturates alter brain functioning. First, the barbiturates may have the ability to bind onto and clog up sodium channels in the axon. By so doing, this will prevent the formation of the action potential by the neuron.[16] This essentially shuts down the affected neuron. It simply cannot fire if its sodium channels are blocked. A second possible mechanism is the apparent ability of the barbiturates to enhance the flow of chloride ions into the neuron. This has the effect of inhibiting the neuron from firing. This action may be accomplished by a direct action of barbiturate molecules on the $GABA_A$ receptor, discussed earlier. There is evidence that barbiturates will bind to a site on the GABA receptor that is different from the benzodiazepine binding site, and by so binding will also enhance the normal functioning of that $GABA_A$ receptor.[17] It is very possible that the barbiturates act both ways to depress brain activity. Appreciate that, in addition to the brain, the barbiturates have the ability to depress the activity of various types of "excitable" tissue, such as muscle.[18] Typically these other tissue types do not have GABA receptors, so the depressant action of the barbiturates does not solely rely on the GABA receptor.

The mechanism of action of the newer anxiolytics will be discussed later.

NONBEHAVIORAL EFFECTS

Some of the nonbehavioral effects following barbiturate administration are:

- a slight decrease in blood pressure and heart rate
- decreased respiration
- an increase in the efficiency of the enzymes in the liver that metabolize drugs

In addition, coma and death can be elicited with high enough doses of the barbiturates.

The benzodiazepines, at moderately high parenteral doses, exert slight decreases in respiration and blood pressure, but these effects are not as intense as those seen with the barbiturates. Other effects include:

- nausea
- headache
- skin rash
- menstrual irregularities

Most important, the benzodiazepines do not have the potential lethality that barbiturates do. Lethal overdose with benzodiazepines is rare. The overwhelming reason why benzodiazepines replaced barbiturates in most medical situations was because benzodiazepines are much safer than barbiturates.

Some of the nonbehavioral effects of the newer anxiolytics are provided later.

WITHDRAWAL

The general characteristic pattern of all withdrawal syndromes, regardless of the class of drug, is the appearance of opposite behaviors during withdrawal than the behaviors elicited by the drug. Also, the severity of withdrawal is directly related to the intensity of drug use. These two characteristics are especially apparent with sedative/hypnotic drug withdrawal.

Since the barbiturates were used to alleviate anxiety, induce sleep, and, in some cases to treat epilepsy, it is not surprising that the withdrawal syndrome for the barbiturates features feelings of anxiety, insomnia, and seizures. Other symptoms include nausea, anorexia, abdominal cramping, and delirium, including visual hallucinations.[19] The seizures can be severe and life-threatening. A difficult withdrawal from barbiturates can be lethal if not medically supervised. It would take chronic long-term use of barbiturates, not characteristic of medically supervised treatment of anxiety but rather more characteristic of drug abuse, to precipitate a life-threatening withdrawal.

The withdrawal syndrome from the benzodiazepines is quite similar to barbiturate withdrawal, with some important differences. The most important difference is that, unlike barbiturate withdrawal, benzodiazepine withdrawal is rarely lethal. Another important difference is the attitude of the medical community and of the public concerning the benzodiazepines, relative to the barbiturates, which impacts the issue of withdrawal. Whereas the barbiturates seem to command a cautious respect of its CNS-depressing properties and potential dangers, the benzodiazepines have lacked this respect. This is illustrated in the unfortunate term "minor tranquilizer,"* which was and still is often used to refer to the benzodiazepines. It was initially thought that there was no withdrawal syndrome associated with the use of benzodiazepines. It now has become clear that there is a withdrawal syndrome similar to barbiturate withdrawal, even following the low dosage levels commonly used to treat anxiety or insomnia.[20] The occurrence of a withdrawal syndrome is not obviated by the newer benzodiazepines with shorter half-lifes but rather is made worse. The shorter the half-life and the higher the daily dose, the more severe the withdrawal.

The withdrawal syndrome for benzodiazepines includes increased anxiety, insomnia, irritability and restlessness, flu-like symptoms (for example, muscle aches), and seizures, if withdrawal is severe. The increased anxiety and insomnia, the most common symptoms, are often referred to as rebound anxiety and rebound insomnia. The shorter half-life benzodiazepines such as triazolam (Halcion®) and the moderate half-life benzodiazepines like alprazolam (Xanax®), have the highest risk for developing both rebound anxiety and insomnia than the longer half-life benzodiazepines.[21]

---

*The term "minor tranquilizer" is an inappropriate term for many reasons. Used to refer to benzodiazepines, minor tranquilizer is contrasted to the term "major tranquilizer," which usually refers to the antipsychotic medications (see chapter 10). Used this way, these terms imply that: 1. the benzodiazepines and the antipsychotic medications are somehow on a continuum—they are not; 2. these two types of drugs share a common mechanism—they do not; and 3. the antipsychotic medications exert their clinical effect by sedation—they do not (see chapter 10).

This is probably due to the fact that blood levels of the drug drop so rapidly for these specific benzodiazepines. The rebound anxiety and insomnia can be seen in between doses, just prior to the next scheduled dose, in people who are not trying to stop using the benzodiazepines but are under treatment. This certainly discourages termination of the medication and encourages not only continued chronic administration but also increased dosages over time. The risk for developing a dependency to the benzodiazepines is high. The occurrence of seizures is usually the result of benzodiazepine medication being discontinued too rapidly.

One of the major improvements in the newer anxiolytics and hypnotics is the apparent absence of any withdrawal syndrome.

THE NEW GENERATION ANXIOLYTICS

Three new families of drugs have been developed specifically to treat anxiety and insomnia, however, these drugs are not similar in structure to the benzodiazepines. The following are examples of these medications:

1. The imidazo-pyridines
   a. Alpidem
   b. Zolpidem
2. The cyclopyrrolones
   a. Suriclone
   b. Zoplicone
3. The azopirones
   a. Buspirone hydrochloride
   b. Isapirone

Both the imidazo-pyridines and the cyclopyrrolones are similar to the benzodiazepines in that they all act on the $GABA_A$ receptor, except the newer drugs do so in a different manner than the benzodiazepines. The cyclopyrrolones are high-affinity full benzodiazepine agonists that bind to the same sites that bind benzodiazepine molecules. In other words, the cyclopyrrolones have a different molecular shape but have the same action as the benzodiazepines. On the other hand, the imidazo-pyridines are termed partial agonists of the benzodiazepine receptor site because these drugs interact with the benzodiazepine receptor complex in only a limited fashion.[22]

Alpidem and zolpidem are specific examples of the imidazo-pyridines. Alpidem has proven to be as effective as conventional benzodiazepines in alleviating anxiety, but without cognitive impairment, motor impairment, or memory deficits.[23,24] In addition, there is no apparent withdrawal syndrome following abrupt discontinuation of alpidem treatment,[25] nor is there rebound insomnia following zolpidem treatment.[26]

Suriclone and zoplicone are specific examples of the cyclopyrrolones. Suriclone is as effective as diazepam in the treatment of anxiety but without the unwanted sedative and other adverse effects that typically accompany benzodiazepines.[27,28]

Furthermore, the rebound insomnia that is common to benzodiazepine treatment is not seen with zoplicone.[26]

The most promising of the newer drug families is the azopirones, specifically buspirone and isapirone. These drugs mark a strategically new way of treating anxiety disorders. Unlike traditional sedatives/hypnotics and other newer unconventional medications discussed above, the azopirones do not act on brain GABA systems but rather on brain serotonin systems.[29] There are many types of serotonin receptors in the brain. One type, the $5HT_{1A}$ receptor, is found in the cerebral cortex and is inhibitory, which means that when activated these receptors will decrease cerebral activity. Buspirone and isapirone bind to and activate these receptors.

Buspirone is quite effective in treating anxiety disorders.[30] It has a relatively short half life of two to four hours, and there have been no overdose fatalities associated with its use, making it a very safe drug.

Buspirone has been shown to be as effective an anxiolytic as diazepam, but unlike the benzodiazepines, buspirone does not induce unwanted sedation, motor impairment,[31] or memory deficits.[32] Furthermore, there does not appear to be any withdrawal syndrome associated with cessation of this treatment.[33] However, it does have its own adverse effects, like headache and nausea.[34] Isapirone has a similar profile. While as effective as diazepam in treating anxiety, isapirone does not have any of the common adverse sedative effects of diazepam but does produce some undesirable gastrointestinal reactions.[35] The azapirones also have a characteristic one-to-three week latency, from the onset of taking the medication to relief of anxiety,[36] which may pose a significant problem in those situations in which relief of anxiety symptoms cannot tolerate a long delay. Despite these few limitations, the use of buspirone and isapirone has increased dramatically, and these new drugs may soon replace the benzodiazepines as the ideal medication for controlling anxiety.

SPECIAL BEHAVIORAL ISSUES

Cross Tolerance and Summation

We have discussed the concept of tolerance in chapter 1. Now, the issue of cross tolerance and summation of drug effects is well-illustrated by the sedatives/hypnotics. Cross tolerance occurs when a tolerance for a particular drug also extends to other drugs in the same class. For example, if a person develops a tolerance to a barbiturate like phenobarbital, then that person will have tolerance to a benzodiazepine like Valium®, even though that person has never taken Valium® before. Just as cross tolerance develops to drugs within the same class, the ingestion of different drugs within the same class sometimes produces a summation of drug effects. For example, if a person takes a dose of barbiturates that induces disinhibition and then takes a dose of methaqualones, the resultant behavior is more like the behavior following a much larger dose of barbiturates. In other words, the sedative hypnotics will add one dose to another, the end behavior essentially reflecting the sum of all the doses taken.

Differential Tolerance

Not all behaviors elicited by the sedatives/hypnotics will develop tolerance at the same rate. The sedating effects of the barbiturates develop tolerance more quickly than do effects of the respiratory depression. Tolerance to the anxiolytic (anti-anxiety) effects of the benzodiazepines develops more slowly than does tolerance to the next-day lethargy following a dose.

The Specific Pharmacological Treatment of Anxiety

The major advances in the treatment of anxiety in the last ten years are reflected in the more precise diagnostic categories for the various types. Furthermore, it now appears that these different subtypes of anxiety disorders respond differently to pharmacological treatments. The following is a summary of the various classifications of anxiety disorders and the medication that seems to work best to treat them.[37]

Panic disorder.   These sudden, unexplainable, and often frequently occurring attacks of terror and feelings of impending doom are relatively short in duration. The symptoms usually include heart palpitations, labored breathing, sweating, dizziness, and intense depersonalization. Benzodiazepines, in particular, alprazolam (Xanax®), and the tricyclic antidepressants, in particular, imipramine (Tofranil®) [see chapter 8], are the more successful medications for this type of anxiety.

Generalized anxiety disorder.   This condition of free floating anxiety does not occur in intense bouts like in panic disorder but may actually be present to some degree in other diagnostically distinct classifications of anxiety. The symptoms include heart palpitations, shortness of breath, sweating, upset stomach, diarrhea, muscle tension and aches, trembling and twitches. Both the long- and short-acting benzodiazepines have traditionally been the first-line medication for generalized anxiety disorder. However, recent reports have described the success of buspirone, the new generation anxiolytic, in treating generalized anxiety disorder. Furthermore, the tricyclic antidepressant imipramine has also been successful. It should be noted that beta blockers like propranolol have never been shown to be useful in treating generalized anxiety disorder but are often still prescribed.

Phobias.   Basically, this condition involves a fearful and disruptive avoidance of a condition or object that is not based on a true threat. It appears in a variety of forms:

- simple phobias, such as claustrophobia (fear of enclosed places) and acrophobia (fear of heights)
- social phobias, like fear of eating in public, using a public restroom, or speaking in public
- agoraphobia, the intense fear of public places

There is little data that directly demonstrates the usefulness of any medication for simple phobias. There is meager evidence that a type of antidepressant medication—the monoamine oxidase inhibitors (MAOIs)—is successful in the treatment of social phobia (chapter 8). Agoraphobia responds somewhat to the tricyclic antidepressant imipramine, but this is not seen in all studies.

Obsessive-compulsive disorder.   This disorder is characterized by overwhelming impulses to ritualistically repeat a certain act over and over again (like hand washing, checking that doors are locked, etc.). The specific antidepressant clomipramine has been the most successful medication in the treatment of obsessive-compulsive disorder.

This brief review illustrates the heterogeneity of anxiety as a behavioral disorder. The success of various medications on different types of anxiety strongly suggests that the brain systems that are responsible for the particular pathologies are in fact different from one another. Research will further define these differences and hopefully yield a specific treatment strategy for the efficient treatment of anxiety.

REVIEW EXAM

1. List the reasons for using the sedatives/hypnotics.
2. Name two pre-barbiturate sedatives/hypnotics.
3. Name one sedative/hypnotic introduced at the time the barbiturates also were introduced.
4. What is the principal reason why the benzodiazepines are preferred over the barbiturates?
5. What are the significant consequences to the high-lipid solubility of the sedatives/hypnotics?
6. What is redistribution?
7. Characterize the biphasic clearance of the barbiturates and benzodiazepines.
8. Give a specific example of a long-, short-, and ultra-short duration barbiturate.
9. What is the half-life of one traditional and one newer benzodiazepine?
10. What are active metabolites?
11. Describe the behaviors that can be elicited with increased dosages of barbiturates.
12. How is the range of behaviors induced with benzodiazepines different than those induced by the barbiturates?
13. Describe disinhibition.
14. How do the benzodiazepines alter sleep patterns?
15. Name the three common adverse behavioral effects of the benzodiazepines.
16. What is the normal role of GABA in brain functioning?
17. Specifically, how do the benzodiazepines effect the GABA receptor?
18. Name the two possible mechanisms by which barbiturates alter brain functioning.
19. Name three nonbehavioral effects induced by barbiturates.
20. List three nonbehavioral effects induced by benzodiazepines, not barbiturates.

21. Name two general characteristics of all withdrawal syndromes.
22. List four symptoms of the barbiturate withdrawal syndrome.
23. Provide four symptoms of the benzodiazepine withdrawal syndrome.
24. How are the imidazo-pyridines and the cyclopyrrolones similar to the benzodiazepines?
25. Behaviorally, how are the imidazo-pyridines and the cyclopyrrolones dissimilar to the benzodiazepines?
26. How does buspirone alter brain functioning?
27. List three ways in which the azapirones differs behaviorally from diazepam.
28. Give two adverse behavioral effects of the azapirones.
29. Describe differential tolerance.
30. Name the major classifications of anxiety disorder and the drug that successfully treats each classification.

REFERENCES

1. GOODMAN, L., & GILMAN, A. (1990). *The Pharmacological Basis of Therapeutics* (8th ed.). New York: Macmillan Publishing Co.
2. SELLERS, E., CARR, G., BERSTEIN, J., SELLERS, S., & KOCH-WESER, J. (1972). Interaction of chloral hydrate and ethanol in man. II. hemodynamics and performance. *Clinical Pharmacology and Therapeutics, 13*, 50–58.
3. ADAM, K., & OSWALD, I. (1984). Effects of lormetazepam and of flurazepam on sleep. *British Journal of Clinical Pharmacology, 17(5)*, 531–538.
4. TSOI, W. (1991). Insomnia: drug treatment. *Annals of the Academy of Medicine, Singapore, 20(2)*, 269–272.
5. WALSH, J., & ENGELHARDT, C. (1992). Trends in the pharmacologic treatment of insomnia. *Journal of Clinical Psychiatry, 53* Suppl., 7–10.
6. MENDELSON, W. (1992). Clinical distinctions between long-acting and short-acting benzodiazepines. *Journal of Clinical Psychiatry, 53* Suppl., 4–7.
7. VAN LAAR, M., VOLKERTS, E., & VAN WILLIGENBURG, A. (1992). Therapeutic effects and effects on actual driving performance of chronically administered buspirone and diazepam in anxious outpatients. *Journal of Clinical Psychopharmacology, 12(2)*, 86–95.
8. CURRAN, H. (1986). Tranquillizing memories: a review of the effects of benzodiazepines on human memory. *Biological Psychology, 23(2)*, 179–213.
9. LISTER, R. (1985). The amnesic action of benzodiazepines in man. *Neuroscience and Behavioral Reviews, 9(1)*, 87–94.
10. SCHARF, M., SASKIN, P., & FLETCHER, K. (1987). Benzodiazepine-induced amnesia. Clinical laboratory findings. *Journal of Clinical Psychiatry, 5*, 14–17.
11. LION, J., AZCARATE, C., & KOEPKE, H. (1975). "Paradoxical rage reactions" during psychotropic medication. *Disease of the Nervous System, 36*, 557–558.
12. WILKINSON, C. (1985). Effects of diazepam (Valium®) and trait anxiety on human physical aggression and emotional state. *Journal of Behavioral Medicine, 8*, 101–114.
13. ROTHCHILD, A. (1992). Disinhibition, amnestic reactions, and other adverse reactions secondary to triazolam: a review of the literature. *Journal of Clinical Psychiatry, 53* Suppl., 69–79.
14. HAEFELY, W., KYBURZ, E., GERECKE, M., & MOHLER, H. (1985). Recent advances in the molecular pharmacology of benzodiazepine receptors and in the structural activity relationships of their agonists and antagonists. *Advances in Drug Research, 14*, 165–322.
15. HAEFLY, W. (1988). Endogenous ligands of the benzodiazepine receptor. *Pharmacopsychiatry, 21(1)*, 43–46.
16. FRENKEL, C., DUCH, D., & URBAN, B. (1990). Molecular actions of pentobarbital isomers on sodium channels from human brain cortex. *Anesthesiology, 72(4)*, 640–649.
17. HAEFELY, W., & POLC, P. (1986). Physiology of GABA enhancement by benzodiazepines and barbiturates. In R. Olse, & J. Venter (Eds.), *Benzodiazepine-GABA Receptors and Chloride Channels: Structural and Functional Properties* (pp. 97–133). New York: Alan R. Liss.

18. HARVEY, S. (1975). Hypnotics and sedatives—the barbiturates. In L. Goodman, & A. Gilman (Eds.), *The Pharmacological Basis of Therapeutics* (5th ed.) (pp. 102–123). New York: Macmillan Publishing Co.

19. LADER, M. (1972). Abuse liability of prescribed psychotropic drugs. In J. Kane & J. Lieberman (Eds.), *Adverse Effects of Psychotropic Drugs* (pp. 77–84). New York: The Guilford Press.

20. SELLERS, E. (1988). Alcohol, barbiturate, and benzodiazepine withdrawal syndromes: clinical management. *Canadian Medical Association Journal*, 139, 113–120.

21. SALZMAN, C. (1992). Behavioral side effects of benzodiazepines. In J. Kane & J. Lieberman (Eds.), *Adverse Effects of Psychotropic Drugs* (pp. 139–152). New York: The Guilford Press.

22. RICHARDS, G., SCHOCH, P., & JENCK, F. (1991). Benzodiazepine receptors and their ligands. In R. Rodgers & S. Cooper (Eds.), *5HT1A Agonists, 5-HT3 Antagonists, and Benzodiazepines. Their Comparative Behavioral Pharmacology* (pp. 1–30). New York: John Wiley & Sons.

23. MORTON, S., & LADER, M. (1992). Alpidem and lorazepam in the treatment of patients with anxiety disorders: comparison of physiological and psychological effects. *Pharmacopsychiatry*, 25(4), 177–181.

24. MORSELLI, P. (1990). On the therapeutic action of alpidem in anxiety disorders: an overview of the European data. *Pharmacopsychiatry*, 23 Suppl.3, 129–134.

25. DIAMOND, B., NGUYEN, H., O'NEAL, E., OCHS, R., KAFFEMAN, M., & BORISON, R. (1991). A comparative study of alpidem, a nonbenzodiazepine, and lorazepam in patients with nonpsychotic anxiety. *Psychopharmacology Bulletin*, 27(1), 67–71.

26. LADER, M. (1992). Rebound insomnia and newer hypnotics. *Psychopharmacology (Berl)*, 108(3), 248–255.

27. ANSSEAU, M., OLI'E, J., VON FRENCKELL, R., JOURDAIN, G., STEHLE, B., & GUILLET, P. (1991). Controlled comparison of the efficacy and safety of four doses of suriclone, diazepam, and placebo in generalized anxiety disorder. *Psychopharmacology (Berl)*, 104(4), 439–443.

28. GERLACH, J., CHRISTENSEN, J., CHRISTENSEN, T., ELLEY, J., JENSEN, J., & LARSEN, S. (1987). Suriclone and diazepam in the treatment of neurotic anxiety. A double blind cross-over trial. *Psychopharmacology (Berl)*, 93(3), 296–300.

29. HOYER, D. (1991). The 5-HT receptor family: ligands, distribution and receptor-effector coupling. In R. Rodgers & S. Cooper (Eds.), *5HT1A Agonists, 5-HT3 Antagonists and Benzodiazepines. Their Comparative Behavioral Pharmacology* (pp. 31–57). New York: John Wiley & Sons.

30. TAYLOR, D. (1988). Buspirone, a new approach to the treatment of anxiety. *FASEB-J*, 2(9), 2445–2452.

31. MATTILA, M., ARANKO, K., & SEPPALA, T. (1982). Acute effects of buspirone and alcohol on psychomotor skills. *Journal of Clinical Psychiatry*, 43, 56–60.

32. LUCKI, I., RICKELS, K., GIESECKE, M., & GELLER, A. (1987). Differential effects of the anxiolytic drugs, diazepam and buspirone, on memory function. *British Journal of Clinical Pharmacology*, 23(2), 207–211.

33. MURPHY, S., OWEN, R., & TYRER, P. (1989). Comparative assessment of efficacy and withdrawal symptoms after 6 and 12 weeks' treatment with diazepam or buspirone. *British Journal of Psychiatry*, 154, 529–534.

34. SCHWEIZER, E., & RICKELS, K. (1991). Serotonergic anxiolytics: a review of their clinical efficacy. In R. Rodgers & S. Cooper (Eds.), *5HT1A Agonists, 5-HT3 Antagonists and Benzodiazepines. Their Comparative Behaviorally Pharmacology.* (pp 365–376). New York: John Wiley & Sons.

35. BORISON, R., ALBRECHT, J., & DIAMOND, B. (1990). Efficacy and safety of a putative axiolytic agent: isapirone. *Psychopharmacology Bulletin*, 26(2), 207–210.

36. RICKELS, K., SCHWEIZER, E., CSANALOSI, I., CASE, W., & CHUNG, H. (1988). Long-term treatment of anxiety and risk of withdrawal: prospective comparison of clorazepate and buspirone. *Archives of General Psychiatry*, 45, 444 – 450.

37. LYDIARD, B., ROY-BURNE, P., & BALLENGER, J. (1988). Recent advances in the psychopharmacological treatment of anxiety disorders. *Hospital and Community Psychiatry*, 39, 1157–1165.

be a temptation to those with limited money or limited access to ethanol. However, methyl alcohol is quite toxic. The metabolism of methyl alcohol produces formic acid and formaldehyde. Both of these substances contribute to the toxicity which follows methanol consumption. Some of the signs of methanol poisoning include vomiting, severe abdominal cramps, blurred vision, which can proceed to blindness, coma, and death.

2. Isopropyl alcohol—propanol is the alcohol commonly found in rubbing alcohol. It is commonly used as a disinfectant or germicide. Propanol is not a very effective disinfectant at concentrations less than 70 percent.[1]

3. Ethyl alcohol—ethanol or grain alcohol is arguably the most widely used drug in the world. Our discussion will focus exclusively on ethanol.

FORMS OF ETHANOL

Ethanol is produced by yeast's interaction with glucose and water, a process called fermentation. In this process, the sugars are converted to ethanol and carbon dioxide by these microorganisms. However, yeast will die in high concentrations of ethanol, so the absolute concentration of ethanol in the fermentation process is about 15 percent, which is the typical concentration in most wines and beers. One way to achieve higher ethanol concentrations is to remove some of the water from the solution that has been fermented, thus making the ethanol concentration higher, a process called distillation. Ethanol has a lower boiling temperature than does water, so when it is boiled the fermented beverage will emit a vapor that has more ethanol than water. By collecting and condensing these vapors in cooling tubes, the resulting beverage will have an appreciably higher content of ethanol. The so-called hard liquors—brandy, whiskey, vodka, rum, and so on, have high ethanol concentrations due to distillation. Another more direct method of achieving a higher ethanol content in fermented beverages is to add ethanol to it. This strategy has been used for ages to yield so-called fortified wines such as sherry and vermouth and is now used on beers and malt beverages.

The actual amount of ethanol in a beverage could be expressed as a percent of the volume of the solution, but often an alternate way of expressing the ethanol content of a beverage is used. The amount of ethanol in a beverage is expressed by its "proof." Proof is two times the absolute percentage of ethanol in the solution. For example, wines and most beers have approximately 15 percent ethanol, or 30 proof, whereas some distilled beverages, for example, specific rums, have ethanol concentrations as high as 75 percent, or 151 proof.

Regardless of how an ethanol beverage is flavored or the form it takes, the critical issue for dosing with ethanol, as with any other drug, is simply how much of the drug, or how many ethanol molecules, is being administered. In the case of ethanol, one has to determine the absolute amount of ethanol that has been consumed. With such a wide variety of ethanol beverages, the issue of equivalency of different ethanol beverages takes some thought. Basically, one needs less of a higher-proof beverage to get the same amount of ethanol that is found in a lower-proof beverage. The thumbnail rule, that one shot (about one ounce) of distilled ethanol or hard liquor is the same as one glass of beer and one cup of wine is not that far off. For a distilled beverage such as gin, that is 94.6 proof or 47.3 percent ethanol—the absolute amount of ethanol in a one-ounce shot glass is approximately 0.47 ounces. In a four-ounce glass of wine, that is 24 proof or 12 percent ethanol—the absolute amount of ethanol is approximately .48 ounces. For a twelve-ounce bottle of beer that contains about 5 percent ethanol, there is approximately .6 ounces of absolute ethanol. These are roughly equivalent doses. However, appreciate the variability of ethanol content in different alcoholic beverages. Distilled ethanol beverages vary from a common 80 proof or 40 percent ethanol content in most rums, vodkas, and tequila, to the 94 to 95 proof or 46 to 48 percent ethanol content in some gins, to 151 proof or 75 percent ethanol content in certain rums. What is important is the actual absolute amount of ethanol that is being consumed.

ABSORPTION AND DISTRIBUTION

Since ethanol is almost exclusively taken orally (Figure 5–1A), our discussion will deal only with this route of administration. Ethanol is absorbed rapidly from the stomach and small intestine. Only about 2 percent to 5 percent of an ingested dose is excreted unchanged from the body, which means that approximately 98 percent to 95 percent of an ingested dose of ethanol is absorbed.

Let us now follow that portion of an ethanol dose which is absorbed. Approximately 20 percent of that dose is absorbed at the stomach, with the remaining 80 percent absorbed in the small intestine. Let us first examine the absorption at the stomach.

At first, absorption from the stomach is rapid, then it slows down. There are two principal factors which modify the absorption of ethanol at the stomach:

1. Volume and concentration of the dose (i.e., beverage)—In general, higher concentrations and larger volumes of ethanol will cause faster absorption. This type of increased absorption, with increasing concentration, does plateau however.
2. Presence of food in the stomach—Food in the stomach will retard ethanol absorption. Drinking on a full stomach will cause slower ethanol absorption (Figure 5–2A).

Absorption of ethanol from the small intestine is rapid and complete, regardless of the food content in it. Although the digestive system is essentially a continuous tube, the stomach does not simply let food stream along into the intestines. A muscle called the pylorus sphincter, at the junction of the stomach and the small intestine, opens and closes to control the flow of food (Figure 5–1B and C). Since the small intestine is so efficient in absorbing ethanol and since about 80 percent of an absorbed ethanol dose is absorbed at the small intestine, the most important factor in determining the overall rate of ethanol absorption is stomach emptying (i.e., pyloric activity) into the small intestine. Any factor that affects stomach emptying will also affect ethanol absorption. For instance, effervescence (i.e., bubbliness) will trigger the pylorus to open, so ethanol beverages that are effervescent, like champagne or other sparkling wines, will reach the small intestine quickly. As a result, intoxication will be induced

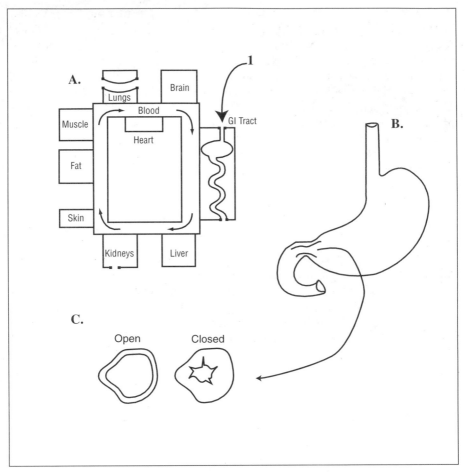

FIGURE 5–1   The Enteral Administration of Ethanol
A. The most common route of administration of ethanol is an enteral—oral—route.
B. The dynamics of the stomach play a key role in the absorption of ethanol. At the junction between the stomach and the small intestine there is a muscle called the pyloric sphincter.
C. When the pylorus is open, stomach contents are allowed to pass into the small intestine. However, when the pylorus is closed, the contents remain in the stomach. Since ethanol is rapidly and completely absorbed from the small intestine, the activity of the pyloric sphincter plays a key role in the speed of ethanol absorption.

more quickly. On the other hand, the simple presence of food will cause the pylorus to close and periodically open, to allow stomach contents to move into the small intestine. It is the combination of these factors influencing absorption at both the stomach and small intestine that accounts for the overall absorption of an ethanol dose observed in the blood (Figure 5–2B).

Once absorbed, a dose of ethanol will be distributed uniformly through all tissue compartments, especially all fluid compartments.

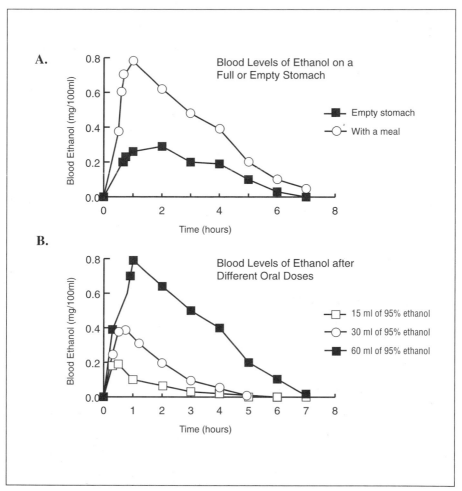

FIGURE 5–2   Factors That Affect Blood Ethanol Levels
A.The presence of food in the stomach will affect ethanol blood levels. Notice the sizable difference in blood levels of ethanol when dosing occurs on an empty or full stomach.
B.The amount of ethanol ingested will also have an impact on the blood levels.

As with other drugs, measuring the levels of ethanol in the body is done by monitoring the amount of ethanol in the blood. Blood levels of ethanol are expressed as grams of ethanol present in 100 mls of blood. For example, 0.03 g percent is 30 mg of ethanol in 100 mls of blood. Since ethanol will be distributed to the fluid compartments in the body, the actual blood level of ethanol will vary from person to person, according to body size. In other words, the larger the absolute size of the fluid compartments, the less ethanol will be left in the blood. The same ethanol dose (i.e., the same number of ethanol molecules) given to two people—one weighing 100 pounds, and the other weighing 200 pounds, will result in higher ethanol blood levels in the smaller person.

BIOTRANSFORMATION

Ethanol molecules are biotransformed by two systems in the liver. The overwhelming majority (approximately 90 percent) of biotransformation is done by the alcohol dehydrogenase system.

Ethanol is converted into acetaldehyde by the enzyme alcohol dehydrogenase. Acetaldehyde is then converted by the enzyme aldehyde dehydrogenase to acetate and acetyl coenzyme A. This is a reaction that cannot be accelerated, nor does it develop tolerance. It will transform approximately 10 mls or 0.3 ounces of absolute ethanol every hour. To dose more than 0.3 ounces every hour will result in the accumulation of ethanol and rising blood levels. We have seen that this small amount of ethanol is approximately one-third of an amount of absolute ethanol in most common drinks.

It should be noted that acetaldehyde is toxic. Normally, acetaldehyde is broken down fairly quickly, so it does not have a chance to accumulate in the body. However, certain medications can alter the breakdown pathway of ethanol. The drug disulfiram or antibuse is used to help people abstain from ethanol. This drug blocks the breakdown of acetaldehyde by blocking aldehyde dehydrogenase activity. The sharply rising blood levels of acetaldehyde cause a person to become sick if he or she consumes ethanol after taking disulfiram. As quickly as five to ten minutes after consuming ethanol, in the presence of disulfiram, the face may be flushed and feel hot, then intense throbbing may be felt in the head and neck, and later, intense headaches, nausea, vomiting, chest pains, vertigo, and confusion may occur. While the use of disulfiram to treat alcoholism is most effective in helping reduce ethanol consumption initially, the use of disufiram alone in long-term treatment has not proven effective.[4]

Recent studies indicate that there may be some alcohol dehydrogenase in the stomach and that there may be sex differences in the actual amount of this gastric component.[5] Women appear to have less gastric alcohol dehydrogenase than do men, which supports the data that, with most factors controlled, women have higher blood levels of ethanol and become intoxicated more rapidly than do men. The existence of a significant amount of alcohol dehydrogenase in the gastric mucosa and the possible sex differences in these levels have yet to be replicated by other investigators.

The other enzyme system that metabolizes ethanol is a subset of the microsomal enzyme systems in the liver. This is called the microsomal ethanol oxidizing system or MEOS. This accounts for approximately 5 percent to 10 percent of ethanol biotransformation. This system is different from the alcohol dehydrogenase system in that it will increase its activity with increased ethanol dosing. Thus, this system may play a role in tolerance and cross-tolerance, as seen in heavy ethanol users.

Let us briefly turn our attention to the small amount of an ethanol dose (approximately 2 to 5 percent of the dose) that is not metabolized and is passed unchanged from the body. This small amount of ethanol is excreted unchanged in the urine, sweat, and expired breath. The level of ethanol in one's breath is, at most, only 0.05 percent of blood levels, so at best it is a crude estimate of actual blood levels. However, because breath levels can be performed in the field relatively easily, as simple as asking someone to blow up a balloon, blood alcohol level tests are now commonly performed by law enforcement officials when attempting to verify whether or not a person is driving while intoxicated.

NONBEHAVIORAL EFFECTS OF ETHANOL

There are some important nonbehavioral effects of ethanol, which include:

1. Increased heat loss and a decrease in body temperature,[6] despite subjective feelings of warmth. The common image of being stranded on a snowy mountain and rescued by a huge Saint Bernard with a case of brandy around its neck, implies that drinking ethanol in a state of hypothermia is helpful. It is not, it only makes matters worse!

2. Intake of small amounts (less than two drinks per day) seems to lower the risk of heart disease.[7] The reported benefits of small doses are provocative and must be carefully considered in light of the next effect.

3. Intake of moderate-to-high amounts increase the risk of heart disease,[8] specifically increased blood pressure.[9] This effect is of particular concern to individuals who are diagnosed as borderline hypertensive. Refraining from ethanol consumption may make a noticeable difference in those individuals.

4. Increased diuresis (urination) by inhibition of ADH (antidiuretic hormone) secretion. This is a direct effect of ethanol on the secretion of this hormone by the hypothalamus.[6]

5. Increased risk for developing a variety of cancers[10] of the mouth, stomach, esophagus, liver, pancreas, rectum, and more.

6. Slight suppression of the immune system.[11] This is not unlike the immune effects of the other sedatives/hypnotics discussed in chapter 4.

7. Liver disease, specifically cirrhosis. The burden of the extra work that must be done by the liver to metabolize ethanol takes its toll.

8. Erosive gastritis (severe irritation of the stomach lining). This is typically seen after chronic use and becomes a matter of vital concern because it can prevent the absorption of vitamins and other nutrients. The consequences of this will be discussed later.

9. Acute toxicity, otherwise known as a hangover. This is a consequence of ingesting too much ethanol. The symptoms include upset stomach, headache, thirst, fatigue, and general malaise.

ETHANOL'S EFFECTS ON THE CENTRAL NERVOUS SYSTEM

Changes in Brain Functioning

That ethanol is able to change brain functioning has been evident for a very long time. However, it is amazing that for a drug as ancient as ethanol the precise effects it has on the brain remains unclear. There have been several promising lines of research that may provide some hints.

One of the earliest-described effects of ethanol has been its ability to somehow change the fluid characteristics of cell membranes, in particular, the membranes of neurons. Recall from chapter 1 that the membranes of cells are a phospholipid bilayer, and the center of the membrane may have a fluid-type consistency. Ethanol dissolves in the center of the membrane and causes an increase in the fluidity of the membrane.[12] How this might account for the profound depressant effects ethanol has on brain functioning remains to be determined.

While a variety of neurotransmitter systems have been hypothesized as mediating the effect ethanol has on the brain, experimental observations have not supported most of these theories. Three brain systems have emerged as potential candidates for ethanol's site of action in the brain: the GABA system, the dopamine system, and the glutamate system.

Since the GABA system has proven to be the site of action for other notable sedatives/hypnotics such as the benzodiazepines and barbiturates, it also has been implicated in the mediation of ethanol's effect on the brain. The data are not clear. Some investigators have found a strong connection between ethanol and the $GABA_A$ and $GABA_B$ systems in the brain.[13,14] However, others have reported that there are no changes in the binding of either benzodiazepines or barbiturates to their respective binding sites on the $GABA_A$ receptor and have concluded that ethanol has no direct effect on the $GABA_A$ receptor.[15] It may be that ethanol modifies the GABA receptor indirectly by its membrane-altering effects.[16]

The dopamine system has been the focus of a great deal of attention, primarily because of its role in mediating positive reinforcement and also because of a provocative literature which suggests the genetic marker for alcoholism may be in dopamine-receptor genes. (The specific topic of genetic markers will be discussed later in this chapter.) There are two types of dopamine receptors in the brain that are of particular interest—the D_1 and D_2 dopamine receptors. Some studies have reported increases in only D_1 dopamine receptors following small doses of ethanol in rats[17] and/or increases in both D_1 and D_2 dopamine receptors following large doses of ethanol in rats,[18] while others have reported decreases in D_1 dopamine receptors.[19] However, there may be some important dietary interactions at play. When diet is strictly controlled, moderate doses of ethanol do not change D_1 nor D_2 dopamine receptors, which suggests that brain dopamine receptors are not likely to play a significant role in the effect of moderate ethanol doses.[20]

Another class of brain receptor that has been implicated in the effects of ethanol is the glutamate system. Neurons that release glutamate as their neurotransmitter typically produce an excitatory effect on the postsynaptic target. The two main categories of receptors for glutamate are the NMDA (N-methyl-D-aspartate) and non-NMDA receptors. The excitation mediated by NMDA receptor activity was inhibited by ethanol at doses that would induce intoxication.[21] This has led to the hypothesis that the intoxicating effects of ethanol may be due to ethanol's ability to inhibit normal levels of excitation produced by NMDA receptors.[22]

The principal problem with these hypotheses concerning the direct mechanism of action of ethanol is that all of the individual brain systems interact with one another, thus to change one will in all likelihood change other systems indirectly. To merely describe changes in brain functioning following ethanol ingestion does not mean the described changes are the mechanism of ethanol's effect, rather than a consequence of some other effect.

Behavioral Consequences

The behavior seen following ethanol intake follows virtually the same pattern as sedative hypnotics, discussed in chapter 4 (see Figure 4–3 for the dose response curves). At low doses, one typically finds a lessening of anxiety and, under certain circumstances, the phenomenon of disinhibition. At higher doses, one finds severe impairment in activities usually associated with higher brain processing, such as speech, planning, and complex motor behavior.[23] This impaired motor behavior, because it affects driving skills, has become a difficult societal problem. The probability of a fatal car accident increases exponentially as the blood alcohol level of the driver increases.[24] Even higher doses will lead to "sedation" or better put—unconsciousness. Since ethanol is taken orally, there is a modicum of protection from ingesting severely high doses of ethanol, because a person will pass out or vomit before reaching that level. However, there are some circumstances, namely rapid drinking without pausing, termed "chugging" or "chugalugging," of distilled beverages in which dangerously high and potentially lethal doses of ethanol can be ingested. Driven usually by peer pressure or curiosity, this type of ethanol intake can result in coma and, in some cases, death. To be certain, there are some individuals who may be so sensitive to the effects of ethanol that they risk coma and death at doses that will produce only mild intoxication in most people. Specific behavioral issues concerning ethanol administration will now be examined.

As stated in chapter 2:

> Among the major determinants of behavior following drug administration is set and setting—the expectations of the user and the immediate environment in which the drug is administered.

This fundamental principle of behavioral pharmacology is well illustrated in the behaviors that follow ethanol ingestion. The long history of ethanol use has provided a vast collection of centuries-old expectations about behaviors that are attributed to the intake of ethanol. This makes it extremely difficult to experimentally determine what the behavioral consequences of ethanol are. The main experimental difficulty is how to directly manipulate or at least control for subject expectation. In other words, if a person is totally convinced that ethanol will cause him or her to be more assertive, then how can an experiment be performed that will control for this strong expectation? The experimental design, called the balanced placebo, has allowed control over subject expectation and has provided surprising results.

The Balanced Placebo Design

Most experiments involved in determining the effects of a specific drug include a placebo group, that is, subjects who receive only the vehicle—the substance in which the drug is mixed but not the drug in question. In human studies, subjects typically are not informed about whether or not they are in the drug or placebo group. This is called a blind study. In some experiments, a third party both assigns and labels the drug and vehicle solutions so the experimenter also does not know which group any particular subject is in. This is called a double blind experiment. In either case, the role of expectation by the subjects is not directly controlled because in both cases subjects may be expecting to receive the drug.

The balanced placebo design[25] directly deals with the subject's expectations. There are two essential components of this design: 1. The subjects must really expect or totally not expect to receive a certain drug; and 2. The presence of the drug must not be easily detected in the solution given to the subjects. An important role of the experimenter then is to convince or fool the subjects into believing the particular conditions of the experiment. Once the experimenter has established two groups with different expectations—the group that expects to receive a certain drug and the group that does not expect to receive it—then each of these groups is divided in two—those subjects who actually receive the drug and those who do not, regardless of their expectations. Figure 5–3 illustrates this 2-by-2 design. Notice there will be two authentic conditions, where subjects get what they expect, and two deceptive conditions—one group expects to receive the drug but will not actually receive it, and one group does not expect to receive the drug but does. Let us examine an early use of the balanced placebo design, which has provided some rather surprising data regarding alcoholism.

Alan Marlatt and his group[26] instructed half of the subjects that they were part of an experiment that would compare the taste of different vodkas. They were in-

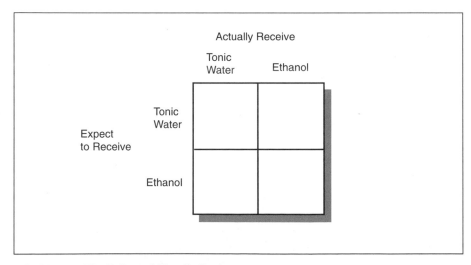

FIGURE 5–3   The Balanced Placebo Design
The balanced placebo design is a 2-by-2 experimental protocol designed to directly manipulate subject expectation. In this particular example, half of the subjects are convinced that they will be receiving a beverage containing ethanol; the other half are convinced that they will be receiving tonic water. Half of each of these expectancy groups will actually receive a beverage containing ethanol; the other half will not.

structed in the taste-rating system and given the appropriate forms to fill out. They were to consume as much of each different vodka as was necessary to complete the comparisons. The other half of the subjects were told that they were part of an experiment that would compare the taste of different tonic waters. They were instructed in the taste-rating system for tonic and given the appropriate forms to fill out. They also were to consume as much of each different tonic water as was necessary to complete the comparisons. Half of the subjects in each of these groups received the vodka solution and the other half received only tonic water. The solution of vodka and tonic, mixed one part vodka to five parts tonic, was chosen because it has been shown that people can detect the presence of ethanol in this solution only by chance, that is, only 50 percent of the time.[26] To maintain the assigned expectancies, those subjects expecting to receive vodka had "new" vodka bottles brought before them, complete with tax seals intact, so they could see that these were fresh bottles. In fact, the subjects who expected vodka but received tonic had vodka bottles with the vodka removed, cleaned, filled with defizzed tonic water, and resealed. Those subjects expecting to receive tonic water had "new" tonic water bottles brought before them. In fact, the subjects who expected tonic water but received vodka had tonic water bottles that had the vodka solution added and resealed with standard soda bottle caps.

Figure 5–4A shows the results of this experiment with social drinkers. Those subjects who expected to receive ethanol drank more than those who expected to drink tonic water, regardless of whether or not they actually did receive ethanol. In other words, it was the expectation of receiving a drug that determined the behavioral outcome, not the actual pharmacological presence of the drug. This is a powerful demonstration of the importance of cognitive factors in behavior following the ingestion of a drug. The CNS processing involved in those cognitive processes that mediate a person's "set" or expectation is a major determinant of behavior following drug administration.

It may be one thing to fool a group of "social drinkers" with this type of balanced placebo experiment but what about a more experienced group of subjects? This same experiment was conducted on a group of "alcoholic" subjects. For this experiment, subjects were classified as "alcoholic" according to a strict criteria. Furthermore, these subjects were "active" alcoholics who were recruited from a bar and not interested in treatment. The result was virtually the same as that of the social drinkers experiment, namely that expectation was the major determinant of behavior following ethanol consumption (Figure 5–4B). These experiments showed that alcoholic subjects expecting to receive tonic water but actually receiving ethanol did not change their consumption patterns. These are important findings that address a pivotal theory held by some theorists and alcohol treatment programs. According to the "loss of control" concept, once ethanol is introduced into the systems of alcoholics, it triggers a series of physiological events which prevents them from being able to stop drinking. This "loss of control" concept had been challenged before,[27] but not as convincingly as in the direct examination of subject expectation in balanced placebo experiments. Thus, the behavior alcoholics exhibit that could be termed "loss of

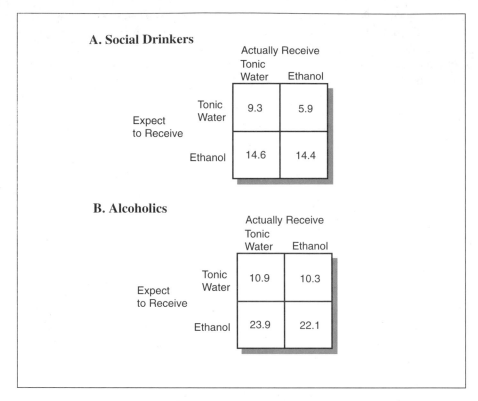

FIGURE 5–4   **The Loss-of-Control Balanced Placebo Experiment**
A balanced placebo design was used to examine the amount of beverage that was consumed in a taste test.
A. Social drinkers drank more when they expected to receive a beverage containing
   ethanol, regardless of whether or not they actually received ethanol.
B. Active alcoholics showed the same basic findings. Namely, they drank more ethanol
   when they expected to receive an ethanol beverage, independent of actually receiving
   ethanol. It is important to note that the alcoholics who expected to receive tonic water
   but actually received ethanol did not exhibit loss-of-control or runaway drinking.

control" in certain situations is not due to some rigid, invariant physiological consequence of ethanol itself.

The balanced placebo design was subsequently used to examine other behaviors, like aggression, sexuality, and even anxiety relief, which have historically been
attributed to the pharmacological actions of ethanol.

The statistics are overwhelming in pointing to the aggression, violence, and
criminal behavior linked to ethanol use. It is assumed that the phenomenon of disinhibition is the fundamental mediator of this effect. Aggressive behavior that is normally suppressed or inhibited by societal and/or moral constraints will be released
when ethanol depresses these inhibitory systems. Animal studies have demonstrated
both an increase in aggressive behavior[28] and a clear decrease in aggression follow-

ing the ingestion of ethanol,[29,30] thus raising the critical question—is there a purely pharmacological induction of violent behavior in humans after ethanol is consumed?

The balanced placebo was used to examine this question, and the results were similar to those of the loss of control experiments. In a balanced placebo type of experiment, subjects who expected to receive ethanol, regardless of whether or not they actually received it, were more aggressive.[31,32] Other experiments have yielded similar results[33] and have proven there is a strong societal expectancy that violent behavior is a consequence of drinking ethanol,[34] which strongly suggests that people who become aggressive after drinking ethanol do so because they believe it will make them more aggressive. How often have the statements, "It wasn't really me, it was the alcohol," or "Well, I had a few drinks and . . ." been offered as excuses for inappropriate aggression?

Despite the numerous studies that have shown subject expectancy to be a critical factor in aggressive behavior, some researchers argue that, at high doses, ethanol may induce aggressive behavior, independent of expectancy.[35]

When the issues of increased sexuality and decreased anxiety following ethanol ingestion were examined using the balanced placebo design, the same type of results emerged. Namely, people who expected to receive ethanol, regardless of whether or not they actually received it, felt more sexually aroused[36] and relaxed[37] than did the subjects who expected to receive tonic water.[38] These findings raise many critical issues not only for the specific topic of ethanol-induced behavior but also for the general topic of any behavior following the ingestion of a drug.

These ethanol expectations are so robust and well-rooted in our culture that they seem to have eclipsed the pharmacological actions of ethanol. We now have a situation in which these expectations may be providing the license to engage in behaviors that are not acceptable. Are we supposed to be less harsh with individuals because ethanol was involved in a date rape, an assault, or spousal abuse? It is human nature to try to get away with inappropriate behavior, and the perennial cry of "It wasn't my fault" will be attempted by many. However, the balanced placebo design experiments relating to ethanol have provided a sobering data base from which to evaluate these age-old pleas.

WITHDRAWAL

The severity of the withdrawal syndrome from ethanol, like other drugs, depends on the duration and intensity of the ethanol dosage. Some symptoms appear early and others appear later, with varying degrees of severity.

The early symptoms include hangover, insomnia, anxiety, agitation, tremor, increased heart rate, and hypertension. These symptoms may last up to two days. Terminating a relatively moderate dependency on ethanol can precipitate a withdrawal that may take a week to resolve. However, the early symptoms of severe withdrawal may also include disorientation and confusion, even hallucinations. The addition of the hallucinations, which may be visual or auditory, and of confusion, would lead to the diagnosis of delirium tremens.

In severe ethanol withdrawal, later symptoms could include fever, electrolyte imbalance, cardiac arrhythmia, and seizures. If not recognized and treated in a hospital, the withdrawal becomes life-threatening. There is a risk of lethality even in medically supervised ethanol withdrawal. The mortality rate in untreated cases of ethanol withdrawal can be as high as 25 percent.[39]

The pharmacological management of ethanol withdrawal typically involves benzodiazepine administration due to the cross-tolerance that develops between ethanol and the benzodiazepines. Parenteral diazepam also is often used to control any seizure activity that may be present. Antipsychotic medications like haloperidol (Haldol®) are given to control hallucinations and thought disorders.[40] Parenteral thiamine is also administered to offset the development of Wernicke's encephalopathy syndrome, which will be discussed in the next section.

In addition to medication, supportive care is an important part of treating ethanol withdrawal. This would include decreasing sensory stimuli, offering reassurance and encouragement, maintaining physical comfort, ensuring enough water is drunk, and orienting the patient to reality. Withdrawal from ethanol is quite difficult and the appropriate supportive care is not a small part of the successful navigation through this process.

NEUROLOGICAL CONSEQUENCES OF CHRONIC ETHANOL USE

Heavy use of ethanol over a long period of time has significant direct and indirect effects on the brain that merit special attention.

Wernicke's Encephalopathy

Chronic excessive use of ethanol results in a pronounced thiamine (vitamin B-1) deficiency, due primarily to the inability of the stomach to absorb thiamine. The chronic erosive and irritating effects of ethanol on the stomach lining is probably the reason for this specific vitamin malabsorption. Thiamine plays a key role in cerebral glucose levels and brain energy metabolism. Prolonged and severe thiamine deficiency, whether induced by ethanol or by other nonpharmacological conditions,[41] will compromise brain energy metabolism and will result in brain cell death.[42] Wernicke's encephalopathy is the term for this type of brain damage. The hallmark symptoms are confusion, ataxia (i.e., poor coordination of arms and legs), and opthalmoplegia (including double vision). Untreated, this syndrome has a mortality rate estimated as high as 17 percent. Massive parenteral doses of vitamin B-1 have proven to be quite successful in alleviating symptoms[43] but cannot reverse the brain damage. The brain areas that are lesioned in Wernicke's encephalopathy include:

those surrounding the ventricles (i.e., the inner caverns) of the brain, in particular, the hypothalamic regions that surround the third ventricle,[44] other critical brain stem areas,[45] with a general loss of white matter under the cerebral cortex,[44] and a specific loss of neurons in the frontal cortex.[46] The mammillary body is one hypothalamic nucleus that is especially affected. One study using magnetic resonance imaging (MRI) estimated that 81 percent of patients with Wernicke's encephalopathy had significantly smaller (less than 50 percent) mammillary bodies compared to age-matched controls.[47]

Korsakoff's Syndrome

If Wernicke's encephalopathy is allowed to advance, it usually progresses to a condition called Korsakoff's Syndrome. The main symptoms in Korsakoff's syndrome are a profound and permanent anterograde amnesia (i.e. an inability to form new memories), a moderate retrograde amnesia (i.e. past memories are no longer accessible) for the more recent past with older memories being more available for recall, and certain personality disturbances with apathy being the principle one. Since Korsakoff's syndrome is a progression from Wernicke's encephalopathy, the brain damage in Korsakoff's syndrome is similar to that described in Wernicke's encephalopathy. Lesions of the mammillary bodies of the hypothalamus, and certain midline portions of the thalamus are particularly pronounced[48]. There is also evidence that the temporal cortex is lesioned in Korsakoff's disease[49]. There is no treatment that can reverse Korsakoff's syndrome.

SPECIAL BEHAVIORAL ISSUES

There are several issues concerning ethanol that merit special treatment.

Is There a Genetic Basis for Ethanol Abuse?

Over the years, a great deal of data has been collected from a variety of different types of human studies, which suggest that ethanol abuse—alcoholism—has a genetic basis. There is the provocative and perennial observation that alcoholism seems to "run in families." Going to Harvard also runs in families, but that is not to suggest that there is a genetic basis for that behavior. The issue of the possible genetics of alcoholism has prompted numerous studies of twins, identical (monozygotic, each sibling having the same genetic material) and fraternal (dizygotic, each sibling having unique genetic material), and of adoptees of alcoholic parents. The essential finding of these studies was that the children of alcoholic parents are more likely, as high as four times more likely, to develop alcoholism themselves.[50,51] Careful consideration of these data bases, however, leads one to conclude that there may be a genetic predisposition in developing alcoholism, but certainly not a strong genetic link.

One typical study[52] compared the sons of alcoholic parents who were adopted by nonrelatives to a matched sample of males who were adopted into similar-income homes. They found that the sons of alcoholics had a higher incidence (ten of fifty-five, or 18 percent) of alcohol-related problems than did the controls, whose incidence rates were four of seventy-eight or 5 percent. On the surface, these data seem to be compelling, however, consider that the overwhelming majority—82 percent—of the sons of alcoholics did not develop drinking problems. Consider also that this high-risk group also had more divorces and a higher incidence of psychological treatment than did the controls, suggesting an instability that may or may not express itself in substance abuse. The low incidence (18 percent) of alcohol-related problems in the high-risk group may not be high enough to argue a strong genetic link, but it was significantly higher than the control group, which does argue a genetic predisposition to problems with alcohol.

Another type of study examines identical twins for concordance—the probability of seeing a certain behavior in each twin. Since these individuals have the same genetic makeup, if one develops alcohol-related drinking problems the likelihood that the other also will develop these problems should be high. In one study,[51] the concordance of alcohol-related drinking problems in identical twins was much higher than the concordance seen in fraternal twins, who do not share the same genetic material. Just like the adoptee study, these data are provocative. The concordance rate in the identical twins was 58 percent. Others have reported similar but lower rates,[53] like 54 percent. This probability is slightly better than chance (50-50); if genetics had a strong influence on the expression of alcohol-related drinking problems then one would certainly expect to see much higher concordance rates in identical twins. These data actually demonstrate the importance of environmental factors in the expression of alcohol-related problems and suggest a genetic predisposition.

It is important to note that certain environmental factors have been shown to influence the development of problems related to drinking alcohol. The presence of marital conflict during childhood and having parents with poor parental skills have proven to be important causal factors in the development of alcohol-related problems.[54] That these conditions may be the common consequences of substance abuse may explain the findings of familial problems with alcohol. Concerning adoption, it has been found that being adopted by a lower-income family increases the likelihood of developing drinking problems later in life, compared to being adopted by a middle-income family, regardless of whether or not the biological parents were alcoholics.[55] These are important factors to consider when evaluating the data concerning the genetic link to the expression of alcohol-related problems.

The search for a genetic link to alcoholism also has focused on describing the physiological differences between the alcoholic and nonalcoholic. One strategy has been to examine the enzymes responsible for ethanol metabolism. One reliable and robust effect that has been described by many researchers is the ethnic difference between Asians and non-Asians in the activity of the enzymes that metabolize ethanol. Many Asians have been shown to be deficient in a functional form of aldehyde dehydrogenase, which breaks down the toxic first metabolite of ethanol metabolism.[56]

The consequence of this is an usually excessive accumulation of acetaldehyde when ethanol is consumed, which leads to ethanol sensitivity. Similar symptoms such as those experienced by people who consume ethanol following disulfiram (antabuse) are common in ethanol-sensitive people. In addition, there also may be variations in alcohol dehydrogenase in these individuals.[57] It has been suggested that the discomfort resulting from the particular genetic variations of these two enzymes may negatively reinforce ethanol consumption in ethanol-sensitive people.[58] In a sense, they may have an endogenous disulfiram reaction that may minimize the risk of developing a heavy ethanol consumption habit. In fact, Asian nations do have unusually low population rates of alcoholism.[58] However, the issue of whether or not aberrant enzymes can account for high ethanol use has not been proven. The genetic variations found in Native American populations do not account for the differences in ethanol sensitivity or rate of alcoholism in these populations, compared to Caucasian groups.[54] The differences in customs and in various cultural attitudes that may play critical roles in the expression of ethanol consumption make the study of different ethnic groups extremely difficult.

Another strategy has been to describe how the alcoholic may be different than matched control subjects who are not alcoholic. The sons of alcoholics seem to show less response to similar doses of ethanol than do matched controls.[59, 60] This data suggests that if ethanol elicits a muted response in these high-risk individuals then they will consume more ethanol and will be more likely to develop a dependency on it. However, direct estimations of the genetic mediation of this effect has led to conflicting findings. It was found that heavy ethanol consumption may have a strong genetic quality,[61] yet, frequency of consumption did not seem to have a strong genetic basis.[62]

One line of evidence that has received a great deal of notoriety has been the reported discovery of the actual genetic material that may be responsible for ethanol dependency. Blum[63] and Noble[64] created a scientific stir when they described a link between the genetic coding for a specific dopamine receptor—the D2 receptor—and alcoholism. However, subsequent research has not confirmed these promising initial observations. With more comprehensive experimental designs and appropriate control groups, the findings of different researchers have revealed no association between the D2 dopamine receptor gene and alcoholism.[65,66,67] In fact, the most recent review of the lack of evidence for a causal D2 genetic link to alcoholism, which appeared in the *Journal of the American Medical Association*, stated that subsequent studies have so convincingly not corroborated Blum's and Noble's initial findings that the issue is all but closed.[68] These later findings did not receive the same popular press coverage as the initial reports, leaving the public somewhat misinformed.

Another line of research focused on the products of ethanol metabolism. It has been shown that acetaldehyde can combine with naturally present catecholamines (see chapter 2) to form a substance called tetrahydroquinolines, or TIQs, which in turn can stimulate brain opiate receptors. Meyers and Melchior found that rats will increase their ingestion of ethanol following injections of TIQs directly into the brain.[69] This has led to the hypothesis that it is the brain system that may be the physiological mediator of heavy ethanol ingestion.[70] While there is meager support for the involvement of brain opiate receptors in alcoholism,[71] the specific role of TIQs in ethanol-consuming behavior under normal conditions (i.e., not injected into the brain), has been challenged in light of the fact that under normal conditions brain levels of TIQs are too low to exert any meaningful effect on brain functioning.[72]

In a separate line of research, investigators have tried to demonstrate that the electrical activity of the brains of alcoholics is different than that of nonalcoholics. Two measures that typically are used are the electroencephalograph (EEG) and the event-related potential (ERP).* Baseline EEG differences between high- and low-risk males were not found in more recent studies.[73,74] However, one of these studies did report EEG differences after a dose of ethanol was administered.[74] The ERP data has been less equivocal. For either visual or auditory ERPs, it seems that alcoholic subjects do indeed have a different ERP pattern to stimuli when compared to nonalcoholic controls.[75,76,74] However, some of these studies were done on abstinent alcoholic subjects, raising the potential experimental confound of possible residual effects on brain function from periods of chronic heavy ethanol use. In other words, would prolonged ethanol use cause these effects as opposed to there being an inherent difference in brain functioning? In addition, these findings may not be specific to alcoholism but might very well include other substance dependency groups. There is data to suggest that various substance dependencies, like ethanol, cocaine, and opiates, may have common biological characteristics.[77] Overall, the ERP data is provocative and needs to be better described in subsequent research.

Several important points can be extracted from this enormous pool of contradictory studies. First and most apparent is that the issue of the genetics of ethanol abuse is not an easily dissected and defined one. There is simply no consistent answer rising above the noise of varying approaches. Second, the notion of the invariant consequence of alcoholism mediated by a person's genes is not supported by the data. The behaviors that lead to ethanol dependency are complex, the result of individual decisions made over time. There is no genetic determination in the choices made. There can be no such thing as a fetal alcoholic. Recall that even for those individuals whose parents are both alcoholics, the overwhelming majority of these people do not develop alcohol-related drinking problems. Third, there is persistent evidence suggesting some sort of genetic involvement in the heavy use of ethanol and perhaps in the development of subsequent dependency. The nature of this involvement is probably best characterized as a genetic predisposition, which implies that if certain conditions exist then heavy use of ethanol may be seen.

The issues surrounding the topic of the genetics of alcoholism are related in many ways to the following question: Is alcoholism a disease?

*When a stimulus presentation elicits an immediate change in the ongoing electrical activity of the brain it is called an evoked response or evoked potential. If, however, the stimulus-induced change is not immediate but occurs somewhat later (in milliseconds), then this change is termed the event-related potential or ERP.

Is Alcoholism a Disease?

There is a divisive issue in the ethanol literature that centers around whether or not one can consider alcoholism a disease. At times, this debate can be extremely emotional and has often polarized therapists and researchers alike. Some consider this issue of the "disease" status of alcoholism a matter of personal choice and conviction, thus outside the rigors of debate. Although it is not clear that the resolution of this issue is really necessary, consider the following.

If one considers a disease to be any abortion of normal functioning, then to say alcoholism is a disease is to say that it is a severe behavioral disorder. There is little debate on this point. However, the nature of the controversy is when the definition of disease is stricter and considered to be a specific abortion of a normal physiological process, with defined, known consequences. Implied is that the expression of a disease is outside the realm of a person's volition and control. The analogy is often made that, "Alcoholism is a disease just like diabetes." This is not an accurate analogy. Ethanol dependency is a complex behavior, shaped not only by the physiology of the individual but also by many social factors such as peer pressure and personal choices made during key moments in life. Such social factors, which play a critical role in the development of alcoholism will not change the expression of insulin-dependent diabetes. As virtually every study on the genetics of alcoholism has shown, alcoholism is not an invariant consequence of one's genes.

The disease model of alcoholism in many ways was a response to the attitude that alcoholism was a moral failing or deficiency. The perception is that more understanding and support would be extended by society and in particular by the medical community if alcoholism were a medical condition. A disease diagnosis somehow legitimizes the resources invested in treating ethanol dependency, since alcoholism would be considered the outcome of an aberrant physiology. The fear is if alcoholism is not a medical condition but is instead the consequence of poor life decisions, society might feel ethanol-dependent people are "getting what they deserve." The issues are not that simple.

People do not choose to become alcoholic. This condition is the confluence of many factors, which include not only the person's physiology, but also certain life events and personal choices made at specific times. The demonstrated genetic predisposition to develop ethanol dependency is only a predisposition and not an invariant determinant of that behavior. Having a physiology that may be more responsive to the positive aspects of ethanol cannot absolve an individual from the responsibility of the choices made that contributed to the development of an ethanol dependency. Nor does that unusual physiology relieve the individual of the responsibility to break that ethanol dependency. Society must never return to the days of hurling moral judgments at those people with ethanol dependencies. These unfortunate individuals who have developed ethanol dependencies are not morally deficient but are suffering from a severe behavioral disorder that is extremely difficult to correct, requiring medical and psychological support.

It is important to note that to maintain that alcoholism is not a disease is in no way minimizing the enormous contribution the support group Alcoholics Anonymous (AA) has made in helping people break ethanol dependencies. Ethanol dependency, namely alcoholism, has devastated lives and is a behavior that is extremely difficult to break. It requires a combination of tremendous commitment by the individual, support from family and friends, and usually total abstinence in order to succeed. AA, with its emphasis on peer support and religion, has helped countless people through these difficult times in their lives. What it takes to break an ethanol dependency may vary from individual to individual. It is the work of rehabilitation therapists to pragmatically discover the appropriate strategy for each person.

REVIEW EXAM

1. Name three common types of alcohol.
2. List the signs of methanol toxicity.
3. What is fermentation?
4. What is distillation?
5. How is "proof" calculated?
6. How much of an ingested ethanol dose is absorbed?
7. How much of an ingested ethanol dose is absorbed in the stomach and in the intestines?
8. What are the two principal factors in the absorption of ethanol at the stomach?
9. How does the activity of the pylorus muscle affect ethanol absorption?
10. What is the most important factor in determining the overall rate of ethanol absorption?
11. Describe the metabolism of ethanol by the alcohol dehydrogenase system.
12. What is the absolute rate of ethanol metabolism by the alcohol dehydrogenase system?
13. How does disulfiram (antabuse) work?
14. How much ethanol metabolism is done by the MEOS system?
15. Name five nonbehavioral effects of ethanol.
16. How does ethanol affect the cell membrane?
17. Name three brain neurotransmitter systems that may be affected by ethanol.
18. Describe the balanced placebo design.
19. Describe the outcome of balanced placebo experiments on ethanol and behavior.
20. Describe the early symptoms of ethanol withdrawal.
21. Describe the symptoms of later, more severe, ethanol withdrawal.
22. Name the medications used in treating ethanol withdrawal.
23. Name the hallmark symptoms of Wernicke's encephalopathy syndrome.
24. What is an effective pharmacological treatment for Wernicke's encephalopathy syndrome?
25. What are the brain lesions in Wernicke's encephalopathy syndome?
    What is "Korsakoff's Syndrome"?
    Name the main symptoms in Korsakoff's syndrome.
26. Describe the evidence that supports the genetic basis of alcoholism.
27. Describe the argument against the genetic basis of alcoholism.

REFERENCES

1. HARVEY, S. (1990). Antiseptics and disinfectants; fungicides; ectoparasiticides. In L. Goodman & A. Gilman (Eds.), *The Pharmacological Basis of Therapeutics*, (8th ed., pp. 964–987). New York: Macmillan Publishing Co.
2. GOLDBERG, L. (1943). Quantitative studies on alcohol tolerance in man. *Acta Physiologica Scandinavia*, 5 (Suppl. 16).
3. WILKINSON, P. Pharmacokinetics of ethanol: a review. *Alcoholism, Clinical and Experimental Research*, 4(1), 6–21.
4. WRIGHT C., & MOORE R. D. (1990). Disulfiram treatment of alcoholism. *American Journal of Medicine*, 88(6), 647–655.
5. FREZZA, M., DIPADOVA, C., POZZATO, G., TERPIN, M., BARAONA, E., & LIEBER, C. (1990). High blood alcohol levels in women. The role of decreased gastric alcohol dehydrogenase activity and first-pass metabolism. *New England Journal of Medicine*, 322(2), 95,99.
6. RITCHIE, J. (1990). The aliphalic alcohols. In L. Goodman & A. Gilman (Eds.), *The Pharmacological Basis of Therapeutics*, (8th ed., pp. 376–380). New York: Macmillan Publishing Co.
7. COATE, D. (1983). Moderate drinking and coronary heart disease mortality: evidence from NHANES I and NHANES I follow-up. *American Journal of Public Health*, 83(6), 888–890.
8. ZAKHARI, S. (1991). Vulnerability of cardiac disease. *Recent Developments in Alcoholism*, 9, 225–260.
9. LEIGH, J., & BERGER, M. (1993). An econometric technique to remove unobserved variables that bias the relationship between alcohol and blood pressure. *Journal of Studies on Alcohol*, 54(2), 225–234.
10. MUFTI, S. (1992). Alcohol acts to promote incidence of tumors. *Cancer Detection and Prevention*, 16(3), 157–162.
11. GROSSMAN, C., MENDENHALL, C., & ROSELLE, G. (1988). Alcohol immune regulation: I. In vivo effects of ethanol on concanavalin A sensitive thymic lymphocyte function. *International Journal of Immunopharmacology*, 10(2), 187–195.
12. HUNT, W. (1985). *Alcohol and Biological Membranes*. New York: Guilford Press.
13. VARGA, K., & KUNOS, G. (1992). Inhibition of baroreflex bradycardia by ethanol involves both $GABA_A$ and $GABA_B$ receptors in the brain stem of the rat. *European Journal of Pharmacology*, 214(2–3), 223–232.
14. TAKADA, R., SAITO, K., MATSUURA H., & INOKI, R. (1989). Effect of ethanol on hippocampal GABA receptors in the rat brain. *Alcohol*, 6(2), 115–119.
15. ULRICHSEN, J., CLEMMESEN, L., BARRY, D., & HEMMINGSEN, R. (1988). The GABA/benzodiazepine receptor chloride channel complex during repeated episodes of physical ethanol dependence in the rat. *Psychopharmacology*, 96(2), 227–231.
16. SUZDAK, P., SCHWARTZ, R., SKOLNICK, P., & PAUL, S. (1988). Alcohols stimulate gamma-aminobutyric acid receptor-mediated chloride uptake in brain vesicles: correlation with intoxication potency. *Brain Research*, 444(2), 340–345.
17. LOGRANO, D., MATTEO, F., TRABUCCHI, M., GOVONI, S., CAGIANO, R., LACOMBA, C., & CUOMO, V. (1993). Effects of chronic ethanol intake at a low dose on the rat brain dopaminergic system. *Alcohol*, 10(1), 45–49.
18. HRUSKA, R. (1988). Effect of ethanol administration of striatal D_1 and D_2 dopamine receptors. *Journal of Neurochemistry*, 50(6), 1929–1933.
19. PELLEGRINO, S., & DRUSE, M. (1992). The effects of chronic ethanol consumption on the mesolimbic and nigrostriatal dopamine systems. *Alcoholism Clinical and Experimental Research*, 16(2), 275–80.
20. HIETALA, J., SALONEN, I., LAPPALAINEN, J., & SYVALAHTI, E. (1990). Ethanol administration does not alter dopamine D_1 and D_2 receptor characteristics in rat brain. *Neuroscience Letters*, 108(3), 289–294.
21. LOVINGER, D., WHITE, G., & WEIGHT, F. (1990). NMDA receptor-mediated synaptic excitation selectively inhibited by ethanol in hippocampal slice from adult rat. *Journal of Neuroscience*, 10(4), 1372–1379.
22. LOVINGER, D., WHITE, G., & WEIGHT, F. (1990). Ethanol inhibition of neuronal glutamate receptor function. *Annals of Medicine*, 22(4), 247–252.
23. PETERSON, J., ROTHFLEISCH, J., ZELAZO, P., & PIHL, R. (1990). Acute alcohol intoxication and cognitive functioning. *Journal of Studies on Alcohol*, 51(2), 114–122.
24. NARANJO, C., & BREMNER, K. (1993). Behavioral correlates of alcohol intoxication. *Addiction*, 88(1), 25–35.

25. MARLATT, A., & ROHSENOW, D. (1980). Cognitive processes in alcohol use: expectancy and balanced-placebo design. In N. Mello (Ed.), *Advances in Substance Abuse: Behavioral and Biological Research* (pp. 159–199). Greenwich, CT: JAI Press.
26. MARLATT, A., DEMMING, B., & REID, J. (1973). Loss of control drinking in alcoholics: an experimental analogue. *Journal of Abnormal Psychology*, 81, 233–241.
27. MERRY, J. (1966). The "loss of control" myth. *Lancet*, 1, 1257–1258.
28. BERRY, M., & SMOOTHY, R. (1986). A critical evaluation of the claimed relationships between alcohol intake and aggression in infrahuman animals. In P. Brain (Ed.), *Alcohol and Aggression* (pp. 84–137). London: Croom Helm.
29. PAIVARINTA, P. (1992). Lack of increased intermale fighting behavior in mice after low ethanol doses. *Pharmacology, Biochemistry and Behavior*, 42(1), 35–39.
30. ALKANA, R., DEBOLD, J., FINN, D., BABBINI, M., & SYAPIN, P. (1991). Ethanol-induced depression of aggression in mice antagonized by hyperbaric exposure. *Pharmacology, Biochemistry and Behavior*, 38(3), 639–644.
31. LANG, A., GEOCHNER, D., ADESSO, V., & MARLATT, A. (1975). Effects of alcohol on aggression in male social drinkers. *Journal of Abnormal Psychology*, 84, 508–518.
32. MARLATT, A., KOSTURN, C., & LANG, A. (1975). Provocation to anger and opportunity for retaliation as determinants of alcohol consumption in social drinkers. *Journal of Abnormal Psychology*, 84, 652–659.
33. DERMEN, K., & GEORGE, W. (1988). Alcohol expectancy and the relationship between drinking and physical aggression. *Journal of Psychology*, 123(2), 153–161.
34. BROWN, S., GOLDMAN, M., INN, A., & ANDERSON, L. (1980). Expectancies of reinforcement from alcohol: Their domain and relation to drinking patterns. *Journal of Consulting and Clinical Psychology*, 48, 419–426.
35. TAYLOR, S., & LEONARD, K. (1983). Alcohol and human physical aggression. *In Aggression: Theoretical and Empirical Reviews* (Vol. 2, pp. 77–102). New York: Academic Press.
36. WILSON, G., & LAWSON, D. (1976). Expectancies, alcohol, and sexual arousal in male social drinkers. *Journal of Abnormal Psychology*, 85, 587–594.
37. WILSON, G., & ABRAMS, D. (1977). Effects of alcohol on social anxiety and physiological arousal: cognitive versus pharmacological processes. *Cognitive Therapy and Research*, 1, 195–210.
38. CROWE, L., & GEORGE, W. (1989). Alcohol and human sexuality: review and integration. *Psychological Bulletin*, 105, 374–386.
39. SCHUCKIT, M. (1989). *Drug and Alcohol Abuse: A Clinical Guide to Diagnosis and Treatment*. New York: Plenum Press.
40. SELLERS, E. (1988). Alcohol, barbiturate and benzodiazepine withdrawal syndromes: clinical management. *Canadian Medical Association Journal*, 139, 113–120.
41. ABARBANEL, J., BERGINER, V., OSIMANI, A., SOLOMON, H., & CHARUZI, I. (1987). Neurologic complications after gastric restriction surgery for morbid obesity. *Neurology*, 37(2), 196–200.
42. BUTTERWORTH, R. (1989). Effects of thiamine deficiency on brain metabolism: implications for the pathogenesis of the Wernicke-Korsakoff syndrome. *Alcohol and Alcoholism*, 24(4), 271–279.
43. LINDBERG, M., & OYLER, R. (1990). Wernicke's encephalopathy. *American Family Physician*, 41(4), 1205–1209.
44. CHARNESS, M. (1993). Brain lesions in alcoholics. *Alcoholism, Clinical and Experimental Research*, 17(1), 2–11.
45. YOKOTE, K., MIYAGI, K., KUZUHARA, S., YAMANOUCHI, H., & YAMADA, H. (1991). Wernicke encephalopathy: follow-up study by CT and MR. *Journal of Computer Assisted Tomography*, 15(5), 835–838.
46. HARPER, C., & KRIL, J. (1990). Neuropathology of alcoholism. *Alcohol and Alcoholism*, 25(2-3), 207–216.
47. CHARNESS, M., & DELAPAZ, R. (1987). Mamillary body atrophy in Wernicke's encephalopathy: antemortem identification using magnetic resonance imaging. *Annals of Neurology*, 22(5), 595–600.
48. MARKOWITSCH, H. (1988). Diencephalic amnesia: a reorientation towards tracts? *Brain Research*, 472(4), 351–370.
49. BLANSJAAR, B., VIELVOYE, G., VAN-DIJK, J., & RIJNDERS, R. (1992). Similar brain lesions in alcoholics and Korsakoff patients: MRI, psychometric, and clinical findings. *Clinical Neurology and Neurosurgery*, 94(3), 197–203.
50. PEELE, S. (1986). The implications and limitations of genetic models of alcoholism and other addictions. *Journal of Studies on Alcohol*, 47, 63–73.

51. SCHUCKIT, M. (1987). Biological vulnerability to alcoholism. *Journal of Consulting and Clinical Psychology,* 55, 301–309.

52. GOODWIN, D., SCHULSINGER, F., HERMANSEN, L., GUZE, S., & WINOKUR, G. (1973). Alcohol problems in adoptees raised apart from alcoholic biological parents. *Archives of General Psychiatry,* 28, 238–243.

53. KAIJ, L. (1960). *Alcoholism in twins. Studies on the Etiology and Sequels of Abuse of Alcohol.* Stockholm: Almquist and Wiksell.

54. ZUCKER, R., & GOMBERG, E. (1986). Etiology of alcoholism reconsidered: the case for a biopsychosocial process. *American Psychologist,* 41, 783–793.

55. CLONINGER, C., GOHAM, M., & SIGVARDSSON, S. (1989). Inheritance of alcohol abuse: cross fostering analysis of adopted men. *Archives of General Psychiatry,* 38, 861–868.

56. CHAMBERS, G. (1990). The genetics of human alcohol metabolism. *General Pharmacology,* 21, 267–272.

57. THOMASSON, H., EDENBERG, H., CRABB, D., MAI, X., JEROME, R., LI, T., WANG, S., LIN, Y., LU, R., & YIN, S. (1991). Alcohol and aldehyde dehydrogenase genotypes and alcoholism in Chinese men. *American Journal of Human Genetics,* 48(4), 677–681.

58. AGARWAL, D., & GOEDDE, H. (1989). Human aldehyde dehydrogenases: their role in alcoholism. *Alcohol.,* 6(6), 517–523.

59. O'MALLEY, S., & MAISTO, S. (1985). Effects of family drinking history and expectancies on response to alcohol in men. *Journal of Studies on Alcohol,* 46, 289–297.

60. SCHUCKIT, M. (1984). Subjective response to alcohol in sons of alcoholics and controls. *Archives of General Psychiatry,* 41, 879–884.

61. CLONINGER, C. (1983). Genetic and environmental factors in the development of alcoholism. *Journal of Psychiatric Treatment and Evaluation,* 5, 487–496.

62. HEATH, A., MEYER, J., JARDINE, R., & MARTIN, N. (1991). The inheritance of alcohol consumption patterns in a general population twin sample: II. Determinants of consumption frequency and quantity consumed. *Journal of Studies on Alcohol,* 52(5), 425–433.

63. BLUM, K., NOBLE, E., SHERIDAN, P., MONTGOMERY, A., RITCHIE, T., JAGADEESWARAN, P., NOGAMI, H., BRIGGS, A., & COHEN, J. (1990). Allelic association of human dopamine D_2 receptor gene in alcoholism. *Journal of the American Medical Association,* 263 (15), 2055–2060.

64. NOBLE, E., BLUM, K., RITCHIE, T., MONTGOMERY, A., & SHERIDAN, P. (1991). Allelic association of the D_2 dopamine receptor gene with receptor binding characteristics in alcoholism. *Archives of General Psychiatry,* 48, 648–654.

65. BOLOS, A., DEAN, M., LUCAS-DERSE, A., RAMSBURG, M., BROWN, G., & GOLDMAN, D. (1991). Population and pedigree studies reveal a lack of association between the dopamine D_2 receptor gene and alcoholism. *Journal of the American Medical Association,* 264, 3156–3160.

66. PARSIAN, A., & CLONINGER, C. (1991). Genetics of high-risk populations. *Addiction Recovery,* 11(6), 9–11.

67. HORGAN, J. (1993). Trends in behavioral genetics: eugenics revisited. *Scientific American,* 268, 122–131.

68. GELERNTER, J., GOLDMAN, D., & RISCH, N. (1993). The A1 allele at the D2 dopamine receptor gene and alcoholism. *Journal of the American Medical Association,* 269(13), 1673–1677.

69. MEYERS, R., & MELCHIOR, C. (1977). Differential actions on voluntary alcohol intake of tetrahydroisoquinolines or a beta-carboline infused chronically in the ventrical of the rat. *Pharmcology, Biochemistry and Behavior,* 7, 19–35.

70. MYERS, R. (1989). Isoquinolines, beta-carbolines, and alcohol drinking: involvement of opioid and dopaminergic mechanisms. *Experientia,* 45(5), 436–443.

71. TOPEL, H. (1988). Beta-endorphin genetics in the etiology of alcoholism. *Alcohol,* 5(2), 159–65.

72. GOLDSTEIN, D. (1983). *Pharmacology of Alcohol,* pp. 27–30. New York: Oxford University Press.

73. COHEN, H., PORJESZ, B., & BEGLEITER, H. (1991). EEG characteristics in males at risk for alcoholism. *Alcoholism, Clinical and Experimental Research,* 15(5), 858–61.

74. VOLAVKA, J., POLLOCK, V., GABRIELLI, W., & MEDNICK, S. (1985). The EEG in persons at risk for alcoholism. *Recent Developments in Alcoholism,* 3, 21–36.

75. PORJESZ, B., & BEGLEITER, H. (1991). Neurophysiological factors in individuals at risk for alcoholism. *Recent Developments in Alcoholism,* 99, 53–67.

76. EMMERSON, R., DUSTMAN, R., SHEARER, D. & CHAMBERLIN, H. (1987). EEG, visually evoked, and event-related potentials in young abstinent alcoholics. *Alcohol,* 4(4), 241–248.

77. GEORGE, F. (1991). Is there a common biological basis for reinforcement from alcohol and other drugs? *Journal of Addictive Diseases,* 10(1-2), 127–39.

CHAPTER SIX
MARIJUANA:
The Outlaw Sedative

GENERAL ISSUES ADDRESSED IN THIS CHAPTER

- The history of Cannabis sativa use
- The nineteenth-century rediscovery of Cannabis sativa in Western medicine and as an intoxicant
- Cannabis sativa's fall from legitimate use as a medicinal agent
- Findings of the 1944 La Guardia Report
- Different preparations of Cannabis sativa
- Various psychoactive components of Cannabis sativa
- Dynamics of Cannabis sativa's absorption and excretion
- Nonbehavioral effects of Cannabis sativa
- How Cannabis sativa may alter brain functioning
- General behavioral profile elicited by Cannabis sativa
- The important role of set and setting for behavior
- Cultural myths that surround Cannabis sativa
- Withdrawal syndrome seen with Cannabis sativa
- Consequences of chronic use of Cannabis sativa
- Issues that surround Cannabis sativa legislation

INTRODUCTION AND HISTORY

Cannabis sativa is arguably the most commonly used illegal drug in the world. It has been estimated that there are close to 300 million users worldwide, with approximately 28 million users in the United States alone. Despite this high use, Cannabis sativa seems to be permanently surrounded by controversy.

Classifying Cannabis sativa is not without dissension. It has definite sedating properties, but as the dose is increased one does not see the family of dose curves described in chapter 4 as with other sedative/hypnotic drugs. However, as the dose of Cannabis sativa is increased, there is a peculiar alteration of perceptions and intoxication which is elicited. It certainly is not a true hallucination, like LSD or mescaline, but there is an altered perception of the environment nonetheless. Most classification schemes list Cannabis sativa as a hallucinogen, undeservingly so, especially considering that there is no cross-tolerance between Cannabis sativa and the more conventional hallucinogens.[1] Perhaps it should be classified not as a sedative nor hallucinogen, but rather as a drug in its own class.

Cannabis sativa has a history unlike that of any other plant or drug. It is one of the oldest purposefully cultivated plants,[2] used for fiber, oil, and medicine.[3] There are many varieties of this species of plant, which is reflected by an additional adjective to the species name. For example, Cannabis sativa indica is that Cannabis sativa grown in India. The rich history of Cannabis sativa can be arbitrarily divided into four periods.

Ancient History

Central Asia is probably the site where Cannabis sativa originated. Before recorded history, Cannabis sativa had been used as a medicine. The earliest written accounts of its use are in China, around 2600 B.C., in the Nei Ching,[4] which is an ancient document about internal medicine, and in 1500 B.C. in the Rh-Ya,[5] which is a compendium of pharmaceutical agents. It was around that time, about 1500–1000 B.C., that Cannabis sativa spread to Southeast Asia, India, and, with the help of Scythian invaders, to Western Europe, Southern Russia, and the Balkans.[6] Both Assyrian and Egyptian written accounts indicate that Cannabis sativa was used extensively as a medicine and used also for its fiber. In India, in the sacred books of the Vedas, Cannabis sativa is referred to as a holy plant. Over the centuries, the medicinal use of Cannabis sativa in India was tethered to religion. Although there is no firm evidence that Cannabis sativa was used in ancient Judea, there are some historical indications that it was. The close ties between Judea and Assyria, as well as ties to Egypt, make it probable that ancient Jewish culture was familiar with Cannabis sativa use. Even more provocative is the contention that a product that was either exported from or at least transported through Judea, and vaguely referred to in the Bible (Ezek., 27:17), was called *pannagh* in Hebrew, which translates to *bhanga* in Sanskrit, *bang* in Persian, and later evolved to *kunnab* in ancient Arabic, then finally to *cannabis* in Greek.[7] The ancient Romans and Greeks certainly used Cannabis sativa as a medicine. The writings of Pliny the Elder, Dioscorides, and Galen all describe conditions that respond to Cannabis sativa treatment.[8] Although its medicinal properties were already well-established, its intoxicating effects were not as well-known. The Scythians used Cannabis sativa in their burial services[8] and in other nonmedicating situations to produce intoxication. In his writings, Galen cautioned that Cannabis sativa use may lead to "senseless talk."[6] By 500 A.D., Cannabis sativa was cultivated as a crop in Europe, used primarily for fiber and medicine.[9]

Middle Ages

From 1000 A.D. to 1300 A.D., Cannabis sativa spread throughout the African continent from the Mediterranean basin.[6] The Middle Ages did not mark any major changes in the use of Cannabis sativa. In Europe and India, there was little difference in cannabis use from the time of Galen. In Arabian culture, cannabis was officially banned, but medically its use was widespread. It was also used as an intoxicant, especially by the lower-class poor. The banishment of cannabis was also established early by Jewish culture. In China, while Cannabis sativa found a legitimate place in medicine, it was a cautious position. Like other intoxicants, Cannabis sativa was not a popular drug in China, probably due to the traditional importance of personal control and introversion.

Seventeenth, Eighteenth, and Nineteenth Centuries in Western Culture

In the years 1600 A.D. through 1700 A.D., Cannabis sativa crossed the Atlantic Ocean with settlers, explorers, and slave merchants to populate the Americas and Australia.

In the nineteenth century, Cannabis sativa was not widely used as either a medicine or recreational intoxicant, even though there was ample information concerning both of these uses. Napoleon's troop movements in the 1800s into Egypt brought back soldiers who regaled the intoxicating properties of hashish.[10] This newfound information gradually spread across French society, Paris in particular, with an overall result of increased popularity among certain circles who took Cannabis sativa to become intoxicated. The most notorious example was the establishment in the mid-1800s of le Club des Hachichins, a group which included noted authors and experimented with hashish to alter consciousness.

Around the same time, in the mid-1800s, there was also a renewed interest in the use of Cannabis sativa in medical practice. This interest was not influenced by its growing popularity as an intoxicant, but rather was the result of the pioneering medical research of the British physician O'Shaughnessy, who published extensive research regarding the use of Cannabis sativa in his practice in India.[11,12] What followed was a deluge of scientific reports concerning the varied uses of Cannabis sativa for numerous conditions.[13,14,15] Cannabis sativa was reestablishing its position in British medicine and drug companies were following the lead. Park-Davis, Lilly, and Squibb all marketed preparations of Cannabis sativa in the 1800s.

In 1892, England formed the Indian Hemp Commission to examine the possible health hazards posed by Cannabis sativa use, especially its high use in India. Two years later, in a seven-volume, 30,000-page report, the Commission concluded that use of Cannabis sativa produced no injurious physical, mental, or moral effects. The report went on to suggest that control of Cannabis sativa should be by taxation, not prohibition.

Despite this renewed acceptance in British medicine, there were not many medical reports from the United States concerning the use of Cannabis sativa for medicinal purposes. However, the use for its fiber in the production of rope, clothes, and paper was well-established by early American settlers, who aggressively cultivated the plant. In fact, until the cotton gin was developed, Cannabis sativa was the major crop in the United States.[16] There seems to be no clear indication that Cannabis sativa was widely used as an intoxicant in the United States at this time. However, the turn of the century witnessed the confluence of various factors that shaped the troubled image Cannabis sativa has today.

The Turn of the Century—the Roots of Our Cultural Reefer Madness

In the late 1800s, the smoking of Cannabis sativa leaves, referred to as marijuana, to produce intoxication was common in South and Central America as well as

Mexico. The importation from the South of this type of "recreational" Cannabis sativa use was attributed to three principal sources: 1. Mexican immigrants; 2. Servicemen whose tours of duty included South and Central America; and 3. Black cavalry soldiers in the Southwest United States.[16] Cannabis smoking by armed service personnel is not unlike the hashish use of the 1800s by overseas service personnel in France. Black cavalry soldiers smoking marijuana with Mexican workers is perhaps more conjecture than demonstrable historical fact. More important is the fact that the influx of Mexican workers to the United States also brought changes in American customs.

During the 1920s, the immigration of Mexican workers into the United States increased significantly.[17] These workers played a major, positive role in the U.S. economy, serving not only as farm workers in the Southern and Midwestern states, but also in the factories of the North.[18] Even though Mexicans were welcomed and needed by employers, communities feared they were the source of much criminal behavior. It was around the 1900s that stories began of criminal behavior attributed to Mexicans under the influence of marijuana. The connection that was made between immigration from Mexico and the introduction of Cannabis sativa was used by some groups to fuel their existing racism. The formation at this time of groups like the Allied Patriotic Societies and the American Coalition, which sought to preserve the "ethnic purity" of America from the possible genetic mixing with Mexicans, highlights this issue.[19] These groups had a vested interest to vilify the Mexican migrant worker—precisely what the role of these radical conservatives in the formation of a societal fear of Cannabis sativa was remains to be determined by historians.

During the early 1900s the border states of Texas, Louisiana, and California were the first to perceive a social problem with marijuana use. This resulted in a state-by-state passage of local legislation, which prohibited the nonmedical use of Cannabis sativa: Texas in 1919, California in 1915, Louisiana in 1924, and New York in 1927.[16] In all of these states, the illicit use of Cannabis sativa was also found in black communities. At this time, there were numerous stories that appeared in the press, relating horrible crimes that were committed as a result of marijuana use. The belief that Cannabis sativa directly caused criminal activity was growing nationwide and provided intense pressure for national legislative action.

One person, Harry Anslinger, played an important role in the early legislation to control Cannabis sativa, as well as in its cultural perception. An Assistant Prohibition Commissioner, Anslinger was relentless in trying to make prohibition work. When this government experiment failed, Anslinger turned his attention and energy to what he perceived to be a major threat to American culture—Cannabis sativa. In 1930, Anslinger became the commissioner of the newly formed Federal Narcotics Bureau (FBN) and began his intense lobbying to prohibit the use of Cannabis sativa. He not only lobbied directly in legislative circles in Washington, D.C., but also wrote many articles for the popular press. His many accounts of criminal behavior induced by Cannabis sativa use, typically, smoking marijuana or hashish, were graphic and intended to shock the reader. The following is an example of this rhetoric:[20]

One summer evening, Moses M. bought his first two marihuana cigarettes for twenty-five cents each. After smoking them, he said, 'I felt just like I was flying.' Moses, crazed with marihuana, went through the window of his hotel room, dropped eighteen feet onto the roof of the garage next door in his bare feet, and then went through the window of K.'s room, crying, 'God told me to kill this man.' Seizing K. by the throat, Moses beat him to death with his fists, after which he broke a chair on his victim's head. Then screaming that he was pursued by Hitler, Moses went through the window and dropped his 200-pound frame to the alley, thirty feet below. In court, Moses had no recollection of the killing and asserted, 'I didn't want to hurt him.'

The overall goal of Anslinger was to stir up the American public to create pressure for the passage of federal prohibition of Cannabis sativa. Independent of the lobbying activity of the FBN were the numerous newspaper stories, especially in the Hearst chain of papers, and in the sensationalistic, perhaps inflammatory, films like "Reefer Madness," "Assassins of Youth," and "Marijuana, Weed with Roots in Hell," all of which provided pressure to make Congress take action. In 1934, in a report to the meeting of the American Psychiatric Association, Dr. Walter Bromberg reported that Cannabis sativa ". . . releases inhibitions and restraints imposed by society and allows individuals to act out their drives openly. . . ."[21] Coupled with the reports from the ongoing examination of Cannabis sativa in the New Orleans area, in which the conclusion was drawn that marijuana caused criminal behavior,[22] the time was right for congressional action, thus, the Marijuana Tax Act was drafted.

The congressional hearings for the Marijuana Tax Act of 1937 saw only one witness who expressed opposition to the legislation—the spokesperson for the American Medical Association, Dr. W. Woodward. Woodward, a lawyer as well as a physician, pointed out that no evidence had been presented that linked Cannabis sativa use to crime, nor was there evidence that its use was prevalent in children.[16] Needless to say, Woodward's testimony did not dissuade the members of the committee. The Marijuana Tax Act passed easily and was enacted in the fall of 1937.

The provisions of this legislation are unusual in that they did not directly outlaw Cannabis sativa use, but rather imposed a tax on its use. If a person was found to possess Cannabis sativa, they would have to produce the proper records of inventory and payment of the appropriate taxes to comply with the law. This legislation proved to be the final blow that essentially ended the legal medicinal use of Cannabis sativa until the 1970s. The use of Cannabis sativa as a medicine in the 1900s was already on the decline for the following reasons:[23]

1. The various specific Cannabis sativa plants have a great deal of variability in their potency, with some specific crops having more psychoactive components than others.

2. Even if the amount of psychoactive components were consistent, Cannabis sativa is unreliable because its principal active component (Δ 9 tetrahydrocannabinol (THC)) would break down at room temperature or when exposed to sunlight. In other words, Cannabis sativa has a short shelf life.

3. The primary active component in Cannabis sativa does not cross the gastrointestinal wall easily, making an enteral (oral) route of administration much less effective than smoking the substance.

4. There were much better drugs entering the market for virtually any condition for which Cannabis sativa would be indicated.

Why would a physician use this unstable drug, which had variable potency and was difficult to absorb from the GI tract, when there were more reliable, specific medications available? It is evident that the passage of the Marijuana Tax Act of 1937 sealed the fate of the legitimate use of Cannabis sativa.

Years later, the U.S. Supreme Court ruled that the Marijuana Tax Act was unconstitutional.

This intense, almost fanatical, campaign by the commissioner of the Federal Bureau of Narcotics, as well as of those who followed his lead in the media, press, and cinema, made the issues surrounding Cannabis sativa use emotional and resistant to logic. The parade of marijuana-induced horrible criminal acts from Harry Anslinger, together with reports from the New Orleans District Attorney's office and reports such as Dr. Bromberg's, all helped to forge a negative image of Cannabis sativa that persists today.

This negative image was challenged almost immediately by the mayor of New York City, Fiorello La Guardia. In September of 1938, La Guardia assembled a thirty-one-member panel of physicians from the N.Y. Academy of Medicine, including pharmacologists, psychologists, sociologists, and chemists, to examine the connection between Cannabis sativa and criminal behavior. The panel deliberated for about six years, aided by the New York City Police Department, and issued its report in 1944. The panel concluded that marijuana use:[16]

1. did not lead to addiction;
2. did not lead to the use of heroin, morphine, or cocaine;
3. was not a determining factor in committing crimes; and
4. was not widespread among children.

The Bureau of Narcotics aggressively rebutted this report in the press and in medical journals.

Appreciate that just ten years prior to the La Guardia Report, the army had conducted two similar investigations (the Panama Canal Studies) and reached the same conclusions, similar to the findings of the Indian Hemp Commisson Report of 1894. Despite these reports, the seemingly indelible negative image of Cannabis sativa, generated in the 1930s, has persisted.

The Comprehensive Drug Abuse Prevention and Control Act of 1970 is the current legislation concerning the legal status of most drugs (see chapter 3). In this scheme, Cannabis sativa—marijuana, hashish, and THC, by name—is listed as Schedule I—the class of forbidden drugs. The drugs in this class are thought to have the highest potential for developing a dependency and have no accepted use in medicine. This classification excludes the use of these drugs by physicians in normal medicating situations. A physician cannot simply write a prescription for Cannabis sativa that can be filled at any drugstore. However, as with any other drug on Schedule

I, researchers have access to these substances for use in conducting experiments, after appropriate applications have been made and approval granted. It was this research provision in the federal drug law that proved to be the mechanism for bona fide medical testing of Cannabis sativa in limited and structured medicating situations.

In 1978, the New Mexico legislature passed a law that had the state's department of health devise a research project to examine the efficacy of Cannabis sativa in treating the nausea induced by cancer chemotherapy. The state then applied to federal agencies for access to Cannabis sativa for this research project.[24] Within the next three years, thirty-one states enacted similar legislation. While these state laws varied somewhat, their common feature was requiring that the state apply for permission to dispense Cannabis sativa to selected patient populations, that is, chemotherapy or glaucoma patients, under the vestiges of a research enterprise. This has enabled a fairly large group of patients nationwide to have legal access to a drug that is technically listed as Schedule I.

To this day, Cannabis sativa remains a Schedule I drug, legally forbidden.

FORMS OF CANNABIS SATIVA

Cannabis sativa is not a self-pollinating plant. The flowers of the female plant contain only the pistils and need the pollen from the stamen of the male plant to reproduce. To this end, the flowering tops of the female Cannabis plant exude a sticky resin to help catch the male's pollen. Because of this sticky resin, probably fertilization is not mediated by flying insects but rather relies on airborne pollen. The female plant is more leafy and bushy on top compared to the male plant. The male will die back soon after flowering, whereas the female will survive much longer after its flowering period.

Perhaps the most common form of Cannabis sativa is the preparation in which the material is dried. Marijuana is the general term for this preparation and may contain any part of the Cannabis sativa plant—the leaves, stems, and even seeds. Marijuana can then be smoked or eaten. Other specific terms for dried Cannabis sativa are ganga, bhang, and sinsemilla. Ganga refers to the resin-rich small leaves and flower brackets of the female. It has relatively more psychoactive components compared to bhang, which is made up of the shoots as well as the leaves, making it less potent than ganga.[1] Sinsemilla refers to the dried preparation of Cannabis sativa before it has gone to seed. It has an even higher content of psychoactive components. Hashish, or charas in the Far East, is the term for the dried extracted resin from the female plant. This form can also be smoked or prepared in foods.

There are many individual components identified in Cannabis sativa. The principal psychoactive component is Δ 9 tetrahydrocannabinol, or simply Δ9-THC. "THC" is often used to refer to Δ9-THC, which is not very precise considering the fact that another psychoactive component is Δ 8 tetrahydrocannabinol (Δ8-THC).

Another notable component is cannabidiol (CBD). Cannabidiol and Δ9-THC comprise up to 95 percent of the active components in Cannabis sativa.[25] However, CBD is not very psychoactive, if at all.[26] This relative difference in psychoactive potency is important because there are appreciable differences in the Δ9-THC-to-CBD ratio in various strains of Cannabis sativa; for instance, the amount of Δ9-THC expressed as a percent of all cannabinoids in Cannabis sativa from India is 1.3 percent, whereas the percent of Δ9-THC in Cannabis sativa from Mexico is 3.7 percent.[6] Recall that this variability in potency was one of the reasons why Cannabis sativa was no longer used in medicine in the 1900s.

ABSORPTION, DISTRIBUTION, AND BIOTRANSFORMATION

The typical routes of administration for Cannabis sativa are: 1. parenteral—pulmonary (smoking); and 2. enteral—oral (eating) (Figure 6–1A). Even though as much as 50 percent of the Δ9-THC is lost in the combustion of the smoking,[27] this is clearly the more efficient route of administration, when speaking of absorption. Smoking marijuana is similar to IV injections of Δ9-THC in terms of its profile in the plasma, whereas an oral dose has a much more erratic plasma level profile.[28] A single IV injection of 1 mg to 5 mg of Δ9-THC will typically yield the following: plasma levels peak immediately to about 100 ng/ml to 500 ng/ml of plasma, followed by a rapid decline to about 5 ng/ml to 10 ng/ml of plasma within one hour, then a much more gradual decline, to about 1 ng/ml to 5 ng/ml of plasma at about four hours.[29] This biphasic clearance pattern reflects the initial rapid movement of Δ9-THC out of blood and into lipid (fat) compartments, not unlike the general pattern seen with other sedatives/hypnotics like the barbiturates and benzodiazepines (see chapter 4). There seems to be some distinct differences in these plasma levels in chronic users of Cannabis sativa and in naive users. While the pattern is essentially the same in form between the two, the absolute plasma levels are somewhat higher for the naive user.[30] Figure 6–2 illustrates these general differences, which are not due to the first phase of the plasma level curve, namely tissue distribution, but rather to the second slower phase, which reflects actual metabolism. The plasma levels following smoking marijuana can be variable according to the level of Δ9-THC in the substance. Figure 6–3 combines the results of two studies[31,32] and illustrates this effect. Notice how similar the clearance curves are compared to those generated by an IV dose of Δ9-THC, illustrated in Figure 6–2.

The overall half-life of Δ9-THC was approximately fifty-seven hours for naive users and twenty-eight hours for chronic users.[30] Some researchers have found similar half-lifes,[33] but others have reported shorter half-lifes of about thirty hours (thirty-three hours for males, twenty-seven hours for females),[34] twenty hours,[35] and some longer, approximately ninety-eight hours (4.1 days), in chronic marijuana smokers.[36]

Absorbed Δ9-THC is lipophilic, which means it will easily dissolve in fat and tends to accumulate in fat depots. The remarkably fast first phase of plasma clearance

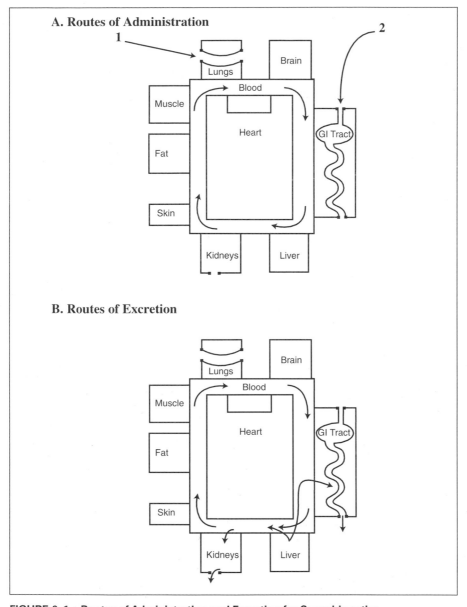

FIGURE 6–1   Routes of Administration and Excretion for Cannabis sativa

A. There are two principal routes of administration for Cannabis sativa: smoking (parenteral—pulmonary) and eating (enteral—oral).

B. The excretion of Cannabis sativa, regardless of the route of administration, is curious. The liver will biotransform it and allow the kidneys to filter and excrete it, as is common with most drugs. However, an unusually large amount of Cannabis sativa metabolites will be sequestered in the bile, which will be released into the GI tract. As a result, there is a large amount of Cannabis sativa metabolites found in feces.

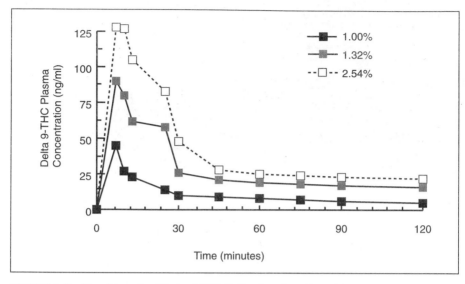

FIGURE 6–2   Blood Levels of Delta-9-THC Following Smoking of Cannabis Sativa
The blood levels of Delta-9-THC following the smoking of Cannabis sativa are dependent on the percentage of Delta-9-THC in the marijuana preparation.

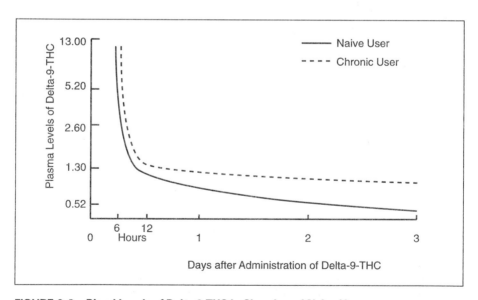

FIGURE 6–3   Blood Levels of Delta-9-THC in Chronic and Naive Users
While the rapid first phase of drug clearance seems similar in chronic and naive users, there appears to be a more efficient clearance in the second, slower phase of the chronic user.

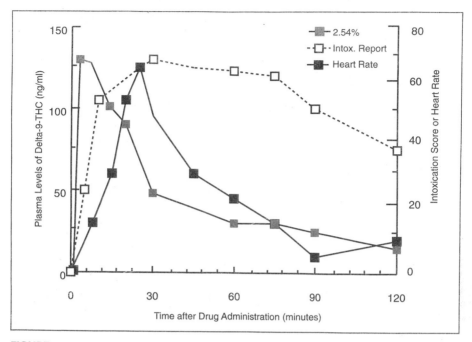

FIGURE 6–4   Blood Levels of Delta-9-THC Plotted with Two Outcomes
The plasma levels of Delta-9-THC are plotted with the onset of two outcomes—heart rate and subjective reports of intoxication. Notice how both the heart rate increases and subjective intoxication peaks after the plasma level of Delta-9-THC peaks.

reflects the speed of this distribution. Despite this intense ability to dissolve in lipids (fats), Δ9-THC does not easily cross into the brain compartment. Approximately 1 percent of an absorbed dose crosses into the brain.[37] As blood levels drop due to ongoing excretion, the Δ9-THC in fat stores will redistribute, that is, move back into circulation, which partially accounts for why Δ9-THC and its metabolites can linger in the blood for so long.

Biotransformation of Δ9-THC occurs principally in the liver. There is a rapid transformation of Δ9-THC to 11-hydroxy-tetrahydrocannabinol (11-OH-Δ9-THC), which is an active metabolite. This metabolite may play a considerable role in the intoxicating effects of Cannabis sativa, because it is twice as psychoactive as Δ9-THC,[26] it can cross into the brain compartment even more quickly than Δ9-THC,[38] and it has an extraordinarily long half-life of over 195 hours or 8.2 days.[39] However, the absolute plasma levels of 11-OH-Δ9-THC are very low, twentyfold less in plasma after smoking,[40] so its overall effect is difficult to assess. The further biotransformation of 11-OH-Δ9-THC yields the inactive metabolite 11-dihydroxy-Δ9-THC.

Regardless of the route of administration, smoking or eating, a considerable portion of the excreted metabolites of Cannabis sativa biotransformation is sequestered in the bile, finds its way into the GI tract, and is excreted in the feces

(Figure 6–1B). One report measured the amount of excreted metabolites in feces to be as high as 65 percent,[29] and others have reported this level to be around 41 percent.[30] The remainder of the metabolites were excreted in the urine.

Correlating pharmacological and psychological effects to plasma levels has been problematic. Neither pharmacological nor psychological effects seem to follow plasma levels too closely (Figure 6–4). Pharmacological effects are maximal within fifteen minutes of smoking, decaying to negligible levels in three hours.[41] Peak subjective perceptions of intoxication also appear later than peak plasma levels of Δ9-THC.[31] These data are in sharp contrast to oral routes of administration of Cannabis sativa, where blood levels do not peak until two to three hours, and the duration of effects can last as long as three to five hours.[1]

The effects of Cannabis sativa on the brain and its behavioral consequences will be discussed after reviewing the nonbehavioral effects of Cannabis sativa.

NONBEHAVIORAL EFFECTS OF CANNABIS SATIVA

Cannabis sativa has many effects, however, the most consistent, regardless of the route of administration, are increased heart rate and reddening of the eyes.[27] The increased heart rate (tachycardia) appears to be dependent on the dose of Δ9-THC.[42] The following are some other principal effects.

Pulmonary Effects

Δ9-THC is an active bronchial dilator, which means regardless of the route of administration, Δ9-THC helps open pulmonary airways. Although millions of people suffer from asthma, the possibility of exploiting this effect to treat respiratory disorders seems unlikely for several reasons. Smoking any substance is certainly not indicated for asthma sufferers. The very process of smoking introduces too many irritating substances to warrant this route of administration. The difficulty of dissolving Δ9-THC and its poor absorption from the GI tract[43] further complicates this particular situation. Oral doses of Δ9-THC were found to be only mildly effective in helping asthma patients. In addition, this effect was somewhat unpredictable and accompanied by central nervous system effects.[44] The preparation of an aerosol inhaler containing Δ9-THC was also tested, with some success, on asthma patients However, it was found that despite its definite bronchial dilation relief, this form of Δ9-THC administration still produced an elevated heart rate, intoxication, and some bronchial irritation.[45] With drugs currently available that treat asthma just as effectively and with less adverse side effects, it seems unlikely that Δ9-THC will be a mainstream treatment option for asthma sufferers.

Another reliable pulmonary effect of marijuana is the impairment of pulmonary function following chronic use.[46] The lungs are a wonderful machine that is not well-designed to withstand long-term inhalation of smoke, as chronic smoking will take its toll. The marijuana-induced impairment of pulmonary function is an effect of the smoking process, not of Δ9-THC itself, since IV Δ9-THC does not affect pulmonary functioning to a great extent.[47]

There is another important concern regarding chronic marijuana smoking—the risk of lung cancer. While there is no direct evidence that this will cause lung cancer, there does appear to be more tar and carcinogenic hydrocarbons in marijuana than tobacco.[48] Given the practice of unfiltered marijuana smoking and of keeping the smoke in the lungs longer, it seems there may be a considerable risk involved in long-term smoking of marijuana.

Effects on Intraocular Pressure

The fluid in the eyes maintains a constant pressure. When the circulatory system, which plays a critical role in the normal turnover of this fluid, fails to adequately drain the older fluid, this pressure builds. If the intraocular pressure gets high enough, it can permanently damage the optic nerve, resulting in blindness. Glaucoma is the condition of having excessive pressure in the eye. It is the leading cause of blindness in the United States. Smoking marijuana decreases intraocular pressure by as much as 30 percent. The effect lasts up to five hours, and tolerance does not seem to develop.[49] The use of Δ9-THC capsules also seems to be effective, but compared to smoking, the onset of relief is delayed, effects last longer, there is greater variability in efficacy, and there are intoxicating effects that are undesirable for many people.[50]

Control of Nausea

The use of pharmacological agents to treat cancer has resulted in intense nausea and vomiting for many. Although there are ancient references to the antiemetic properties of Cannabis sativa, it was rediscovered as an antiemetic agent by several sources in the early 1970s and first reported in 1975.[51] This was the fundamental rationale for the movement of many states in initiating programs in which Cannabis sativa is legally dispensed to certain patient populations. There have been many studies, with varying conclusions, concerning the efficacy of Cannabis sativa in alleviating the nausea and vomiting often induced by cancer chemotherapy. A review of a majority of these studies[52] reveals that Δ9-THC is a more effective antiemetic than some of the more traditional ones used, but less effective than others. It is likely that the different agents used for chemotherapy for different types of cancer may induce nausea and vomiting through different mechanisms, thus the prospect of having one antiemetic be best for all chemotherapy situations is rather remote.

A separate issue concerning the antiemetic properties of Cannabis sativa involves the choice of the route of administration. It seems that an enteral (oral) route is not advisable for a person who is about to vomit but that a parenteral (smoking) route would be better. One of the few studies that directly examined this issue found that smoking marijuana, with its faster absorption rate, was more efficient in achieving the appropriate antiemetic blood levels of Δ9-THC than was taking capsules of Δ9-THC.[53] However, the usual problems with this route also means there are definite disadvantages, including the risk of contaminated marijuana cigarettes, the potential variability between lots, and the fact that some patients find smoking itself to be nauseating.[53]

There is an additional major drawback in using Cannabis sativa as an antiemetic, in that tolerance develops to this antiemetic effect,[53] making this treatment strategy pharmacologically difficult at best.

Immune Suppression

There has been an unclear research literature concerning possible immune suppression by Cannabis sativa. Cell-mediated immunity was found to be significantly deficient in chronic marijuana users,[54] and marijuana users seem to have fewer T (thymus-derived) cells.[55] However, other studies have reported no differences in immunocompetence in marijuana users.[56,57] Regardless of these reports, there is no evidence that marijuana users are any more susceptible to viral infections or cancer, which both are associated with lowered T cell counts.[58] Thus, the functional significance of any immune effects of Cannabis sativa may be negligible.

It should be noted that Cannabis sativa has been shown to suppress tumor growth. Administration of Δ9-THC in mice not only increased survival time but actually reduced tumor size by 25 percent to 82 percent.[59]

Testosterone Levels

There has been a series of apparently contradictory findings concerning Cannabis sativa's effects on endocrine functioning, in particular, on testosterone levels. The effects of Cannabis sativa appear to be cyclical. Although there may be acute decreases in blood testosterone and in lutenizing hormone, there are no differences after several weeks of chronic marijuana use. However, later, there are decreases in testosterone, lutenizing hormone, and follicle stimulating hormone.[60] Regardless of the timing of these effects, plasma hormone levels usually remain within a range considered normal for most individuals.

Sleep

A reliable effect of Cannabis sativa on sleep is a decrease in REM (rapid eye movements) sleep[61] seen with another sedative/hypnotic, the barbiturates (chapter 4). However, unlike other sedatives/hypnotics, the benzodiazepines, Cannabis sativa does not affect Stage 4 (slow wave) sleep.

Food Consumption

The consistent report of increased food intake following ingestion of Cannabis will be discussed in detail under Behavioral Consequences.

In addition to the preceding effects, general motor effects also have been reported, such as incoordination (ataxia), muscle weakness, and tremor.[41] It is important to note what physiological functions are not changed by Cannabis sativa, like pupil diameter, body temperature, respiration,[41] blood glucose levels, and insulin secretion.[62]

It also is important to note that there is virtually no lethality associated with Cannabis sativa use. Overdose of Cannabis sativa in any form, marijuana or hashish included, by any route of administration does not lead to death.

How Cannabis sativa affects the brain will be reviewed next.

EFFECTS ON THE CENTRAL NERVOUS SYSTEM

Radioactively labeled Cannabis sativa seems to concentrate in the frontal and parietal cerebral cortex, in critical limbic structures like the hippocampus, amygdala, and septum, and in motor areas like the basal ganglia.[63] The identification in recent years of an actual cannabinoid receptor has raised the possibility of the involvement of an endogenous cannabinoid substance in normal brain functioning. The cannabinoid receptor has its highest densities in the globus pallidus (the "output" nucleus of the basal ganglia), the substantia nigra, the hippocampus and cerebellum, and the forebrain in general.[64] This particular distribution suggests that an endogenous cannabinoid may be involved in the mediation of motor behavior and cognitive functioning. It is noteworthy that the brain stem in general has a very low density of cannabinoid receptors, which may account for the lack of lethality with Cannabis sativa use. However, the brain stem has critical areas that mediate emesis, that is, nausea and vomiting, and these data suggest the antiemetic effects of Cannabis sativa have to be mediated in higher brain areas.

There has been some evidence that chronic (and not acute) Cannabis sativa use may specifically increase the efficiency of benzodiazepine receptor binding in the frontal cortex.[65] This would suggest that the anti-anxiety effects of Cannabis sativa may be mediated by the GABA system in the brain. It has also been indicated that the cannabinoid receptor may be co-localized with dopamine receptors, specifically the D_1 dopamine receptor.[66] Two types of cannabinoid receptors have been identified: 1. the CB1 type that is in the central nervous system; and 2. the CB 2 type that is the peripheral nervous system.[67] Furthermore an endogenous cannabinoid has also been found and named anandamide (arachidonylethanolamide). Anandamide is produced in neurons,[68] binds to cannabinoid receptors[69] and appears to have similar effects to Δ9-THC.[70] Future research will better localize and decipher the distribution and functional interaction of the cannabinoid receptor in the brain.

BEHAVIORAL CONSEQUENCES

The behavior following administration of Cannabis sativa has characteristics that are truly unique, some similar to the behavior seen following the administration of other sedatives/hypnotics (chapter 4). A general sedating and relaxing effect is produced at lower doses, as well as an anti-anxiety effect. As with the other sedatives/hypnotics, as the dose is increased, disinhibition may be seen, which is expressed as a paradoxical increase in behavior due to the depression of inhibition. The sedation/intoxication following any behavioral disinhibition may be exhibited as increased relief from anxiety, feelings of well-being, periods of decreased behavior, characterized by silence and introspection, and times of increased activity and jocularity. There are apparent short-term memory deficits and changes in time estimation after ingesting marijuana. As with any sedative/hypnotic, Cannabis sativa may impair motor skills, driving skills, in particular.[67] Furthermore, there may be mood shifts. It is important to remember that these cognitive effects of Cannabis sativa are so subject to user expectation and the environment in which the drug is taken that such a list of behaviors should not be considered an invariant sequence of events but rather a list of possible behavioral outcomes.

The consistent reports of increased appetite and food consumption, sometimes referred to as the "munchies," is curious. This increase in food consumption associated with cannabis intake has been known for some time.[68] Recent studies have verified this behavioral change[69] and have suggested that the increased caloric intake is due to increased consumption of snack foods, not of regular meals.[70] In fact, satiety mechanisms themselves may not be altered at all by cannabis intake.[71] It also has become more apparent that the variability in the behavioral effects of cannabis is due to set and setting.[69,71]

Perhaps more than with any other drug, the factors of set (the user's expectations) and setting (the environment in which the drug is taken) exert a powerful influence on the behavioral effects of Cannabis sativa. Unlike any other sedative or central nervous system depressant, the intoxication following Cannabis sativa seems to be under the volitional control of the user, which means a person can essentially overcome the sedating effects at will and appear normal if the situation so demands.[27] The variability observed among subjects and even within the same subject raises doubts that the behaviors traditionally attributed to Cannabis sativa are actually a pure pharmacologically induced outcome of the drug.

Rigorous psychological testing of the effects of Cannabis sativa has been plagued not only by the variability among and within subjects but by the problems of consistency of the potency of the Cannabis sativa tested and the variability due to the different routes of administration used in experiments (i.e., an enteral (oral) versus a parenteral (smoking) route).

Among the most important behavioral studies concerning Cannabis sativa are the two series of experiments by Reese Jones, which address the issues of subject expectation and environmental factors more directly than any other previous studies.[72] The data in the Jones' studies challenge many traditionally accepted beliefs concerning the behavioral outcomes following Cannabis sativa use.

The purpose of the first experiment was to examine the level of intoxication produced by smoking a given amount of Cannabis sativa. In this study, the subjects were 100 male volunteers between the ages of twenty-one and thirty, all of whom had experience smoking marijuana. There were three main types of dependent measures:

1. Intoxication as reported by the subject on a scale of 0 to 100 (100 being the most intoxicated the person has ever been, 0 being the least); 2. A 272-item questionnaire (the Subjective Drug Effects Questionnaire—SDEQ); and 3. A host of physiological parameters, including pulse rate and salivary flow. The subjects were asked to smoke either the marijuana cigarette, containing 9 mg of Δ9-THC, or the placebo cigarette in a rigorously controlled protocol, in which the number of seconds of inhalation as well as the number of seconds the smoke was held in the lungs before exhalation were recorded. The placebo control is notable, in that placebo cigarettes were made from marijuana that had all of the active components extracted, the leaves rehydrated, dried, and made into cigarettes. There were no measurable active cannabinoids present in the placebo cigarettes. Thus, smoking them would produce all of the visual and olfactory cues of smoking marijuana, without the intake of any psychoactive components. It is this manipulation of subject expectancy that makes these studies such a unique and significant contribution in understanding the behavioral effects of Cannabis sativa.

The mean subjective intoxication scores, based on a scale of 0 to 100, were 61 for the marijuana and 34 for the placebo. While these scores indicate that the marijuana was judged to be more intoxicating than the placebo, the range of scores was striking, with the placebo receiving scores from 0 to 90 and the marijuana receiving scores of 0 to 95. This means that for some who were smoking the placebo, which had no psychoactive agents, it was intensely intoxicating, whereas for those who were smoking the marijuana it was not intoxicating at all. Despite this range, the physiological measures indicated that after smoking marijuana the pulse rate significantly increased and salivary flow significantly decreased, which was not seen after smoking the placebo.

To determine if the amount of experience with Cannabis sativa use may account for the variability of the intoxication scores, twenty-five frequent and twenty-five infrequent users from the 100 subjects were identified and their data analyzed separately. Table 6–1 summarizes this analysis. Notice that it was the infrequent and not the experienced frequent user who was able to distinguish the marijuana from the placebo. This seems to be the case only in smoking marijuana, because in another experiment[72] in which Cannabis sativa was given orally in an extract, neither group had any difficulty distinguishing cannabis from the placebo (Table 6–1). When one examines the physiological and performance data according to the amount of prior experience with Cannabis sativa, it appears the effects are much more intense for the infrequent user and that the development of tolerance is robust (Table 6–2). Notice that for virtually every one of these measures, physiological as well as behavioral, the more experienced marijuana users had less intense effects than did the less experienced users. These data do not support the notion of reverse tolerance and suggest the phenomenon of reverse tolerance does not apply to any behavior other than perhaps the perception of intoxication—even then it may not be a truly pharmacologically induced effect.

Thus, it appears that subjective expectation plays a key role in the intoxication induced by Cannabis sativa. The infrequent users have not had enough experience to

TABLE 6–1

	EXPERIENCE LEVEL	
	FREQUENT (>7 CIGARETTES/WEEK)	INFREQUENT (<2 CIGARETTES/MONTH)
Intoxication Rating		
Smoking 1 gm of 9% Delta 9-THC	52	67
Smoking the Placebo Cigarette	48	22
Intoxication Rating		
Oral Intake of 25 mg Delta 9-THC	32	72
Oral Intake of the Placebo	5	2

form the appropriate associations between the environmental cues (i.e., the sights and smells) and the experience of intoxication.

In an experiment designed to examine the effects of environment on Cannabis sativa intoxication,[72] subjects were asked to smoke marijuana in two different conditions, one week apart: 1. in a four-person group setting that was unstructured and allowed personal interactions to occur; and 2. alone in a laboratory with only the research assistant present. Even though both the intoxication scores and increases in pulse rate did not differ between the two conditions, there were significant differences in the expression of intoxication. According to the SDEQ scores, there was a

TABLE 6–2

	EXPERIENCE LEVEL	
	FREQUENT (>7 CIGARETTES/WEEK)	INFREQUENT (<2 CIGARETTES/MONTH)
Measures		
Increase in Pulse Rate	17.3	31.2
Salivary Flow	.9	1.8
Digit Substitution Errors	2	8
Complex Reaction Time	21	52

significant characterization of intoxication in the group setting as "euphoric," with more perceptual and thinking changes compared to the individual setting. Moreover, when tested individually, subjects appeared generally sedated, relaxed, and drowsy. These same subjects given the same dose of Cannabis sativa in a group setting acted differently. They were active, euphoric, and elated, complete with the uncontrolled laughter often reported as a cardinal sign of Cannabis sativa intoxication.

Collectively, these studies dramatically emphasize the importance of set (expectation) and setting (environment) in the behavioral expression following a drug, especially one like Cannabis sativa. The marked physiological changes induced by Cannabis sativa produce such an ambiguous type of intoxication that cognitive factors play a major role in its interpretation.

The effects of Cannabis sativa on memory, short-term memory in particular, merit some attention. Interference with memory processes is common in some of the other sedatives/hypnotics. As discussed in chapter 4, the benzodiazepines have a reliable effect on memory, and the barbiturates as well as the other anticonvulsants also impair memory formation.[73] The effects of Cannabis sativa on short-term memory, when the studies are properly controlled (see under Special Issues, "Consequences of Long-Term Heavy Use of Cannabis Sativa"), may not be detectable in normal everyday life.

It should be noted that even in studies of the chronic heavy use of Cannabis sativa, usually in the form of marijuana, there are virtually no reports of true hallucinations on the level of LSD, mescaline, or psilocin. The classification of Cannabis sativa as a hallucinogen by most schemes illustrates the historic credibility our culture has given to older apocryphal accounts of Cannabis sativa-induced hallucinations.

CULTURAL MYTHS

There are several myths concerning the behavior that is elicited by Cannabis sativa, which may have originated from casual observations but nevertheless have persisted despite experimental evidence to the contrary.

One of the earliest myths is that Cannabis sativa precipitates aggressive behavior. Although not exclusively the product of the Federal Bureau of Narcotics rhetoric campaign of the 1930s, this popular misconception has been difficult to alter. The evidence linking Cannabis sativa use to crime is virtually nonexistent.[78] In fact, studies have reported the opposite. The typical effect of Cannabis sativa use is a decrease in expressed and experienced hostility.[46] Among a prison population, regular marijuana users were better-socialized and better-adjusted, compared to other prison population subgroups.[79]

The myth of a phenomenon called reverse tolerance will be discussed in the next section, Tolerance and Withdrawal.

Another popular myth regarding Cannabis sativa has been the idea that this drug has the pharmacological property of causing a so-called amotivational syndrome. Simply described, the amotivational syndrome is when the chronic use of Cannabis sativa, usually marijuana and hashish, leads to a condition of apathy, dullness, and a compulsive interest in the substance, which may progress to the point where the individual is no longer motivated to participate in life's activities, such as school or work. The observation that Cannabis sativa may drive individuals to exhibit this behavioral pattern has been made since antiquity.[80] More recently, the connection between amotivated behavior and Cannabis sativa use has been made in India,[81] Egypt,[82] and in a population of U.S. soldiers in West Germany.[83] The central issue, which is extremely difficult to resolve experimentally, is to determine whether the personal dynamics of an individual is directly responsible for the amotivation, and not the drug used. The choice made by an amotivated person to remain in a constant state of intoxication is symptomatic of a personality disorder or, at the very least, of an inappropriate way to cope with a difficult environment. The actual substance used, whether Cannabis sativa or ethanol, barbiturates or benzodiazepines, is a matter of circumstance. Amotivation also occurs in individuals who do not use any chemical substances. Many investigators have not found evidence to support Cannabis sativa use directly inducing amotivational syndromes,[84,85] including two studies conducted in closed wards.[86,46] In fact, one ward study[46] found that the chronic-use marijuana group was more motivated based on their work performance than a matched chronic ethanol group. Furthermore, it was first reported in 1890 by the British Indian Hemp Commision and later corroborated by Jamaican and Costa Rican studies regarding the effects of long-term Cannabis sativa use (see following, Consequences of Long-Term Heavy Use of Cannabis Sativa) that Cannabis sativa increases staying power on a job and relieves fatigue.[58] In Jamaica, employers would supply ganja to workers to "get more work out of them."

Thus, while people who are amotivated may use Cannabis sativa, it appears very unlikely that chronic use of Cannabis sativa is the one causal factor in the expression of this behavior. The induction of an amotivational syndrome in people who if not for this drug would be normally motivated cannot reasonably be considered a pharmacological property of Cannabis sativa.

Finally, still another myth of Cannabis sativa is that this drug is a gateway substance to other drug dependencies (or addictions). While it is true that many users of so-called harder drugs, namely heroin and cocaine, also are very likely to use Cannabis sativa, it is not true that Cannabis sativa use will cause an individual to use other drugs. The La Guardia Report in 1944 concluded that marijuana smoking does not lead to opiate addiction.[16] Two longitudinal studies described the progression of legal drug use into illegal drug use in high school students[87,88] and found that the most common entry drug to illegal drug use was alcohol, primarily beer and wine. Appreciate that these data do not mean drinking beer and wine will cause individuals to use harder drugs, but rather that a large proportion of those people who went on to hard drugs had earlier experiences with ethanol. The causal role of beer, wine, or Cannabis sativa in the progression to illegal drug use simply has not been proven.

TOLERANCE AND WITHDRAWAL

The development of tolerance to the effects of Cannabis sativa is robust and has been well-described. In descriptive field studies, the Indian Hemp Commission report of 1894, a report on chronic hashish users in Greece,[89] and a West Germany report on American soldiers stationed there,[90] note the development of tolerance. In laboratory clinical experiments,[80] the tolerance that develops to repeated Cannabis sativa use has been seen in most measures taken (Table 6–2).

There is a unique phenomenon that has been attributed to Cannabis sativa use,[41] called reverse tolerance. Recall that tolerance is the decrease in a drug's effects, with repeated doses. Reverse tolerance is the increase in a drug's effects, with repeated doses. While there have been numerous reports of tolerance following Cannabis sativa use, there has never been an unequivocal experimentally demonstrated case of reverse tolerance. Apparently, this phenomenon, which is totally based on apocryphal accounts, only addresses the situation of people not being able to get intoxicated on their first exposure to smoking marijuana. This may be the case behaviorally, but given the ambiguous nature of the intoxication produced by Cannabis sativa, reverse tolerance is certainly not a pharmacological property of the drug but rather a result of the many cognitive factors involved in the intoxication experience.

There is a withdrawal syndrome that has been described in abrupt cessation of Cannabis sativa use. An oral dose of 30 mg of Δ9-THC was given every four hours a day for thirty days, and a sudden stop in dosing produced the following symptoms: irritability, decreased appetite, nausea, vomiting, diarrhea, salivation, sweating, and some disruption of sleep.[91] These are not unlike the withdrawal symptoms seen after a moderate dependency to sedatives/hypnotics. However, other researchers have reported much milder withdrawal. Following the chronic use of five marijuana cigarettes a day for over sixty days, the reported withdrawal was less intense and produced fewer symptoms[92] than did the withdrawal described earlier. Another study observed only restlessness and weight loss in its withdrawal syndrome.[46] The reports of chronic Cannabis sativa use in Costa Rica and Jamaica (see Consequences of Long-Term Heavy Use of Cannabis Sativa) did not indicate any withdrawal syndromes in those populations.

Despite the rather moderate withdrawal following chronic Cannabis sativa use, there is some evidence for the potential of developing a dependency on it. There have been several reports of chronic Cannabis sativa users who have wanted to stop but were unable to do so without a great deal of difficulty.[82,93,90]

SPECIAL ISSUES

Consequences of Long-Term Heavy Use of Cannabis Sativa

In order to determine the outcome of prolonged Cannabis sativa use, three studies focused on chronic users in Jamaica, Costa Rica, and Greece.

In the Jamaican study,[94] thirty heavy users (with an average duration of seventeen years of daily ganja smoking) were compared to thirty nonusers in the area. The use of other drugs, including ethanol, was infrequent. This study lasted three years and made neuropsychological, personality, neurological, psychiatric, and anthropological evaluations. There were no physiological or psychological differences between the groups, except that the user group had decreased pulmonary function, as one would suspect with a smoking habit. There was no evidence for any signs of an amotivational syndrome. In fact, the users and their employers reported that the cannabis helped them work better. In addition, increased appetite, enhanced auditory functioning, and even altered time sense were not found in users of high-potency Cannabis sativa.[95]

In the Greek study,[96] forty-seven chronic hashish users, who used for more than ten years (with the exception of ethanol, no other addictive substances were used) were compared to forty nonusers of hashish. Only moderate ethanol use was allowed, and subjects who used ethanol heavily were excluded from the study. The measure taken in this study was the WAIS (Wexler Adult Intelligence Scale) which consisted of a neurological examination, psychiatric interview, physical exam, and social history. By design, most of these measures were taken immediately after all subjects were asked to smoke marijuana or a placebo cigarette. Performance on psychological tests following marijuana intake was often similar to performance following placebo smoking. There was no evidence of any brain damage and no indicator of any organic brain syndrome. The chronic users did not exhibit memory loss, disorientation, or any kind of confusion consistent with known organic psychoses. The effects of smoking marijuana on EEG and psychological testing were transient and no longer measurable four hours after the drug was taken. Basically, this study, like other studies in the United States,[97,98] failed to find any true pharmacological toxicity due to long-term Cannabis sativa use as reflected in the nervous system or the mental status of the user. The investigators concluded:

> We are not impressed that the range of dangers—physical, psychological, and behavioral—ascribed to cannabis use are inherent in the chemical or pharmacological properties of these substances.

In the first Costa Rican study,[99] eighty-four chronic marijuana users, with the average duration of Cannabis sativa use being seventeen years and the average use about ten marijuana cigarettes a day, were matched to 156 nonuser controls. From this population, a matched subsample of forty-one users and controls was selected for specific testing. In addition to eyesight, pulmonary function, and sleep EEG, psychological function was measured by the following battery: verbal memory and learning, examined with three separate tests, nonverbal memory and learning examined with three separate tests, and the WAIS, to measure intellectual performance. Despite the unusually heavy Cannabis sativa use for such a long time, all of the comparisons between users and nonusers showed no differences. There were no significant differences between users and their controls on any of the sixteen major variables which made up the neuropsychological memory tests. Across the different stimuli presented, there were no significant differences in memory and learning between the two groups. Concerning the WAIS, the fourteen variables that made up the various scales and subtests to measure intelligence all showed no significant differences between user and nonuser groups.

There was a follow up[100] to the Costa Rican study that targeted those measures from the original study which indicated a trend, though not significant, that chronic marijuana users were indeed deficient in memory and learning. A portion of the subjects from the original study was found and recruited into the new experiment, twenty-seven users and thirty nonusers. This time, more sophisticated cognitive tests were added to the testing battery. All of the tests that were given in the original study still showed no differences between the user and nonuser groups. Only the new tests indicated that compared to nonusers, chronic users learned lists of unrelated words more slowly and had slower rates of processing in tasks that required sustained attention. Since it took a second set of testing with specialized tests to detect learning differences in the chronic-use marijuana group, the authors concluded that these effects, these deficits in learning, are subtle and subclinical, meaning that these effects probably would not impact day-to-day life in a real world outside the laboratory.

Notably absent from these reports is that any kind of psychoses was evident in any of the subjects, which does not support the notion that chronic use will somehow induce brain damage that progresses to psychosis.

Why Cannabis Sativa Commands Cultural Concern

The manner in which our culture has dealt with and continues to deal with Cannabis sativa provides us with a wealth of insights concerning many topics beside the pharmacology of this drug, in particular, the legislative process.

One topic is the generation of publicity, which targets the public and subsequently state and national legislatures. The strategy used by government officials in the Federal Bureau of Narcotics was one of presenting unscientific and unreliable data as truth. The parade of gory crimes that were said to be committed because of Cannabis sativa use is now so ridiculous that one wonders how this practice went on so long. While this strategy was successful in having legislation passed to outlaw Cannabis sativa, the price for this "victory" was high. The loss of credibility was perhaps the most tragic casualty in the "Marijuana—Assassins of Youth" rhetoric campaign of the 1930s.

There are two related topics concerning the legal status of Cannabis sativa: 1. Should Cannabis sativa be completely legalized?; and 2. Should Cannabis sativa be rescheduled to allow more widespread medical use?

Currently Cannabis sativa is listed on Schedule I, the legal classification for drugs that have a high abuse potential and have no accepted medical use. The statewide movement of the late 1970s to establish research programs in which Cannabis sativa would be dispensed to selected patient populations seemed to usher in a period of decriminalization of Cannabis sativa. Not only were states passing laws that would minimize penalties for simple possession, but the federal government initiated the Compassionate Investigational New Drug program to facilitate these state programs. However, in the early 1990s, it became politically advantageous to appear "hard on drugs." This "tough on crime" theme has been extended to the laws concerning Cannabis sativa. Many states have recriminalized possession of Cannabis sativa, and in March 1992 high-ranking officials of the Bush administration unilaterally and without public hearing ended the Compassionate IND program. The processing of literally hundreds of applications for legitimate access to Cannabis sativa for medical treatment was abruptly terminated.[101]

It is not within the scope of this book to review the arguments for and against the legalization of Cannabis sativa. Certainly both positions have merit, and either position can mount a compelling case. Independent of the legal status is the issue of the vigor with which the current laws are enforced. The enormous commitment of money, people, and, in many cases the loss of life, to the control of a drug that poses such a minimal physical threat to its user perhaps needs to be reevaluated.

However, given the data which indicates that cannabis may have medical usefulness in treating such conditions as glaucoma, and the accompanying nausea of chemotherapy in cancer patients, it becomes increasingly difficult to defend the Schedule I classification of Cannabis sativa and the recent curtailment of its availability for experimental treatment. The drugs classified in Schedule II have a high potential for developing a dependency, yet are prescribed by physicians as they judge appropriate in the treatment of certain medical conditions. There is no reason to believe that physicians will not exercise this proper judgment in the case of Cannabis sativa.

There have been numerous commissions which have examined the safety and possible usefulness of Cannabis sativa, including the Indian Hemp Commission Report (1894), two Panama Canal Zone reports (1930), the La Guardia Report (1944), reports from New Zealand, Canada, and England (1970), the World Health Organization Report (1981), and the National Academy of Science Report to Congress (1982). All of these reports reach similar conclusions—that there is no threat to society from Cannabis sativa use, and that there is nothing dangerously inherent about this drug. Why Western culture is so persistent in its total ban on Cannabis sativa remains extremely difficult to understand.

REVIEW EXAM

1. How would you classify Cannabis sativa? Why?
2. Where and when did Cannabis sativa originate?
3. When did Cannabis sativa regain a role in medicine in England?
4. What were the three sources for Cannabis sativa importation into the United States?
5. What role did Harry Anslinger play in Cannabis sativa legislation?
6. What were the reasons for the decline of Cannabis sativa as a medicine in the 1900s?
7. What were the findings of the LaGuardia Report?

8. What are the differences between male and female Cannabis sativa plants?
9. What are the active components of Cannabis sativa?
10. What is the half-life of Cannabis sativa? Describe its clearance from the blood.
11. When are the peaks effects felt following the smoking and ingestion of Cannabis sativa?
12. Name the most consistent effects of Cannabis sativa.
13. What are the pulmonary and immune effects of Cannabis sativa?
14. What are the effects of Cannabis sativa on intraocular pressure and sleep?
15. Where are the cannabinoid receptors in the brain?
16. What is the common behavioral profile following Cannabis sativa use?
17. What are the findings of the Jones' experiments on set and setting?
18. Describe the four cultural myths concerning Cannabis sativa.
19. Describe the withdrawal syndrome in heavy Cannabis sativa use.
20. Describe the findings of the three major studies of chronic heavy use of Cannabis sativa.

REFERENCES

1. JAFFE, J. (1980). Drug addiction and drug abuse. In L. Goodman & A. Gilman (Eds.), *The Pharmacological Basis of Therapeutics* (6th ed., pp. 535–588). New York: Macmillan Publishing Co.
2. SCHULTES, R. (1970). Random thoughts and queries on the botany of cannabis. In C. Joyce & S. Curry (Eds.), *The Botany and Chemistry of Cannabis* (pp. 11–38). London: Churchill.
3. SCHULTES, R., & HOFMANN, A. (1980). *The Botany and Chemistry of Hallucinogens.* Springfield, IL: Charles C. Thomas.
4. MECHOULAM, R. (1986). The pharmacohistory of Cannabis sativa. In R. Mechoulam (Ed.), *Cannabinoids as Therapeutic Agents* (pp. 1–19). Boca Raton, FL: CRC Press.
5. EMBODEN, W. (1972). Ritual use of Cannabis sativa L.: A historical ethnographic survey. In P. Furst (Ed.), *Flesh of the Gods.* New York: Praeger.
6. PATRIS, M., & NAHAS, G. (1984). Botany: The unstable species. In G. Nahas (Ed.), *Marihuana in Science and Medicine* (pp. 3–36). New York: Raven Press.
7. RABIN, C. (1966). Rice in the Bible. *Journal of Semitic Studies*, 11, 2.
8. BRUNNER, T. (1973). Marijuana in Ancient Greece and Rome? The literary evidence. *Bulletin of the History of Medicine*, 47, 344.
9. GODWIN, H. (1967). Pollen analytic evidence for the cultivation of cannabis in England. *Review of Palaeobotany and Palynology*, 4, 71–80.
10. ROUYER, M. (1810). Sur le medicaments usuels des Egyptiens. *Bulletin de Pharmacie*, 2, 25.
11. O'SHAUGNESSY, W. (1843). On the Cannabis indica or Indian hemp. *Pharmacol. J. Trans.*, 2, 594.
12. O'SHAUGNESSY, W. (1842). On the preparation of the Indian hemp or Gunjah (Cannabis indica). *Trans. Med. Phys. Soc. Bombay*, 8, 421-461.
13. M'MEENS, R. (1860). Report on the committee on Cannabis indica. Transactions of the fifteenth annual meeting of the Ohio State Medical Society, 15, 75–100.
14. CHRISTISON, A. (1851). On the natural history, action, and uses of Indian hemp. *Mon. J. Med. Sci.*, 13, 26.
15. REYNOLDS, R. (1859). On some of the therapeutic uses of Indian hemp. *Archives of Medicine*, 2, 154.
16. SLOMAN, L. (1979). *Reefer Madness—Marijuana in America.* New York: Grove Press.
17. MUSTO, D. (1987). *The American Disease—Origins of Narcotic Control* (pp. 210–229). New York: Oxford University Press.
18. SAMORA, J. (1969). *Los mujados: The Wetback Story* (pp. 38–46). Notre Dame, IN: University of Notre Dame Press.
19. TAYLOR, P. (1930, April). More bars against the Mexicans? *Survey,* p. 26.
20. ANSLINGER, H., & TOMKINS, W. (1953). *The Traffic in Narcotics.* New York: Funk.
21. BROMBERG, W. (1934). Marihuana intoxication. *American Journal of Psychiatry*, 91, 303–330.

22. STANLEY, E. (1931). Marihuana as a developer of criminals. *American Journal of Police Science*, 2, 252.
23. *Marjuana and Health* (1975). Fifth Annual Report to the United States Congress from the Secretary of Health, Education, and Welfare, p. 119.
24. ROFFMAN, R. (1982). *Marijuana As Medicine* (pp. 1–27). Seattle, WA: Madrona Publishers.
25. DOORENBOS, N., FETTERMAN, P., QUIMBY, M., & TURNER, C. (1971). Cultivation, extraction, and analysis of Cannabis sativa L. *Annals of the New York Academy of Science*, 191, 3–14.
26. WALL, M. (1971). The in vitro and in vivo metabolism of tetrahydrocannabinol (THC). *Annals of the New York Academy of Science*, 191, 23–39.
27. SCHWARTZ, R. (1987). Marijuana: an overview. *Pediatric Clinics of North America*, 34 (2), 305–317.
28. AGURELL, S., LINDGREN, J., & OHLSSON, A. (1979). Introduction to quantification of cannabinoids and their metabolites in biological fluids. In G. Nahas & W. Paton (Eds.), *Marijuana: Biological Effects* (pp. 3–13). Oxford: Pergamon Press.
29. HARVEY, D. (1984). Chemistry, metabolism, and pharmacokinetics of the cannabinoids. In G. Nahas, & D. Harvey, & M. Paris (Eds.), *Marijuana in Science and Medicine* (pp. 37–107). New York: Raven Press.
30. LEMBERGER, L., AXELROD, J., & KOPIN, I. (1971). Metabolism and disposition of tetrahydrocannabinols in naive subjects and chronic marijuana users. *Annals of the New York Academy of Science*, 191, 142–154.
31. PEREZ-REYES, M., GUISEPPI, S., DAVIS, K., SCHINDLER, V., & COOK, C. (1982). Comparison of effects of marijuana of three potencies. *Clinical Pharmacology and Therapeutics*, 31 (5), 617–624.
32. BARNETT, G., CHIANG, C., PEREZ-REYES, M., & OWENS, S. (1982). Kinetic study of smoking marijuana. *Journal of Pharmacokinetics and Biopharmaceutics*, 10 (5), 495–506.
33. HOLLISTER, L. (1971). Status report on clinical pharmacology of marijuana. *Annals of the New York Academy of Science*, 191, 132–141.
34. WALL, M., & PEREZ-REYES, M. (1981). The metabolism of Δ9-tetrahydrocannabinol and related cannabinoids in man. *Journal of Clinical Pharmacology*, 21, 178S–189S.
35. OHLSSON, A., LINDGREN, J., WAHLEN, A., AGURELL, S., HOLLISTER, L., & GILLESPIE, H. (1982). Single dose kinetics of deuterium labelled Δ1-tetrahydrocannabinol in heavy and light cannabis users. *Biomedical Mass Spectrometry*, 9, 6–10.
36. JOHANSSON, E., ARGUELL, S., HOLLISTER, L., & HALLDIN, M. (1988). Prolonged apparent half-life of delta-1-tetrahydrocannabinol in plasma of chronic marijuana users. *Journal of Pharmacy and Pharmacology*, 40, 374–375.
37. GILL, E., & JONES, G. (1972). Brain levels of Δ1-tetrahydrocannabinol and its metabolites in mice—correlation with behavior and the effect of the metabolite inhibitors SKF-525A and piperonyl butoxide. *Biochemical Pharmacology*, 21, 2237–2248.
38. LEMBERGER, L., & RUBIN, A. (1975). The physiologic disposition of marijuana in man. *Life Science*, 17, 1637–1642.
39. HUNT, C., JONES, R., HERNING, R., & BACHMAN, J. (1981). Evidence that cannabidiol does not significantly alter the pharmacokinetics of tetrahydrocannabinol in man. *Journal of Pharmacokinetics and Biopharmaceutics*, 9, 245–260.
40. WALL, M., & BRINE, D. (1979). Applications of mass spectrometry in cannabinoid research. In G. Nahas & W. Paton (Eds.), *Marijuana: Biological Effects* (pp. 15–43). Oxford: Pergamon Press.
41. WEIL, A., ZINBERG, N., & NELSEN, J. (1968). Clinical and psychological effects of marijuana in man. *Science*, 162, 1234–1242.
42. GRAHAM, J. (1986). The cardiovascular action of cannabinoids. In R. Mechoulam (Ed.), *Cannabinoids As Therapeutic Agents* (pp. 1–19). Boca Raton, FL: CRC Press.
43. PEREZ-REYES, N., LIPTON, M., TOMMOUS, M., WALL, M., BRINE, D., & DAVIS, K. (1973). Pharmacology of orally administered Δ9-THC. *Journal of Clinical Pharmacology and Therapeutics*, 14, 48–55.
44. ABBOUD, R., & SANDERS, H. (1976). Effect of oral administration of Δ9-THC on airway mechanics in normal and asthmatic subjects. *Chest*, 70, 480.
45. TASKIN, D., REISS, S., SHAPIRO, B., CALVARESE, B., OLSEN, J., & LODGE, J. (1977). Bronchial effects of aerosolized Delta-9-tetrahydrocannabinol in healthy and asthmatic subjects. *American Review of Respiratory Disease*, 115, 57–65.

46. MENDELSON, J., ROSSI, A., & MEYER, R. (Eds.) (1974). *The Use of Marijuana, Psychological and Physiological Inquiry.* New York: Plenum Press.

47. MALIT, L., JOHNSTONE, R., BOURKE, D., KULP, R., KLEIN, V., & SMITH, T. (1975). Intravenous Delta-9-tetrahydrocannabinol: effects on ventilatory control and cardiovascular dynamics. *Anesthesiology*, 42 (6), 666–673.

48. ROFFMAN, R. (1982). *Marijuana As Medicine* Seattle, WA.: Madrona Publishers. (pp. 62–75).

49. HELPER, R., FRANK, I., & PETRUS, R. (1976). Ocular effects of marijuana smoking. In Braude, M., & Szara S (Eds.), *Pharmacology of Marijuana*, (pp. 815-824) Raven Press: New York.

50. PURNELL, W., & GREGG, J. (1972). Delta-9-tetrahydrocannabinol, euphoria, and intraocular pressure in man. *Annals of Opthamology*, 7, 921–922.

51. SALLAN, S., ZINBERG, N., & FREI, E. (1975). Antiemetic effects of delta-9-tetrahydrocannabinol in patients receiving cancer chemotherapy. *New England Journal of Medicine*, 293, 795–797.

52. CAREY, M., BURISH, T., & BRENNER, D. (1983). Delta-9-THC in cancer chemotherapy: research problems and issues. *Annals of International Medicine*, 198, 106–114.

53. Chang, A., Shiling, D., Stillman, R., Goldbverg, N., Seipp, C., Barofsky, I., Simon, R., & Rosenberg, S. (1979). Delta-9-Tetrahydrocannabinol as an antiemetic in cancer patients receiving high dose methotrexate. *Annals of International Medicine*, 91, 819–824.

54. NAHAS, G., SUCIU-FOCA, N., ARMAND, J., & MORISHIMA, A. (1974). Inhibition of cellular mediated immunity in marijuana smokers. *Science*, 183, 419–420.

55. PETERSEN, B., LEMBERGER, L., GRAHAM, J., & DALTON, B. (1975). Alterations in the cellular-mediated immune responsiveness of chronic marijuana smokers. *Psychopharmacology Communications*, 1, 67–74.

56. SILVERSTEIN, M., & LESSIN, P. (1974). Normal skin test response in chronic marijuana users. *Science*, 186, 740–742.

57. LAU, R., LERNER, C., TUBERGEN, D., BENOWITZ, N., DOMINO, E., & JONES, R. (1975). Non-inhibition of phytohemagglutin (PHA) induced lymphocyte transformation in humans by Delta-9-tetrahydrocannabinol (delta-9-THC). *Federation Proceedings*, 34, 783.

58. *Marjuana and Health* (1975). Fifth Annual Report to the United States Congress from the Secretary of Health, Education, and Welfare, p. 111.

59. HARRIS, L., MUNSON, A., & CARCHMAN, R. (1976). Antitumor properties of cannabinoids. In M. Braude & S. Szara (Eds.), *Pharmacology of Marijuana*, (pp. 749–762) New York: Raven Press.

60. KOLODNY, R., MASTERS, W., KOLODNER, R., & TORO, G. (1974). Depression of plasma testosterone levels after chronic intensive marijuana use. *New England Journal of Medicine*, 290, 872–874.

61. TASSINARI, C., PERAITA-ADRADOS, G., AMBROSETTO, G., & GASTAUT, H. (1974). Effects of marijuana and delta-9-THC at high doses in man. A polygraphic study. *Electroencephalography and Clinical Neurophysiology*, 36 (1), 94.

62. PODOLSKY, S., PATTAVINA, C., & AMARAL, M. (1971). Effect of marijuana on the glucose tolerance test. *Annals of the New York Academy of Science*, 191, 54–60.

63. MCISSAC, W., FRITCHIE, G., IDANPANN-HEIKKILA, J., HO, B., & ENGLERT, L. (1971). Distribution of marijuana in monkey brain and concomitant behavioral effects. *Nature*, 230, 593–594.

64. HERKENHAM, M., LYNN, A., LITTLE, M., JOHNSON, M., MELVIN, L., DE COSTA, B., & RICE, K. (1990). Cannabinoid receptor localization in brain. *Proceedings of the National Academy of Sciences of the United States of America*, 87 (5), 1932–1936.

65. SETHI, B., TRIVEDI, J., KUMAR, P., GULATI, A., AGARWAL, A., & SETHI, N. (1986). Antianxiety effect of cannabis: involvement of central benzodiazepine receptors. *Biological Psychiatry*, 21, 3–21.

66. HERKENHAM, M., LYNN, A., DE COSTA, B., & RICHFIELD, E. (1991). Neuronal localization of cannabinoid receptors in the basal ganglia of the rat. *Brain Research*, 547 (2), 267–274.

67. PRILLER, J., BRILEY, E., MANSOURI, J., DEVANE, W., MACKIE, K., & FELDER, C. (1995). MEAD ethanolamide, a novel eicosanoid, is an agonist for the central (CB1) and peripheral (CB2) cannabinoid receptors. *Molecular Pharmacology*, 48(2), 288–292.

68. DI-MARZO, V., FONTANA, A., CADAS, H., SCHINELLI, S., CIMINO, G., SCHWARTZ, J., & PIOMELLI, D. (1994). Formation and inactivation of endogenous cannabinoid anandamide in central neurons. *Nature*, 372(6507), 686–691.

69. FELDER, C., JOYCE, K., BRILEY, E., MANSOURI, J., MACKIE, K., BLOND, O., LAI, Y., MA, A., & MITCHELL R. (1995). Comparison of the pharmacology and signal transduction of the human cannabinoid CB1 and CB2 receptors. *Molecular Pharmacology*, 48(3), 443–450.

70. HOWLETT, A. (1995). Pharmacology of cannabinoid receptors. *Annual Review of Pharmacology and Toxicology,* 35, 607–634.

71. KLONOFF, H. (1974). Marijuana and driving in real-life situations. *Science,* 186, 317–324.

72. HOLLISTER, L. (1971). Hunger and appetite after single doses of marijuana, alcohol, and dextroamphetamine. *Clinical Pharmacology and Therapeutics,* 12(1), 44–49.

73. KELLY, T., FOLTIN, R., EMURIAN, C., & FISCHMAN, M. (1990). Multidimensional behavioral effects of marijuana. *Progress in Neuro-Psychopharmacology and Psychiatry,* 14(6), 885–902.

74. FOLTIN, R., FISCHMAN, M., & BYRNE, M. (1988). Effects of smoked marijuana on food intake and body weight of humans living in a residential laboratory. *Appetite,* 11(1), 1–14.

75. MATTES, R., ENGELMAN, K., SHAW, L., & ELSOHLY, M. (1994). Cannabinoids and appetite stimulation. *Pharmacology, Biochemistry and Behavior,* 49(1).

76. JONES, R. (1971). Tetrahydrocannabinol and the marijuana-induced social "high," or the effects of mind on marijuana. *Annals of the New York Academy of Science,* 191, 155–165.

77. REYNOLDS, E., & TRIMBLE M. (1985). Adverse neuropsychiatric effects of anticonvulsant drugs. *Drugs,* 29 (6), 570–581.

78. GOODE, E. (1974). The criminogenics of marijuana. *Addictive Diseases,* 1 (3), 297–322.

79. MCGUIRE, J., & MEGARGEE, E. (1974). Personality correlates of marijuana use among youthful offenders. *Journal of Consulting and Clinical Psychology,* 42 (1), 124–133.

80. ROSENTHAL, F. (1971). *The Herb Hashish versus Medieval Muslin Society.* Leiden: E.J. Brill.

81. CHOPRA I., & CHOPRA, R. (1967). The use of cannabis drug in India. *Bulletin on Narcotics, 9,* 4–29.

82. SOUEIF, M. (1967). Hashish consumption in Egypt with special reference to psychosocial aspects. *Bulletin on Narcotics, 19,* 1–12.

83. TENNANT, F., & GROESBECK, C. (1972). Psychiatric effects of hashish. *Archives of General Psychiatry,* 27, 133–136.

84. BRILL, N., & CHRISTIE, R. (1974). Marijuana use and psychosocial adaptation. *Archives of General Psychiatry,* 31, 713–719.

85. MIRANNE, A. (1979). Marijuana use and achievement orientation of college students. *Journal of Health and Social Behavior,* 20, 194–199.

86. MILES, G. (1975). A selective review of studies of long-term use of cannabis on behavior, personality, and cognitive functioning. In P. Connel & N. Dorn (Eds.), *Cannabis and Man,* (pp. 66–86). Edinburgh: Churchill Livingstone.

87. KANDEL, D., & FAUST, R. (1975). Sequence and stages in patterns of adolescent drug use. *Archives of General Psychiatry,* 32, 923–932.

88. SINGLE, E., KANDEL, D., & FAUST, R. (1974). Patterns of multiple drug use in high school. *Journal of Health and Social Behavior,* 15 (4), 344–357.

89. MIRAS, C. (1969). Experience with chronic hashish smokers. In J. Wittenburn, H. Brill, J. Smith, & S. Wittenborn (Eds.), *Drugs and Youth* (pp. 191–198). Springfield, IL: Charles C. Thomas.

90. TENNANT, F., PRELE, M., PRENDERGAST, T., & VENTRY, P. (1971). Medical manifestations associated with hashish. *Journal of the American Medical Association,* 216, 1965–1969.

91. JONES, R., & BENOWITZ, N. (1976). The 30-day trip—clinical studies of Cannabis tolerance and dependence. In M. Braude & S. Szara (Eds.) *Pharmacology of Marijuana* (pp. 627–641). New York: Raven Press.

92. NOWLAN, R., & COHEN, S. (1977). Tolerance to marijuana: heart rate and subjective "high." *Clinical Pharmacology and Therapeutics,* 22, 550–556.

93. FREEDMAN, I., & PEER, I. (1968). Drug addiction among pimps and prostitutes in Israel. *International Journal of Addiction,* 3, 271–300.

94. RUBIN, V., & COMITAS, L. (1975). *Ganga in Jamica: A Medical Anthropological Study of Chronic Marijuana Use.* The Hague: Mouton.

95. *Marjuana and Health* (1975). Fifth Annual Report to the United States Congress from the Secretary of Health, Education, and Welfare, p. 92.

96. STEFANIS, C., DORNBUSH, R., & FINK, M. (1977). *Hashish: Studies of Long-Term Use.* New York: Raven Press.

97. HANNERZ, J., & HINDMARSH, T. (1983). Neurological and neuroradiological examination of chronic cannabis smokers. *Annals of Neurology,* 13 (2), 207–210.

98. WERT, R., & RAULIN, M. (1986). The chronic cerebral effects of cannabis use. I. methodological issues and neurological findings. *International Journal of Addiction,* 21 (6), 605–628.

99. RANDAL, R., & O'LEARY, A. (1993). *Marijuana As Medicine: Initial Steps*. Washington D.C.: Galen Press.

100. CARTER, W., COGGINS, W., & DOUGHTY, P. (1976). *Chronic Cannabis Use in Costa Rica*. Report submitted to NIDA in fulfillment of Contract No. NO1-MH3-0233(ND).

101. PAGE, J., FLETCHER, J., & TRUE, W. (1988). Psychosociocultural perspectives on chronic cannabis use: the Costa Rican follow-up. *Journal of Psychoactive Drugs*, 20, 57–65.

CHAPTER SEVEN
OPIATES:
Drugs That Block Pain

GENERAL ISSUES ADDRESSED IN THIS CHAPTER

- Categorizing opiates based on structure
- How opiate use became widespread
- The evolution of opiate control legislation
- How the opiates are introduced and excreted
- The spectrum of effects induced by opiates
- The role of brain stem mechanisms
- Peripheral effects of opiates
- Characteristics of several morphine-like substances
- Classes of opiate receptors and what each class mediates
- Types of endogenous opiates
- Characteristics of opiate antagonists and mixed agonists/antagonists
- Withdrawal syndromes for morphine, methadone, and meperidine
- The issues of pharmacologically treating opiate withdrawal
- The role of expectation in opiate overdose
- The normal role of opiates in brain pleasure systems
- Opiate-based designer drugs

LIST OF SPECIFIC OPIATES

1. Natural Opiates (those found in nature):
   a. Morphine
   b. Codeine
   c. Papaverine
2. Synthetic Opiates
   A. Semisynthetic Opiates (those structurally similar to the natural opiates)
      a. Heroin (Diacetylmorphine)
      b. Hydromorphone (Dilaudid®)
      c. Dihydrocodeine (Percodan®)
      d. Pentazocine (Talwin®)
      e. Levorphanol (Levo-Dromoran®)
      f. [Dextro methorphan®]
   B. Those substances not structurally similar to the natural opiates:
      1. The Phenylpiperideines
         a. Meperidine (Demerol®)
         b. Loperamide (Imodium®)
         c. Diphenoxylate hydrochloride (combined with atropine is Lomotil®)
         d. Fentanyl (Sublimaze®)
      2. Methadone (Dolophine®)
      3. Propoxyphene (Darvon®)

3. Opiate Antagonists
   1. Pure Opiate Antagonists
      a. Naloxone (Narcan®)
      b. Naltrexone (Trexan®)
   2. Partial Opiate Antagonists
      a. Cyclozacine
      b. Butophanol (Stadol®)

INTRODUCTION

As the name implies, drugs in the opiates class are either directly derived from opium or have similar effects.* Perhaps the best-known behavioral consequences of any drug are relief from pain and euphoria following opiate administration. Opium is the milky juice in the seed pod of the opium poppy. After the petals of the flower fall, this juice then can be harvested by cutting a shallow gash along the seed pod and allowing the juice to slowly seep out. The juice dries to a gummy consistency which can be further processed into several forms.

The active components in opium that are most medically beneficial are morphine, which is approximately 25 percent of opium by weight, codeine, approximately 0.5 percent, and papaverine, approximately 0.5 percent.[1] Papaverine is a muscle relaxant that does not cross into the brain compartment, thus it exerts no direct effects on the brain.[2] However, morphine and codeine have profound effects on the brain and also on behavior.

One way of categorizing the opiates is by the structure of the molecules of the individual opiate types. The opiates found in opium, namely morphine and codeine, have a distinct molecular shape. In fact, codeine and morphine are almost structurally identical except for the presence of a methyl group—a CH_3—in codeine (Figure 7–1). The outcome of this seemingly small difference is in a significant functional dissimilarity between these two compounds. Codeine is in general less pharmacologically active than morphine.[2] Even though it may be a weaker analgesic compared to morphine, codeine is still very potent as a pain reliever. In addition, being less pharmacologically active can have its advantages. For instance, the respiratory depression effects of codeine are much less than with morphine.[2]

Alterations of this molecular shape produce substances that belong in the semisynthetic opiate category. The addition of two acetyl groups (CH_3CO) to the morphine molecule results in a different compound called heroin.

There are drugs that have been synthesized that do not resemble the molecular structure of natural opiates, but nevertheless seem to have very similar effects on brain functioning and behavior as do the natural opiates. These drugs can be categorized as synthetic opiates that are not structurally similar to the opiates. Two types

---

*The term "narcotic" also is sometimes used for the drugs in this class. While it technically should only refer to opiates, it has become synonymous with "dangerous drug" and has been used when referring to any drug that dulls the senses. This unfortunate loss of precision and the negative associations now implied with this name have rendered the term "narcotic" useless.

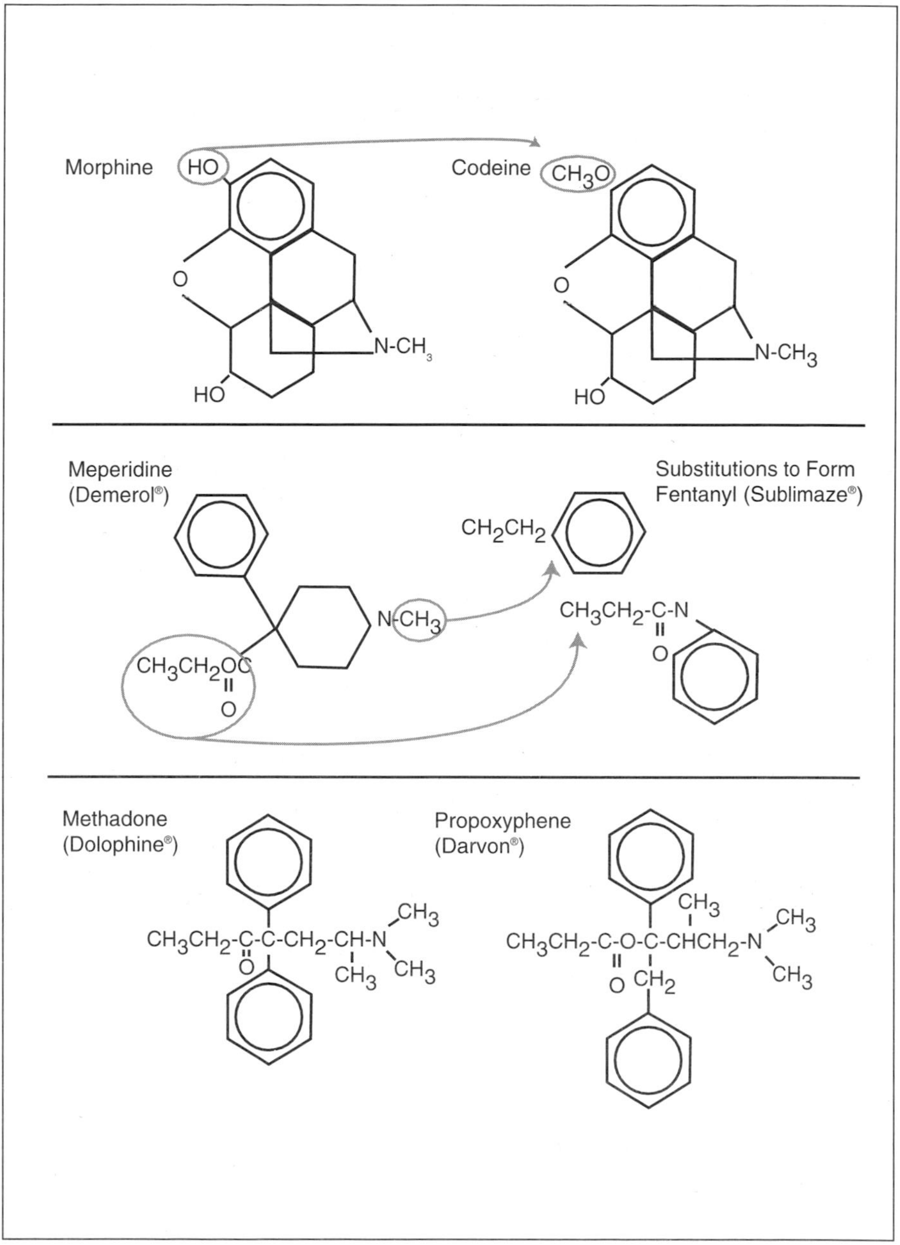

FIGURE 7-1 Molecular Shapes of Some Opiates
Notice how the molecular structure of two of the natural opiates, morphine and codeine, are very similar.
Notice how certain variations of a known opiate can yield another opiate with different characteristics.
Methadone and Darvon® are structurally similar, but the behavioral outcomes are quite different.

of these molecular structures are illustrated in Figure 7–1. One is the phenyl-piperideines, two specific examples of which are meperidine (Demerol®) and fentanyl (Sublimaze®). Notice how two substitutions of side chains to the common molecular shape will produce an entirely different substance. Also illustrated are methadone (Dolophine®) and propoxyphene (Darvon®), which are structurally related to each other. The functional differences between meperidine and fentanyl as well as between methadone and propoxyphene are appreciable.

HISTORY

Opium has an ancient history, dating back to the third century B.C.[1] Opium has been used by the ancient Egyptian, Greek, and Roman cultures. The use and cultivation of opium had become as vast as the breadth of the Roman Empire. However, its spread to the Arab world was especially significant. It was the extensive commercial network of Arabian traders that enabled opium to spread from Africa to India and China.

Throughout the world, the use of opium steadily grew. By the mid-sixteenth century, opium was a common medicine in Europe, used to treat a variety of conditions. While the next 200 years witnessed the continued growth of opium use, it was the events of the nineteenth and early twentieth centuries that caused a dramatic change in the perception of opium.

The 1800s

In the early 1800s the specific psychoactive components of opium were isolated: morphine in 1803, codeine in 1832. This dramatically changed the medicinal use of opiates. By the mid-1800s, the use of pure components and not crude opium was the norm in medical practice. The invention of the hypodermic syringe in the mid-1800s also played a role in the changing use of opiates. In the nineteenth century, the nonmedicinal, recreational use of opiates began to adopt a rather high profile in Europe, with several leading literary figures indulging in opiate use. The danger in developing a dependency on opium was also becoming as apparent as the medical usefulness of it.

In China, the emperor was concerned about the dangers of the popular practice of smoking opium, which was introduced around the end of the eighteenth century. His ban on opium smoking was not heeded by the populace, and the demand for opium increased. This problem was further complicated by the fact that the importation of opium was controlled by British companies. The increasing outflow of monetary resources, namely silver, and the increasing dependence on Britain, led to more severe limitations on trade with the British. The international relations between the two countries became so strained that it resulted in armed conflict—the so-called Opium Wars (1839–1842 and 1856–1860). This is a good example of how nonpharmacological factors, in this case, financial and political, have an enormous impact on the regulation of certain drugs.

In America, the dynamics of opiate use and its legislative control were somewhat more complex. As with other countries around the world, there was an initial period of totally unrestricted importation and marketing of opium. One result was that the American people were deluged by a host of tonics and elixirs that were touted to cure a seemingly endless list of ailments. These tonics and "cures" typically contained varying amounts of opiates. Thus, during the 1800s, there was an extraordinarily high level of opiate consumption in America, which began to rise in the 1840s and continued to climb, peaking around 1896.[3] Two specific reasons for this pattern of consumption of opiates were the high use of opiates by physicians in medicating situations and the self-medicating practices of Americans with tonics and other commercially available medications. Since the ingredients were regarded by manufacturers as industrial secrets and were not printed on the label, these medications were termed "patent medications." The use of these medications grew at such a fast rate that by the end of the 1800s patent medications were at their peak and probably contained the highest levels of opiates.[3] These medications could be purchased in any store, or by mail order. Even heroin could be bought this way after 1898. Opiates and cocaine became a part of everyday life for many Americans, even though their presence for the most part went undetected.

The Civil War was initially considered to be a causal factor in the alarming increase of opiate use in America. The use of morphine to control the pain of wounded soldiers on the battlefield served to induce opiate dependency in a large population of individuals that otherwise might not have begun an opiate habit. It now appears that the use of morphine as pain medication during the Civil War was at best a minor contributing factor in this developing habit. For one, the portion of the overall population with an addiction to morphine was not as severe as in European countries, like Great Britain, Germany, France, Italy, and Russia, all of which also experienced armed conflict and used morphine as battlefield analgesics.[3] In addition, the growth of opium imports was increasing prior to the Civil War and continued afterward at a similar rate.[3]

In any event, America's increasing appetite for opiates had grown to the point that approximately 250,000[3] to one million Americans[4] had developed dependencies on opiates.

However, in the 1800s, concern about opiate use began to surface. By the late 1800s, the fear of morphine addiction was being articulated by physicians more emphatically, especially with the increased use of injectable morphine. The public was calling for the control of these substances through legislation. Around the 1890s, the legislative control of opiates and cocaine was initiated by several states. Typically, these early attempts called for physicians to be the sole distributors of opiates. However, patent medications were still a viable source of opiates, and variability between states that did pass some legislation produced a situation in which neighboring states with more lax prescription constraints would attract those persons seeking opiate prescriptions. The need for federal legislation was apparent.

The 1900s

The beginning of the twentieth century marked the advent of federal legislation to control substances that were thought harmful to the public. The opiates and cocaine were the substances of greatest concern. In the early 1900s, there was a pronounced timidity by the federal government concerning drug legislation, because federal control over opiate use and over physicians' practices of dispensing opiates was considered unconstitutional. Supported by several Supreme Court rulings, the gradual testing of the constitutional waters accelerated over a short time to form the legislation that is now in place.

In 1906, the Pure Food and Drug Act was passed. It required the manufacturers of patent medicines to state on their products the amount of opiates, alcohol, cocaine, and even Cannabis sativa extract found in the product. The assumption was that an informed consumer would discriminate and not buy medication that was potentially harmful or habit-forming. The Act also made it illegal for a manufacturer to claim that a medicine or tonic was not habit-forming if it contained opiates, alcohol, cocaine, or Cannabis sativa extract.

In 1914, the Harrison Narcotic Act was passed. This legislation taxed and did not directly restrict opiate distribution. All professionals who dealt with opiates had to register by applying for permits from the Treasury Department for acquiring and dispensing opiates, paying a tax for each transaction.

In 1922, the Narcotic Import and Export Act was passed, which restricted importation of crude opium for legitimate medical use only. Two years later, in 1924, the Heroin Act was passed, which made it illegal to manufacture or possess heroin, except for government-approved research. Legislation in subsequent years primarily made the penalties for these regulations more severe. In the 1920s and 1930s, compared to opiate use in the 1800s, a decline was seen in its use in America, reaching a level of use that seemed prevalent only in selected portions of the population.[3]

ABSORPTION, DISTRIBUTION, AND BIOTRANSFORMATION

There are five possible routes of administration for the opiates (Figure 7–2), one enteral and four parenteral. Enterally, opiates taken orally can be absorbed from the GI tract, though not easily. There are several parenteral routes: 1. Topical, via nasal mucosa (some snuffs have been thought to have contained opiates); 2. Topical, that is, on the skin in the form of a patch (transdermal). The opiate fentanyl (Sublimaze®) is being used in patches to control chronic pain; 3. Pulmonary, that is, through the lungs (opium smoking was popular at the turn of the century in some circles); and of course, 4. Directly into the circulation—IV, into a muscle—IM, and sometimes under the skin—SQ.

As we saw earlier, the route of administration will impact the onset and duration of a drug's effects. An IM injection of morphine will induce peak analgesia in about half the time as a higher morphine dose taken orally.

Although morphine distributes fairly evenly in most tissue compartments like the kidneys, spleen and lungs, it does not accumulate in any tissue compartment, not even the brain. In fact, morphine is not very lipid-soluble and has a relatively difficult time crossing the blood-brain barrier. Because of this there is little preventing the

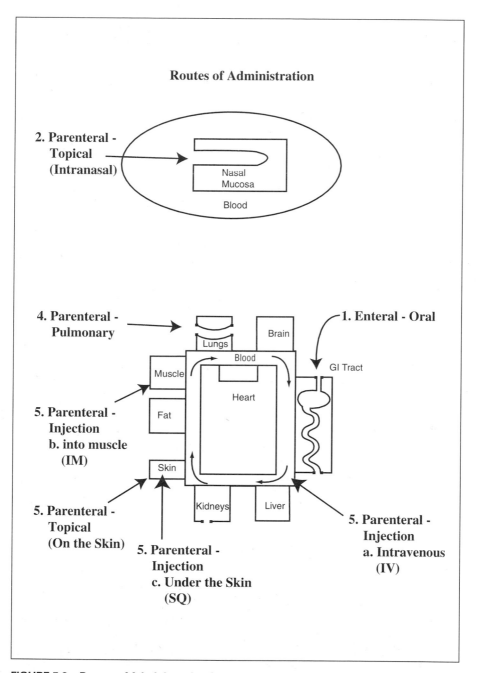

FIGURE 7-2   Routes of Administration for the Opiates
The opiates can be administered using many different routes. They can be swallowed (en-teral—oral), injected (parenteral—injection), smoked (parenteral—pulmonary), snorted (parenteral—topical), and even placed on the skin in drug skin patches (parenteral—topical).

liver from biotransforming it and the kidneys from filtering and excreting it. The following half-lifes reflect this relatively quick excretion:

Morphine—two to three hours
Codeine—three hours
Meperidine—three hours

In contrast to these opiates, methadone has a long half-life, approximately twenty-four hours. This is one of the principal reasons why it is used to help individuals overcome opiate dependency.

Most morphine excretion is done by the kidneys, but a small percentage of excreted morphine (less than 7 percent) is found in the feces, as a result of small amounts being absorbed in the bile. Even though morphine is excreted rapidly and fairly completely, metabolites of the dose can be detected in the urine several days after a dose.

The duration of the effects of a dose of most opiates is typically four to five hours. Methadone, of course, is longer, meperidine (Demerol®) somewhat shorter.

BEHAVIORAL AND NONBEHAVIORAL EFFECTS

Morphine has profound effects both on the central nervous system and on the gastrointestinal tract. Let us first review the general behavioral profile induced by opiates. After a moderate dose of morphine (5 mg to 10 mg), the following may be observed:

- analgesia (insensitivity to pain in a conscious person)
- decreased anxiety
- depressed respiration
- pupil constriction (the telltale indicator of opiate use)
- constipation
- decreased sensitivity to stimuli
- impaired ability to concentrate
- drowsiness, sometimes unconsciousness, or sleep
- heavy limbs and warm body sensations
- itching of the face and nose
- euphoria or dysphoria
- nausea and vomiting

As the dose of morphine is increased, there is no appearance of categorically different behaviors but rather an intensification of behaviors, present even at low doses. The increased doses cause these effects to become more pronounced. The euphoria (or dysphoria) is intensified, analgesia is heightened, nausea is more pronounced, and respiration is further depressed.

If the dose of an opiate is sufficiently high, acute toxicity may develop. In the nontolerant person this could happen after as little as 100 mg administered enterally and as little as 30 mg parenterally. The following are the typical presenting symptoms:

- stupor or coma
- pinpoint pupils
- profoundly depressed respiration (as low as two to four/min.)
- drop in blood pressure
- drop in body temperature
- flaccid skeletal muscles
- depressed urine formation

The three critical signs to which emergency room personnel are sensitive and are diagnostic for opiate toxicity are: coma, respiratory depression, and pinpoint pupils.

Many of these effects on the CNS are the result of the morphine directly acting on specific brain stem systems. For example, pupil constriction induced by opiates is the result of opiates acting on those specific brain stem nuclei that control pupil diameter, and not the result of opiate peripheral action on the muscles of the eye.

Depressed respiration and nausea also are the result of direct effects on the brain stem areas involved in these particular activities. More specifically, morphine reduces the responsiveness of certain brain stem areas to carbon dioxide (CO_2) in the blood.[5] In addition, certain opiates have antitussive, cough-suppressing effects,[6] also due to opiates acting on those brain areas involved in the so-called cough reflex.

It also is important to note that opiates do not directly alter all brain stem systems. For example, blood pressure and heart rate are not substantially altered. There may be some minor alterations in the cardiovascular system following the use of opiates that are caused by severe respiratory depression, induced by the opiates. This is important because cardiovascular functions are controlled by areas in the brain stem. The reason opiates will affect some brain stem areas and not others has to do with the peculiar distribution of opiate receptors in the brain.

The ability of the opiates to induce analgesia seems to be the result of the way the CNS processes pain. Pain is a critical sensation for survival, and its CNS-processing is redundant and complex.[7] Some of the principal areas involved include the substantia gelatinosa in the spinal cord, the reticular formation, the central gray (sometimes referred to as the periaqueductal gray), the intralaminar nuclei of the thalamus, the amygdala, the hypothalamus, and the cerebral cortex. There are receptors for opiates at virtually every level of the CNS involved in pain perception. From the moment pain stimuli enter the CNS and synapse in the spinal cord, endogenous opiates are involved in the processing. It is important to note that the relief of pain by opiates is selective, so other sensory systems like vision, touch, and hearing are not altered.

There are two notable peripheral effects of the opiates, one on the intestines and one in the skin. Opiates exert a powerful effect on gastrointestinal motility, which has made the opiates an ancient medication for diarrhea. The opiates affect the stomach as well as the intestines. They cause the stomach to delay emptying and severely decrease the contractions of the small and large intestines which are responsible for the movement of food through the tract.[1] The slowing of movement allows for the more complete absorption of water.

Opiates cause the blood vessels in the skin to dilate. The skin of the face and neck appear to be sensitive to this vasodilation, which often results in the perception of warmth and feeling of being flushed.[1]

Variants of Morphine

The search for a powerful pain reliever that is not habit-forming has been and continues to be the principal motivation for much pharmacological research. The results to date have generated a host of agents that have distinctive properties which are useful in particular medical situations. The following are just a few of such agents.

1. Heroin. First developed by the Bayer company in 1989, it was considered nonaddictive and a possible treatment for people with morphine dependencies. The tremendous risk of developing a dependency on heroin outweighed its analgesic properties and led to its rigorous control. It is a Schedule I substance. Perhaps the most notable difference between heroin and morphine is heroin's higher lipid solubility, thus its ability to cross the blood-brain barrier. Heroin can cross the blood-brain barrier almost 100 times faster than morphine.[8]

2. Meperidine (Demerol®). Introduced in 1939, meperidine is structurally dissimilar to morphine. Despite this molecular difference, meperidine binds to opiate receptors and has analgesic effects. The difference between meperidine and morphine is that meperidine acts faster and its duration of effects are shorter than morphine. This makes meperidine the drug of choice for many medicating situations in which a short period of analgesia is desired.

3. Diphenoxylate (Lomotil® when combined with atropine). A variation of meperidine, diphenoxylate has potent antidiarrhea effects without many of the other opiate effects seen with morphine. At doses that control diarrhea, there are none of the subjective effects seen with morphine doses. This is a Schedule V substance.

4. Loperamide (Imodium®). Loperamide is also a variation of meperidine and like diphenoxylate, it has antidiarrhea properties.[9] It also does not have the opiate effects of morphine at doses that treat diarrhea. It has a fairly long half-life of seven to twelve hours, which is advantageous in treating GI tract problems.

5. Fentanyl (Sublimaze®). In the structural family of the phenylpiperidine compounds, along with meperidine, diphenoxylate, and loperamide, is fentanyl (Sublimaze®). Fentanyl has a relatively short duration of action, one to two hours,[10] but it is extremely powerful as an analgesic. It is more powerful than morphine[11] or heroin[12] for pain relief. Although initially fentanyl was used in acute short-term situations, like postoperative pain control,[13] fentanyl has been found to be useful in controlling chronic pain.[14] Packaged in a patch to be worn on the skin, transdermal fentanyl has been effective in controlling chronic cancer pain as well.[15] Unfortunately, it has become a popular opiate for abuse, sometimes referred to as China white,[11] and has encouraged the illegal development of chemical variations of its molecular structure (see the Special Issues section later).

THE MEDIATING MECHANISMS OF OPIATE ACTIVITY

In the last two decades, a great deal has been learned about specifically how the brain operates relative to opiate compounds. In the 1970s, it was discovered that an opiate, typically morphine, binds to certain brain receptors.[16,17] This was a remarkable discovery—that the brain has receptors that are sensitive to an exogenous substance like morphine. This suggested to researchers that the brain must have its own opiate-like compounds that stimulate these receptors. In 1975, the first descriptions of endogenous substances that bind to opiate receptors were reported.[18] What followed was an explosion of information concerning the brain opiate system. We shall briefly review two general areas: the description of the receptors for opiate molecules and the classes of opiate substances that are made in the brain.

The Opiate Receptor Types

The receptor structures that recognize opiates, whether natural, synthetic, or endogenous, are distributed throughout the CNS and in the periphery in the intestines. As the molecular technology describing these structures continues to improve, there will probably be even more precise classifications, as well as new types discovered. The following are five different subclasses of opiate receptors:

1. Mu (μ) receptors—μ1 and μ2 receptors
2. Sigma (Σ) receptors—the PCP/Σ receptor and the Σ PCP insensitive receptor
3. Kappa (k) receptor
4. Delta (Δ) receptor
5. Epsilon (μ2) receptor

All of these receptors are involved in one way or another in the mediation of analgesia.[19,20] The mu receptor in particular plays a critical role in mediating analgesia.[21] The potency of individual analgesics seems to correlate to how well these molecules bind to mu receptors.[7] However, not all of these receptors are involved in mediating all of the other effects the opiates elicit. For example, the respiratory depression so distinctive of opiate use is mediated by mu, sigma, and delta receptors, but the kappa receptor may not be involved at all with respiration.[22] The sigma receptor may actually cause acceleration of respiration.[19] The gastrointestinal effects of the opiates seem to be mediated by a combination of mu receptor activity at the brain level and mu and kappa receptors in the intestines.[19] The antidiarrhea effects of loperamide appear to be specifically mediated by mu receptors.[19]

Compared to the other opiate receptors, the sigma receptors are peculiar in several ways. The drug phencyclidine hydrochloride (PCP, or angel dust) binds to the PCP/sigma receptor and not to other opiate receptor types. The PCP/sigma receptor does mediate analgesia at low doses, however, with higher doses of PCP, the PCP/sigma receptor may cause a peculiar intoxication that involves hallucinations.[23] None of the effects of the PCP/sigma receptor are reversible by the typical opiate antagonists like naloxone.

Opiate Agonists/Antagonists

Cyclozacine is an antagonist for the mu receptor and an agonist for the kappa and sigma receptors. This means it can block the effects of morphine and heroin that drive mu receptors. However, by virtue of being kappa and sigma receptor agonists, cyclozacine also can induce a certain level of analgesia, as well as respiratory depression and pupil constriction, by stimulating the kappa and sigma receptor types.[1] Cyclozacine has a half-life of approximately ten hours and a fairly long duration of action of about twenty-four hours.

Butophanol (Stadol®) is also a mu receptor antagonist and a kappa and sigma receptor agonist. Butophanol has been used as an analgesic, because it has a similar profile as does morphine in its onset and duration of analgesia. However, the respiratory depression with butophanol is less severe than with morphine or heroin,[29] and the subjective effects are different than those reported with morphine.[30] Butophanol has been found especially useful for controlling pain during childbirth[31] and in alleviating postoperative-anesthesia shaking.[32]

WITHDRAWAL

Morphine/Heroin Withdrawal

Let us first examine the withdrawal syndrome for morphine or heroin. The specific character and severity of the syndrome depend mostly on two factors: the intensity of the dosing and the health of the user. The following is a general profile of common features observed in heroin/morphine withdrawal.

These features progress in three general stages:

1. About eight to twelve hours after the last scheduled dose tearing (lacrimation), runny nose (rhinorrhea), yawning, and sweating are seen.
2. In the next stage, about twelve to fourteen hours after the last dose, there may be a tossing, restless sleep (yen sleep)
3. As the withdrawal worsens and peaks, usually in forty-eight to seventy-two hours after the last dose, dilated pupils, increased irritability, tremors, insomnia, marked anorexia, intense yawning, severe sneezing, tearing, nausea and vomiting, diarrhea, increased heart rate and blood pressure, marked chilliness, waves of goose bumps, abdominal cramping, aches in bones and muscles, muscle spasms, and orgasms (in both men and women) are seen.

Untreated, these symptoms will run their course and resolve in seven to ten days.

It has been suggested that brain norepinephrine systems may be involved in the withdrawal process. The "locus coeruleus" is one of the most important nuclei in the brain that uses norepinephrine (NE) as a neurotransmitter. During withdrawal, the activity of locus coeruleus neurons increases, mediated by an NMDA (N-methyl-D-aspartate) pathway from a neighboring nucleus called the nucleus paragigantocellularis.[33] Moreover, a nonopiate drug called clonidine (Catapres®), which stimulates alpha-adrenergic receptors in the locus coeruleus, reduces the symptoms of heroin withdrawal.[34] Whether the activity of locus coeruleus is causal or simply reflects some other brain activity remains to be determined.

Meperidine Withdrawal

Withdrawal from meperidine (Demerol®) is somewhat different than withdrawal from morphine or heroin.[35] It begins sooner (within three hours of the last dose), and will resolve sooner, in four to five days. Compared to heroin and morphine withdrawal, some of the symptoms such as diarrhea, pupil dilation, and nausea may be less severe, but at its most severe point, some of the symptoms like muscle twitching and nervousness may be worse.

Methadone Withdrawal

The withdrawal syndrome for methadone has virtually the same symptoms as for morphine and heroin, but there are some important differences. Methadone withdrawal develops more slowly (approximately twenty-four to forty-eight hours after the last dose), and it is usually less intense than withdrawal from morphine and heroin. The peak discomfort may be reached by the third day and may not change much for the duration of the withdrawal. Moreover, methadone withdrawal lasts considerably longer than morphine and heroin withdrawal, up to forty-two to forty-nine days. It is the significantly less severe withdrawal from methadone that is the critical rationale for using it to help individuals break a morphine or heroin dependency. In addition, unlike the other opiates commonly used to maintain dependencies, methadone is effective taken orally, so it may also help extinguish the general behavior of injecting drugs. Finally, the effects of methadone last longer than the effects of morphine or heroin, thus requiring fewer doses, which might also be helpful in breaking the high habit strength of a drug dependency.

Opiate Withdrawal

Several strategies have developed in the pharmacological treatment of individuals who want to break their opiate dependencies.

In one strategy, it is assumed that the severe negative aspects of morphine withdrawal or, more commonly, heroin withdrawal, may prevent many from attempting to withstand this process. In order to make withdrawal less aversive, the individual is switched to methadone, an opiate that has a milder withdrawal. Typically, the user will go off IV heroin, and as soon as withdrawal symptoms begin, oral methadone is given at a dose that will allay the symptoms. The methadone may be maintained at that dose for a short time, and then a gradual decrease, approximately 5 mg a day, is initiated until the individual is not taking any methadone,[36] thus the methadone withdrawal syndrome begins. Recall that the withdrawal from heroin resolves in about ten days, while the withdrawal from methadone can last up to four times as long. The high drop-out rate from withdrawal programs suggests[37] that this longer withdrawal, albeit less severe, may not be desirable.

injection every day, but alternating each day between the two injection rooms. The injections continued for thirty days, which means the drug group received fifteen injections of heroin in the course of this study. The dose was gradually increased from 1 mg/kg to 8 mg/kg for the last two injections.

After thirty days of injections, all of the animals were given a very large parenteral IV dose of heroin (15 mg/kg). Half of the animals in both groups were injected in each of the two rooms. This means some animals were given heroin in the room that was associated with the vehicle injection.

Table 7–1 shows the essential results. Most of the animals in the group that had not received heroin before the high dose of 15 mg/kg on test day died; the mortality rate for this group was 96 percent. Compare this to the animals that were given heroin every other day for thirty days and were given the high dose on test day in the heroin room. Those animals had significantly fewer deaths; the group mortality rate was 32 percent—only one-third of the control heroin naive animals. These data demonstrate the robust tolerance that develops with repeated heroin administrations. In this case, the tolerance that developed to the life-threatening aspects of chronic heroin use was protective to these surviving animals. However, the data for those animals that were given heroin every other day for thirty days but were given the high dose on test day in the vehicle room were surprising. These animals had a group mortality rate of 64 percent, which was double the rate for the other drug group. Even though the drug history was identical for these two groups, it was the difference in expectation that caused such a difference in mortality. The animals that were given the heroin on test day in the vehicle room did not experience the proper environmental cues to initiate the compensatory response necessary to avoid an overdose. In the morphine experi-

TABLE 7–1

GROUP	PERCENT OF ANIMALS IN A GROUP THAT DIED FROM HEROIN OVERDOSE
Controls Heroin—Naive Animals that received the vehicle every day and on Day 31 received the high dose of heroin in either room.	96.1
Heroin—Experienced Animals that received heroin on alternate days and on Day 31 received the high dose of heroin in the usual heroin room.	32.4
Heroin—Experienced Animals that received heroin on alternate days and on Day 31 received the high dose of heroin in the unusual vehicle room.	64.3

Note: 1. This was clearly a lethal dose to inexperienced animals.
2. Fifteen drug administrations were enough to develop tolerance to the lethality.
3. Lethality doubled when the animals were injected in the wrong room, that is, a place the animals did not expect to receive heroin.

ment reviewed in chapter 2, it was shown that the compensatory response of the animals began as soon as the animals were in the injection room and prior to the actual injection.[44] Perhaps in the heroin overdose study, surviving the high heroin dose may have depended on engaging the compensatory response(s) prior to the injection. Many of the animals injected in the vehicle room could not initiate a compensatory response in time to prevent a lethal overdose. Regardless of the timing or the precise mechanism, these data dramatically illustrate the role of expectation and learning in the outcome of a drug administration .

These data directly address the problematic issue of overdose deaths in heroin addicts. Why is it that a chronic heroin user who has developed tolerance will die with a dose of heroin that she or he tolerated the previous day? Siegel interviewed ten heroin users who survived near heroin overdose situations.[46] He found that in fact many of these users had reported that some aspect of their drug dosing routine had been different in their near-overdose. Whatever the specific missing cues were, their brains had not received the significant stimuli to anticipate a dose and initiate a compensatory response for that drug dose.

The Role of Opiates in the Pleasure System of the Brain

Intense euphoria seems to be one of the principal effects of opiate use and also one of the reinforcing factors that may account for the easy development of dependencies on the opiates. This has led researchers to examine the brain systems that mediate pleasure and reward. As was outlined in chapter 2, one of the principal components of the brain pleasure system are the cell bodies of dopamine-containing cells in the Ventral Tegmental Area (VTA) of the midbrain, which projects to the nucleus accumbens in the telencephalon and the nucleus Accumbens goes on to project to a variety of structures, including the cerebral cortex. Endogenous opiates play a critical role in this pleasure system.[47] There are mu (μ) receptors in the area of the VTA, which help drive the VTA dopamine neurons as well as mu receptors in the nucleus accumbens.[48] Thus, the opiates can directly drive the nucleus accumbens in a dopamine independent way[49] and can indirectly drive the nucleus accumbens by inhibiting those cells that normally inhibit the dopamine cells of the VTA. Thus, the intense positive feelings that many opiate users report following opiate administration may in part be the result of directly driving one of the brain's pleasure systems.

Opiate-Based Designer Drugs

One basic strategy in pharmacological research is to take a drug with a known medical usefulness and alter its molecular shape to see if the resulting new drug will have more potent positive clinical effects and fewer negative effects than the original compound. The development of the synthetic opiates is a good example. This is a necessarily involved and lengthy process with a great deal of testing, because companies must be sure the resulting new compound will not be harmful.

Unfortunately, the possibility of developing more useful medications has been perverted by some by the lure of developing a more euphoric drug of abuse. Illegal chemical enterprises that modify the chemical structure of existing drugs have produced a host of drug "analogs," which have been termed designer drugs. Designer drugs are illegal variations of existing, usually controlled substances.[50] This has raised two major issues of concern, one a legal hazard, and one a health hazard.

Since the seemingly small variations on a molecular structure can produce a new substance with very different characteristics (Figure 7–1), the development, sale, and use of designer drugs has become problematic in law enforcement. At issue is whether or not designer drugs can be controlled by law. A designer drug is essentially a brand-new drug. Only the drugs listed in the Schedule system set up by the Comprehensive Drug Abuse Prevention and Control Act of 1970 have been identified and classified at the appropriate level of control. It would be an impossible task, given the current system of drug scheduling, to attempt to identify and schedule every possible variation of controlled substances. This issue will have to be resolved in the coming years.

The possible health hazards of designer drugs cannot be emphasized enough. The tragic case of the use of a meperidine analog dramatically illustrates this point. Analogs of meperidine include fentanyl, which is more potent than heroin. Perhaps motivated to produce a similar substance, an illegal meperidine analog, MPTP (1-methly-4-phenyl-1,2,3,6-tetrahydroperidine), was introduced and used by several unfortunate individuals.[51] This designer drug proved to be a selective neurotoxin, that is, a substance that destroys only certain types of neurons in the brain. The dopamine cells of the nigrostriatal pathway were selectively destroyed by MPTP,[52] resulting in a disabling condition identical to Parkinson's disease.[51] While providing a significant new tool in the research on Parkinson's disease,[53] this designer drug permanently crippled those who used it. This is the inherent health risk of designer drugs— namely, that the user cannot predict how this substance will affect his or her brain or if there will be any other kind of toxicity. There has been no extensive testing or safety screening for these compounds, and the user essentially becomes an unwitting subject in a very risky experiment.

Although the risk of permanent neurotoxicity may seem to be a compelling reason not to use designer drugs, there has been a flurry of designer drug variants of fentanyl.[54] There have not been reports of acute toxicity, like that following MPTP, to these new types of drugs, but the risk of chronic or late-onset toxicity remains.

REVIEW EXAM

1. Name the opiates found in nature.
2. Name two opiates that are structurally similar and not similar to the natural opiates.
3. Name two reasons for the high use of opiates in America in the late 1800s.
4. What did the Pure Food and Drug Act of 1906 require?
5. Name the four routes of administration for the opiates.
6. What is the half-life of morphine?
7. Characterize the effects of a moderate dose of morphine.

8. Name the signs of acute opiate toxicity.
9. Describe the peripheral effects of opiates.
10. How are the actions of fentanyl different from those of morphine?
11. Name the different classes of opiate receptors.
12. Which of these receptor types from question 11 mediate analgesia?
13. Name the three classes of endogenous opiates.
14. What is the difference between neurons that use endorphins and those that use enkephalins as neurotransmitters?
15. Describe the actions of butophanol.
16. Describe the withdrawal syndrome for morphine and how it differs from meperidine withdrawal.
17. Describe the various strategies of treating opiate withdrawal with drugs.
18. What are the advantages and disadvantages of methadone maintenance programs?
19. What were the basic findings of the Seigel experiments on heroin overdose?
20. Describe the involvement of the opiates and the brain structures that mediate reward.
21. Describe the outcome of MPTP use.

REFERENCES

1. JAFFE, J. & MARTIN, W. (1980). Opioid analgesics and antagonists. In A. Gilman, L. Goodman, & A. Gilman (Ed.), *The Pharmacological Basis of Therapeutics (6th ed.,* pp. 494–534). New York: Macmillan Publishing Co.
2. LENZ, G., EVANS, S., WALTERS, D., & HOPFINGER, A. (Eds.).(1986). *Opiates* (pp. 1–28). New York: Academic Press.
3. MUSTO, D. (1987). *The American Disease—Origins of Narcotic Control.* New York: Oxford University Press.
4. ABEL, E. (1980). *Marijuana: The First Twelve Thousand Years.* New York: Plenum Press.
5. ECHENHOFF, J., & OECH, S. (1960). Effects of narcotics upon respiration and circulation in man— a review. *Clinical and Pharmacological Therapy,* 1, 483–524.
6. Merck Sharp and Dohme Research Laboratories, Medical Literature Department (1970). *Codeine and Certain Other Analgesic and Antitussive Agents.* Rahway, NJ: Merck and Co. Inc.
7. JESSELL, T., & KELLY, D. (1991). Pain and analgesia. In E. Kandel, J. Schwartz, & T. Jessell (Eds.), *Principles of Neural Science* (3rd ed. pp. 385–399). New York: Elsvier.
8. ANGIER, N. (1990). Storming the walls. *Discover,* 11(5), 67–72.
9. AWOUTERS, F., MEGENS, A., VERLINDEN, M., SCHUURKES, J., NIEMEGEERS, C. & JANSSEN, P. (1993). Loperamide. Survey of studies on mechanism of its antidiarrheal activity. *Digestive Diseases and Sciences,* 38(6), 977–995.
10. GOVONI, L., & HAYES, J. (1988). *Drugs and Nursing Implications* (6th ed.). Norwalk, CT: Appleton and Lange.
11. KHURI, E. (1989). Narcotic Poisoning. In *Conn's Current Therapy.* Philadelphia, PA: W.B. Saunders.
12. KIRSCH, M. (1986). *Designer Drugs.* Minneapolis, MN: CompCare Publications.
13. WILLENS, J., & MYSLINSKI, N. (1993). Pharmacodynamics, pharmacokinetics, and clinical uses of fentanyl, sufentanil, and alfentanil. *Heart and Lung,* 22(3), 239–251.
14. YEE, L., & LOPEZ, J. (1992). Transdermal fentanyl. *Annals of Pharmacotherapy,* 26(11), 1393–1399.
15. SIMMONDS, M., & RICHENBACHER, J. (1982). Transdermal fentanyl: long-term analgesic studies. *Journal of Pain and Symptom Management,* 7(3 Suppl), S36–39.
16. PERT, C., & SNYDER, S. (1973). Opiate receptor: demonstration in nervous tissue. *Science,* 179, 1011–1014.
17. TERENIUS, L. (1973). Characteristics of the "receptor" for narcotic analgesics in synaptic plasma membrane fraction from rat brain. *Acta Pharmacologia et Toxicologia,* 33(5), 377–384.

18. HUGHES, J. (1975). Isolation of an endogenous compound from the brain with pharmacological properties similar to morphine. *Brain Research*, 88, 295–308.
19. HAMMOND, D. (1986). Biological effects of opiates. In G. Lenz, S. Evans, D. Walters, & A. Hopfinger (Eds.), *Opiates* (pp. 29–44). New York: Academic Press, Inc.
20. HAYES, S., & VOGELSANG, J. (1991). Opiate receptors and analgesia: an update. *Journal of Post Anesthesia Nursing*, 6(2), 125–128.
21. HERZ, A., & MILLAN, M. (1990). Opioids and opioid receptors mediating antinociception at various levels of the neuraxis. *Physiologia Bohemoslovaca*, 39(5), 395–401.
22 SHOOK, J., WATKINS, W., & CAMPORESI, E. (1990). Differential roles of opioid receptors in respiration, respiratory disease, and opiate-induced respiratory depression. *American Review of Respiratory Disease*, 142(4), 895–909.
23. ITZHAK, Y. (1988). Multiple opioid-binding sites. In G. Pasternak (Ed.), *The Opiate Receptors* (pp. 95–142). Clifton, NJ: The Humana Press.
24. LENZ, G., EVANS, S., WALTERS, D., & HOPFINGER, A. (Eds.). (1986). *Opiates* (pp. 459–512). New York: Academic Press, Inc.
25. SZEKELY, J. (1983). In J. Szekely & A. Ronai (Eds.), *Opiate Peptides* (Vol. 2, p. 109). Boca Raton, FL: CRC Press.
26. RONAI, A. (1983). In J. Szekely & A. Ronai (Eds.), *Opiate Peptides* (Vol. 3, p 107). Boca Raton, FL: CRC Press.
27. BLOOM, F. (1988). Neuropeptides. In *The Biology of the Brain: From Neurons to Networks* (pp. 114–130). New York: W. H. Freeman Book Company.
28. MISRA, A. (1978). Metabolism of opiates. In M. Adler, L. Manara, & R. Shomanin (Eds.), *Factors Affecting the Action of Narcotics* (pp. 297–343). New York: Raven Press.
29. NAGASHIMA, H., KARAMANIAN, A., MALOVANY, R., RODNAY, P., ANG, M., KOERNER, S., & FOLDER, F. (1976). Respiratory and circulatory effects of intravenous butophanol and morphine. *Clinical Pharmacology and Therapeutics*, 19, 738–745.
30. VOGELSANG, J., & HAYES, S. (1991). Butophanol tartrate (Stadol®): a review. *Journal of Post-Anesthesia Nursing*, 6(2), 129–135.
31. HAYES, S. & VOGELSANG, J. (1991). Opiate receptors and analgesia: An update. *Journal of Post Anesthesia Nursing*, 6(2), 125–128.
32. VOGELSANG, J., & HAYES, S. (1992). Butophanol tartrate (Stadol®) relieves postanesthesia shaking more effectively than meperidine (Demerol®) or morphine. *Journal of Post-Anesthesia Nursing*, 7(2), 94–100.
33. RASMUSSEN, K. (1991). Afferent effects on locus coeruleus in opiate withdrawal. *Progress in Brain Research*, 88, 207–216.
34. GOLD, M., REDMOND, C., & KLEBER, H. (1978). Clonidine blocks opiate withdrawal symptoms. *Lancet*, 2, 599–602.
35. ISABEL, H, & WHITE,W. (1953). Clinical characteristics of addictions. *American Journal of Medicine*, 14, 558–565.
36. MIRIN, S., WEISS, R., & GREENFIELD, S. (1991). Psychoactive substance use disorders. In A. Golenberg, E. Bossuk, & S. Schoonover (Eds.), *The Practioner's Guide to Psychoactive Drugs* (3rd ed.). New York: Plenum Medical Book Co.
37. BAEKELAND, F., & LUNDWALL, L. (1975). Dropping out of treatment: a critical review. *Psychology Bulletin*, 82, 738–783.
38. GOSSOP, M. (1988). Clonidine and the treatment of the opiate withdrawal syndrome. *Drug and Alcohol Dependence*, 21(3), 253–259.
39. GOLDSTEIN, A. (1976). Heroin addiction: sequential treatment employing pharmacological supports. *Archives of General Psychiatry*, 33, 353–358.
40. JENICKE, M. (1989). Drug Abuse. In E. Rubenstein & D. Federman (Eds.), *Scientific American Medicine*. New York: Scientific American Press.
41. YOUNGSTROM, N. (1990). The drugs used to treat drug abuse. *American Psychological Association Monitor*, 21(10), 19.
42. LENZ, G., EVANS, S., WALTERS, D., & HOPFINGER, A. (1986). *Opiates*. (pp. 400–447). New York: Academic Press.
43. GOLDSTEIN, A. (1991). Heroin addiction: neurobiology, pharmacology, and policy. *Journal of Psychoactive Drugs*, 23(2), 123–133.
44. HINSON, R., & SIEGEL, S. (1983). Anticipatory hyperexcitability and tolerance to the narcotizing effect of morphine in the rat. *Behavioral Neuroscience*, 97, 759–767.

45. SIEGEL, S., HINSON, R., KRANK, M., & MCCULLY, J. (1982). Heroin "overdose" death: contribution of drug-associated environmental cues. *Science*, 216, 436–437.
46. SIEGEL, S. (1984). Pavlovian conditioning and heroin overdose: reports by overdose victims. *Bulletin of the Psychonomic Society,* 22 (5), 428–430.
47. KOOB, G. (1992). Neural mechanisms of drug reinforcement. *Annals of the New York Academy of Science*, 654, 171–190.
48. NORTH, R. (1992). Cellular actions of opiates and cocaine. *Annals of the New York Academy of Science*, 654, 1–6.
49. STINUS, L., CADOR, M., & MOAL, M. (1992). Interaction between endogenous opioids and dopamine within the nucleus accumbens. *Annals of the New York Academy of Science*, 654, 254–273.
50. JERRARD, D. (1990). "Designer drugs": a current perspective. *Journal of Emergency Medicine*, 8(6), 733–741.
51. LANGSTON, J., BALLARD, P., TETRUD, J., & IRWIN, I. (1983). Chronic Parkinsonism in humans due to a product of meperidine-analog synthesis. *Science*, 219(4587), 979–980.
52. JAVITCH, J., UHL, G., & SNYDER, S. (1984). Parkinsonism-inducing neurotoxin, N-methyl-4-phenyl-1,2,3,6-tetrahydropyridine: characterization and localization of receptor binding sites in rat and human brains. *Proceedings of the National Academy of Science of the United States of America*, 81(14), 4591–4595.
53. KOPIN, I. (1987). MPTP: an industrial chemical and contaminant of illicit narcotics stimulates a new era in research on Parkinson's disease. *Environmental Health Perspectives*, 75, 45–51.
54. GALLAGHER, W. (1986). The looming menace of designer drugs. *Designer,* 7(8), 24–35.

CHAPTER EIGHT
STIMULANTS:
Drugs That Energize

GENERAL ISSUES ADDRESSED IN THIS CHAPTER

- Various routes of administration for the stimulants
- The wide spectrum of half-lifes for the stimulants
- The similar molecular structure of the stimulants to normally occurring structures
- Possible mechanisms of action of amphetamine
- Importance of dopamine in the action of amphetamines
- Similarities in the mechanisms of action of other stimulants compared to amphetamine
- Possible mechanisms of action of the methylxanthines
- Role of the sympathetic nervous system in the action of the stimulants
- Common behavioral and nonbehavioral consequences following ingestion of the stimulants
- Specific behavioral effects for particular stimulants
- Toxic reactions to cocaine, amphetamines, and caffeine
- Legitimate medical uses for the stimulants
- Withdrawal syndrome for amphetamines and cocaine
- The role of brain pleasure systems and stimulants
- The amphetamine psychosis
- Freebaseing cocaine and smoking methamphetamine

LIST OF DRUGS

1. Amphetamine
2. Methamphetamine
3. Cocaine
4. Methylphenidate (Ritalin®)
5. Nicotine
6. Synthetic cocaine derivatives: novocaine (Procaine®), lidocaine (Xylocaine®)
7. Phenylpropanolamine
8. Methylxanthines: caffeine, theophylline, theobromine
9. Khat

INTRODUCTION

There are a variety of substances that have the overall effect of stimulating or "energizing" the user. Most people have experienced these drugs in one form or another, and some do so on a regular basis. Whether drinking a cup of coffee, cocoa, or tea, smoking a cigarette, having a tooth numbed by the dentist for a filling, eating a piece of chocolate, or taking a cold capsule, there are many ways of sampling these stimulant-type drugs. Typically, fatigue can be allayed, behavior sometimes is sped up, and in some cases euphoria can be induced. In addition, one stimulant, cocaine and its synthetic derivatives, can block the conduction of pain when applied locally. Several of these substances are found in nature, for example cocaine, methylxanthines, nicotine, and khat, while others are purely synthetic, like amphetamine and metham-phetamine. The use of tobacco is so common worldwide that it is easy to forget it is nothing more than a convenient delivery system for the drug nicotine. Not unlike another culturally accepted drug, ethanol, nicotine often is not even thought of as a drug. The medical usefulness of some of these substances has been known for centuries and has contributed to the development in modern medicine of successful treatment strategies for certain psychopathologies. In addition, unraveling how these drugs alter the brain has provided significant clues to the more global aspects of how the central nervous system functions normally.

Although the diverse collection of substances previously mentioned share a common behavioral outcome, they differ in their individual histories and in the way they alter brain functioning.

HISTORY

The history of the stimulants follows very different courses. The origins of cocaine, nicotine, and the methylxanthines are ancient stories. The development of amphetamine and methamphetamine on the other hand is a relatively new story, in which there was a search for a synthetic form of an ancient natural medicine. In addition, the more recent issues concerning cocaine abuse closely parallels the history of the opiates, discussed in chapter 6.

Cocaine

Well before 500 A.D., the practice of chewing coca leaves for their stimulating and euphoric effects was established in the tribes that inhabited the Andes mountains of Peru.[1] When the Spanish conquered the Inca Empire in the sixteenth century and exploited the populace for labor, they realized how important cocaine was to the fabric of these people's lives, people who had to live in rather challenging conditions. Despite their reports of the stimulating effects of the coca leaf, Europeans were unimpressed. This was due in part to the fact that the samples of coca leaves which were brought back were probably inactive, because the cocaine in the harvested leaves breaks down rather quickly and would not have survived the long distance to Europe. It was not until samples of the live plant were returned around 1750[1] and, more importantly, when the extraction of cocaine from the leaves was accomplished in the mid 1800s,[2] that Europeans discovered the wonders of cocaine. Then, the history of cocaine use follows a similar course to that of the opiates (see chapter 7), namely an initial period of unrestricted use and many outlandish claims, followed by a period of strong regulation and control of distribution. Although by the mid to late 1800s, cocaine was being used to treat many clinical conditions, two effects had become quite apparent: its local anesthetic properties and its CNS-stimulating effects. Cocaine was the first local anesthetic. In 1880, von Anrep became the first person to describe cocaine's anesthetic properties when locally applied,[3] but many incorrectly attribute this discovery to Sigmund Freud and/or Karl Koller, who in 1884, were more effective in their advocacy of cocaine's anesthetic properties.[2] The acceptance of cocaine as an anesthetic for surgical procedures was quick, and by the beginning of the 1900s, cocaine was used in a variety of surgical situations, and the search for synthetic forms of cocaine had already begun.[3] By 1906, both novocaine and lidocaine (Xylocaine®) had been synthesized.

The CNS-stimulating properties of cocaine and the euphoria it produced, made this a popular drug in the mid to late 1800s. With advocates as prestigious as Sigmund Freud, cocaine was being used clinically to treat many clinical conditions, from timidity to hay fever to alcohol and morphine addictions. The drug company Parke-Davis aggressively marketed cocaine in a variety of forms, including a hypodermic syringe kit for those who preferred injections. As with the opiates at this time, cocaine distribution was not restricted, so access was virtually unlimited. It should not be surprising then that cocaine found its way into a variety of elixirs and tonics, the most famous examples being Vin Mariani and Coca-Cola®. In 1863, Angelo Mariana developed a mixture of bordeaux wine and cocaine, which was quite popular and received endorsements from Thomas Edison to Pope Leo, who bestowed the papal medal to Mariana for his accomplishment. In 1885, John Pemberton mixed cocaine with the kola nut and syrup and developed a soda fountain drink that has become one of the icons of American beverages. From this widespread consumption of cocaine in America in the mid to late 1800s, reports of the negative aspects of cocaine use also became apparent. Fear of developing dependencies, reports of psychotic episodes, and a host of severely adverse effects prompted legislation to control and regulate the use of cocaine. As we have seen with the campaign to draft legislation to control marijuana and, to some extent, in the effort to control opiates, the movement to pass laws regulating any drug often identifies that drug with minority and/or foreign groups that are already the object of fear and social restraints. The evolution of legislation to regulate cocaine use followed this unfortunate pattern and took on a racial tone.[4] Stories were reported that cocaine use in Southern blacks was reaching epidemic levels and that it was responsible for a crime wave in the South. In the early 1900s, such prestigious and accepted publications like the *Journal of the American Medical Association*, the *New York Tribune, Literary Digest*, the *New York Times*, and even *Good Housekeeping* spoke of the new addiction to cocaine by Southern blacks and the resultant crime wave. This alleged high use in blacks was shown simply not to be the case when records in Georgia were directly examined in 1914.[4] However, the fear of what was termed the "cocainized black," with super-human strength and cunning, led many police jurisdictions in the South to switch to higher-caliber weapons because blacks under the influence of cocaine were so difficult to "stop." Tragically, this wave of unfounded cocaine stories also coincided not only with the passage of laws that created legal segregation and restricted voting privileges for blacks, but with illegal lynchings and violence directed toward blacks.

The legislation to control cocaine use appeared under the same laws as the opiates, discussed earlier. First, the Pure Food and Drug Act of 1906 required labels that stated the amounts of cocaine in the product, made it illegal to claim that a product was not habit-forming if it had cocaine in it, and attempted to limit cocaine imports for medicinal use only.[1] The Harrison Narcotic Act of 1914 levied taxes on the exchange of certain drugs that would require the application of permits and essentially discouraged use by providing a great deal of paperwork. This legislation was directed to opiates but was extended to include cocaine as well. The labeling of cocaine as a narcotic by this legislation was pharmacologically inaccurate and confusing, ultimately diluting the term narcotic to dangerous drug. Finally, the Comprehensive Drug Abuse Prevention and Control Act of 1970 created a scheme of drug classifications according to each drug's potential for forming dependencies and for each drug's medical usefulness. It also made possession of cocaine a federal offense.

Amphetamine and Methamphetamine

The first synthesis of amphetamines occurred in 1887,[5] however, its importance went unnoticed. Around the same time, the active compound in ma huang, an ancient Chinese medication, was isolated from the ephedra plant,[6] and its significance also laid dormant until the investigations of Chen and Schmidt in the 1920s. These investigators made two critical observations: 1. the active compound in ma huang was similar to norepinephrine (the compound made in the CNS) in the way it could stimulate the cardiovascular system; and 2. this compound was effective when given orally.[7] Alles and Leake then began attempts to produce a synthetic form of ephedrine and found that the compound that seemed to be a good match was dl-phenylisopropylamine or amphetamine.[8] It is interesting to note that methamphetamine had been synthesized earlier, in 1914,[9] and independently in Japan in 1919.[10] It was in the 1930s that the legitimate clinical use of amphetamines as a sympathomimetic, that is, a drug that mimics an aroused sympathetic flight-or-fight nervous system, gained acceptance and widespread popularity. Its bronchodilator abilities were described early,[11] as were its CNS-stimulating properties,[12] including its ability to induce anorexia.[13] With this initial widespread use, there also came the first reports of amphetamine abuse.[14] Because amphetamines were used to treat a variety of clinical conditions, primarily respiratory problems like asthma, certain sleep disorders, obesity, and lethargy, amphetamines did not acquire the intense negative image of cocaine. For example, during World War II, amphetamines as well as methamphetamines were used to allay battle fatigue and increase stamina in troops.[15] After the war, in Japan, the surplus methamphetamine supply was then sold legally, over-the-counter, and became a major factor in Japan's first substance abuse problem in its history.[16] Other countries experienced similar "waves" of amphetamine and methamphetamine abuse during this post-war period.[14] While the development of more specific and effective stimulant drugs to treat certain disorders has obviated the clinical use of amphetamine or methamphetamine in most cases, the popularity of these stimulants as drugs of abuse remains relatively high.

Phenylpropanolamine

Phenylpropanolamine (PPA) was first synthesized in 1912,[17] thus it has a history as long as the amphetamines. The history of PPA illustrates the changing role that some agents experience over time in the medical community. The early research of PPA in the 1930s focused on its autonomic effects, namely pupil dilation;[18] increased blood pressure;[19] relaxation of bronchial smooth muscles and antitussive properties;[20] and decongestant properties.[21] Then, in 1939, there was a landmark report by Hirsch,[22] in which he concluded that PPA was as effective an appetite suppressant as amphetamines, without any of the side effects. The tradition of using PPA as an appetite suppressant began, and PPA was considered safe enough to be allowed in many over-the-counter preparations. Currently, PPA is used in many over-the-counter cold remedy preparations, as well as many preparations that are supposed to control appetite, thereby enabling the user to diet more effectively and lose weight.

Methylxanthines

The methylxanthines refer to a class of drugs that are found in certain plants. Collectively, the worldwide popularity of the various beverages containing methylxanthines exceeds all other drugs. Typically there are three methylxanthines of interest—caffeine, theophylline, and theobromine. Although these common beverages contain all three methylxanthines to varying degrees, individual beverages are now associated with one particular methylxanthine, that is, coffee with caffeine, tea with theophylline, and cocoa and chocolate with theobromine.

Caffeine.   Coffee comes from the shrub *Coffea arabica* or *Coffea canephora robusta*, which grows between the Tropic of Cancer and the Tropic of Capricorn. The actual discovery of coffee was not recorded accurately but it is shrouded in various apocryphal accounts. One common story attributes its discovery to a herd of sheep grazing on wild coffee plants in Arabia, with the sheep remaining active through the night. This drew the attention of a prior at a nearby monastery, who had the berries picked and made into a beverage to help him through his nightly prayers.[23] Despite the religious prohibition of any intoxicant for most Arabs, coffee had become a part of Arabian life by the fifteenth century and was actively traded by Arabian merchants. By the seventeenth century, coffee had become quite popular in Europe, as coffeehouses where people would congregate, often discussing political issues while consuming coffee, became a widespread phenomenon.[24] In the late seventeenth century, European traders brought the plant to their tropical colonies to establish plantation enterprises.[25] Around this time, the coffee plant was also introduced to the Americas and to the Caribbean. Brazil began its cultivation of coffee in the early eighteenth century, becoming one of the leading coffee suppliers in the world. Beginning with the events leading up to the American Revolution, to the present, coffee has enjoyed a long-standing popularity in the United States, rooted in the close association between tea consumption and England and its need to sever all ties with its mother country.[26]

Theophylline.   Worldwide consumption of tea as a beverage is second only to water.[27] By definition, tea is the beverage made by simmering the leaves of the plant *Camellia sinensis* in hot water. It is the presence of methylxanthines, one of which is theophylline, in these leaves that distinguish them as tea. One can make a similar beverage from other plants, for example, certain herbs, but this is not considered tea. The main reason for these types of preparations is to avoid the consumption of the methylxanthines.

Camellia sinensis is a plant native to China, India, Burma, Thailand, Laos, and Vietnam. Legend has it that in 2737 B.C., when river water was being boiled for the Emperor Shen Nung, certain leaves fell into the boiling water and gave the water a distinctive pleasurable taste.[27] The first actual written accounts of tea date around 350 A.D. in China. Although used as a medicine initially, by the fifth century, tea had become a nonmedicinal beverage. It took some time for tea to become as popular in Japan. First introduced to Japan by the Chinese in the seventh century, tea had not become an integral part of Japanese life until the thirteenth century.[27] It was in the seventeenth century that tea consumption spread significantly to Europe and the colonies in America.[27] By the eighteenth century, it had surpassed coffee consumption in England due to a variety of reasons, not the least of which was the direct economic profits to English business interests.[24] The cultivation of tea has also spread to areas other than the Orient to keep up with the increasing worldwide demand. In the 1800s, plantations were established in India and Ceylon, and in the 1900s significant plantations were established in Africa and South America.[27]

Theobromine.   Cocoa and chocolate products come from the tree *Theobroma cacao*, which means "food of the gods," a term that is certainly not difficult to understand for the uncountable number of chocolate lovers in the world. Although believed to have originated from the Amazon forests,[28] the cocoa tree was cultivated by the Aztecs and Mayans and may have been part of their religious ceremonies.[29] There is no historical account of these sacred trees anywhere else in the world except this Central American/Yucatan area before the early 1500s, when Spanish explorers arrived. Although Christopher Columbus was credited with being the first person to actually bring cacao to Spain from the Americas in 1502, Europeans did not know what to do with this odd "bean." It was Cortez who learned from the Aztecs how to prepare cacao beverages that the Aztecs called "chocolatl," meaning "warm drink." He returned to Spain in 1528, and the processing of "chocolatl" was modified by adding sugar to it, making this beverage a commercial success.[30] Because the processing procedure was kept an industrial secret, it was not until the 1600s that chocolate was introduced into Italy, France, and then England, where "chocolate houses" soon came into being. It was the increasing demand for chocolate in the seventeenth century that led to new cultivation sites and producers, so by the eighteenth century there were new manufacturing methods and preparations, such as the development of milk chocolate by the Swiss in 1876.[30]

Maté.   For a number of people in South America, maté is the primary source of caffeine. The beverage is prepared from the leaves of the holly *Ilex paraguariensis,* which is native to a relatively small area of South America in southern Brazil and

Paraguay.[31] Maté was used by inhabitants of this area well before the Spanish invaders arrived in the sixteenth century. It remains today a common beverage in the area.

Nicotine.   The cultimavation of tobacco in the Americas is an ancient tradition, comparable to that of corn (maize), chocolate, and certain hallucinogens. One form of tobacco, *Nicotiana rustica,* dates back approximately to 5000 B.C.[32] Nicotine was used in the aboriginal cultures of North, Central, and South America in religious rituals conducted by the community shaman for healing and divining and not as a recreational substance for consumption by the general population. Among the many things brought back to Europe by the expeditions of Columbus and subsequent explorers was the practice of smoking tobacco. Initially, tobacco was considered an intoxicating substance like other hallucinogens, and its use was opposed by the Church. Despite the obstacles presented by the Church and some governments, tobacco use in Europe grew rapidly, primarily becuase of its medicinal properties. In the sixteenth and seventeenth centuries, tobacco became accepted as a recreational drug in Europe, Asia, Japan, China, and Russia.[33] The development in the late 1800s and early 1900s of the efficient manufacturing of cigarettes may have been the most significant factor in the universal popularity of tobacco. Originally, cigarettes were manufactured by hand. The new cigarette-making machines were capable of making over 100,000 cigarettes a day. Thus, they become a relatively inexpensive and convenient nicotine delivery system that was more readily available economically and socially to more people than ever before. Other factors in the sharp increase in cigarette smoking were the introduction in 1913 of a cigarette that was a blend of American tobaccos and the repeal of many state laws that made selling cigarettes illegal.[34] From 1913 to 1963, the use of cigarettes in the United States grew at an unprecedented rate.[35] It was not until the late 1960s that cigarette consumption declined, due to the realization of tobacco's toxicity. Although cigarette use may be declining, the use of chewing tobacco, so-called "smokeless tobacco," has found new life. Prior to the popularity of the machine-made cigarette, chewing tobacco was once one of the principal methods of ingesting tobacco. Now, this former method has found a following in the younger segment of the population. Initial estimates not only indicate extremely high use of smokeless tobacco in the United States but also that the highest rates of use are by adolescents and young adult males.[36]

Khat.   Chewing the leaves of the khat bush for its stimulating and euphoric properties has been popular in Eastern Africa and on the Arabian peninsula for centuries.[37] Since World War II, the popularity of this particular drug has increased, especially in Somalia,[38] so much so that within the last twenty years it has reached epidemic proportions in that country.[39] The recent military humanitarian food relief by the United Nations in Somalia brought the practice of chewing khat leaves to the attention of many Westerners. The use of this specific drug had been somewhat confined to those geographical areas in which the khat bush grew, because only the fresh leaves are active.[40] However, the speed of air transport has resulted in the appearance of active khat in various European countries.[37]

for the smoke that is directly drawn by the smoker from the burning tobacco, whether the source is a cigarette, cigar, or pipe. Sidestream smoke is the smoke from burning tobacco that is not directly drawn from the source but rather is inhaled by anyone in the immediate area. Nicotine also can be absorbed in the mucosal layers of the mouth in chewing or smokeless tobacco and cigars. Finally, nicotine can be absorbed from the skin, which is the site for nicotine skin patches used in certain medical treatments and the site of absorption in some cases of nicotine toxicity associated with specific pesticides.[41]

The excretion of the stimulants is performed primarily by the kidneys, following the usual biotransformation by the liver to make the drugs more water-soluble. However, the excretion of amphetamines by the kidneys is unusual in that it is dependent on the acidity of the urine.[43] When the urine is acidic then the half-life of amphetamines is seven to fourteen hours, whereas the half-life is sixteen to thirty-four hours if the urine is basic (less acidic). In the case of nicotine, only about 10 percent of absorbed nicotine passes unchanged in the urine; the remaining 90 percent is metabolized by the liver. Initially, there is a rapid distribution of nicotine to various body compartments, especially the brain compartment.[41] Following a parenteral dose of nicotine, the half-life is thirty to sixty minutes;[42] however, if one waits for the distribution to body compartments to equalize, the half-life is somewhat longer, approximately 120 minutes.[41]

The following are the half-lifes for some of the other stimulants:

- cocaine—forty minutes
- methylphenidate (Ritalin®)—one to two hours
- caffeine—two to four hours
- phenylpropanolamine—four to four and one-half hours

It is important to note that cocaine has a much shorter half-life than the amphetamines, which is also reflected in the duration of the effects elicited of each.

Let us now examine how these stimulant drugs alter brain functioning.

EFFECTS ON THE CENTRAL NERVOUS SYSTEM (CNS)

It is important to realize that the molecular structure of many of the stimulants is remarkably similar to the structure of a particular class of neurotransmitters—the monoamines. Thus, to understand how specific stimulants alter brain functioning we need to briefly review the way neurons, which use monoamines as neurotransmitters, communicate. Recall from chapter 2 that there are certain neurons in the CNS that use a class of neurotransmitters called biogenic amines or monoamines. There are three monoamines—norepinephrine (NE, or noradrenlin), dopamine (DA), and serotonin (5-HT). Neurons that use monoamines will synthesize and release one of these compounds when they fire. Figure 8–2 shows the molecular shapes of substances that are normally made in the brain (i.e., NE and DA), stimulants that exist in nature (i.e., ephedrine, the methylxanthines, and cocaine), and synthetic stimulants. Notice the amazing similarities between norepinephrine, which is made and used in the brain, and epinephrine, which is used in the peripheral nervous system, and the synthetic stimulants amphetamine, methamphetamine, and phenylpropanolamine.

When monoamine neurons fire, they release neurotransmitters onto the surface of its targets, which contains specialized receptors for that particular neurotransmitter molecule. Given the fairly high firing rates of neurons in the CNS, it is critical that the synapse be returned to its prefiring state to allow the neuron to fire again, if necessary. Normally this recovery phase occurs very quickly, so within a few milliseconds, the neuron is capable of firing again. In neurons that use monoamines as neurotransmitters, one of the important aspects of the recovery phase involves the removal of the released neurotransmitter molecules from the synapse. This is accomplished by a specialized membrane mechanism that has a high affinity for the neurotransmitter molecules. This specialized presynaptic membrane protein has a binding site that faces into the synapse, onto which the neurotransmitter molecule will attach. The membrane protein will then "pull" the released neurotransmitter molecule rapidly back into the neuron and off the receptors. This process is called reuptake and is the principal mechanism of inactivating a synapse in which monoamines are used. This reuptake process is altered by certain stimulant drugs.

The mechanism of how amphetamines alter brain functioning is perhaps the best-described. There are several ways amphetamines alter CNS functioning:

1. Blocking the reuptake of monoamine neurotransmitters.[2] Perhaps the most robust effect of the amphetamines is to block the reuptake process so that monoamine neurotransmitter molecules stay in the synapse longer and stimulate the postsynaptic receptors longer. Realize the term "block" means severely hamper, not a complete cessation of the reuptake process.

2. Causing more neurotransmitters to be released.[44] The amphetamines will actually cause more neurotransmitter molecules to be released. It is important to note that this enhanced release of monoamine neurotransmitters pertains only to the neurotransmitter molecules that are released when the neuron fires.[45] Amphetamines may also cause the spontaneous release or leaking of neurotransmitter molecules in the absence of the neuron's firing.[46]

3. Directly stimulating the receptors on the postsynaptic surface.[47] It appears the amphetamine molecule is similar enough to the molecular shape of the monoamine neurotransmitter molecules that it can itself stimulate the postsynaptic receptors that are normally stimulated by the monoamine neurotransmitters.

4. Amphetamines may hamper the activity of an enzyme—monoamine oxidase.[2] This putative mechanism may relate to the enhanced release of the neurotransmitter molecules mentioned above. Monoamine oxidase (MAO) resides in the presynaptic terminal and destroys any monoamine neurotransmitter molecules that are not in the vesicles, which store neurotransmitter molecules until the neuron fires. If MAO is hampered, it is possible that more neurotransmitter molecules could survive longer, resulting in more

actions of caffeine: 1. The mobilization of intracellular calcium and inhibition of the enzyme phosphodiesterase, which is necessary to prevent some neurons from having too much of a particular type of stimulating substance.[57] These last two actions occur only at high doses of caffeine, higher than typical dose ranges. Since blocking adenosine receptors occurs at lower doses of caffeine, this leads one to believe that the adenosine receptor blockade is what accounts for the typical stimulation induced by caffeine.

One of the major neurotransmitters in both the CNS and PNS is acetylcholine (ACh). There are two main classes of ACh receptors, and one class is those ACh receptors that are stimulated by nicotine. The other type of ACh receptor is stimulated by muscarine. The mechanism of action for the effects following nicotine administration is the result of the absorbed nicotine stimulating the receptors in the central nervous system and peripheral nervous system as well. The distribution of neurons that use ACh as a neurotransmitter provides some clues about the behavioral effects of nicotine. These ACh neurons are in the cerebral cortex, the cortex of the cerebellum, and in a variety of individual nuclei, from the telencephalon just below the cerebral cortex to the nuclei in the brain stem. Two particular ACh nuclei seem to be involved in memory; one is the septal nucleus, which projects to the hippocampus, the other is the nucleus basalis, which projects to much of the frontal cortex.

The mechanism by which khat alters brain functioning has only been researched relatively recently. It appears that khat is similar to the amphetamines. It has been shown that it causes the release of NE and DA from presynaptic terminals,[58] and that it blocks the reuptake of dopamine.[59]

EFFECTS ON THE PERIPHERAL NERVOUS SYSTEM (PNS)

Until now, our focus has been on the CNS, that is the brain and spinal cord. Recall from chapter 2 that the peripheral nervous system (PNS) is composed of the neurons and fibers that bring in sensory information from the various sensing organs and directly innervate the muscles as well as the internal organs. An important component of the PNS is the autonomic nervous system (ANS), which has two parts—the sympathetic and parasympathetic divisions. It is the sympathetic division of the ANS that is affected by the stimulants.

When activated, the sympathetic nervous system induces the so-called flight or fight response, which essentially prepares the body to resolve a potential life-threatening situation. This sympathetic arousal response includes dilating pupils for better vision, increasing heart rate, widening bronchial passages to better oxygenate the blood, and diverting blood flow from digestion to muscle mass. Norepinephrine (NE) is one of the neurotransmitters that mediates the sympathetic response, the same NE that is one of three monoamines in the CNS. NE then is a neurotransmitter in the CNS and sympathetic portion of the PNS. A drug that will enhance the normal activity of the monoamines in the CNS also will usually enhance the activity in the sympathetic division of the PNS. Essentially, these drugs will elicit a sympathetic response. They have been referred to as sympathomimetics.

The autonomic nervous system and central nervous system interact by a two-neuron or two-synapse circuit. Acetylcholine is the neurotransmitter used for the first synapse, by both the sympathetic and parasympathetic divisions. Furthermore, ACh is used in the second synapse of the parasympathetic division. The most prominent effect that nicotine exerts on the PNS is a biphasic effect on the autonomic ganglia. A biphasic small dose of nicotine produces excitation; larger doses produce depression of the autonomic ganglia.[42] Another PNS effect of nicotine occurs at the synapse, where muscles are activated by nerve, the nerve-muscle synapse. Nicotine has an initial excitatory action, followed by a paralysis of the muscle due to an inhibitory action.

NONBEHAVIORAL AND BEHAVIORAL CONSEQUENCES

Some of the general physiological effects of dosing with amphetamines, methamphetamines, and cocaine are typical of a sympathetic arousal state:

- increased blood pressure
- increased respiration and relaxed bronchial muscles to enhance adequate oxygen supply
- pupil dilation
- increased blood glucose
- increased heart rate
- blood flow is shunted to skeletal muscles and away from digestion

The general behavioral effects also are consistent with a sympathetic response:

- alertness or decreased fatigue and an increased ability to concentrate
- insomnia
- elevation of mood, to the point of euphoria
- anorexia

Amphetamines

Despite the initial reports in the late 1920s[60] and early 1930s[61] that amphetamines did not have any physiological activity, including subjective effects, the euphoric, arousing, and anorexic effects of the amphetamines have been well-documented since the mid and late 1930s.[13,62,63] Since the effects of amphetamines have been studied so thoroughly, let us use them as an example of a prototype sympathomimetic.

Subjective effects of amphetamines.   One of the robust effects of amphetamines that was described early on[64] was the sense of an increased alertness and a decreased ability to fall asleep. One can understand why amphetamines have been used by those people who are involved in tasks that produce fatigue: long-distance petite, nor does it lead to any differences in acute caloric intake.[82] It is difficult to critically examine one parameter like body weight in chronic smokers. It has been shown that chronic smokers as a group are different from the nonsmoking population in more ways than the habit of cigarette smoking. Chronic smokers have attitudes and exhibit behaviors on several dimensions that may impact the risk of coronary heart disease,[83] thus may confound a controlled examination of body weight over time. The effects of nicotine on metabolic rates may be a way of accounting for body weight differences in chronic smokers. Energy expenditure in a twenty-four-hour period is increased in smokers,[84] and this increase also has been reported at rest[85] and during activity.[86] Moreover, smoking seems to change fuel metabolism, specifically increasing fat oxidation.[87] However, the increase in energy expenditure in chronic smokers has not been reported in all studies.[88]

Sleep.   Nicotine, via skin patches, has been found to both decrease total sleep time and the percent of time spent in REM sleep, and increase the initial latency to fall asleep.[89] Furthermore, smoking has been associated with sleep disturbances such as initial difficulty in falling asleep and sleep fragmentation.[90]

Khat

Khat (or chat) has been called a natural amphetamine because of its similar structure to amphetamines, its mechanisms of action, and its overall effects on behavior. Khat produces a sympathetic activation with increased blood pressure and heart rate.[91] Behaviorally khat induces alertness, perceived increased intellectual efficiency, euphoria, and anorexia.[92]

TOXIC REACTIONS TO THE STIMULANTS

While the effects of stimulants on certain neurons in the brain result in increased activation and in some cases feelings of euphoria, these drugs will exert significant effects on organ systems outside of the brain, which are the basis for the toxic reactions to these drugs. The toxicity following cocaine use is the most severe and illustrates this principle best. The norepinephrine (NE) terminals in the heart and blood vessels (see Effects on the Peripheral Nervous System (PNS) preceding), when overstimulated by cocaine, lead to a toxic reaction that often is fatal. One action of cocaine is to cause a vasoconstriction; in other words, the NE terminals in the smooth muscles of blood vessels will contract, causing the diameter of the vessels to decrease. This action results in increased blood pressure. Another action of cocaine is on the NE terminals on the heart, which results in an increased heart rate and in irregular heart beats (i.e. cardiac arrhythmia). The most common peripheral signs of toxicity following cocaine use are heart attack (i.e., acute myocardial infarction), cardiac arrhythmia, and even rupture of the aorta, which is the first large blood vessel leaving the heart. There are two important points to note concerning these toxic reactions. First, they may occur in people who are otherwise healthy young adults, with no preexisting heart problems. Second, the route of administration need not be as intense as freebasing or IV administration to precipitate toxic reactions; they may even occur after intranasal administration.

There also are two common CNS toxic reactions to cocaine: seizures, which may occur as late as thirty minutes after a dose of cocaine; and ruptures in the blood vessels inside the CNS, which is probably a secondary effect due to the rapid increase in blood pressure following cocaine use.

The toxic reactions following amphetamine use are similar to those seen following cocaine use, although somewhat less severe. They include headache, tremor, dizziness, extreme agitation, chest pain, heart palpitations, irregular heart rhythms, nausea, vomiting, diarrhea, abdominal cramps, and in some extreme cases, convulsions leading to death.[93]

There also is some evidence that amphetamines and methamphetamines will actually destroy dopamine and serotonin neurons in the brain. While this is seen in animals, it is not clear that this neurotoxicity occurs in humans.[94]

The toxicity associated with nicotine merits special attention. Nicotine itself can produce profound toxicity, due primarily to the suppression of muscle activity at the nerve muscle synapse, in particular, the muscles of respiration. Many insecticides contain nicotine for this lethal suppression of breathing. Acute nicotine poisoning typically involves the accidental ingestion of such pesticides or of tobacco products.[42] The onset of symptoms is rapid and includes abdominal pain, nausea and vomiting, diarrhea, headaches, and a decrease in blood pressure. Death also may be rapid, the result of the nicotine-induced suppression of breathing. The lethal dose of nicotine is about 60 mg,[42] which far exceeds the typical dose from an individual cigarette, but raises another issue—the toxicity of tobacco. It is unfortunate that tobacco is the principal source of obtaining nicotine, because it is considered by many to be one of the most toxic substances in our culture,[95] containing a variety of dangerous compounds. In particular, inhaling the smoke of burning tobacco will significantly increase the risk for developing many different types of cancer. The risk of lung cancer, specifically, has been found to be directly related to the tar content of cigarettes,[96] also associated with cigar and pipe smoking.[97] Smoking has also been shown to be related to stroke,[98] and cancer of the pancreas.[99] Furthermore, this increased risk is long-lasting. Former smokers have to abstain from smoking for ten years for the risk of pancreatic cancer to match nonsmoking controls.[99] Moreover, anyone who is inhaling smoke from burning tobacco is subject to tobacco toxicity. Substances that cause cancer are termed carcinogens. Lung carcinogens are certainly present in sidestream smoke,[100] and certain lung carcinogens have been shown to be present in nonsmokers who are exposed to environmental tobacco smoke.[101] These and many other similar findings raise serious public health issues concerning the air we breathe. The toxicity associated with smokeless or chewing tobacco is primarily cancer of the mouth and the entire oral cavity,[36] serious noncancerous conditions like loss of bone in which teeth are set, infection of the gums (i.e., gingivitis), and leukoplakia, which produces precancerous white patches in the mouth.[102]

Toxic reactions to caffeine include a racing heart (or tachycardia), insomnia, an extremely excited-agitated state, ringing in the ears, and, on rare occasions, death.[73] The toxic reactions to theophylline can be more severe and include headache, dizziness, heart palpitations,* vomiting, convulsions, and sometimes death.[73] These reactions typically occur when extremely high doses are consumed.

MEDICAL USES

There are several medical situations in which amphetamines and other stimulants are successfully used in pharmacological treatment.

Treatment of Narcolepsy

Narcolepsy is a chronic lifelong sleep disorder that affects almost a quarter of a million Americans.[103] The symptoms include excessive daytime sleepiness, uncontrollable sleep attacks, and cataplexy, which is the sudden loss of muscle tone and voluntary movement. These sleep attacks may be precipitated by emotional stress or high carbohydrate meals.[15] The use of amphetamines to treat narcolepsy was first described in 1935,[13] and narcolepsy remains perhaps the only bona fide reason for specifically prescribing them. Despite the success of amphetamine treatment, the use of methylphenidate (Ritalin®) to treat narcolepsy has become more common[104] because of its fewer unwanted side effects.[15,105]

Treatment of Attention Deficit Disorder (ADD)

Learning disorders that involve problems of attention include Attention Deficit Disorder (ADD) without hyperactivity, or Attention Deficit Hyperactivity Disorder (ADHD), a condition formerly termed hyperactivity in children. Oddly enough, this condition is treated successfully by stimulant medications. Some of the clinical features of hyperactivity are: distractibility, short attention span, inability to sit still, outbursts of anger, and unpredictable mood changes. It is not clear why a CNS-stimulant would lead to improvement in hyperactivity.

Use of amphetamines in treating this condition began in the mid 1930s. Dr. C. Bradley operated a home for behaviorally disordered children and decided that a new drug on the medical scene might offer them some help.[106] Without any strong logical or medical rationale, other than, "Let's see if this drug will improve their individual conditions," Dr. Bradley administered amphetamines for one week to thirty children who had major behavioral disturbances. Fourteen children responded in a striking manner, from the first day of amphetamine treatment. There was a very apparent increase in interest in school material, as well as increased performance in all subjects. This remarkable improvement disappeared the first day amphetamine treatment was discontinued. Thus was born the still puzzling medicating paradox of giving a stim-

---

*Tachycardia is the term for a rapid increase in heart rate, whereas palpitations refer to a pounding heart.

ulant to help manage a hyperactive child. This paradox applies to CNS depressants as well. The barbiturates that typically depress the CNS (chapter 3) have the unlikely effect of making children who are diagnosed with hyperactivity even more active.[107]

The amphetamines, in addition to improving attention deficits and hyperactivity in children, also have certain unwanted effects. The anorexic effects of amphetamines are particularly problematic in a population of growing children who need adequate levels of nutrition. One of the more serious effects of amphetamine medication in young children is suppression of growth, which has been seen in as many as 75 percent of children.[108] Other unwanted effects include insomnia, tachycardia,[107] and the development of motor tics, which is uncommon.[109] Methylphenidate (Ritalin®) is another stimulant that does not seem to have the problems amphetamine medication does, thus it has become the drug of choice for the treatment of ADD.[109] However, there may be some risk of liver problems with methylphenidate, so pemoline (Cylert®) has become the second-choice medication for ADHD.[109]

It should be noted that if a child increases his or her attention span in response to amphetamine treatment, this cannot be considered proof that the child must have ADD or another type of learning disorder. The work of Judith Rapoport and her colleagues at the National Institute of Health showed that when low doses of amphetamines were given to a population of children who had no learning disabilities their attention span increased.[110] Thus, this response to amphetamines cannot be used as a diagnostic indicator that a child has ADD or a learning disorder.

In the last few years it has become apparent that the problem of ADD does not really end in childhood. As many as 70 percent of children with ADD will show signs of it when they reach adulthood.[111] The use of methylphenidate has been successful in the treatment of adults with ADD.

Treatment of Obesity

In their initial study on narcolepsy in 1935, Prizimetal and Bloomberg observed that one of their patients no longer experienced an insatiable appetite and, in fact, lost weight while on amphetamines.[13] In 1937, the first formal proposal was introduced to use amphetamines for the treatment of obesity,[112] followed by the first clinical report in 1938,[113] which was a resounding success, also enthusiastically endorsing the use of amphetamines to treat obesity. Since eating is not compatible with the sympathetic response of the fight or flight reaction that amphetamines elicit, the rationale for this use is quite sound. However, the hazards of chronic cardiovascular stress, insomnia, the euphoria that might lead to dependency, and the inducement of some severe behavioral anomalies, prompted the medical community to discontinue this medicating practice. It is considered unethical and also illegal to prescribe amphetamines specifically for weight control. The focus then shifted to other stimulants that might also have anorexic properties. We shall consider one in particular—phenylpropanolamine (PPA).

It had been known since the early PPA studies of the 1930s that unlike other drugs used to induce a sympathetic response, which were not effective if taken orally, PPA *was* effective when orally administered.[19] This is an important characteristic for a drug if it is to be part of a viable far-reaching treatment strategy. This set the stage for the 1939 Hirsch Report, which compared the efficiency of amphetamines and PPA in the treatment of obesity and found them comparable, with PPA having fewer adverse effects.[22] Since that report, the use of PPA in weight control has remained a tradition in American self-medicating practices. To this day, over-the-counter appetite suppressants have PPA as the active ingredient. This use of PPA went unchallenged until the late 1950s, when direct clinical experiments raised doubts about its effectiveness in controlling weight gain.[114] In 1965, the Federal Trade Commission conducted hearings about the effectiveness of PPA in weight control, and the Food and Drug Administration conducted similar reviews in 1978, 1979, and 1982. All of these reviews reached the same conclusion—that PPA can be considered an effective treatment strategy for controlling appetite.[115] However, the unambiguous demonstration of PPA to control overeating in a well-controlled clinical experiment has yet to be accomplished.

Treatment of Respiratory Disorders

Another former legitimate use of amphetamines was to increase bronchial passages in asthma patients. Inhalers once contained amphetamines. As with the use of amphetamines in the treatment of obesity, the risk of dependency and abuse far outweighed the clinical benefits and resulted in the termination of this medicating strategy. The methylxanthine theophylline is a useful medication for asthma and for other respiratory problems.[73] In addition, theophylline is used to stimulate respiration in emergency situations, typically in infants born prematurely.[73] On the over-the-counter level, the use of PPA as a decongestant has a long history. Still used today in such products as Contac® and in most cold relief medications, PPA has proven to be a useful drug. Specific prescription drugs, which have been developed to work on particular receptors in the bronchial passages, have proven to be especially effective in treating respiratory disorders. These drugs include albuterol (or salbutamol), terbutaline sulfate (Brethine®), and metaproterenol sulfate (Alupent®).[93]

Local Anesthesia

When directly applied to the axons of neurons, cocaine and its synthetic derivatives (like procaine—Novocain®) block those channels in the axon that actively allow sodium ions to flow.[116] The result of this local blocking action is the prevention of the "action potential," which is the electrical output signal of the neuron marking its firing. If this occurs in neurons that convey pain information, then local anesthesia is produced. The particular numbing action of cocaine occurs only when it is directly applied to neuronal axons and does not occur in the CNS with conventional dosing procedures. It should be noted that the use of cocaine (and its derivatives) as a peripheral nerve block is common in a wide range of medical and dental situations.

Perhaps the most familiar situation is that of a dentist numbing a tooth with an injection of Novocain®.

Experimental Treatment for Alzheimer's Disease

Alzheimer's disease is a devastating disorder that inflicts the elderly. The deterioration of memory and other cognitive functions are hallmark symptoms of Alzheimer's disease. One aspect of the neuropathology that may be mediating this disorder is a loss of cells in one particular nucleus, the nucleus basalis. These neurons use ACh as a neurotransmitter. There have been some initial studies that have reported an improvement in learning[117] and in cognitive functioning[118] in Alzheimer's patients who have been given nicotine via nicotine skin patches.

Notable Failures in Medical Treatment

While the use of amphetamines in the treatment of obesity or weight control was a notable failure in that the risks far exceeded the benefits, there is another notable failure in the medical use of stimulants. The clinical disorder of depression is not successfully treated with amphetamines or cocaine. While amphetamines may offer a transient euphoria to depressed patients, this relief is not long-lasting.[119] Cocaine, with an even shorter duration of action than amphetamines, has also been unsuccessful in treating depression and may even worsen an existing depression.[120]

WITHDRAWAL

Just like the withdrawal syndromes for most drugs, regardless of the class of drug, the symptoms of a particular withdrawal syndrome are typically the opposite of those effects elicited by that drug, and the severity of a withdrawal syndrome seems to be related to the intensity and duration of drug use. Since amphetamines elicit increased activation, euphoria, sleeplessness, and decreased appetite, the withdrawal syndrome for amphetamines commonly is characterized by symptoms such as tiredness, fatigue (sometimes referred to as the amphetamine crash), depression, and increased appetite.[121] There is no potential life-threatening withdrawal like that seen with the barbiturates or opiates,[122] however, the depression of an amphetamine withdrawal can be so intense that the withdrawing user may be at risk for suicide.[123]

The withdrawal syndrome from cocaine raises an extremely important issue concerning the relationship between tolerance, withdrawal, and dependency (see chapter 2). Tolerance develops quite rapidly to subjective effects, as well as to heart effects following either intranasal or parenteral dosing of cocaine; this rapid tolerance is termed tachyphylaxis. However, cocaine withdrawal, which is similar to that observed following amphetamine use but less severe, is so mild that some do not consider it a true withdrawal syndrome.[124] The lack of a strong, clearly demonstrable withdrawal syndrome may incorrectly lead to the conclusion that one cannot develop a dependency or addiction, to cocaine. This is clearly not the case. The powerfully reinforcing properties of cocaine have led to the development of very intense dependencies. Thus, the concept of dependency need not be so tightly associated with the occurrence of a withdrawal syndrome.

Withdrawal from nicotine may include several of the following symptoms: weight gain,[80] irritability and restlessness, difficulty concentrating, and of course an intense craving for nicotine. These symptoms are not restricted to smoking tobacco but also have been described in withdrawal from smokeless or chewing tobacco.[125] Nicotine skin patches significantly help in the withdrawal process and aid in achieving smoking abstinence. Concurrent behavioral therapy will approximately double the success rate of nicotine patches alone.[126] Two additional withdrawal treatment strategies are noteworthy. Clonidine[127] and naloxone[128] treatment both have reportedly helped in the withdrawal process perhaps by producing a decreased craving for nicotine. Clonidine stimulates a subclass of norepinephrine receptors, called alpha adrenergic receptors, and naloxone is a pure opiate receptor antagonist. That neither of these agents directly act on ACh systems illustrates how different neurotransmitter systems in the CNS interact with each other.

Withdrawal from caffeine is much less severe than from amphetamines. The most common symptoms include headache and irritability.[129]

SPECIAL ISSUES

Brain Mechanisms of Reinforcement or Pleasure

An important component of the medial forebrain bundle (MFB), which appears to be one of the principal brain mechanisms that mediates pleasure, is the dopamine system that originates in the midbrain.[130] The dopamine cell bodies of this system, which are in the ventral tegmental area (VTA) and project to the nucleus accumbens and to the frontal cortex, may be critical for the experience of pleasure.[131] Two types of drugs, opiates and stimulants, appear to stimulate this so-called pleasure pathway, thus this may be why people develop dependencies on these drugs.

Studies indicate that: 1. Both the opiates and stimulants, in particular cocaine, exert their effects on this common reinforcement/pleasure brain system;[132] and 2. There is a functional interaction between opiates and cocaine at this VTA dopamine system.[133] Even though the VTA system is composed of dopamine neurons, injections of opiates directly onto the nucleus accumbens also drive this reinforcement/pleasure brain system.[134] This may be due to the presence of opiate receptors on the neurons in the VTA and in the interneurons in the nucleus accumbens.[135] Cocaine's rewarding properties appear to be directly associated with its effect of stimulating the neurons in the VTA.[136] Moreover, there is a difference between cocaine and the amphetamines in the pattern of dopamine level increases measured in the nucleus accumbens and prefrontal cerebral cortex,[137] which may account for the differences in the rewarding properties of amphetamine and cocaine. There is even some evidence that the powerfully reinforcing properties of nicotine also may be due to nicotine interacting with the VTA.[138]

The Amphetamine Psychosis

Just a few years after the initial reports of successful amphetamine treatment for narcolepsy (see preceding) came the first report of a type of psychotic reaction to amphetamines in some patients.[139] This psychotic reaction was first experimentally induced in 1944[140] and later induced in nonschizophrenic volunteers in 1968[141] and 1970.[142] This psychotic reaction was called the "amphetamine psychosis," but it has also been shown to be elicited by methamphetamine,[122] cocaine,[143] and methylphenidate.[144]

In one of the initial descriptions of a population of drug abusers with amphetamine psychosis, the progression of amphetamine use/abuse that finally precipitated the condition involved the following sequence:[72]

1. Oral dosing of amphetamines would accelerate to up to 250 mg a day, as tolerance developed;
2. The user then progressed to parenteral IV dosing to improve the quality of the euphoria, initially at doses of 20 mg to 40 mg, three or four times a day;
3. As the user became tolerant to the IV doses, amphetamines would be injected more frequently, peaking every two hours, around the clock, for several days. This type of dosing pattern was termed "runs."
4. Exceedingly tolerant users would dose 100 mg to 300 mg of methamphetamine during these runs (the highest dose in this particular report was 1,000 mg of methamphetamine IV every two hours). It was during these intense runs that a paranoid schizophrenic reaction would be likely to occur.

The initial IV dose of amphetamine would provide a "sudden, generalized, overwhelming, pleasureful feeling . . . ," but tolerance developed quickly to this euphoria. Most of the subjects report enhanced interest, increased performance, and more sexual satisfaction. There also was an increase in motor behavior, an activity that was initially purposeful but later became compulsive exercises in stereotypical behavior. The desire for food was so completely suppressed that users on long runs had to consciously force themselves to eat. The profound suppression of food intake is curious, because starvation typically will induce a state of acidosis, which in turn would cause more amphetamines to be excreted faster. Thus, the user would have to increase the next dose to maintain the euphoria. In this group of users, typically in the second or third day of a run, a deep and profound paranoia would develop and intensify as the run continued. The paranoia in this particular group differed from some of the other reports, in that the paranoia elicited by these users always focused on their own illegal activities, and they were aware that their paranoia was induced by the amphetamines. The users did not sleep during a run, which made them exhausted. The IV injections of amphetamines were the only thing that kept users awake. Once users stopped injecting amphetamines, sleep would overwhelm them. Depending on the duration of the run, users could sleep for up to four days. Upon awakening, users would be hungry, but more important the paranoia typically would have disappeared. This state of intense paranoia seemed to be totally drug-induced.

However, given the nature of subjects who are multiple drug users, it is difficult to interpret reports of amphetamine use in the streets. It was not until rigorous laboratory experiments that were conducted on carefully screened "normal" volunteer subjects, in which chronic amphetamine administration also caused paranoid reactions, that the suggestion of a true and reversible drug-induced model for a mental disorder gained attention.

Based on all of these data bases, a general picture emerged concerning the paranoia induced by amphetamines. Typically, continuous dosing with amphetamines or certain other stimulants precipitates a condition that is clinically indistinguishable from a paranoid schizophrenic reaction. There is considerable variability in the dosing that will lead to an amphetamine psychosis reaction. Usually, chronic administration of amphetamines is needed, however, a single dose of 55 mg has been shown to elicit this reaction.[145] On the other hand, some individuals seem quite resistant to this particular reaction. For example, chronic IV methamphetamine administration to cumulative levels of 1,000 mg to 5,000 mg did not result in amphetamine psychosis,[146] nor did a case in which over 800 mg of amphetamine a day for over ten years was maintained.[145] Furthermore, after experiencing an amphetamine psychosis reaction, there seems to be a considerable risk of experiencing another reaction with only one dose.[122] It also has been reported that the amphetamine psychosis lasts longer in individuals whose urine is alkaline, which suggests that this reaction is dependent on the actual blood level of amphetamine.[147] It is important to note here that children treated with chronic moderately high doses of amphetamines rarely experience this amphetamine psychosis.[148]

The following are general features of amphetamine psychosis:

1. Paranoid ideation is the most consistent feature of this reaction. There can be well-formed delusions of persecution. If severe enough, the delusions might cause a person to progress beyond a confused state to panic and possibly violent behavior.[149]
2. Stereotypical behavior is another hallmark of this reaction. This would include those motor behaviors that are seemingly meaningless repetitions of ordinary, simple motor tasks, such as rocking, twirling a lock of hair, and stacking and restacking items in a cupboard. This repetitive behavior can become even more complex, like taking apart the machinery of a clock, motorcycle or car, or an appliance and reassembling it, over and over again.
3. Hallucinations also are quite prevalent. These can be auditory as well as visual. In fact, the nature of auditory hallucinations typically include a voice that commands an individual to do something. There also can be paresthesia, where sensations of tingling, crawling skin are experienced, which can precede the expression of amphetamine psychosis.[150]

These signs of amphetamine psychosis make this reaction extremely similar to the clinical indications of paranoid schizophrenia, with some notable exceptions, the primary one being that as the drug clears from the body, a person returns to a predrug state. It is difficult to say that the person returns to "normal," since we are typically dealing with a person who is chronically using many illegal drugs, and one can argue that such a person is not the norm. Recall, however, that even in volunteers who have been psychologically screened and are considered "normal," the amphetamine psychosis can be elicited. In these individuals, their psychotic reactions were over as they cleared the drugs and returned to their normal states in as short as eight hours.[150] Other characteristics that make amphetamine psychosis unique from true paranoia are: 1. the consciousness of the person remains clear; 2. the person can recall all of the events that happened during the psychotic reaction; and 3. there probably is not a fundamental thought disorder in these people,[151] although some would argue this point.[152]

There is no other class of drug that will mimic a mental disorder as completely as the stimulants and amphetamine psychosis. The amphetamine psychosis has provoked some major hypotheses concerning the underlying brain pathology involved in certain mental disorders. Most notably, the amphetamine psychosis has been used by many to support the so-called dopamine theory of schizophrenia, in which the root pathology mediating schizophrenia is thought to be an overactive dopamine system. This topic will be discussed further in chapter 10.

Freebasing Cocaine and Smoking Methamphetamine

While smoking is an ancient route of drug administration, not all drugs are available in a form that can be smoked. The coca leaf contains so little cocaine, less than 1 percent,[153] that smoking it would not deliver enough of the drug to make it a viable route of administration. Primarily born out of illegal use, cocaine and methamphetamine have been processed to yield a form that will deliver high doses of the drug when smoked.

Because pure cocaine, whether in the coca leaf or isolated, is not stable, it cannot survive the time it takes to harvest, export (or smuggle), and distribute to the ultimate users. For this reason, cocaine is converted to a very stable form by adding sodium hydrochloride to the molecule. This the stable white powder form of cocaine that is easily transported and directly snorted. If the sodium hydrochloride portion is subsequently removed by an additional step, the resulting substance is the pure cocaine molecule, in the form of crystals. The is freebased cocaine.

Initially, the method to free processed cocaine from its hydrochloride salt was rather dangerous. At one point, the extraction involved having the cocaine in ether, which is subsequently evaporated, yielding the freebased cocaine. Ether is quite volatile, and there have been numerous accounts of these illegal operations exploding. The freebase cocaine crystals are volatile when heated; that means that under intense heat, such as the heat of a butane blowtorch, this form of freebased cocaine yields a vapor that is extremely intoxicating. The speed and intensity of this type of dosing (sometimes referred to as freebasing or simply basing) cannot be overstated. The subjective euphoria is comparable to an IV injection of cocaine. Essentially, one can experience the intense high of an IV injection without the risks involved in actually injecting oneself.[154] The effects, including euphoria, occur instantaneously and can literally knock the user down if he or she is standing when freebasing cocaine.

There are certain other risks that merit attention. The practices and traditions of illicit drug users often create additionally dangerous situations. The intense heat needed to smoke freebase cocaine results in the inhalation of hot smoke. To cool this smoke, users often make use of water-pipe devices. It became popular in certain circles to fill these smoking devices with liquor or another distilled ethanol beverage. A distilled ethanol beverage with a high ethanol content is quite flammable, a feature that is exploited by certain dramatic recipes (i.e., crêpe suzette, baked Alaska, etc.). Operating a butane blowtorch in close proximity to a volatile fluid is a risky proposition. The serious accidental burning of actor Richard Pryor while he was smoking freebased cocaine "through" 151-proof rum was such a situation.

Another much less dangerous method of attaining freebase cocaine involves the use of baking soda rather than ether. In this method, the resulting clumps of freebased cocaine contain enough residual baking soda that a crackling sound is made when it is smoked, thus giving it its street name—crack. Crack is freebased cocaine that went through a sodium bicarbonate (baking soda) method of freebasing.

Methamphetamine can be processed to yield a form that is smokable. The process is somewhat different than that of freebasing cocaine in that the methamphetamine molecule has sodium hydrochloride added to it. The resulting methamphetamine takes the form of crystals, referred to as "ice." The combustion of the methamphetamine crystals in the smoking process also is different from the combustion of freebased cocaine. Whereas very little of smoked freebased cocaine condenses in cooler air, smoked methamphetamine readily condenses to a solid crystal form when cooled.[154] This means that when methamphetamine is smoked, considerable amounts will condense in the mouth and throat, which will be absorbed on those particular mucosal membranes as a topical administration. The consequences of having this rather peculiar absorption situation, namely an initial pulmonary route that is quite rapid and a subsequent topical absorption at the mouth and throat, are that the blood levels of methamphetamine following smoking rise very quickly and are then sustained in circulation, which is not the pattern of smoking freebased cocaine.[154] Repeated smoking of methamphetamine produces the danger of accumulating toxic levels that will not recede quickly.

Nicotine Use—Providing Insight to Addiction

Despite all of the studies and publicity concerning the health hazards of smoking and the immediate aversive reactions people have to it, cigarette smoking remains a widespread practice throughout the world. Most smokers are smart individuals who are certainly capable of making sound decisions, yet they persist in a behavior that they know is harmful and will shorten their lives. This is the nature of drug addiction and dependency. Witnessing a person who is trying to break a methamphetamine or cocaine dependency may not be in the realm of most individuals. However, most of us have either experienced firsthand or have had a family member or friend who has had a nicotine dependency. Seeing the resolve and energy involved in breaking a nicotine dependency and suffering through the relapses and setbacks common to this process may serve to provide us with a better perspective about the dynamics of recovery from other substance dependencies.

Author's Comment: The news accounts of relatively high-profile athletes succumbing to lethal overdoses of cocaine merit some thought. Any drug that can drive the cardiac system as intensely as the amphetamines, cocaine, and methamphetamine may dangerously overstimulate the heart muscle in some individuals who have very sensitive hearts. Indeed, when an individual experiments with these types of drugs, he or she is essentially gambling that his or her heart is not easily harmed by them. Some unfortunate trained athletes, in peak physical condition, have lost that gamble.

REVIEW EXAM

1. Name the early legislative attempts to control cocaine use.
2. Name two observations made in the 1920s about the effects of ma huang.
3. Why did amphetamine use not have as negative a stigma as cocaine did in the 1940s?
4. What replaced amphetamine as a diet pill?
5. Name the three methylxanthines.
6. Name the four routes of administration for the stimulants.
7. How is the excretion of amphetamines unique from the other stimulants?
8. What is the half-life of cocaine? Of coffee?
9. Name the three principal actions of an amphetamine that account for its behavioral effects.
10. Name the principal action of the methylxanthines that account for its behavioral effects.
11. Describe a typical sympathetic response.
12. Name two of the prominent subjective effects of amphetamines.
13. Name the four typical sympathetic effects of the methylxanthines.
14. Describe the central nervous system's toxic reaction to cocaine.
15. Name the five medicinal uses of the stimulants.
16. Describe the withdrawal syndrome for the amphetamines.
17. Describe the interaction between opiates and stimulants on brain reward systems.
18. What are the general features of "amphetamine psychosis"?
19. What is freebase cocaine?

REFERENCES

1. BROWN, R. (1990). Pharmacology of cocaine abuse. In K. Redda, C. Walker, & G. Barnett (Eds.), *Cocaine, Marijuana, Designer Drugs: Chemistry, Pharmacology, and Behavior* (pp. 39–51). Boca Raton, FL: CRC Press.
2. PATRICK, R. (1977). Amphetamine and cocaine: biological mechanisms. In J. Barchas, P. Berger, R. Ciaranello, & G. Elliot (Eds.), *Psychopharmacology—From Theory to Practice* (pp. 331–340). New York: Oxford University Press.

3. RITCHIE, J., & GREENE, N. (1980). Local Anesthetics. In A. Gilman & L. Goodman (Eds.), *The Pharmacological Basis of Therapeutics* (6th ed. pp. 300–320). New York: Macmillan Publishing Co., Inc.

4. MUSTO, D. (1987). *The American Disease—Origins of Narcotic Control*, (pp. 1–23). New York: Oxford University Press.

5. EDELEANU, L. (1887). Ueber einige derivate der phenylmethylacrylsaure und der phenylisobuttersaure. *Chemische Berichet*, 20, 616.

6. NAGAI, N. (1887). Ephedrine. *Pharm. Ztg.*, 32, 700.

7. CHEN, K., & SCHNIDT, C. (1930). Ephedrine and related substances. *Medicine (Baltimore)*, 9, 1.

8. LEAKE, C. (1970). The long road for a drug, from idea to use. In F. Ayd & B. Blackwell (Eds.), *Discoveries in Biological Psychiatry* (pp. 68–84). Philadelphia, PA: Lippincott Co.

9. SCHMIDT, E. (1914). Ueber das ephedrin und pseudoephedrin. *Archives of Pharmacology*, 252, 120.

10. BURTON, B. (1991). Heavy metals and organic contaminants associated with illicit methamphetamine production. In M. Miller & N. Kozel (Eds.), *Methamphetamine Abuse: Epidemiologic Issues and Implications—National Institute of Drug Abuse Research Monograph 115* (p. 48). Washington, DC: U.S. Government Printing Office.

11. PINESS, G., MILLER, H., & ALLES, G. (1930). Clinical observations on phenylaminoethanol sulphate. *Journal of the American Medical Association*, 94, 790.

12. ALLES, G. (1933). The comparative physiological actions of dl-phenylisopropylamines. I. pressor effect and toxicity. *Journal of Pharmacology and Experimental Therapeutics*, 47, 339.

13. PRINZMETAL, M., & BLOOMBERG, W. (1935). The use of Benzedrine® for the treatment of narcolepsy. *Journal of the American Medical Association*, 105, 2051.

14. CALDWELL, J. (1980). Amphetamines and related stimulants: some introductory remarks. In J. Caldwell (Ed.), *Amphetamines and Related Stimulants: Chemical, Biological, Clinical, and Sociological Aspects* (pp. 1–11). Boca Raton, FL: CRC Press.

15. SILVERSTONE, T., & WELLS, B. (1980). Clinical psychopharmacology of amphetamine and related compounds. In J. Caldwell (Ed.), *Amphetamines and Related Stimulants: Chemical, Biological, Clinical, and Sociological Aspects* (pp. 147–159). Boca Raton, FL: CRC Press.

16. SUWAKI, H. (1991). Methamphetamine abuse in Japan. In M. Miller & N. Kozel (Eds.), *Methamphetamine Abuse: Epidemiologic Issues and Implications—National Institute of Drug Abuse Research Monograph 115* (pp. 84–98). Washington, DC: U.S. Government Printing Office.

17. CALLIESS, F. (1912). Ueber einge abkommlinge des propiophenons. *Archives of Pharmacology*, 141–154.

18. AMATSU, H., & KUBOTA, S. (1913). Ueber die pharmakologischen wirkungen des ephedrins und mydriatins. *Kyoto Igakkai Zasshi*, 14, 77–78.

19. CHEN, K., CHANG-KENG, W., & HENRIKSEN, E. (1929). Relationship between the pharmacological action and the chemical constitution and configuration of the optical isomers of ephedrine and related compounds. *Journal of Pharmacology and Experimental Therapeutics*, 36, 363–400.

20. HASAMA, B. (1930). Beitrage zur erforschung der bedeutung der chemischen konfiguration fur die pharmakologischen wirkungen der adrenalinahnlichen stoffe. *Archives of Experimental Pathology and Pharmacology*, 153, 161–186.

21. STOCKTON, A., PACE, P., & TAINTER, M. (1931). Some clinical actions and therapeutic uses of racemic synephrine. *Journal of Pharmacology and Experimental Therapeutics*, 41, 20.

22. HIRSCH, L. (1939). Controlling appetite in obesity. *Journal of Medicine, Cinncinati*, 20, 84–85.

23. RICHIE, J. (1980). Central Nervous System Stimulants: The Xanthines. In A. Gilman & L. Goodman (Eds.), *The Pharmacological Basis of Therapeutics* (6th ed., pp. 367–378). New York: Macmillan Publishing Co.

24. WHITE, J. (1991). *Drug Dependence* (pp. 1–55). Engelwood Cliffs, NJ: Prentice Hall.

25. SPILLER, M. (1984). The coffee plant and its processing. In *The Methylxanthine Beverages and Foods: Chemistry, Consumption, and Health Effects—Progress in Clinical and Biological Research* (Vol. 158, pp. 75–89). New York: Alan R. Liss—Inc.

26. QUIMME, P. (1976). *The Signet Book of Coffee and Tea* (Ch. 8). New York: New American Library.

27. GRAHAM, H. (1984). Tea: the plant and its manufacture; chemistry and consumption of the beverage. In *The Methylxanthine Beverages and Foods: Chemistry, Consumption, and Health Effects—Progress in Clinical and Biological Research* (Vol. 158, pp. 29–74). New York: Alan R. Liss, Inc.

28. CHAAT, E. (1954). *Cocoa*. New York: Interscience.

29. COOK, R. (1972). *Chocolate Production and Use*. New York: Books for Industry.

30. SHIVELY, C., & TARKA JR., S. (1984). Methylxanthine composition and consumption patterns of cocoa and chocolate products. In *The Methylxanthine Beverages and Foods: Chemistry, Con-*

sumption, and Health Effects—Progress in Clinical and Biological Research (Vol. 158, pp. 149–178). New York: Alan R. Liss, Inc.

31. Graham, H. (1984). Mate. In *The Methylxanthine Beverages and Foods: Chemistry, Consumption, and Health Effects—Progress in Clinical and Biological Research* (Vol. 158, pp. 179–183). New York: Alan R. Liss, Inc.

32. Furst, P. (1976). Tobacco: Proper food of the gods. In P. Furst (Ed.) *Hallucinogens in Culture* (pp. 23–32). Novato, CA: Chandler & Sharp Publishers, Inc.

33. WHITE, J. (1991). *Drug Dependence* (pp. 30–34). Englewood Cliffs, NJ: Prentice Hall.

34. SLADE, J. (1993). Nicotine delivery devices. In C. Orleans & J. Slade (Eds.), *Nicotine Addiction: Principles and Management* (pp. 3–23). New York: Oxford University Press.

35. SLADE, J. (1989). The tobacco epidemic: lessons from history. *Journal of Psychoactive Drugs*, 21(3), 281–291.

36. CULLEN, J., BLOT, W., HENNINGFIELD, J., BOYD, G., MECKLENBURG, R., & MASSEY, M. (1986). Health consequences of using smokeless tobacco: summary of the Advisory Committee's report to the Surgeon General. *Public Health Report*, 101(4), 355–373.

37. NENCINI, P., GRASSI, M., BOTAN, A., ASSEYR, A., & PAROLI, E. (1989). Khat-chewing spread to the Somali community in Rome. *Drugs and Alcohol Dependence*, 23(3), 255–258.

38. ELMI, A. (1983). The chewing of khat in Somalia. *Journal of Ethnopharmacology*, 8(2), 163–176.

39. ELMI, A., AHMED, Y., & SAMATAR, M. (1987). Experience in the control of khat-chewing in Somalia. *Bulletin on Narcotics*, 39(2), 51–57.

40. KALIX, P., BRENNEISEN, R., KOELBING, U., FISCH, H., & MATHYS, K. (1991). Khat, an herbal drug with amphetamine properties. *Schweizerische Medizinische Wochenschrift*, 121(43), 1561–1566.

41. HENNINGFIELD, J., COHEN, C., & PICKWORTH, W. (1993). Psychopharmacology of nicotine. In C. Orleans & J. Slade (Eds.), *Nicotine Addiction: Principles and Management* (pp. 24–45). New York: Oxford University Press.

42. TAYLOR, P. (1980). Ganglionic stimulating and blocking agents. In A. Gilman & L. Goodman (Eds.), *The Pharmacological Basis of Therapeutics* (6th ed., pp. 211–219). New York: Macmillan Publishing Co.

43. VREE, T., & HENDERSON, P. (1980). Pharmacokinetics of amphetamines: in vivo and in vitro studies of factors governing their elimination. In J. Caldwell (Ed.), *Amphetamines and Related Stimulants: Chemical, Biological, Clinical, and Sociological Aspects* (pp. 147–159). Boca Raton, FL: CRC Press.

44. GLOWINSKI, J., & AXELROD, J. (1965). Effects of drugs on the uptake, release, and metabolism of ³H-norepinephrine in the rat brain. *Journal of Pharmacology and Experimental Therapeutics*, 149, 43–49.

45. VON VOIGHTLANDER, P., & MOORE, K. (1973). Involvement of nigrostriatal neurons in the in vivo release of dopamine by amphetamine, amantadine, and tyramine. *Journal of Pharmacology and Experimental Therapeutics*, 184, 242.

46. FELDMAN, R., & QUENZER, L. (1984). *Fundamentals of Neuropsychopharmacology* (pp. 151–206). Sutherland, MA: Sinauer Assoc., Inc.

47. CALDWELL, J., & SEVER, P. (1974). The biochemical pharmacology of abused drugs. I. amphetamines, cocaine, and LSD. *Clinical Pharmacology and Therapeutics*, 16, 625–638.

48. JONSSON, L., ANGGARD, E., & GUNNE, L. (1971). Blockade of intravenous amphetamine euphoria in man. *Clinical Pharmacology and Therapeutics*, 12, 889.

49. GUNNE, L., ANGGARD, E., & JONSSON, L. (1972). Clinical trials with amphetamine-blocking drugs. *Psychiatria, Neurologia, Neurochirurgia*, 75, 225.

50. PORRAS, A., & MORA, F. (1993). Dopamine receptor antagonist blocks the release of glycine, GABA, and taurine produced by amphetamine. *Brain Research Bulletin*, 31(3-4), 305–310.

51. KNEPPER, S., GRUNEWALD, G., & RUTLEDGE, C. (1988). Inhibition of norepinephrine transport into synaptic vesicles by amphetamine analogs. *Journal of Pharmacology and Experimental Therapeutics*, 247(2), 487–494.

52. BARNETT, G., & RAPAKA, R. (1990). Designer drugs: an overview. In K. Redda, C. Walker, & G. Barnett (Eds.), *Cocaine, Marijuana, Designer Drugs: Chemistry, Pharmacology, and Behavior* (pp. 163–174). Boca Raton, FL: CRC Press.

53. ELLINWOOD, E. (1980). Neuropharmacology of amphetamines and related stimulants. In J. Caldwell (Ed.), *Amphetamines and Related Stimulants: Chemical, Biological, Clinical, and Sociological Aspects* (pp. 69–84). Boca Raton, FL: CRC Press.

54. CHIN, J. (1989). Adenosine receptors in brain: neuromodulation and role in epilepsy. *Annals of Neurology*, 26(6), 695–698.

55. SCHWABE, U., LORENZEN, A., & GRUN, S. (1991). Adenosine receptors in the central nervous system. *Journal of Neural Transmission, Supplementum*, 34, 149–155.
56. DODD, S., HERB, R., & POWERS, S. (1993). Caffeine and exercise performance. An update. *Sports Medicine*, 15(1), 14–23.
57. NEHLIG, A., DAVAL, J., & DEBRY, G. (1992). Caffeine and the central nervous system: mechanisms of action, biochemical, metabolic, and psychostimulant effects. *Brain Research. Brain Research Reviews*, 17(2), 139–170.
58. KALIX, P. (1992). Cathinone, a natural amphetamine. *Pharmacology and Toxicology*, 70(2), 77–86.
59. WAGNER, G., PRESTON, K., RICAURTE, G., SCHUSTER, C., & SEIDEN, L. (1982). Neurochemical similarities between d,l cathinone and d-amphetamine. *Drugs and Alcohol Dependence*, 9(4), 279–284.
60. MILLER, H., & PINESS, G. (1928). A synthetic substitute for ephedrine. *Journal of the American Medical Association*, 91, 1033.
61. PINESS, G., MILLER, H., & ALLES, G. (1930). Clinical observation of phenylaminoethano sulphate. *Journal of the American Medical Association*, 94, 790.
62. NATHANSON, M. (1937). The central action of beat-aminopropylbenzene (Benzedrine®). *Journal of the American Medical Association*, 108, 528.
63. DAVIDOFF, E., & REIFNSTEIN, E. (1937). The stimulating action of benzedrine sulfate. *Journal of the American Medical Association*, 108, 1770.
64. BAHSEN, P., JACOBSEN, E., & THESLEFF, H. (1938). The subjective effect of beta-phenylisopropylaminsulfate on normal adults. *Acta Medica Scandinavica*, 97, 89.
65. GUNNE, L., ANGGARD, E., & JONNSON, L. (1972). Clinical trials with amphetamine-blocking drugs. *Psychiatria, Neurologia, Neurochirurgia*, 75, 225–226.
66. EVANS, M., MARTZ, R., LEMBERGER, L., RODDA, B., & FORNEY, R. (1976). Effects of dextroamphetamine on psychomotor skills. *Clinical Pharmacology and Therapeutics*, 19, 777.
67. TYLER, D. (1947). The effect of amphetamine sulfate and some barbiturates on the fatigue produced by prolonged wakefulness. *American Journal of Physiology*, 150, 253.
68. CROW, T., & BURSILL, A. (1970). An investigation into the effects of methamphetamine on short-term memory in man. In E. Costa & S. Garattini (Eds.), *Amphetamine and Related Compounds* (p. 889). New York: Raven Press.
69. CUTHBERSTON, D., & KNOX, J. (1947). The effects of analeptics in the fatigued subject. *Journal of Physiology*, 106, 42.
70. SMITH, G., & BEECHER, H. (1959). Amphetamine sulfate and athletic performance: objective effects. *Journal of the American Medical Association*, 170, 542.
71. WEISS, B., & LATIES, V. (1962). Enhancement of human performance by caffeine and the amphetamines. *Pharmacology Reviews*, 14, 1.
72. KRAMMER, J., FISCHMAN, V., & LITTLEFIELD, D. (1967). Amphetamine abuse. *Journal of the American Medical Association*, 201, 305–309.
73. RALL, T. (1980). Central nervous system stimulants—the xanthines. In A. Gilman & L. Goodman (Eds.), *The Pharmacological Basis of Therapeutics* (6th ed., pp. 592–607). New York: Macmillan Publishing Co., Inc.
74. WEST, R., & HACK, S. (1991). Effect of cigarettes on memory search and subjective ratings. *Pharmacology, Biochemistry and Behavior*, 38(2), 281–286.
75. PRITCHARD, W., ROBINSON, J., DEBETHIZY, J., DAVIS, R., & STILES, M. (1995). Caffeine and smoking: subjective, performance, and psychophysiological effects. *Psychophysiology*, 32(1), 519–527.
76. STOUGH, C., MANGAN, G., BATES, T., & PELLETT, O. (1994). Smoking and Raven IQ. *Psychopharmacology, Berlin*, 116(3), 382–384.
77. KADOYA, C., DOMINO, E., & MATSUOKA, S. (1994). Relationship of electroencephalographic and cardiovascular changes to plasma nicotine levels in tobacco smokers. *Clinical Pharmacology and Therapeutics*, 55(4), 370–377.
78. STEVENS, H. (1976). Evidence that suggests a negative assocation between cigarette smoking and learning. *Journal of Clinical Psychology*, 32(4), 896–898.
79. KERR, J., SHERWOOD, N., & HINDMARCH, I. (1991). Separate and combined effects of the social drugs on psychomotor performance. *Psychopharmacology-Berlin*, 104(1), 113–139.
80. GREEN, M., & HARARI, G. (1995). A prospective study of the effects of changes in smoking habits on blood count, serum limpids and lipoproteins, body weight, and blood pressure in occupationally active men. The Israeli CORDIS Study. *Journal of Clinical Epidemiology*, 48(9), 1159–1166.

81. PERKINS, K., EPSTEIN, L., SEXTON, J., SOLBERG-KASSEL, R., STILLER, R., & JACOB, R. (1992). Effects of nicotine on hunger and eating in male and female smokers. *Psychopharmacology-Berlin*, 106(1), 53–59.

82. PERKINS, K., SEXTON, J., DIMARCO, A., & FONTE, C. (1994). Acute effects of tobacco smoking on hunger and eating in male and female smokers. *Appetite*, 22(2), 149–158.

83. CASTRO, F., NEWCOMB, M., MCCREARY, C., BAEZCONDE-GARBANATI, L. (1989). Cigarette smokers do more than just smoke cigarettes. *Health Psychology*, 8(1), 107–129.

84. WARWICK, P., & BUSBY, R. (1993). Prediction of twenty-four-hour energy expenditure in a respiration chamber in smokers and nonsmokers. *European Journal of Clinical Nutrition*, 47(8), 600–603.

85. COLLINS, L., CORNELIUS, M., VOGEL, R., WALKER, J., & STAMFORD, B. (1994). Effect of caffeine and/or cigarette smoking on resting energy expenditure. *International Journal of Obesity and Related Metabolic Disorders*, 18(8), p. 551–556.

86. HULTQUIST, C., MEYERS, A., WHELAN, J., KLESGES, R., PEACHER-RYAN, H., & DEBON, M. (1995). The effect of smoking and light activity on metabolism in men. *Health Psychology* 14(2), 124–131.

87. JENSEN, E., FUSCH, C., JAEGER, P., PEHEIM, E., & HORBER, F. (1995). Impact of chronic cigarette smoking on body composition and fuel metabolism. *Journal of Clinical Endocrinology and Metabolism*, 80(7), 2181–2185.

88. WARWICK, P., EDMUNDSON, H., & THOMSON, E. (1995). No evidence for a chronic effect of smoking on energy expenditure. *International Journal of Obesity and Related Metabolic Disorders*, 19(3), 198–201.

89. DAVILA, D., HURT, R., OFFORD, K., HARRIS, C., & SHEPARD, J. JR. (1994). Acute effects of transdermal nicotine on sleep architecture, snoring, and sleep-disordered breathing in nonsmokers. *American Journal of Respiratory and Critical Care Medicine*, 150(2), 469–474.

90. WETTER, D., & YOUNG, T. (1994). The relation between cigarette smoking and sleep disturbance. *Preventive Medicine*, 23(3), 328–334.

91. BRENNEISEN, R., FISCH, H., KOELBING, U., GEISSHUSLER, S., & KALIX, P. (1990). Amphetamine-like effects in humans of the khat alkaloid cathinone. *British Journal of Clincial Pharmacology*, 30(6), 825–828.

92. NENCINI, P., & AHMED, A. (1989). Khat consumption: a pharmacological review. *Drug and Alcohol Dependency*, 23(1), 19–29.

93. WEINER, N. (1980). Norepinephrine, epinephrine, and the sympathomimetic amines. In A. Gilman & L. Goodman (Eds.), *The Pharmacological Basis of Therapeutics* (6th ed., pp. 138–175). New York: Macmillan Publishing Co., Inc.

94. RICAURTE, G., & MCCANN, U. (1992). Neurotoxic amphetamine analogues: effects in monkeys and implications for humans. *Annals of the New York Academy of Science*, 648, 371–382.

95. LAGRUE, G., BRANELLEC, A., & LEBARGY, F. (1993). Toxicology of tobacco. *Revue du Praticien*, 43(10), 1203–1207.

96. KAUFMAN, D., PALMER, J., ROSENBERG, L., STOLLEY, P., WARSHAUER, E., & SHAPIRO, S. (1989). Tar content of cigarettes in relation to lung cancer. *American Journal of Epidemiology*, 129(4), 703–711.

97. HIGGINS, I., MAHAN, C., & WYNDER, E. (1988). Lung cancer among cigar and pipe smokers. *Preventive Medicine*, 17(1), 116–128.

98. COLDITZ, G., BONITA, R., STAMPFER, M., WILLETT, W., ROSNER, B., SPEIZER, F., & HENNEKENS, C. (1988). Cigarette smoking and risk of stroke in middle-aged women. *New England Journal of Medicine*, 318(15), 937–941.

99. JI, B., CHOW, W., DAI, Q., MCLAUGHLIN, J., BENICHOU, J., HATCH, M., GEO, Y., & FRAUMENI, J. (1995). Cigarette smoking and alcohol consumption and the risk of pancreatic cancer: a case-control study in Shanghai, China. *Cancer Causes and Control*, 6(4), 369–376.

100. CHORTYK, O., & CHAMBERLAIN, W. (1990). A study on the mutagenicity of tobacco smoke from low-tar cigarettes. *Archives of Environmental Health*, 45(4), 237–244.

101. HECHT, S., CARMELLA, S., MURPHY, S., AKERKAR, S., BRUNNEMANN, K., & HOFFMANN, D. (1993). A tobacco-specific lung carcinogen in the urine of men exposed to cigarette smoke. *New England Journal of Medicine*, 329(21), 1543–1546.

102. SEVERSON, H. (1993). Smokeless tobacco: risks, epidemiology, and cessation. In C. Orleans & J. Slade (Eds.), *Nicotine Addiction: Principles and Management* (pp. 262–278). New York: Oxford University Press.

103. BERGSTROM, D., & KELLER, C. (1992). Narcolepsy: pathogenesis and nursing care. *Journal of Neuroscience Nursing*, 24(3), 153–157.

104. Chaudhary, B., & Husain, I. (1993). Narcolepsy. *Journal of Family Practice*, 36(2), 207–213.
105. YOSS, R., & DALY, D. (1968). On the treatment of narcolepsy. *Medical Clinics of North America*, 52, 781.
106. BRADLEY, C. (1937). The behavior of children receiving Benzedrine®. *American Journal of Psychiatry*, 94, 577–585.
107. SCHAIN, R. (1972). *The Neurology of Childhood Learning Disorders* (pp 129–138). Baltimore, MD: The Williams & Wilkins Co.
108. GREENBERG, L., DEEM., M., & MCMAHON, S. (1972). Effects of dextroamphetamine, chlorpromazine, and hydroxyzine on behavior and performance in hyperactive children. *American Journal of Psychiatry*, 129, 532.
109. STEVENSON, R., & WOLRAICH, M. (1989). Stimulant medication therapy in the treatment of children with attention deficit hyperactivity disorder. *Pediatric Clinics of North America*, 36(5), 1183–1197.
110. RAPOPORT, J., BUCHSBAUM, M., ZAHN, T., & WEINGARTNER, H., LUDLOW, C., & MIKKELSEN, E. (1978). Dextroamphetamine: cognitive and behavioral effects in normal prepubertal boys. *Science*, 199, 560–563.
111. BELLAK, L., & BLACK, R. (1992). Attention deficit hyperactivity disorder in adults. *Clinical Therapeutics*, 14(2), 138–147.
112. Davidoff, E., & Reifenstein, E. (1937). The stimulating action of Benzedrine® sulfate. *Journal of the American Medical Association*, 108, 528.
113. LESSES, M., & MYERSON, A. (1938). Benzedrine sulfate as an aid to the treatment of obesity. *New England Journal of Medicine*, 218, 119.
114. FAZEKAS, J., EHRMANTROUT, W., & CAMPBELL, K. (1959). Comparative effectiveness of phenylpropanolamine and dextroamphetamine in weight reduction. *Journal of the American Medical Association*, 170, 1018–1021.
115. LASAGNA, L. (1988). *Phenylpropanolamine—a Review* (pp. 1–20). New York: John Wiley & Sons.
116. MATTHEWS, J., & COLLINS, A. (1983). Interactions of cocaine and cocaine congeners with sodium channels. *Biochemical Pharmacology*, 32, 455.
117. WILSON, A., LANGLEY, L., MONLEY, J., BAUER, T., ROTTUNDA, S., MCFALLS, E., KOVERA, C., & MCCARTEN, J. (1995). Nicotine patches in Alzheimer's disease: pilot study on learning, memory, and safety. *Pharmacology, Biochemistry and Behavior*, 51(2–3), 509–514.
118. LEVIN, E. (1992). Nicotinic systems and cognitive function. *Psychopharmacology-Berlin*, 108(4), 417–431.
119. HARE, E., DOMINIAN, J., & SHARPE, L. (1962). Phenelzine and dextroamphetamine in depressive illness. *British Medical Journal*, 1, 9.
120. RODRIGUEZ, M. (1990). Treatment of cocaine abuse: medical and psychiatric consequences. In K. Redda, C. Walker, & G. Barnett (Eds.), *Cocaine, Marijuana, Designer Drugs: Chemistry, Pharmacology, and Behavior* (pp. 97–111). Boca Raton, FL: CRC Press.
121. KRAMER, J. (1969). Introduction to amphetamine abuse. *Journal of Psychedelic Drugs*, 2, 8.
122. BELL, D. (1973). The experimental production of amphetamine psychosis. *Archives of General Psychiatry*, 29, 35–40.
123. Connell, P. (1958). *Amphetamine Psychosis*. Maudsley Monograph, No. 5. London: Oxford University Press.
124. FISCHMAN, M. (1984). The behavioral pharmacology of cocaine in humans. In J. Grabowski (Ed.), *Cocaine: Pharmacology, Effects, and Treatment of Abuse. National Institute of Drug Abuse Research Monograph 50* (p. 72). Washington, DC: U.S. Government Printing Office.
125. HATSUKAMI, D., ANTON, D., KEENAN, R., & CALLIES, A. (1992). Smokeless tobacco abstinence effects and nicotine gum dose. *Psychopharmacology-Berlin*, 106(1), 60–66.
126. PALMER, K., BUCKLEY, M., & FAULDS, D. (1992). Transdermal Nicotine. A review of its pharmacodynamic and pharmacokinetic properties, and therapeutic efficacy as an aid to smoking cessation. *Drugs*, 44(3), 498–529.
127. ORNISH, S., ZISOOK, S., & MCADAMS, L. (1988). Effects of transdermal clonidine treatment on withdrawal symptoms associated with smoking cessation. A randomized, controlled trial. *Archives of Internal Medicine*, 148(9), 2027–2031.
128. GORELICK, D., ROSE, J., & JARVIK, M., (1988–89). Effect of naloxone on cigarette smoking. *Journal of Substance Abuse*, 1(2), 153–159.
129. GOLDSTEIN, A., KAISER, S., & WHITBY, O. (1969). Psychotropic effects of caffeine in man. IV. Quantitative and qualitative differences associated with habituation to coffee. *Clinical Pharmacology and Therapeutics*, 10, 489–497.

130. MILIARESSIS, E., EMOND, C., & MERALI, Z. (1991). Reevaluation of the role of dopamine in intracranial self-stimulation using in vivo microdialysis. *Behavioral Brain Research*, 46(1), 43–48.

131. HOEBEL, B., HERNANDEZ, L., SCHWARTZ, D., MARK, G., & HUNTER, G. (1989). Microdialysis studies of brain norepinephrine, serotonin, and dopamine release during ingestive behavior. Theoretical and clinical implications. *Annals of the New York Academy of Science*, 575, 171–193.

132. KORNETSKY, C., & PORRINO, L. (1992). Brain mechanisms of drug-induced reinforcement. *Research Publications-Association for Research in Nervous and Mental Disease*, 70, 59–77.

133. HEIDBREDER, C., GEWISS, M., LALLEMAND, S., ROQUES, B., & DE WITTE, P. (1992). Inhibition of enkephalin metabolism and activation of mu- or delta-opioid receptors elict opposite effects on reward and motility in the ventral mesencephalon. *Neurophamacology 31(3)*, 293–298.

134. WISE, R. (1989). Opiate reward: sites and substrates. *Neuroscience and Biobehavioral Reviews*, 13(2–3), 129–133.

135. STINUS, L., CADOR, M., & LE MORAL, M. (1992). Interaction between endogenous opioids and dopamine within the nucleus accumbens. *Annals of the New York Academy of Science*, 654, 254–273.

136. FIBIGER, H., PHILLIPS, A., & BROWN, E. (1992). The neurobiology of cocaine-induced reinforcement. *Ciba Foundation Symposium*, 166, 96–124.

137. MOGHADDAM, B., & BUNNEY, B. (1989). Differential effect of cocaine on extracellular dopamine levels in rat medial prefrontal cortex and nucleus accumbens: comparison to amphetamine. *Synapse*, 4(2), 156–161.

138. CORRIGALL, W., COEN, K., & ADAMSON, K. (1994). Self-administered nicotine activates the mesolimbic dopamine system through the ventral tegmental area. *Brain Research,* 653(1–2), 278–84.

139. YOUNG, D., & SCOVILLE, W. (1938). Paranoid psychosis in narcolepsy and the possible dangers of Benzedrine® treatment. *Medical Clinics of North America,* 22, 637.

140. ANNUAL REPORT OF THE U.S. HEALTH SERVICE (1944). Washington, DC: U.S. Government Printing Office.

141. Griffith, J., Cavanaugh, J., & Oates, J. (1968). Paranoid episodes induced by drugs. *Journal of the American Medical Association*, 205, 39.

142. ANGRIST, B., & GERSHON, S. (1970). The phenomenology of experimentally induced psychosis— preliminary observations. *Biological Psychiatry*, 2, 95–107.

143. POST, R. (1975). Cocaine psychoses: a continuum model. *American Journal of Psychiatry, 132*, 225–231.

144. MCCORMICK, T., & MCNEEL, T. (1963). Acute psychosis and Ritalin® abuse. *Texas State Journal of Medicine*, 59, 99.

145. DAVIS, J., & SCHLEMMER, F. (1980). The amphetamine psychosis. In J. Caldwell (Ed.), *Amphetamines and Related Stimulants: Chemical, Biological, Clinical, and Sociological Aspects* (pp. 161–173). Boca Raton, FL: CRC Press.

146. SMITH, D. (1969). Physical versus psychological dependence and tolerance in high-dose methamphetamine abuse. *Clinical Toxicology*, 2, 99.

147. ANGGARD, E., GUNNE, L., JONNSON, L., & NIKLASSON, F. (1970). Pharmacokinetic and clinical studies on amphetamine dependent subjects. *European Journal of Clinical Pharmacology*, 3, 3.

148. BARKLE, R. (1977). A review of stimulant drug research with hyperactive children. *Journal of Child Psychology and Psychiatry*, 18, 137.

149. RYLANDER, G. (1972). Psychoses and the punding and choreiform syndrome in addiction to central stimulant drugs. *Psychiatria, Neurologia, Neurochirurgia*, 75, 203–212.

150. GRIFFITH, J., CAVANAUGH, J., HELD, J., & OATES, J. (1972). Dextromphetamine—evaluation of psychomimetic properties in man. *Archives of General Psychiatry*, 26, 97–100.

151. BELL., D. (1965). Comparison of amphetamine psychosis and schizophrenia. *British Journal of Psychiatry*, 3, 701.

152. ANGRIST, B., SATHANANTHAN, G., WILK, S., & GERSHON, S. (1974). Amphetamine psychosis: behavioral and biochemical aspects. *Journal of Psychiatric Research*, 11, 13.

153. RIVIER, L. (1981). Analysis of alkaloids in leaves of cultivated erythroxylum and characterization of alkaline substances used during coca chewing. *Journal of Ethnopharmacology*, 3, 313–335.

154. COOK, E. (1991). Pyrolytic characteristics, pharmacokinetics, and bioavailability of smoked heroin, cocaine, phencyclidine, and methamphetamine. In M. Miller & N. Kozel (Eds.), *Methamphetamine Abuse: Epidemeological Issues and Implications* (pp. 6–23). Washington, DC: U.S. Government Printing Office.

CHAPTER NINE
DRUGS USED TO TREAT MENTAL DISORDERS

GENERAL ISSUES ADDRESSED IN THIS CHAPTER

- The serendipitous discovery of the antipsychotics
- The principal symptoms of schizophrenia
- Variability in the absorption and clearance of the antipsychotics
- How antipsychotics block dopamine receptors in the brain
- A review of brain dopamine systems and dopamine receptor types
- Behavioral and nonbehavioral consequences of the antipsychotic medication
- The four common adverse behavioral motor problems associated with antipsychotic medication
- The dopamine theory of schizophrenia
- The significance of the new antipsychotic—clozapine
- The principal symptoms of mood disorder
- How the traditional tricyclic antidepressants alter brain functioning
- How the monoamine oxidase inhibitors and heterocyclic antidepressants alter brain functioning
- Behavioral and nonbehavioral consequences of the antidepressant medications
- The cheese reaction to the monoamine oxidase inhibitors
- The various adverse behavioral effects associated with the tricyclic antidepressants
- The monoamine and beta-adrenergic theories of mood disorders
- Electroconvulsive shock therapy (ECT)
- The concerns surrounding Prozac®
- Behavioral and nonbehavioral consequences of lithium medication
- How lithium alters brain functioning
- Adverse effects associated with lithium medication

LIST OF DRUGS

I. Antipsychotic Medications
   1. Phenothiazines—Chlorpromazine (Thorazine®)
      a. Thioridazine (Mellaril®)
      b. Trifluoperazine hydrochloride (Stelazine®)
      c. Fluphenazine (Prolixin®)
   2. Butyrophenones—Haloperidol (Haldol®)

II. Antidepressant Medications
   1. Tricyclic Antidepressants
     A. Secondary Amines
       a. Desipramine (Norpramin®)
       b. Nortriptyline (Aventyl®)
       c. Protriptyline (Vivactil®)
     B. Tertiary Amines
       a. Imipramine (Tofranil®)
       b. Amitriptyline (Elavil®)
       c. Doxepin (Sinequan®)
   2. Monoamine Oxidase Inhibitors—Tranylcypromine sulfate (Parnate®)

3. Heterocyclic Antidepressants—Trazodone (Desyrel®)
   a. Fluoxetine (Prozac®)
   b. Sertraline (Zoloft®)

III. Lithium

INTRODUCTION

Up to now, we have been reviewing how drugs influence behavior in a variety of medicating and illicit situations. In this chapter, we find the unique situation in which drugs are used to improve the abnormal behavior of individuals with psychological pathologies. In chapter 4 we saw that the treatment of anxiety disorders typically uses the benzodiazepines and, more recently, newer drugs such as the azopirones (buspirone), the imidazo-pyridines (zolpidem), and the cyclopyrrolones (suriclone and zoplicone). This chapter will focus on severe mental illness, specifically psychoses and affective disorders (depression and mania). They will be discussed separately, since different drugs are used to treat each condition. In addition, lithium is discussed specifically. Let us begin with psychoses.

ANTIPSYCHOTIC MEDICATIONS

The antipsychotics have been referred to as the major tranquilizers, which is not an accurate term. It implies that they only help calm individuals who are uncontrollably agitated. While this is true in some cases, this class of drug accomplishes more. The antipsychotics also help withdrawn and behaviorally retarded individuals in that they help them become less withdrawn and exhibit *more* behavior. Thus, the term tranquilizer really does not convey the full behavioral scope of these drugs.

HISTORY

One major class of antipsychotic medication is the phenothiazines. The discovery of their antipsychotic properties was accidental. Phenothiazine, first synthesized in 1883 in a chemical study of dyes, was initially examined as a possible medication for treating clinical conditions like parasitic worms and also as an antihistamine in the 1940s.[1] Around this time, in France, a naval surgeon named Laborit was experimenting with different drug combinations, which included antihistamines, to extend and strengthen anesthesia.[2] In the 1950s, Laborit tried a new antihistamine, chlorpromazine (Thorazine®), and discovered a peculiar behavioral outcome. Chlorpromazine had the unique characteristic of producing tranquilization in patients without loss of consciousness.[2] Patients' apparent lack of concern about their immediate environment was called artificial hibernation or the hibernation syndrome, or a *lobotomie pharmacologique.*[3] These observations eventually led clinicians to experiment with using chlorpromazine to calm agitated mentally disordered patients. In the next few years, the ensuing clinical trials, done first on manic patients then on other types, including schizophrenics, led to the discovery that chlorpromazine was a potent antipsychotic with effects not seen previously with any drug.[4] It was in a 1952 report that Daly and his colleagues coined the term "neuroleptic" for drugs that reduced neurological activity.

Around this time, in 1953, a young physician returned to work in his family's small pharmaceutical company. Because of limited facilities and resources, he developed a strategy that is the basis for designer drugs today, namely to take a known drug, slightly modify its structure, then test it as a "new" drug. The opiate drug meperidine (Demerol®) was modified and two compounds were developed: one was diphenoxylate, or Lomotil®, a potent antidiarrheal drug and another was an analgesic.[1] This analgesic was further modified until ultimately a drug was developed which had a profile, based on tests with animals, that was similar to other antipsychotic drugs. This drug, a variant of meperidine, is called haloperidol (Haldol®). It was first tested clinically in 1958 and found to be even more potent an antipsychotic than chlorpromazine, thus, by the 1960s, haloperidol was a common medication in Europe.[1] It is interesting that the two major classes of antipsychotic medications were both discovered accidentally.

Since this time, many medications have been synthesized and, with only one noted exception, all of the newer medications are no more effective than the original drugs.[5]

CLASSIFICATION OF SCHIZOPHRENIC DISORDERS

Schizophrenia, the most common form of psychosis, is actually a group of disorders. The DSM-II-R categorizes the schizophrenias into five essential subtypes, based on the specific symptoms shown by each. They are:

1. Disorganized type
2. Catatonic type
3. Paranoid type
4. Undifferentiated type
5. Residual type

Symptoms include the following:

1. Hallucinations. These are disturbances in perception in which the person experiences a perception in the absence of actual stimuli. Although hallucinations may occur in any sensory modality, auditory hallucinations are most common.
2. Delusions. These are distortions of reality that lead to misevaluations and erroneous conclusions. A common example of delusions are ideas of reference, in which personal significance is attached to unrelated events, like the evening newscaster is thought to be talking directly to the patient, trying to get a message to him or her.

3. Disturbances of thought, language, and communication. The logic and reasoning exhibited by these patients is faulty and is reflected in their speech. Their language is severely impaired and difficult to follow because of the odd associations.

4. Disturbances of emotion. This can be seen as either tremendous swings, from happy to sad, triggered by situations that would not normally elicit such a strong response or seen as a person's having little emotion, or flat affect.

ABSORPTION, DISTRIBUTION, AND EXCRETION

The phenothiazines and haloperidol are both readily absorbed from the GI tract, making the enteral oral route the easiest and most convenient route of administration. Parenteral injection routes, typically intramuscular (IM) and intravenous (IV) also are used in some situations in which a more rapid onset of effects is required. For example, an oral dose of chlorpromazine will achieve peak blood levels in about two hours, whereas a parenteral IM dose will have peak blood levels in fifteen minutes.[6] However, regardless of the route, the antipsychotic drugs, compared to other drug classes, have the greatest variability in terms of dose, absorption, and other therapeutic indicators.[1] Table 9–1 shows the total twenty-four-hour drug dose for several typical antipsychotic medications. Note that the daily dose range for chlorpromazine (Thorazine®) is 50 mg to 400 mg, whereas the daily dose for haloperidol (Haldol®) is only 2 mg to 6 mg.

Absorption from a single oral dose also has a great deal of variability, not only from one person to another but also in the same individual from one single dose to another.[3] Even after chronic daily administration of 300 mg of chlorpromazine* for one month, the blood levels of chlorpromazine measured in thirty-two patients showed a twelvefold difference between the lowest and highest values.[3]

The half-life of the antipsychotics also is quite variable among subjects, with some estimates of half-life being in the four-to-six hour range[1] and other estimates in the ten-to-twenty hour range.[6] The antipsychotics are very lipid-soluble and as such will tend to accumulate in fat depots and have biphasic clearance profiles from the blood. For chlorpromazine, the biphasic clearance is first rapid, with a half-life of approximately two hours and then is slower, with an approximate half-life of thirty hours.[6]

The antipsychotics are metabolized primarily by the enzymes in the liver and excreted primarily by the kidneys in the urine, but small quantities are sequestered in the bile and excreted in the feces.[6] Chlorpromazine and trifluoperazine (Stelazine®) have many metabolites, several of which are active.[3] Haloperidol (Haldol®) and other selective antipsychotics are metabolized entirely to nonactive metabolites. If drug administration is discontinued for chlorpromazine, for example, the actual drug levels in the blood will of course drop, but the metabolites will linger and be detectable in the urine for several months.[3]

---

*Chlorpromazine is perhaps the most extensively studied of the antipsychotic medications. Much less can be said about the other specific drugs in this class.

**TABLE 9–1   Relative doses of typical antipsychotic drugs
(for people who are not hospitalized)**

ANTIPSYCHOTIC DRUGS	DOSE RANGE (TOTAL MG/DAY)
Chlorpromazine (Thorazine®)	50–400
Trifluoperazine (Stelazine®)	4–10
Haloperidol (Haldol®)	2–6

MECHANISMS OF ACTION

The antipsychotic drugs affect not only the brain but also the peripheral nervous system. In the PNS, antipsychotic drugs have two principal actions: 1. They block acetylcholine (ACh) receptors; and 2. They block alpha-adrenergic receptors.[6] As we shall see, these effects on the PNS account for many of the effects listed in the section below.

Effects on the central nervous system.   Even though the phenothiazines and the butyrophenones are structurally dissimilar, the antipsychotic drugs, as a class, share a common mechanism of action on the brain—they block dopamine receptors. The better an individual drug is at blocking dopamine receptors, the more efficient that drug will be in the clinical treatment of psychoses.[7] This correlation is so strong that the success of a drug in human clinical use can be predicted with a great deal of accuracy, based on dopamine receptor blocking done in animal tissue studies.[8] This robust effect has led to the so-called dopamine theory of schizophrenia. Simply stated, this hypothesis essentially proposes the following: Since the drugs that are effective in treating psychoses have as their principal action the blockage of brain dopamine receptors, then psychoses, like schizophrenia, may be the result of abnormally overactive brain dopamine systems. We will consider this hypothesis in more detail later. Figure 9–1 illustrates the structural similarity between the dopamine molecule and a typical antipsychotic chlorpromazine. By turning the chlorpromazine molecule ninety degrees, one can better see the physical commonality in these two molecules. Brain dopamine systems and the various brain dopamine receptors will be reviewed next.

Dopamine Systems

Recall from chapter 2 that there are several specific brain nuclei whose cells use dopamine as a neurotransmitter. The three most prominent are:

1. The nigrostriatal dopamine pathway. Its cell bodies are in the nucleus of the substantia nigra in the midbrain. Its axons are sent to two nuclei, the striatum, in the telencephalon. This system is critically involved in motor behavior and is the system that is damaged in Parkinson's disease.
2. The mesolimbic and mesocortical systems. Its cell bodies are in the ventral tegmentum in the midbrain. Its axons are sent to either the prefrontal cerebral cortex (mesocortical system) or to a variety of limbic nuclei (mesolimbic system). This system seems to be involved in emotional behavior and may be the brain system that is abnormal or functioning abnormally in psychoses. This is the target system for antipsychotic medication.

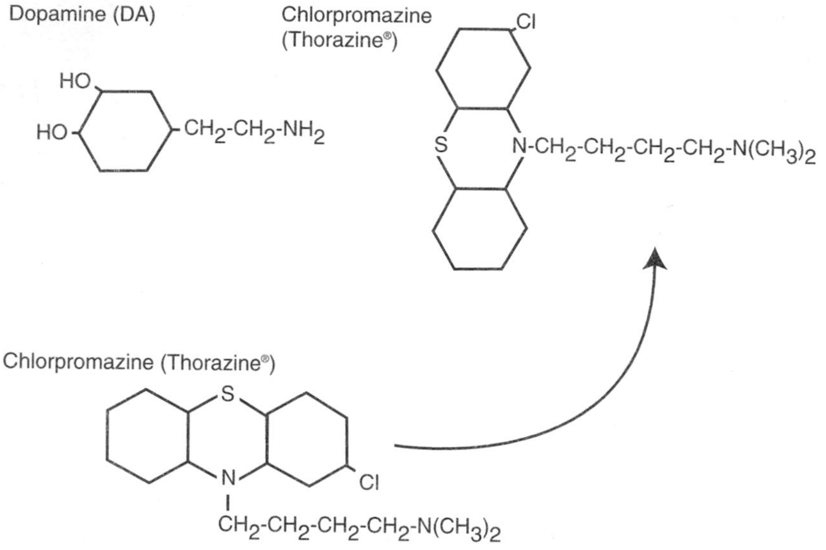

FIGURE 9–1   The Similarity of Chlorpromazine to Dopamine
By turning the molecular structure of chlorpromazine, one can better see how its center portion is similar in structure to dopamine.

3. The tubero-infundibular system. Its cell bodies are in the hypothalamus just above the pituitary. Its axons are sent a short distance to an area that has a special blood vessel link with the pituitary. Essentially, this system plays a role in the hypothalamus-pituitary interactions that maintain appropriate hormone levels in the blood.

All of these systems use dopamine as a neurotransmitter, thus all of their targets have dopamine receptors at those particular synapses. While the most likely systems that may be pathological in psychoses are the mesolimbic and mesocortical systems, the antipsychotic medications, with the possible exception of clozapine, will block dopamine receptors in all of these systems, resulting in a variety of motor problems (see the Adverse and Toxic Effects section later in this chapter). However, there are several types of receptors for dopamine, and the antipsychotics affect them differently.

Dopamine Receptor Types

There have been six dopamine receptor subtypes that have been characterized in the brain: D_1, D_{2a}, D_{2b}, D_3, D_4, and D_5.[9] These different subtypes can be functionally classified by how they are affected by the antipsychotics and anatomically by where they are found in the brain. The D_1 and D_5 receptors are not blocked very well by the phenothiazine and butyrophenone antipsychotics. Both of the D_2 receptors are the principal sites of action for the phenothiazines and butyrophenones. These receptors are found in the cerebral cortex, in critical limbic structures involved with emotion, and in the striatum, which is involved with motor behavior. In addition to being on the postsynaptic surface, the D_{2b} receptors appear to be on the presynaptic terminals of the dopamine cells and act as inhibitory autoreceptors for them. The D_3 and D_4 receptors also are found in limbic areas and in the cerebral cortex, but not in motor areas like the striatum. The phenothiazine and butyrophenone antipsychotic medications show very little binding to the D_3 and D_4 receptor types. However, clozapine, one of the newer antipsychotic medications, blocks the D_3 and D_4 receptors best and only weakly blocks the D_2's receptor types. It is this differential blockade of dopamine receptors that results in clozapine treatment having very few motor problems commonly associated with the more traditional antipsychotic medications.

NONBEHAVIORAL AND BEHAVIORAL CONSEQUENCES OF ANTIPSYCHOTIC DRUGS

There is a variety of effects of the antipsychotics that relates to their anticholinergic properties, including dry mouth or decreased salivation, constipation, and blurred vision.[3] The blocking of alpha-adrenergic receptors by the antipsychotics results in some distinctive cardiovascular effects, like an increased heart rate (tachycardia), a mild decrease in blood pressure, postural hypotension*,[6] and peripheral vasodilation, which causes mild hypothermia.[10] The severity of these effects varies among the particular antipsychotic medications.

Behaviorally, the antipsychotics typically induce a tranquilized state without loss of consciousness, a condition that was originally termed artificial hibernation— an indifference to the immediate environment. Some of the antipsychotics, chlorpromazine in particular, will induce sedation, whereas some, like trifluoperazine, are more likely to induce agitation.[3]

Of course, the most profound behavioral effect of these drugs is the relief of psychotic symptoms in mentally disordered patients. Even though discovered by accident, the success of this class of drugs in the treatment of psychoses is an accomplishment of enormous importance. Prior to this alternative, care of severely mentally disordered patients was essentially only custodial. These drugs have brought patients back into life and within reach of conventional therapy.

The symptoms that appear to respond well to the antipsychotic drugs include hallucinations, acute delusions, hostility, flat affect, and general withdrawal.[6] Moreover, these drugs also seem to alleviate the primary core symptoms, such as thought disorder and paranoia, although this has been challenged by some.[3] Clearly, the

*Also referred to as orthostatic hypotension, this term refers to the condition in which a person experiences lightheadedness or dizziness when standing up from a sitting or reclined position.

antipsychotic medications do not actually cure psychoses, but rather are an absolutely essential part of a treatment strategy that helps control the disorder.

In addition to treating various psychotic conditions, the antipsychotic medications also have been used to treat Tourette's syndrome, a disorder in which the patient has uncontrolled motor tics, sudden nonverbal vocalizations like barks and grunts, and unpredictable outbursts of foul language.[1] Antipsychotic drugs also have been used to treat nausea and vomiting due to a variety of causes.[6]

WITHDRAWAL AND TOLERANCE

Since antipsychotic drugs are used to reverse or correct a given set of behaviors that are already established in a patient, the issues of drug dependency and withdrawal are somewhat complex. Certainly, if antipsychotic medication is discontinued the psychotic behavior invariably returns. This does not constitute a withdrawal syndrome, since it was present prior to the administration of the drug. When directly examined in animals, there is virtually no withdrawal syndrome associated with the discontinuation of antipsychotic medication, and with the exception of some muscle discomfort, the same is true for humans.[6]

Tolerance develops for the sedation often seen with antipsychotic medications and cross-tolerance develops between the antipsychotics.[6] Tolerance does not develop to the antipsychotic relief these drugs render, which means that the dose does not have to be increased over the years of treatment.

ADVERSE AND TOXIC EFFECTS

In terms of lethality, the antipsychotics are remarkably safe. It is difficult for adults to die from overdoses of antipsychotics alone. For example, a single dose of 10,000 mg (that is, 10 grams) of chlorpromazine did not result in death.[6] However, there is a rare condition called the malignant syndrome, in which following antipsychotic medication a person experiences rigidity, fever, and hypertension, among other symptoms, which may progress to coma and even death.[11]

Another relatively rare reaction to antipsychotic medication is agranulocytosis, which is a severe decrease in white blood cells, usually in response to a fever. Although this can become a potentially fatal reaction, if detected in its early stages recovery is quick and complete. The incidence rate of agranulocytosis ranges from reports of one case in 10,000 for antipsychotic medications in general,[6] eleven cases in 1,000,[12] and eighteen cases in 3,000[13] for patients specifically receiving chlorpromazine. Typically, this reaction occurs in the first three months of treatment.[14]

A less severe adverse reaction to antipsychotic medications is skin photosensitivity,[6] abnormal accumulations of pigment in the skin [3] and, in some cases, the eye.[1]

By far the most significant type of adverse effect associated with the antipsychotics is a variety of abnormal motor behaviors, most of which occur soon after antipsychotic treatment has begun. The incidence of some motor disturbance induced by medication has been reported to be as high as 90 percent of all people who receive this medication[15] and one of the major reasons why patients do not comply with drug treatments.[16] Four of the most common reactions are reviewed next.

Acute Dystonia or Dystonic Reactions

Dystonia is a syndrome of sustained muscle contraction that usually results in bizarre appearances, depending on the muscle groups involved.[17] When dystonia affects the muscles of the face, the patient may grimace or the jaw may spasm open or closed. When the neck muscles are affected, the neck might be severely twisted or pulled either forward or backward. The muscles of the trunk also can be affected, resulting in odd postural stands. In addition, the tongue muscles can be the site for dystonia. One of the characteristics of dystonia is that the patient can often exert some control over the muscle spasm by touching the affected area, so that a dystonic reaction can be ended by the patient.

The risk of developing dystonia is highest within the first five days of beginning antipsychotic treatment.[18] Parenteral administration, either IV or IM, of anticholinergic agents like benztropine (Cogentin®) or antihistamines like diphenhydramine (Benadryl®) can provide immediate relief of these symptoms.[19] However, the most effective treatment of this antipsychotic-induced dystonia is to gradually discontinue the medication, which is not always an option given the severity of the psychoses being treated.[20]

Akathisia

Akathisia refers to a compulsion to move. There is no specific muscle group involved, nor is there a specific motor behavior, but rather akathisia is an intense feeling of restlessness experienced by the patient. Acute akathisia is the most common of the early-onset motor abnormalities induced by the antipsychotic medications.[21] The incidence rate is approximately 20 percent for patients placed on antipsychotics.[22] One study reported an incidence rate of 75 percent.[23] It usually occurs within five to forty days after the onset of antipsychotic medication.[18] Akathisia usually is seen as a constant movement by the patient, such as continuous pacing, shifting the weight from one foot to the other, continually crossing and uncrossing the legs when seated, changing one's stance, etc. These symptoms often are interpreted incorrectly as anxiety or as a worsening of the psychotic condition. The only clearly effective treatment for akathisia is a reduction in or discontinuation of the medication, which as mentioned earlier, may not be a realistic option in the overall treatment of a psychotic individual.

Parkinson Syndrome or Parkinsonism

Within five to thirty days after antipsychotic medication has been initiated, a patient may express a disorder that is indistinguishable from true Parkinson's disease in its clinical symptoms. The typical signs which characterize Parkinson's disease are akinesia or bradykinesia, rigidity, and tremor at rest.[24] Tremor at rest may often disappear or be reduced when purposeful activity is engaged in, but the condition becomes more intense during times of stress. Bradykinesia is a lack of spontaneous movement due to difficulty initiating voluntary movement. Rigidity is the result of an increase in muscle tone to the point that passive movement of limbs is resisted. The akinesia associated with Parkinson's Syndrome is especially debilitating, since it may often express itself as a lack of emotion, diminished gesturing, impaired social ability, and a general lack of concern.[19] The treatment for this drug-induced condition is the same as the treatment for true Parkinson's disease. There are several anticholinergic medications that have proven helpful. Two in particular include benztropine (Cogentin®) and procyclidine (Kemadrin®).[19]

The causal pathology in Parkinson's disease is a loss of cells in the substantia nigra, which use dopamine as a neurotransmitter (see chapter 2 and the section Dopamine Systems preceding). The antipsychotic medications mimic this disorder because their primary action is to block dopamine receptors, thus those motor areas in the brain which have dopamine receptors for the input of the substantia nigra also are blocked. The result, both in true Parkinson's disease and in the recipient of antipsychotic medication is that critical motor processing takes place without input from the substantia nigra.

Tardive Dyskinesia

As the name implies, this is a late-onset motor disorder that occurs after a relatively long time on antipsychotic medication. There is no doubt that the longer a person is given antipsychotic medication, the greater the risk for developing tardive dyskinesia. However, it has been extremely difficult to precisely describe the parameters of this relationship. Prospective studies have reported incidence rates for tardive dyskinesia that increase with drug exposure time.[25,26,27,28] Figure 9–2 summarizes the cumulative rates.

Tardive dyskinesia is a disorder that involes involuntary abnormal movements, typically of the mouth and tongue, for example, lip smacking and pursing, and the tongue darting out of the mouth. In some cases, other parts of the body are affected, such as the limbs. One peculiar aspect of this motor disorder is that the patient can voluntarily control the symptoms by attending to them.[18] The proposed mechanism for tardive dyskinesia is that following prolonged blockage of dopamine receptors, some aspect of the dopamine system may become hypersensitive or supersensitive.[29]

Unlike the other behavioral adverse reactions listed earlier, this syndrome may be irreversible in some patients.[18] This is an especially important issue since there is no effective treatment for tardive dyskinesia. The only accepted successful treatment strategy has been to discontinue the medication, which of course runs the risk of having the original psychosis emerge.[30]

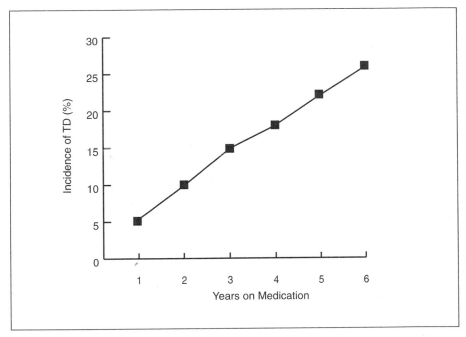

FIGURE 9–2   Incidence Rates of Tardive Dyskinesia
The longer a person is maintained on antipsychotic medication, the greater the risk for developing tardive dyskinesia. (The box marks the incidence rate after only three years of chronic antipsychotic medication.)

SPECIAL ISSUES

The Dopamine Theory of Schizophrenia

Essentially, this theory proposes that schizophrenia specifically and psychoses in general are the result of overactive dopamine systems in the brain. The initial support for this theory came from the two following facts: 1. Those drugs that offer the most effective relief from this disorder block dopamine receptors; and 2. Overstimulating the dopamine systems in the brain with stimulants leads to the amphetamine psychosis (see chapter 8). The more recent research efforts which support the dopamine theory of schizophrenia have resulted in ambiguous findings.

The New Generation Antipsychotics

Clozapine is a new antipsychotic that may mark the most significant advance since the initial development of antipsychotic medication. Compared to traditional antipsychotics, clozapine has been reported to be more effective in the treatment of psychoses,[31,32] and induces fewer[33] and less tardive dyskinesia.[34] Not only has cloza-pine been shown to be more effective than traditional antipsychotics like chlorpro-mazine,[35] but it also has been shown to be effective in patients who do not respond to the typical antipsychotic medications.[36]

The significance of this relatively new, so-called atypical antipsychotic lies in clozapine's unique property of blocking the D_3 and D_4 dopamine receptor types, while having only a minimal effect on the D_2 receptor type.[9] The motor effects fol-lowing antipsychotic medication are due primarily to the D_2 receptors in motor sys-tems like the nigrostriatal pathway.[37] The phenothiazines and haloperidol block the D_2 receptors in these motor areas as effectively as they block D_2 receptors in the lim-bic/emotional areas. Clozapine, on the other hand, does not bind to the D_2 receptors in these motor areas very well,[38] thus does not cause the motor problems seen with the more traditional antipsychotics.

Clozapine appears to have two other significant effects on brain functioning. It blocks the specific serotonin receptor types 5HT2 and 5HT1c.[39] It is not clear if this action of clozapine relates to either its antipsychotic properties or its lack of motor effects. Clozapine also blocks muscarinic acetylcholine receptors.[40] As we have seen, the use of anticholinergic drugs seems to alleviate the motor problems of antipsy-chotic medications. By having this built-in feature, clozapine may itself correct for any detrimental D_2 receptor blockade.

Even though clozapine may not have the motor problems associated with the other antipsychotic medications, it does have other adverse effects, the most serious being agranulocytosis. While the occurrence of agranulocytosis can happen with conventional antipsychotics, the rate is much higher with clozapine, approximately 1 to 2 percent.[41] The development of agranulocytosis induced by clozapine use follows a similar time course as that of the conventional antipsychotics, namely within the first few months of treatment.[36]

Other less severe adverse effects associated with clozapine treatment include seizure, increased heart rate, hypotension, weight gain, and increased salivation.[33]

ANTIDEPRESSANTS

The affective disorders are disorders of mood, like depression and mania. The inci-dence rate of these debilitating disorders can be as high as 10 percent of the general population of Western countries.[42] As with the antipsychotic medications, the dis-covery of the drugs used to treat affective disorders were discovered accidentally.

Basically, there are four classes of drugs used in the treatment of affective dis-orders:

1. Traditional tricyclic antidepressants (TCA)
2. Monoamine oxidase inhibitors (MAOIs)
3. Newer heterocyclic antidepressants
4. Lithium

Since lithium is used to treat mania, in particular, it will be discussed in a separate section.

HISTORY

The parent compound for the tricyclic antidepressants was synthesized in 1889. It was not until the 1940s that a derivative, imipramine, was examined as a possible antihistamine. When the findings were released that another suspected antihistamine, chlorpromazine, actually had antipsychotic effects, imipramine was tested again in 1958. Khun found that imipramine was not an effective antipsychotic but did seem to render relief to the depressed patients in the sample.[43] Since then there have been numerous studies indicating how effective tricyclic antidepressants are in the treatment of affective disorders.

Around this time, the serendipitous discovery of the antidepressant properties of another drug also were made. The drug, iproniazid, which was developed and being used to treat tuberculosis, had another effect—patients who received it experienced an elevation in mood, to the point of euphoria. It soon was discovered that iproniazid severely hampered the action of an enzyme—monoamine oxidase (MAO). By 1957, the successful use of monoamine oxidase inhibitors (MAOIs) to treat depression was reported.

There was another serendipitous discovery that also happened around this time. Hypertensive patients had been given a drug called reserpine, which seemed to cause these otherwise normal patients to experience profound depression. While this discovery did not directly impact the development of newer drugs, it provided another set of data which supported the monoamine theory of affective disorders.

CLASSIFICATION OF MOOD DISORDERS

The basic behavioral disturbance in this disorder is a profound alteration of mood. This alteration can be expressed as a pathologically depressed, elevated, or manic mood. In the depressed mood, the main symptoms include a profound loss of pleasure, an intense apathy, nonintentional change in weight (increase or decrease), change in sleep (either insomnia or hypersomnia), suicidal ideation or thoughts of death. In the manic mood, the main symptoms include feelings of grandiosity, periods of excessive talking, decreased need for sleep, distractibility, and engaging in risky behavior (financial, business, or sexual indiscretions). There are five basic subclassifications of these disorders, depending on the occurrence of a manic period: 1. bipolar disorder; 2. major depressive disorder (formerly referred to as unipolar); 3. cyclothymic disorder; 4. bipolar disorder NOS (not otherwise specified); and depressive disorder NOS.

ABSORPTION, DISTRIBUTION, AND BIOTRANSFORMATION

As a group, the antidepressant drugs used to treat mood disorders, formerly referred to as affective disorders, are readily absorbed from the GI tract. The TCAs are usually completely absorbed from an oral administration within ten hours and peak plasma concentrations are reached within two hours.[44] Distribution is fairly even throughout body compartments except in the case of imipramine, in which there is an unusually high concentration in the brain.[44]

Biotransformation for both TCAs and MAOIs is done in the liver. The metabolism of many of the TCAs produces active metabolites. For example, imipramine metabolism yields desimipramine; amitriptyline metabolism yields nortriptyline; doxepin metabolism yields nordoxepin. Although these metabolites are active, their role in the clinical effectiveness of the TCAs has yet to be determined.[6] Typically, the metabolism of the MAOIs does not yield active metabolites.

The following is a representative sample of the half-lifes of the TCAs:[45]

1. Imipramine—thirteen hours
2. Amitriptyline—fifteen hours (Nortriptyline—thirty-one hours)
3. Desipramine—eighteen hours
4. Doxepin—seventeen hours
5. Protriptyline—seventy-eight hours
6. Trazadone—five hours
7. Fluoxetine—forty-eight hours (and as long as six days after chronic treatment)[46]
8. Sertraline—twenty-four hours[46]

EFFECTS ON THE CENTRAL NERVOUS SYSTEM

Tricyclic Antidepressants

The TCAs can be subdivided into two categories according to their molecular structure and precise action on synaptic functioning in the brain. Structurally, the TCAs can be subdivided into two classes:

1. TCAs with one methyl group (CH_3), referred to as secondary amines—specifically, desipramine and protriptyline
2. TCAs with two methyl groups, referred to as tertiary amines—specifically, imipramine, amitriptyline, doxepin, and clomipramine[47]

After a neuron has fired, it releases neurotransmitter molecules into the synaptic cleft to interact with special postsynaptic receptors on the target surface. Neurons must then engage a mechanism to terminate this action and get ready for the next firing (i.e., the next action potential) (see chapter 2). Neurons in the brain that use the monoamines, namely norepinephrine (NE), dopamine (DA), or serotonin (5HT) as neurotransmitters terminate the action of their neurotransmitter molecules by a reuptake process. The released neurotransmitter molecules that are in the synapse are actively taken back into the presynaptic terminal by an active membrane transport mechanism. The TCAs block this reuptake system. The result of the TCAs' hampering of this reuptake process is that the neurotransmitter molecules remain on the postsynaptic receptors longer. Thus, the principal functional consequence of TCAs is the immediate enhancement of monoamine transmission. Recall from our discussion of the stimulants that one of the mechanisms of the action of amphetamines is also a hampering of the reuptake process in monoamine neurons.

It is important to note that the specific monoamines are affected differently by the TCAs. The TCAs belonging to the one methyl group, secondary amines, namely desipramine and protriptyline, block the reuptake of norepinephrine (NE) much more efficiently than serotonin (5HT). The TCAs belonging to the two methyl group, tertiary amines, that is, imipramine, amitriptyline, doxepin, and clomipramine, block the reuptake of serotonin (5HT) much more efficiently than norepinephrine (NE). Appreciate that both norepinephrine and serotonin reuptake systems are blocked by the TCAs. The main difference between the subclasses of TCAs is one of relative degree.

Monoamine Oxidase Inhibitors

As their name implies, these drugs block the enzyme monoamine oxidase (MAO). This enzyme exists in the presynaptic terminal of the neurons that use monoamines as neurotransmitters. This enzyme will break down monoamine neurotransmitter molecules in the cytoplasm, not yet in the synaptic vesicle. By breaking down so-called free-floating neurotransmitter molecules, MAO decreases the absolute amount of molecules available for packaging into synaptic vesicles. Ultimately then, MAO regulates the amount of neurotransmitter molecules that are released when the cell fires. By inhibiting this action of MAO, the MAO inhibitors (MAOIs) will cause the release of more monoamine neurotransmitter molecules with each action potential.

Heterocyclic Antidepressants

These newer medications, like fluoxetine (Prozac®) and maprotiline, are like the traditional tricyclic antidepressants in that they also block the reuptake process of certain monoamine neurons. These drugs are different because they have been developed to be even more specific to one monoamine system than are the traditional TCAs. For example, maprotiline is approximately 600 times more selective for blocking NE reuptake than 5HT reuptake, compared to desipramine,[48] and fluoxetine is approximately 30 times more effective in blocking the reuptake of serotonin than NE reuptake.[48] Sertraline (Zoloft®), like fluoxetine (Prozac®), is another specific serotonin reuptake blocker.

Note that for all three classes of antidepressants, the immediate effect on brain functioning is the enhancement of communication with those neurons that use monoamines as a neurotransmitter.

The long-term consequences of blocking monoamine reuptake, whether NE or 5HT, may be one of the causal factors in the clinical efficacy of these antidepressant medications. This will be discussed later in the Special Issues section.

BEHAVIORAL EFFECTS

There are few behavioral effects of antidepressant drugs in those individuals who are not suffering from clinical depression, and these can be characterized as generally unpleasant. There may be sedation, decrease in blood pressure, and dry mouth.[6] Doxepin may be more sedating than imipramine in these control populations.[47] This is especially striking considering that amphetamines and cocaine also block monoamine reuptake (see chapter 8), yet the antidepressants do not induce the euphoria of the stimulants. This suggests that it may be the other actions of the stimulants which account for their high reinforcing properties.

In patient populations that are depressed, the antidepressants will relieve the symptoms of their depression. A characteristic common to all of the antidepressant medications is that there is a ten-to-fourteen day delay from the onset of taking the medication and the onset of clinical relief. The elevation of mood as a result of the alleviation of depression is not euphoric, such as with the stimulants cocaine and amphetamines, but rather is an absence of severe depression. While the antidepressant medications have consistently been shown to be more effective than placebo treatments, approximately 30 percent of patients will not positively respond to these medications.[47] The considerably high spontaneous improvement rate, approximately 31 percent in populations receiving only the placebo,[49] or other nonpharmacological interventions, indicate that mood disorders are a heterogeneous collection of disorders with a variety of treatment strategies available to the attending practitioner.

WITHDRAWAL

The withdrawal symptoms from abruptly stopping tricyclic antidepressant medications are similar to a severe flu reaction: headache, chills, diarrhea and vomiting, abdominal cramps, dizziness, insomnia, and irritability.[50]

Abrupt withdrawal from MAOI medication has not been considered a serious problem.[51] The symptoms include nausea, headaches, palpitations, sweating, and muscle weakness.[52]

ADVERSE AND TOXIC EFFECTS

General Toxicity

Unlike the antipsychotics, overdoses of the TCAs can be fatal. This is especially problematic when one considers that one of the common characteristics of the population being treated with TCAs is suicidal tendencies. Suicides are common with TCA medication.[53] If given more than a week's supply, a depressed patient will have enough of the drug to achieve a fatal overdose,[6] so care must be exercised to prevent this situation. The MAOIs also are quite lethal at doses well within the availability of the patient.[54]

The TCAs induce a variety of effects on the autonomic nervous system. They include: dry mouth, increased heart rate (tachycardia), decreased blood pressure (hypotension), postural hypotension, constipation, dizziness, vomiting,[53] and urinary retention.[6]

The MAOIs have a similar profile of autonomic effects as do the TCAs. These signs include: dizziness, postural hypotension, dry mouth, constipation, difficulty in urination, inhibited orgasm, and impotence.[53] A massive overdose can result in convulsions and death.[6]

The most serious toxic reaction to the MAOIs is a hypertensive crisis sometimes referred to as the "Cheese Reaction." Our food sometimes contains certain agents called "pressor" agents which if left uncontrolled would elicit the sympathetic nervous system to rapidly raise blood pressure. Normally, there is MAO in the liver and in the gut to metabolize these compounds in our food and thus prevent this increase in blood pressure.[54] When MAOIs are given in the treatment of depression, all MAO is inhibited including this peripheral MAO. Thus the consumption of foods rich in these pressor agents would lead to a sharp increase in blood pressure. Tyramine, a product of the fermentation process, is the most common dietary pressor agent responsible for a MAOI induced hypertensive reaction. Foods rich in tyramine include: aged cheeses especially cheddar and Swiss, red wines, red wine vinegars, beer, homemade yogurt, and any food with Brewer's yeast.[54] Thus the term "Cheese" reaction is not accurate.

There are three progressively more severe stages to this reaction.[53]

1. Stage one: Sudden throbbing headaches are commonly reported, along with nausea, vomiting, and sweating. These signs may disappear within a few hours if no further tyramine-containing food is ingested.
2. Stage two: Severe hypertension, palpitations, and chest pains, along with headache and sweating, and potential collapse are seen here.
3. Stage three: All of the above symptoms are experienced, as well as intracranial bleeding, which is fatal.

Drugs that induce sympathetic reactions, like amphetamines and cocaine, also precipitate a hypertensive crisis if taken in combination with MAOIs.[53]

Tricyclic Antidepressants

There are several adverse behavioral consequences with the tricyclic drugs.

1. Aggression. There are certain people with personality disorders who are at risk for showing increased aggression in response to antidepressant medication. One study reported that almost half of the patients with previously diagnosed borderline personality disorder showed increased paranoia and became more suicidal, hostile, and impulsive

while on antidepressant drugs.[55] This medication-induced increased aggression appears to occur only in those individuals who may be predisposed to aggression prior to the medication.[51]

2. Weight gain. Weight gain is one of the more common effects of chronic antidepressant medication.[56] The incidence of either weight gain and/or carbohydrate craving may be as high as 50 percent in certain populations.[51]

3. Jitteriness syndrome. Just after the initiation of antidepressant medication, typically those drugs which have a more direct effect on the norepinephrine system, like imipramine, desipramine, and protriptyline,[56] the patient sometimes will suddenly experience an intense feeling of restlessness, increased energy, and irritability.[57] This usually will resolve within a day.[58]

4. Sleep effects. The TCAs will reliably suppress REM sleep.[59] This effect is immediate and seems to correlate with the eventual clinical effectiveness in treating the depression.[60] There also is an increase in nocturnal myoclonus, which is the strong leg contraction or kick that occurs during sleep.[61] This effect appears to occur with those antidepressants that more directly affect the serotonin system, such as clomipramine.[62] The patient is usually unaware of this nocturnal myoclonus and it is the patient's bed partner that brings this condition to the attention of the attending physician.[62]

The MAOIs have similar adverse behavioral effects as do the TCAs, including weight gain,[51] suppressing REM sleep,[59] inducing mania,[63] and even antisocial behavior, in some rare cases.[64]

SPECIAL ISSUES

The Monoamine Theory of Affective Disorders

Essentially, this theory suggests that affective disorders like depression are the result of a chemical, that is a neurotransmitter, imbalance or deficit in the brain. Specifically, the monoamine theory holds that affective disorders are the result of either an underactive monoamine system in the brain or that levels of monoamine neurotransmitter molecules in the brain are too low. The monoamine theory is based on a variety of sources, including the initial observations of patients treated with reserpine and the MAOI iproniazid (see above), as well as the later evidence that successful medications that reverse depressive symptoms all seem to enhance monoamine activity. The major shortcoming of this theory is that it fails to explain why there is a ten-to-fourteen day delay from the onset of taking medication to the onset of clinical improvement. The medications typically enhance monoamine systems immediately, yet the person does not experience relief for two weeks.

Recent advances in the technology of directly studying specific receptors in the brain have led to an alternate theory.

The Beta-Adrenergic Theory of Affective Disorders

There are two specific receptor types for norepinephrine—the alpha- and beta-adrenergic receptors. Each has a distinctive distribution in the peripheral nervous system and the central nervous system. It is important to consider a general characteristic shared by most receptors, that is, not all of them are functional at any one point in time. In other words, a given population of receptors will have a portion that is not active, and the brain will regulate just how many receptors are active according to its needs.

One long-term consequence of chronic antidepressant medication is the decreased number, referred to as a down regulation, of beta-adrenergic receptors in the brain.[65] This down regulation, which takes approximately ten to fourteen days to accomplish, is found not only with drugs that block the reuptake of norepinephrine but also with a variety of antidepressants that do not directly alter norepinephrine. The specific serotonin reuptake blockers, like fluoxetine (Prozac®) and sertraline (Zoloft®), also cause the eventual down regulation of beta-adrenergic receptors in the brain, as do the MAOIs and even the nonpharmacological treatment ECT.[65] Thus, it appears that the norepinephrine and serotonin systems in the brain interact with each other in such a way that altering one will impact the other, and the common outcome for these medications centers around the beta-adrenergic receptors in the brain. For example, the administration of both fluoxetine and desipramine not only enhanced the antidepressant results of the medications, but also was one-third faster than either medication alone.[66]

Recent research has been describing the precise role of serotonin in the clinical effectiveness of antidepressants. Traditional tricyclic antidepressant medications and ECT, in addition to the down regulation of beta-adrenergic receptors, will also enhance serotonin receptor sensitivity on the cerebral cortex,[67] specifically the 5-HT1A serotonin receptor.[68] It appears that the serotonin-norepinepherine interaction that may mediate the clinical relief of antidepressant medications is a down regulation of the beta-adrenergic receptors and an increase in serotonin receptor activity.[69] Postmortem biochemical analyses of the brains of suicide victims indicate that the prefrontal cortex has lower levels of 5HT transport activity[70] and higher beta-adrenergic receptor binding.[71]

Electroconvulsive Shock Therapy (ECT)

Based on the observations of the Hungarian physician von Meduna in the early 1900s, it was believed that seizures protected patients from severe psychiatric pathology, thus the strategy of inducing seizures for therapeutic reasons began. At first, seizures were pharmacologically induced, but in 1938 the use of electroconvulsive techniques were introduced into clinical medicine.[72] Originally, ECT was done without anesthesia or other medications. The procedure now involves the use of muscle relaxants and some anesthesia to prevent bone fractures during the convulsions and to prevent anxiety surrounding the procedure.[72] The optimal ECT schedule is considered to be a series of two seizures a week for three to four weeks.[73] Bilateral ECT, that is, causing the entire brain to go into seizure, is slightly more effective than unilateral ECT, which causes only one hemisphere of the brain to go into seizure.[74] Modern ECT is considered safe and effective,[75] with positive response rates as high as 95 percent.[74] ECT is believed to induce more rapid relief than the standard two-week delay of the antidepressants, which becomes critical when dealing with some suicidal patients. However, this alleged rapid clinical response and success in suicidal patients has not been observed by all.[47] Although ECT has been suggested for patients who do not respond to antidepressant medications, the positive response rate to ECT by medication-resistant patients is quite low, around 50 percent.[76]

Despite the new ECT techniques, which obviate many of the major problems with ECT, there remain two significant concerns. First, ECT will invariably induce confusion and a loss of memory surrounding the ECT treatment, which becomes progressively more severe with increased sessions.[72] Second, without additional pharmacological support, the relapse rate of patients with successful ECT six months later is significantly higher than with those patients with additional antidepressant medication.[77]

The precise mechanism by which ECT provides clinical relief is not known. However, ECT, like traditional antidepressant medication, does cause a down regulation of beta-adrenergic receptors[65] and enhances 5HT sensitivity in the cerebral cortex.[67]

Concerns Surrounding Prozac®

Despite press accounts of aggressive and suicidal effects induced by fluoxetine (Prozac®), controlled examinations of these allegations do not support these observations. The adverse behavioral effects associated with the traditional antidepressants do not appear to be different than those attributed to Prozac®. One study examined over 1,000 cases of patients medicated with Prozac® and found no differences between Prozac® and other antidepressant medications in the incidence of new suicidal ideation.[78] As discussed earlier, the occurrence of aggressive behavior following the administration of antidepressant medication is restricted to certain patient populations that have borderline personality disorders. This effect is not specific to fluoxetine but rather to this class of medication.

It is important to remember that one of the core symptoms of severe affective disorders include suicidal ideation. The practitioner must always be vigilant to its appearance at any time during the course of treatment.

LITHIUM® AND MANIA

The antidepressant medications listed earlier are not useful in the treatment of mania. Lithium is the principal medication that will effectively treat mania, with a success rate as high as 95 percent.[74] In addition, lithium may even prevent the occurrence of bipolar swings into depression from a manic phase.[79]

HISTORY

The discovery of lithium was not as serendipitous as the other medications discussed in this chapter. In Australia, in the 1940s, John Cade developed a hypothesis stating that mania was the result of some endotoxin produced by manic patients. Using an animal model, Cade found that the urea from the urine of manic patients was one toxic substance. His subsequent experiments to increase the solubility of urates led to the discovery of lithium as a potential sedating candidate.[80] Although Cade's initial clinical trials of using lithium on manic patients were overwhelmingly successful, it took almost twenty years before the worldwide medical community accepted its use in the treatment of mania. There were several reasons for this unusually long delay.[47] The initial Cade clinical reports were published in local Australian medical journals, not the more widely read international journals. The use of lithium as a sodium substitute in the 1940s resulted in several fatalities, casting a negative shroud on this drug. Financially, lithium could not be patented, thus it was not commercially profitable for drug companies. Despite these difficulties, the use of lithium in treating mania has become the first-line medication worldwide.

ABSORPTION, DISTRIBUTION, AND EXCRETION

Lithium is almost exclusively given orally. It is completely absorbed from the GI tract, is almost entirely excreted by the kidney at a moderate rate, and has a half-life of approximately twenty-four hours. The excretion of lithium is influenced by the sodium balance in the patient. When sodium intake is low, lithium is retained longer. If sodium intake is increased, lithium is excreted more rapidly.[80] Lithium tends to accumulate in the kidneys.[79]

BEHAVIORAL AND NONBEHAVIORAL EFFECTS

In nonmanic individuals, lithium may elicit subjective feelings of fatigue, lethargy, and decreased ability to concentrate, as well as decreased memory functioning.[79] In the manic patient, lithium can help control manic episodes and even prevent the occurrence of future manic swings.[74] For the manic patient, this means that they are able to experience a level of control over their positive emotions that was not previously there. It is important to note that, like the antidepressants, lithium has a six-to-ten day delay from the onset of medication and relief of symptoms.[47]

Lithium has a poor therapeutic index, which means that the dose required to relieve manic symptoms is very close to adverse and even toxic levels. At clinical dose levels, manic patients will typically experience the effects mentioned above and more. The most frequently observed side effect to lithium therapy is tremor, which is typically seen early in treatment and will abate within the first two weeks of treatment.[81] Other signs include dry mouth, frequent urination,[74] and GI tract upset, seen as nausea, vomiting, or diarrhea, due to the fact that lithium irritates the GI tract.[80]

EFFECTS ON THE CENTRAL NERVOUS SYSTEM

Lithium has a variety of effects. Precisely which one(s) account for the clinical relief of mania has yet to be determined. Lithium, a positively charged ion, can substitute for other positively charged ions like sodium, potassium, calcium, and magnesium,[79] all of which play critical roles in brain functioning. Lithium can be transported by the sodium-potassium-ATPase pump in neurons,[79] which maintains the proper ionic environment of the neuron so it is able to communicate. Lithium enhances the reuptake of norepinephrine (NE) at the synapse and may even decrease the amount of NE released when the cell fires.[80] Lithium will also decrease the synthesis and release of acetylcholine (ACh) at those synapses that use ACh.[79] It increases the reuptake of serotonin as well.[80] The amount of calcium in the presynaptic terminal is a necessary factor in the release of any neurotransmitter, and lithium will decrease the amount of calcium available presynaptically.[79] Which of these effects, if any, is responsible for the clinical actions of lithium is not known.

WITHDRAWAL

There are no reports of any withdrawal syndrome associated with the abrupt discontinuation of lithium treatment.

TOXIC EFFECTS

We have listed some of the adverse effects usually observed with lithium treatment. As we have also mentioned, clinical doses of lithium are close to toxic levels. The first symptoms that precede a toxic reaction to lithium are a worsening of the hand tremor or having the tremor spread to other parts of the body, incoordination, inability to articulate, due to spasticity in the muscles used for speaking, disorientation, muscle twitching, dizziness, and involuntary contractions of the face muscles.[79]

If the condition is allowed to continue, severe lithium toxicity would elicit confusion, convulsions, delirium, and eventually coma and death.[79] This is why monitoring the patient and blood levels of lithium is so important during treatment.

REVIEW EXAM

1. What is the hibernation syndrome?
2. Describe the difference between hallucinations and delusions.
3. Name the typical routes of administration for the antipsychotic medications.
4. What are the common half-lifes for the antipsychotics?
5. What are the specific effects of the antipsychotics on the PNS and CNS?
6. What are the dopamine systems that may be involved in psychotic behavior?
7. Characterize the dopamine receptors that are affected by the antipsychotic medications.
8. Name three nonbehavioral effects following antipsychotic medication.
9. Which psychotic symptoms seem to respond to the antipsychotic medications?
10. Characterize each of the four motor problems associated with the antipsychotic medications.

11. Describe the dopamine theory of schizophrenia.

12. How does clozapine differ from the other antipsychotic medications?

13. Describe the principal symptoms of depressed and manic mood disorders.

14. Compare the half-life of traditional tricyclic antidepressants to that of Prozac® and Zoloft®.

15. Describe how the two types of tricyclic antidepressants alter brain functioning at the synapse.

16. How do the newer heterocyclic antidepressants alter brain functioning at the synapse?

17. Describe the withdrawal symptoms associated with the antidepressants.

18. Describe the nonbehavioral adverse effects of the tricyclic antidepressants and of the MAOIs.

19. Describe the three stages of the cheese reaction.

20. Describe two of the four adverse behavioral effects associated with the antidepressants.

21. Compare the monoamine theory of mood disorder with the beta-adrenergic theory of mood disorder.

22. What are the main advantages and disadvantages of electroconvulsive shock therapy (ECT)?

23. How does sodium intake influence lithium excretion?

24. Name the subjective feelings that lithium elicits from normal nonmanic individuals.

25. How does lithium alter brain functioning?

26. What are the signs that precede a toxic reaction to Lithium®?

REFERENCES

1. HOLLISTER, L. (1977). Antipsychotic medications and treatment of schizophrenia. In J. Barchas, P. Berger, R. Ciaranello, & G. Elliot (Eds.), *Psychopharmacology: From Theory to Practice* (pp. 121–150). New York: Oxford Press.

2. RIFKIN, A. (1987). Extrapyramidal side effects: a historical perspective. *Journal of Clinical Psychiatry,* 48 (Suppl. 9), 3–6.

3. LADER, M. (1983). Antipsychotic drugs. In *Introduction to Psychopharmacology* (pp. 51–67). Kalamazoo, MI: The Upjohn Co.

4. DELAY, J., DENIKER, P., & HARL, J. (1952). Utilisation en therapeutique psychiatrique d'une phenothiazine d'action centrale elective. *Annals of Medical Psychology,* 110, 112–117.

5. HOLLISTER, R. (1987). Strategies for research in clinical psychopharmacology. In H. Meltzer (Ed.), *Psychopharmacology: The Third Generation* (pp. 31–38). New York: Raven Press.

6. BALDESSARINI, R. (1980). Drugs and the treatment of psychiatric disorders. In A. Gilman & L. Goodman (Eds.), *The Pharmacological Basis of Therapeutics* (6th ed., pp. 391–447). New York: Macmillan Publishing Co., Inc.

7. CREESE, I., BURT, D., & SNYDER, S. (1976). Dopamine receptor binding predicts clinical and pharmacological potencies of antischizophrenic drugs. *Science,* 192, 481–482.

8. CREESE, I. (1985). Receptor binding as a primary drug screen. In H. Yamamura, S. Enna, & M. Kuhar (Eds.), *Neurotransmitter Receptor Binding* (pp. 189–233). New York: Raven Press.

9. KANDEL, E. (1991). Disorders of thought: schizophrenia. In E. Kandel, J. Schwartz, & T. Jessell (Eds.), *Principles of Neural Science* (3rd ed., pp. 853–868). Norwalk, CT: Appleton and Lange.

10. BYCK, R. (1975). Drugs and the treatment of psychiatric disorders. In A. Gilman & L. Goodman (Eds.), *The Pharmacological Basis of Therapeutics* (5th ed., pp. 152–200). New York: Macmillan Publishing Co., Inc.

11. MELTZER, H. (1973). Rigidity, hyperpyrexia, and coma following fluphenazine enanthate. *Psychopharmacologia,* 29, 337–346.

12. CARFAGNO, S., & MCGEE, J. (1961). Granulocytopenia due to chlorpromazine: a report of 11 cases. *American Journal of Medical Science,* 241, 44–54.

13. PISCIOTTA, A., EBBE, S., LENNON, E., METZGER, G., & MADISON, F. (1958). Agranulocytosis after administration of phenothiazine derivatives. *American Journal of Medicine, 25,* 210–223.
14. HOLLISTER, L. (1958). Allergic reactions to tranquilizing drugs. *Annals of Internal Medicine, 49,* 17–29.
15. CASEY, D. (1991). Neuroleptic drug-induced extrapyramidal syndromes and tardive dyskinesia. *Schizophrenia Research, 4,* 109–120.
16. VAN PUTTEN, T. (1974). Why do schizophrenic patients refuse to take their drugs? *Archives of General Psychology, 31,* 67–72.
17. FAHN, S. (1988). Concept and classification of dystonia. In S. Fahn, C. Marsden, & D. Caline (Eds.), *Advances in Neurology* (pp. 2–8).
18. KLEIN, D., GITTELMAN, R., QUITKIN, F., & RIFKIN, A. (Eds.). (1980). *Diagnosis and Drug Treatment of Psychiatric Disorders: Adults and Children* (2nd ed., pp. 174–214). Baltimore, MD: Williams & Wilkins.
19. LAVIN, M., & RIFKIN, A. (1992). Neuroleptic-induced Parkinsonism. In J. Kane & J. Lieberman (Eds.), *Adverse Effects of Psychotropic Drugs,* (pp. 175–188).
20. BURKE, R. (1992). Neuromuscular effects of neuroleptics: dystonia. In J. Kane & J. Lieberman (Eds.), *Adverse Effects of Psychotropic Drugs* (pp. 189–200). New York: Gilford Press
21. BARNES, T. (1992). Neuromuscular effects of neuroleptics: akathisia. In J. Kane & J. Lieberman (Eds.), *Adverse Effects of Psychotropic Drugs* (pp. 201–217). New York: Gilford Press
22. AYD, F. (1961). A survey of drug-induced extrapyramidal reaction. *Journal of the American Medical Association, 175,* 1054–1060.
23. VAN PUTTEN, T., MAY, P., & MARDER, S. (1984). Akathisia with haloperidol and thiothixene. *Archives of General Psychiatry, 41,* 1036–1039.
24. BIANCHINE, J. (1980). Drugs for Parkinson's disease: centrally acting muscle relaxants. In A. Gilman & L. Goodman (Eds.), *The Pharmacological Basis of Therapeutics,* (6th ed. pp. 475–493). New York: Macmillan Publishing Co., Inc.
25. YASSA, R., NAIR, V., & SCHWARTZ, G. (1984). Tardive dyskinesia: a two-year follow-up study. *Psychosomatics, 25,* 852–855.
26. SALTZ, B., WOERNER, M., KANE J., LIEBERMAN, J., ALVIN, J., BERGMANN, K., BLANK, K., KOBLENZER, J., & KAHANER, K. (1991). Prospective study in tardive dyskinesia in the elderly. *Journal of the American Medical Association, 266,* 2402–2406.
27. KANE, J., WOERNER, M., WEINHOLD, P., WEGNER, J., & KINON, B. (1984). Incidence of tardive dyskinesia: five-year data from a prospective study. *Psychopharmacology Bulletin, 20(3),* 387–389.
28. KANE, J., WOERNER, M., & BORENSTEIN, M. (1986). Integrating incidence and prevalence of tardive dyskinesia. *Psychopharmacology Bulletin, 22(1),* 254–258.
29. GERLICH, J., REISBY, N., & RANDRUP, A. (1974). Dopaminergic hypersensitivity and cholinergic hypofunction in the pathophysiology of tardive dyskinesia. *Psychopharmacologia, 34,* 21–35.
30. KANE, J., & LIEBERMAN, J. (1992). Tardive dyskinesia. In J. Kane & J. Lieberman (Eds.), *Adverse Effects of Psychotropic Drugs* (pp. 235–245). New York: Gilford Press
31. CONLEY, R., SCHULZ, S., BAKER, R., COLLINS, J., & BELL J. (1988). Clozapine efficacy in schizophrenic nonresponders. *Psychopharmacology Bulletin, 24(2),* 269–274.
32. KANE, J., HONIGFELD, G., SINGER, J., & MELTZER, H. (1989). Clozapine for the treatment-resistant schizophrenic: results of a U.S. multicenter trial. *Psychopharmacology, 99,* S60–S63.
33. SAFFERMAN, A., LIEBERMAN, J., KANE, J., SZYMANSKI, S., & KINON, B. (1991). Update on clinical efficacy and side effects of clozapine. *Schizophrenia Bulletin, 17,* 247–262.
34. LIEBERMAN, J., SALTZ, C., JOHNS, C., POLLACK, S., BORENSTEIN, M., & KANE, J. (1991). The effect of clozapine on tardive dyskinesia. *British Journal of Psychiatry, 158,* 503–510.
35. CLAGHORN, J., HONIGFELD, G, & ABUZZAHAB, F. (1987). The risks and benefits of clozapine versus chlorpromazine. *Journal of Clinical Psychopharmacology, 7,* 377–384.
36. MELTZER, H. (1992). Pattern of efficacy in treatment-resistant schizophrenia. In H. Meltzer (Ed.), *Novel Antipsychotic Drugs* (pp. 33–46). New York: Raven Press.
37. SEEMAN, P., LEE, T., CHAN-WONG, M., & WONG, K. (1976). Antipsychotic drug doses and neuroleptic/dopamine receptors. *Nature, 261,* 717–718.
38. FARDE, L., WIESEL, F., NORDSTROM, A., & SEDVALL, G. (1989). D-1 and D-2 dopamine receptor occupancy during treatment with conventional and atypical neuroleptics. *Psychopharmacology, 99,* S28–S31.

39. MELTZER, H. (1992). The mechanism of action of clozapine in relation to its clinical advantages. In H. Meltzer (Ed.), *Novel Antipsychotic Drugs* (pp. 2–13). New York: Raven Press.
40. MILLER, R., & HILEY, C. (1976). Antimuscarinic properties of neuroleptics and drug-induced Parkinsonism. *Nature, 248,* 596–597.
41. KRUPP, P., & BARNES, P. (1989). Leponex-associated agranulocytopenia: a review of the situation. *Psychopharmacology, 99,* S118–S121.
42. HENINGER, G. (1993). The biologic basis of major affective disorders: an overview. In *Neurobiology of Affective Disorders* (pp. 2–6). New York: Raven Health Care Communications, a division of Raven Press.
43. KHUN, R. (1958). The treatment of depressed states with G22355 (imipramine hydrochloride). *American Journal of Psychiatry, 115,* 459–464.
44. LADER, M. (1983). *Introduction to Psychopharmacology* (pp. 68–89). Kalamazoo, MI: The Upjohn Co.
45. BENET, L., & SHEINER, L. (1980). Design and optimization of dosage regimens: pharmacokinetic data. In A. Gilman & L. Goodman (Eds.), *The Pharmacological Basis of Therapeutics* (6th ed., pp. 1675–1737). New York: Macmillan Publishing Co., Inc.
46. VAN HERTEN, J. (1993). Clinical pharmacokinetics of selective serotonin reuptake inhibitors. *Clinical Pharmacokinetics, 24*(3), 203–220.
47. KLEIN, D., GITTELMAN, R., QUITKIN, F., & RIFKIN, A. (Eds.). (1980). Review of the literature on mood-stabilizing drugs. In *Diagnosis and Drug Treatment of Psychiatric Disorders: Adults and Children* (2nd ed., pp. 268–408). Baltimore, MD: Williams & Wilkins.
48. FRAZER, A. (1993). Regionally selective effects in brain of typical and atypical antidepressants. In *Neurobiology of Affective Disorders* (pp. 17–21). New York: Raven Health Care Communications, a division of Raven Press.
49. KLERMAN, G., & COLE, J. (1965). Clinical pharmacology of imipramine and related antidepressant compounds. *Pharmacology Reviews, 17,* 101–141.
50. SHATAN, C. (1966). Withdrawal symptoms after abrupt termination of imipramine. *Canadian Psychiatric Association Journal, 11* (suppl.), S150–S158.
51. FRENKEL, A., QUITKIN, F., & RABKIN, J. (1992). Behavioral side effects associated with antidepressants and lithium. In J. Kane & J. Lieberman (Eds.), *Adverse Effects of Psychotropic Drugs* (pp. 111–127). New York: Gilford Press
52. PALLADINO, A. (1983). Adverse reactions to abrupt discontinuation with phenelzine. *Journal of Clinical Psychopharmacology, 3,* 206–207.
53. KLEIN, D., GITTELMAN, R., QUITKIN, F., & RIFKIN, A. (Eds.) (1980). Side effects of mood-stabilizing drugs and their treatment. In *Diagnosis and Drug Treatment of Psychiatric Disorders: Adults and Children* (2nd ed., pp. 449–492). Baltimore, MD: William & Wilkins.
54. MCGRATH, P., & HARRISON, W. (1992). Cardiovascular effects of monoamine oxidase inhibitor antidepressants and Lithium. In J. Kane & J. Lieberman (Eds.), *Adverse Effects of Psychotropic Drugs* (pp. 298–317). New York: Gilford Press
55. SOLOFF, P., GEORGE, A., NATHAN, R., SCHULZ, P., & PEREL, J. (1986). Paradoxical effects of amitriptyline on borderline patients. *American Journal of Psychiatry, 143,* 1603–1605.
56. COLE, J., & BODKIN, J. (1990). Antidepressant drug side effects. *Journal of Clinical Psychiatry, 51,* 21–26.
57. ZITRIN, C., KLEIN, D., & WOERNER, M. (1980). Treatment of agoraphobia with group exposure in vivo and imipramine. *Archives of General Psychiatry, 37,* 63–72.
58. ZUBENKO, G., COHEN, B., & LIPINSKI, J. (1987). Antidepressant-related akathisia. *Journal of Clinical Psychopharmacology 7,* 254–257.
59. KUPFER, D., SPIKER, D., COBEL, P., & MCPARTLARD, R. (1978). Amitriptyline and EEG sleep in depressed patients. *Sleep, 1*(2), 149–159.
60. KUPFER, D., SPIKER, D., COBEL, P., NEIL, J., ULRICH, R., & SHAW, D. (1981). Sleep treatment prediction in endogenous depression. *American Journal of Psychiatry, 138,* 429–434.
61. LIPPMAN, S., MOSKOVITZ, R., & O'TUAMA, L. (1977). Tricyclic-induced myoclonus. *American Journal of Psychiatry, 134, 90–91.*
62. *CASAS, M., GARCIA-RIBERTA, C., ALVAREZ, E., UDINA, C., QUERALTO, J., & GRAU, J. (1987). Myoclonic movements as a side effect of treatment with therapeutic doses of clomipramine. International Clinical Psychopharmacology, 2, 333–336.*
63. PICKAR, D., MURPHY, D., COHEN, R., CAMPBELL, I., & LIPPER, S. (1982). Selective and nonselective monoamine oxidase inhibitors: behavioral disturbances during their administration to depressed patients. *Archives of General Psychiatry, 39,* 535–540.

64. SHEEHAN, D., CLAYCOMB, J., & KOURETAS, N. (1980–81). Monoamine oxidase inhibitors: prescription and patient management. *International Journal of Psychiatry in Medicine,* 10, 99–121.
65. SULSER, F. (1993). The aminergic "link hypothesis" of affective disorders: a molecular view of therapy-resistant depression. In *Neurobiology of Affective Disorders* (pp. 7–12). New York: Raven Health Care Communications, a division of Raven Press.
66. NELSON, J., MAZURE, C., BOWERS, M., & JATLOW, P. (1991). A preliminary open study of the combination of fluoxetine and desipramine for rapid treatment of major depression. *Archives of General Psychiatry,* 48, 303–307.
67. DE MONTIGNY, C. (1984). Electroconvulsive shock treatments enhance responsiveness of forebrain neurons to serotonin. *Journal of Pharmacology and Experimental Therapeutics,* 228, 230–234.
68. CHAPUT, Y., DE MONTIGNY, C., & BLIER, P. (1991). Presynaptic and postsynaptic modifications of the serotonin system by long-term administration of antidepressant treatments: an in vivo electrophysiological study in the rat. *Neuropsychopharmacology,* 5, 219–229.
69. DE MONTIGNY, C. (1993). Is the serotonin system still a promising target for the future of pharmacotherapy of affective disorders? In *Neurobiology of Affective Disorders* (pp. 22–26). New York: Raven Health Care Communications, a division of Raven Press.
70. MANN, J., & ARANGO, V. (1992). Integration of neurobiology and psychopathology in a unified model of suicidal behavior. *Journal of Clinical Psychopharmacology,* 12 (suppl.), 2S–7S.
71. MANN, J. (1993). The organization of noradrenergic and serotonergic receptor systems in the cerebral cortex of suicide victims: implications for the pathogenesis of suicidal behavior and depression. In *Neurobiology of Affective Disorders* (pp. 26–30). New York: Raven Health Care Communications, a division of Raven Press.
72. GULEVICH, G. (1977). Convulsive and coma therapies and psychosurgery. In J. Barchas, P. Berger, R. Ciaranello, & G. Elliott (Eds.), *Psychopharmacology: From Theory to Practice* (pp. 514–526). New York: Oxford Press.
73. SHAPIRA, B., CALEV, A., & LERER, B. (1991). Optimal use of electroconvulsive therapy: choosing a treatment schedule. *Psychiatric Clinics of North America,* 14(4), 935–946.
74. DAVIS, G., & GOLDMAN, B. (1992). Somatic therapies. In H. Goldman (Ed.), *Review of General Psychiatry* (3rd ed., pp. 370–390). Norwalk, CT: Appleton and Lange.
75. KHAN, A., MIROLO, M., HUGHES, D., & BIERUT, L. (1993). Electroconvulsive therapy. *Psychiatric Clinics of North America,* 16(3), 497–513.
76. DEVANAND, D., SACKEIM, H., & PRUDIC, J. (1991). Electroconvulsive therapy in the treatment-resistant patient. *Psychiatric Clinics of North America,* 14(4), 905–923.
77. SEAGER, C., & BIRD, R. (1962). Imipramine with electrical treatment in depression—a controlled trial. *Journal of Mental Science* 108, 704–707.
78. FAVA, M., & ROSENBAUM, J. (1991). Suicidality and fluoxetine: is there a relationship? *Journal of Clinical Psychiatry,* 52, 108–111.
79. LADER, M. (1983). Lithium. In *Introduction to Psychopharmacology* (pp. 90–94). Kalamazoo, MI: The Upjohn Co.
80. SACK, R., & DE FRAITES, E. (1977). Lithium and the treatment of mania. In J. Barchas, P. Berger, R. Ciaranello, & G. Elliott (Eds.), *Psychopharmacology: From Theory to Practice* (pp. 208–225). New York: Oxford Press.
81. LEMUS, C., & LIEBERMAN, J. (1992). Neuromuscular effects of antidepressants and lithium. In J. Kane & J. Lieberman (Eds.), *Adverse Effects of Psychotropic Drugs* (pp. 165–174). New York: Gilford Press

CHAPTER TEN
HALLUCINOGENS:
Drugs That Uniquely Alter Consciousness

GENERAL ISSUES ADDRESSED IN THIS CHAPTER

- Two ways of categorizing the various types of hallucinogens
- The aboriginal history of many of the hallucinogens
- The distribution and clearance of LSD, mescaline, and psilocin
- The pronounced effects of LSD, mescaline, and psilocin on the peripheral nervous system
- The effects of LSD, mescaline, and psilocin on the central nervous system
- The individual behavioral consequences of LSD, mescaline, and psilocin
- Tolerance to the use of LSD, mescaline, and psilocin
- Particular issues involved with dimethyltryptamine (DMT) and bufotenin
- The issue of flashbacks
- Pharmacological and behavioral consequences of phencyclidine (angel dust) use
- The misinformation concerning phencyclidine- (angel dust) induced aggression
- Designer drugs that are similar to the amphetamines and norepinephrine (NE)
- Pharmacological and behavioral consequences of MDA and MDMA (ecstasy) use
- Agents that alter the central nervous system and acetylcholine (ACh) system
- The peculiar case of *Amanita muscaria*—a hallucinogenic mushroom of the Euro-Asian continents
- Morning glory seeds (ololiuqui)—possible ancient hallucinogen

LIST OF DRUGS

1. Structurally similar to serotonin
   a. Lysergic acid diethylamide (LSD)
   b. Psilocin (from psilocybin)
   c. Dimethyltryptamine (DMT)
   d. Bufotenin (5-hydroxy-DMT)
   e. Lysergic acid amide
2. Structurally similar to norepinephrine
   a. Mescaline
   b. Designer drugs: DOM, MDMA (ecstasy), MDA
3. Drugs that block acetylcholine receptors
   a. Atropine
   b. Scopolamine
4. Miscellaneous
   a. Ibotenic acid
   b. Muscimol
   c. Phencyclidine (Sernyl, PCP, "angel dust")

INTRODUCTION

A hallucination is a perception of an object, sound, and/or another sensation that is not based on reality; in other words, a person sees things that are not really there, hears sounds in the absence of anything capable of generating sounds, or feels touch sensations in the absence of anything actually touching the skin. There are certain mental disorders and some epileptic conditions for which experiencing hallucinations is not uncommon. In addition, certain drugs will produce hallucinations in otherwise normal people and are aptly named hallucinogens.

Western culture has never accepted the use of hallucinogens, and despite the fact that these drugs pose no threat of lethality, as a class, hallucinogens are feared and strictly forbidden. In the United States, the major hallucinogens are classified as Schedule I—the drugs with the highest perceived potential of dependency which carry the strictest penalties for possession. The term hallucinogens conjures up a cultural image of drug abuse and of teenagers being incapacitated by a stupor of kaleidoscopic distortions. To view hallucinogens merely as drugs of abuse is to not fully appreciate their long history and functional role in aboriginal cultures in Central and South America (see the next section on history).

Two of the principal classes of hallucinogens are structurally similar to the naturally existing brain neurotransmitters serotonin (5-HT) and norepinephrine (NE). Figures 10–1 and 10–2 illustrate these structural similarities, Figure 10–1 for those hallucinogens similar to 5-HT and Figure 10–2 for those similar to NE. Notice how a common trend in both of these classes of hallucinogens is the addition of methyl groups (CH_3) to the basic molecular shape. For example, note how the addition of methyl groups to the basic serotonin molecule yields psilocin, and, when added to the basic norepinephrine molecule, yields mescaline. How this seemingly minor change in the shape of a normal neurotransmitter can produce a drug with such intense behavioral consequences remains a mystery.

These molecular similarities are the basis for one classification scheme of hallucinogens in which these drugs are subclassified: 1. Those hallucinogens that are structurally similar to serotonin; 2. Those hallucinogens that are structurally similar to norepinephrine; and 3. Those hallucinogens that are not structurally similar to either of these neurotransmitters. Some would include a fourth class of hallucinogens, which are blockers of the acetylcholine receptor.

The hallucinogens are not equally capable of producing frank hallucinations. Another categorization of hallucinogens could be a functional one, namely what drugs produce the most potent hallucinations. The major hallucinogens are LSD, mescaline, and psilocin. Clearly, no other drugs are as powerful as these. Just how to subdivide the remaining hallucinogens in terms of their potency in producing hallucinations is difficult. The next tier* of hallucinogens may include phencyclidine

---

*The term minor hallucingens should be avoided since it may minimize the concern one should have for any of the drugs in this class and give the wrong impression that there is no risk involved in taking them.

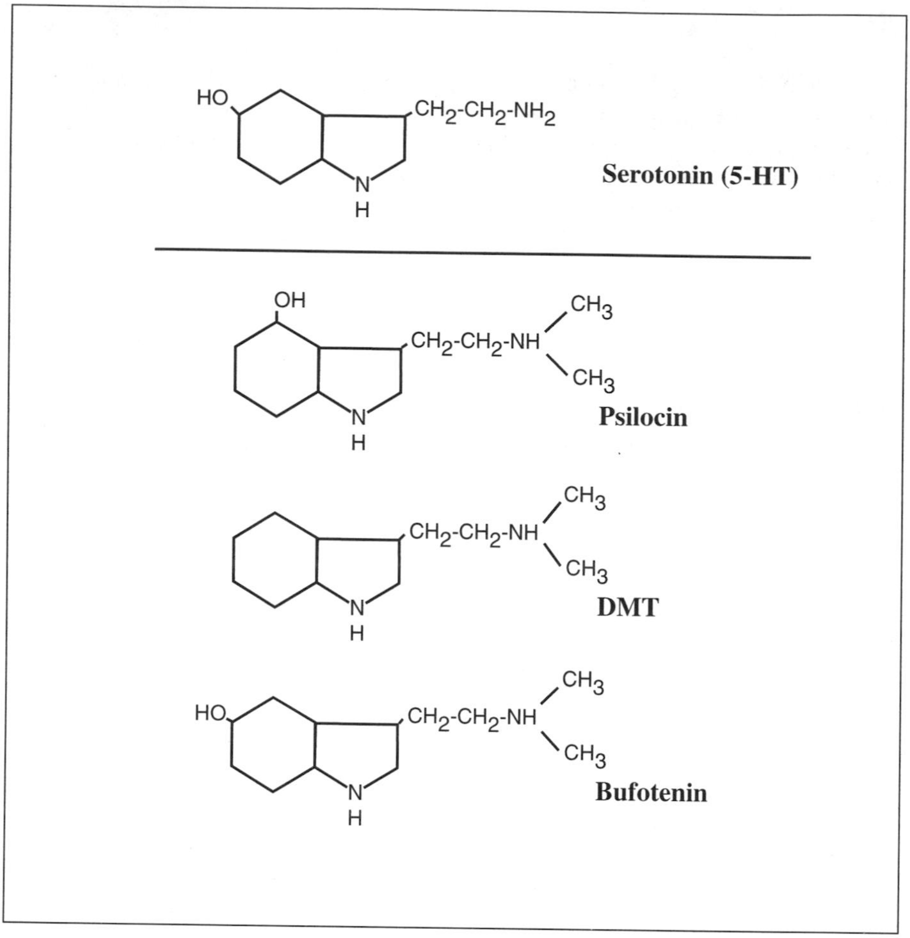

FIGURE 10–1   The Molecular Shape of Serotonin and Certain Hallucinogens
The addition of methyl groups (CH_3) to the serotonin molecule produces hallucinogens like psilocin, DMT, and bufotenin.

("angel dust"), which is in a class by itself, the reasons for which will be discussed in the Special Issues section later. The following tier may include DMT, bufotenin, ibotenic acid, muscimol, and the "designer drugs," which are analogs of NE. The last tier may include lysergic acid amide, myristicin, and the acetylcholine receptor blockers. Such a functional breakdown would not be without argument as hallucinations are such a subjective outcome. There are some who would say that ethanol produces hallucinations, that is, the folklore of little pink elephants associated with ethanol intoxication. Another sedative, marijuana, is categorized incorrectly by many as a hallucinogen, even though its ability to induce true hallucinations is comparable to ethanol. Also consider the fact that initially tobacco was considered a hallucinogen by the Spanish conquistadors when they first observed the practice of smoking.

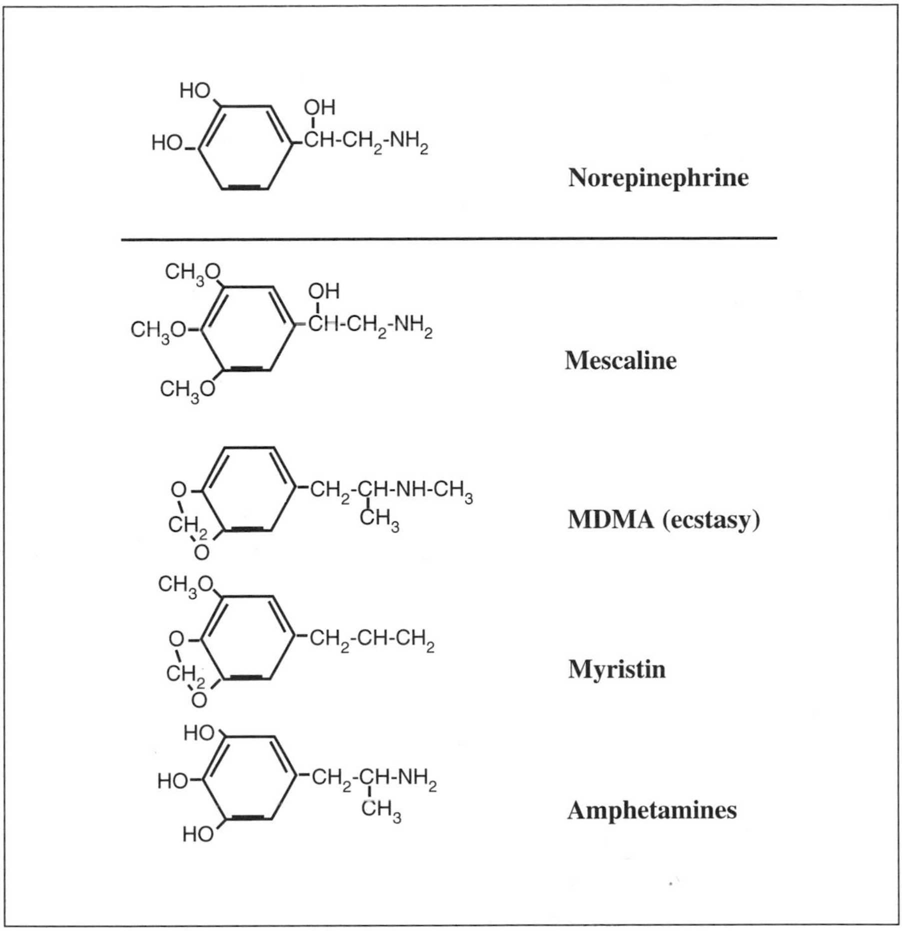

FIGURE 10–2   The Molecular Shape of Norepinephrine and Certain Hallucinogens
Just as with serotonin, the addition of methyl groups to the norepinephrine molecule
also produces hallucinogens like mescaline. Notice that myristin, one of the components
of nutmeg, is similar to MDMA (ecstasy).

SOURCES AND HISTORY

With the noted exceptions of phencyclidine and the designer drugs that are analogs of norepinephrine/amphetamine, the other hallucinogens are found extensively in nature. The worldwide distribution of plants that are sources of hallucinogens present an interesting question. There are almost 100 different species of hallucinogenic plants in the "new" world, that is, the Americas, which is in sharp contrast to the mere handful, less than ten, of plant sources of hallucinogens in the "old" world, namely Euro-Asian continents.[1] This striking disparity in world distribution begs an explanation. Some have hypothesized that the Judeo-Christian, Islamic, and other religious traditions of the old world did not (and still do not) provide a place in their culture for hallucinogenic experiences, whereas the aboriginal religious cultures of South, Central, and North American natives did.[1] These new world cultures valued the role of the shaman, who was the seer, spiritual leader, and advisor of the tribe. The use of hallucinogens in this spiritual sense was essential in communicating with spirits and deities.[2] Thus, hallucinogenic use was not in the context of abuse or recreation but rather in a religious ritual that demanded respect.

The Sacred Mushrooms of Ancient Central America— The Source of Psilocin

It is difficult to precisely date the use of mushrooms in religious ceremonies in aboriginal tribes that populated what is now Mexico, Central America, and northern South America. It was the Spanish conquerors in the seventeenth century who first described the intoxicating mushrooms that were religiously respected by the Indians of central Mexico.[3] The cultural belief that certain mushrooms were sacred is believed to have been established in 1000 B.C..[4] The Aztec term for these hallucinogenic mushrooms is teonanacatl (meaning "God's flesh"), and they were used to communicate with the spirits and gods. The importance of specific mushrooms to the society is evidenced by the numerous cultural images of mushrooms, especially the discovery of mushroom sculptures found in burial[5] and other archeological sites. These stone mushrooms have been found in Guatemala,[6] Mexico,[7] El Salvador,[8] Honduras, and Peru.[5] So accurate are these sculptured images that the specific types of mushrooms can be identified. The species of hallucinogenic mushrooms are the *Psilocybe* family, *Psilocybe mexicana* especially, and *Stropharia cubensis*.[9]

Peyote Cacti—The Source of Mescaline

The use of hallucinogenic cacti has an ancient tradition in South, Central, and North America, as well as in Mexico. The art, primarily done on pottery and textiles, of the aboriginal people of the Andes depicts hallucinogenic cacti as early as 1000 B.C.[10] In Mexico, similar images of these cacti date to around 100 B.C.[11] The religious use of hallucinogenic cacti spread from the aboriginal tribes of Mexico, referred to as "mescaleros," to other native American cultures in North America and as far north as Canada.[11] The colonization, that is, conquering, of this area by the Spanish in the seventeenth century was accompanied by the introduction of Christianity into these cultures. Although the Catholic Church prohibited the use of hallucinogens, especially in what was considered "pagan rituals," the religious use of hallucinogenic cacti resisted this pressure and remains today. The use of hallucinogenic cacti by the Native American Church in its ceremonies has been the center of a prolonged legal battle that is still active. The most recent ruling of the Supreme Court is that the use of peyote can be banned, even within the context of religious use, by the Native American Church.[12]

Perhaps the best-known of the hallucinogenic cacti is *Lophophora williamsii*, also known as peyote. Distinctive because of its lack of spines, this cactus grows in the deserts of southern North America, Central America, and Mexico. The term peyote, which is derived from the Aztec word *peyotl,* refers to a variety of medicinal plants, in addition to *Lophophora williamsii.* Some have argued that the term *hikuri* is a more accurate word for *Lophophora williamsii.*[11]

Rye Grain Fungus and the Discovery of LSD

Lysergic acid diethylamide (LSD) is sometimes referred to as a semisynthetic substance because one of its principal components is a natural product from a fungus that grows especially well on rye grain and on other grains and grasses. The particular fungus or ergot is *Claviceps purpura,* and it contains lysergic acid.

Whether or not lysergic acid in this form can itself be hallucinogenic is doubtful, however, there is a literature concerning ergot poisoning or ergotism, that might provide some insight into this matter.[13,14] Cultivating and preparing grains for bread and other food stuffs has an ancient history, and one would reason that accounts of fungal contamination of these grains should have as long a history. While there are many suggestive historical references from ancient Greek, Roman, and Chinese sources, not only of ergot poisonings but also of the medicinal use of ergot preparations, it was not until the Middle Ages that better accounts were available. From the 900s A.D. through the 1300s A.D. there were numerous accounts of ergot poisonings throughout Europe, presumably due to eating fungus-infested grains. There appeared to be two forms of ergotism, one gangrenous, the other convulsive. In the gangrenous form, all body parts—hands and limbs, as well as parts of the face—were susceptible to cell death and eventual erosion. This was accompanied by a horrible smell and preceded by an excruciating, burning pain. This pain sensation was the basis for the many early names given to ergotism: Ignis sacer (sacred fire), ignis plaga (the fire plague), and ignis judicialis (the fire of justice). In addition, a host of the local patron saints to whom the individual community prayed became associated with ergotism outbreaks, producing such names as St. Martial's Fire, St. Martin's (Martin of Tours) Fire, the Virgin Mary's Fire, and perhaps the most popular, St. Anthony's Fire. In the convulsive form, ergotism had been described as severe, uncontrollable convulsions that could begin as a spasming of the hands or feet to simple spasms of the extremities that lasted only minutes.[14] Muscle spasms could in some cases affect the muscles of the face and vocal cords, which would produce visually impressive effects.[14] One of the reported outcomes of these convulsions was dementia in severe cases or mental dullness in less severe cases.[14]

Despite the fact that the cause of ergotism and the establishment of preventive measures occurred in Europe in the 1600s, outbreaks of ergotism persisted throughout the nineteenth century. Also of interest is that in the Middle Ages only the gangrenous type of ergotism was initially reported, but gradually there were more and more reports of the convulsive type, so by the 1700s the overwhelming majority, over 85 percent, reported ergotism of the convulsive type.[13]

One particular incident concerns the witchcraft trials in Salem, Massachusetts, in 1692. Eight girls were exhibiting odd behavior, including convulsions. The town officials considered these convulsions to be the work of local witches and subsequently executed nineteen people for practicing witchcraft.[15] Examination of the court proceedings and of the weather and farming records of that area led one investigator to suggest that the "possessed" girls may have been suffering from ergotism, the ingestion of a grain infected with the ergot fungus.[16] It is impossible to determine with certainty what exactly happened in Salem at that time and if ergotism was indeed involved. However, a similar incident occurred in Fairfield County, Connecticut, around this time, which led other investigators also to suspect ergot poisoning.[17]

The importance of the history of ergotism, in particular, the convulsive type, is demonstrated by the fact that something in this natural fungus can exert a powerful effect on the central nervous system. The experiments on this ergot fungus in the early 1940s yielded a compound that has the most potent effects on the brain than any drug ever examined.

The actual synthesis of LSD by Dr. Albert Hofmann occurred in 1938, but its discovery was not to happen until 1943.[18] In early spring of that year, Dr. Hofmann suddenly felt strange and went home, where he experienced an unusual intoxication, which progressed to "fantastic images." Recovering from this first-ever LSD "trip," which lasted only two hours, Hofmann guessed correctly that he must have ingested something at work. He thought the ergot derivatives he had been working on might be responsible. To test that hypothesis he purposefully consumed what he thought was a small dose but in fact was a very large dose of LSD. This time, the LSD intoxication lasted much longer, about six hours, and was quite intense. The specific description of his LSD experience is discussed later. This accidental ingestion and accurate deduction by Dr. Hofmann launched an entire field of research into hallucinogenic agents. It is important to remember that World War II was in its final stages and the military potential of LSD compelled officials to classify the work on LSD. It was not until 1947 that the general scientific and public communities heard of the effects of the hallucinogenic. The popularity of LSD as a recreational substance peaked in the late 1960s and early 1970s, fueled by strong advocates as well as by the example of highly visible popular performing artists and by the popularity of hippie/flower children types of lifestyles. While the popularity of LSD has dropped considerably since then, its use by young people has waxed and waned over the years. An important part of the history of LSD is the research conducted by the U.S. army, which began in the 1950s.[19] Some of this research involved exposing individuals to LSD without their knowledge, and the apparent attempt of the army to mass-produce millions of doses of LSD raised critical issues of the ethics and the morality of this type of research.[20]

An "Old World" Hallucinogenic Mushroom—*Amanita Muscaria*

The ancient legends of the Koryack tribes of the Siberian forests tell of a magic plant, which sprouted from the spittle of a god, that would enable anyone who consumed it to have a variety of powers, among which would be the ability to see the future or communicate with the underworld.[21] This plant was the distinctive mushroom *Amanita muscaria,* also known as "fly-agaric." In fact, it may very well be that *Amanita muscaria* is the sacred hallucinogenic plant of the ancient aboriginal Indo-European tribes, which would date its use to before 2000 B.C..[22] The use of *Amanita muscaria* by Siberian tribes continued through the nineteenth century, when the modernization of these areas by outside commercial traders and political events introduced ethanol as an alternate intoxicant.[21]

The Minor Hallucinogens—DMT and Bufotenin

Aboriginal tribes form Mexico, Central, and South America had used hallucinogenic snuffs in various religious and hunting rituals. Pipes, spoons, and other devices apparently designed for snuffing, a type of ancient snuffing paraphernalia if you will, have been recovered from various archeological expeditions in those areas. These discoveries have helped date the use of hallucinogenic snuffs there. One of the earliest snuffing artifacts was recovered in Peru and is dated to approximately 1600 B.C.[23] Similar artifacts have been found in Costa Rica, Chile, Argentina, and Brazil.[24] The evidence for ancient snuffing devices in Mexico is curious. Archeological findings in Oaxaca and Olmec indicate that snuffing may have been a part of that culture early on, around 2000 B.C., but by 1000 A.D. this method of intoxication ceased.[23]

Although there may be a variety of sources of these ancient hallucinogenic snuffs, there appear to be two plants of particular importance: 1. *Anadenanthera peregrina* and *Anadenanthera colubrina*; and 2. a variety of species of the *Virola* tree, especially *Virola theidora.* The seeds of the A. peregrina and A. colubrina contain both dimethyltryptamine and bufotenin, while the bark of the Virola tree also contains the highest concentrations of these agents, as well as 5-methoxy-dimethyl-tryptamine, still another potential hallucinogen.[25]

It should be noted that bufotenin also is found in the skin of certain toads, among which is *Bufo marinus;* and 5-methoxy-dimethyl-tryptamine has been isolated in the skin of the toad *Bufo alvarius.* That aboriginal cultures of Mexico knew this and made use of this source of hallucinogens is suggested by the archeological discovery, dating to approximately 1250 B.C., of the skeletal remains of a great many toads, specifically *Bufo marinus,* at an Olmec ceremonial site.[26]

Since the most potent hallucinogens are LSD, mescaline, and psilocin, these drugs will be discussed in detail first. Of these three hallucinogens, LSD has been the most studied.

LSD, MESCALINE, AND PSILOCIN ABSORPTION, DISTRIBUTION, AND BIOTRANSFORMATION

LSD, mescaline, and psilocin can all be absorbed rapidly from the GI tract, thus oral administration is the most common method used. As we shall see later, oral routes are not always the most efficient for the other hallucinogens.

LSD distributes well to the various tissue compartments but only about 1 percent of an ingested dose crosses into the brain compartment, and the highest concentrations are in the liver.[15] This is a striking characteristic when one considers the extremely low doses that are ingested. Doses of LSD that are capable of inducing effects can be as small as 20 micrograms,[27] but usually range from 50 to 100 micrograms.[28] There is no other drug that can elicit such dramatic effects in such minute quantities.

Excretion is rather fast for the hallucinogens, as is reflected in their relatively brief half-lifes. The half-life for LSD has been reported to be as short as three hours[15] and as long as five hours.[29] It is not certain what the precise half-lifes are for mescaline and psilocin. Much of mescaline is excreted unchanged, and it has been shown that peak excretion occurs within six hours.[30] The duration of the effects of these drugs is relatively short. For LSD, it is approximately twelve hours, similar to the six to eight hours of effects elicited by mescaline.[31] Psilocin, however, has a shorter duration of effects, approximately two to four hours.[31]

EFFECTS ON THE PERIPHERAL NERVOUS SYSTEM

One common feature of LSD, mescaline, and psilocin is that they each elicit a pattern similar to a sympathetic arousal state. Thus, the peripheral nervous system appears to be a major target for these drugs. The specific behaviors observed after ingestion include: increased heart rate, dilated pupils, restlessness or arousal, increased body temperature, headache, sweating and chills, and nausea.[15]

This stimulation of the sympathetic nervous system is not like the sympathomimetic properties of the stimulants amphetamines or cocaine (see chapter 8). In the case of the stimulant drugs, direct stimulation of peripheral structures like the heart was the cause of severe toxicity. The hallucinogens are quite different. There is virtually no direct lethality associated with LSD, mescaline, or psilocin.[32] There have been no reports of human lethality attributed directly to any of these drugs.* However, given the intensity of some of the hallucinatory responses by some individuals, the risk of experiencing a panic reaction is relatively high. If adequate support is not available to a user undergoing a panic reaction, that person may engage in behavior that may lead to serious injury. One of the truly regrettable and arguably one of the most immoral episodes in armed forces drug research was the experiments in which individuals were given LSD without their consent or knowledge. One result was a suicide by a person who was overcome by intense hallucinations, without receiving any context or support.[19] Such a dire reaction is certainly not an invariant consequence of hallucinogen use and not a pharmacological outcome of the drug. As we have seen above, Hofmann experienced high-dose LSD hallucinations without

---

*There was an infamous case in which an elephant was given an inappropriately high dose of LSD in an attempt to elicit a behavioral pattern similar to that of elephants that seasonally "run amuck." Dr. J. West calculated the dose based on what was given to small rodents. Such a common "milligram of drug per kilogram of body weight" dosing protocol cannot be translated across species, and the result was the death of the elephant.

preparation or support, and he did not have a panic reaction. However, individuals will vary in terms of their specific reactions to the types of hallucinations experienced under the influence of these drugs, and the possibility of panic reactions must be prepared for prior to taking a drug of this kind.

EFFECTS ON THE CENTRAL NERVOUS SYSTEM

The specific effects of hallucinogens on brain functioning has been extensively studied in those hallucinogens that structurally resemble serotonin, in comparison to those hallucinogens that are structurally related to norepinephrine.

LSD and psilocin.   The effects of these hallucinogens appear to be mediated by serotonin (5-HT) receptors.[33] Recall that there are a variety of serotonin receptor types. Of interest to this discussion are the 5-HT-2 and 5-HT-1A and 5-HT-1C receptors. The 5-HT-2 and 5-HT-1A receptors are located throughout the brain but are found in particularly high densities in the cerebral cortex and in several key limbic structures.[34] It is important to note that the specific receptors suspected to be involved in the mediation of the effects of hallucinogens are not located in the cerebral cortical areas that process sensory information, be it visual or auditory cortices.

LSD appears to be a specific 5-HT-2 receptor antagonist and a 5-HT-1A and 5-HT-1C agonist.[35] In fact, the potency of LSD, and of DMT, to induce hallucinations is correlated to how vigorously these drugs bind to 5-HT-2 receptors.[36] The consequence of antagonizing or hindering 5-HT-2 receptors and of agonizing or driving 5-HT-1A and 5-HT-1C has been difficult to assess. The overall effect seems to be a dampening of serotonin activity. Chronic doses of LSD or psilocin induce the "down regulation," that is, decreased number of 5-HT-2 receptors without effecting 5-HT-1A or 5-HT-1C, or norepinephrine or dopamine receptors.[37] Moreover, LSD has been found to suppress serotonin transmission in general.[38]

Mescaline.   It is not clear precisely what brain receptors are directly affected by mescaline. In the periphery, it has been shown that mescaline blocks the release of acetylcholine (ACh) in muscle.[39] In the brain, mescaline does not effect 5-HT-2 receptors as does LSD or psilocin.[37]

BEHAVIORAL CONSEQUENCES

In addition to the sympathetic responses discussed preceding, the other main behavioral effect of this class of drugs is a profound distortion of perception, typically visual perceptions.* There are several distinct features of the behavioral consequences following LSD, mescaline, and psilocin, thus these agents will be individually addressed.

*If one defines hallucination in a very strict way as the perception of objects without any reality base, then none of the drugs in this class actually induce true hallucinations. Rather, these drugs will cause the distorted perceptions of objects that are really there.

LSD.   One of the few phenomenological accounts of the behavioral consequences of LSD not tainted by user expectation or the environment in which the drug
was taken are the accounts of Dr. Albert Hofmann, when he accidentally ingested
LSD and became the first person to experience this potent drug. With his precise
notes of that event and subsequent experiments with LSD, there is some critical information beyond the mere documentation of symptoms. The very first experience,
the accidental ingestion of LSD, caused Dr. Hofmann to leave work early because of
a feeling of restlessness and dizziness. At home, Dr. Hofmann experienced a state of
drunkenness that he characterized as not unpleasant, intense kaleidoscopic experiences of fantastic images and colors, and a state similar to an overactive imagination.[15] Nobody knows just how much LSD was ingested to induce this, the world's
first LSD experience. However, the following Monday, Dr. Hofmann purposefully
ingested 0.25 mg (or 250 micrograms) to see if in fact the LSD was the cause of his
unusual experience. His subsequent LSD experience was more intense than the first
one. This time the visual distortions were constantly changing in color, as if the objects were being reflected on water. It was not a pleasant experience. Moreover, Dr.
Hofmann noted that auditory stimuli were converted into visual effects. The next
morning, Dr. Hofmann was fine, showing no lingering effects of the experience.
Three significant findings from Dr. Hofmann's first LSD experiences merit attention:
1. He did not have a panic reaction; 2. He was fully recovered by the next morning;
and 3. He apparently did not experience flashbacks later on. These are important
points, given the misinformation that government agencies had distributed concerning the dangers of LSD use.

There are several general characteristics of an LSD experience. Perhaps the
principal characteristic is that objects are perceived in a distorted way, which has
been described as a kaleidoscopic display of colors and form, or similar to the re-
flections from curved mirrors often used in amusement parks and funhouses. Cross
modal experiences such as seeing sound and hearing colors also are often described.
There appears to be a strong emotional component to an LSD experience, which can
be intensely positive or negative and can swing in either direction during the experience. While there may be an impairment of intellectual processing, consciousness is
not lost, nor is volitional and cognitive control. For example, a person on the verge of
a panic reaction can respond to the comforting words of a supportive friend. The intoxication following LSD has been described as a state of drunkenness, independent
of the occurrence of hallucinations. The reported disintegration of time may be a
common feature of intoxication in general, since this also is reported with marijuana
use and ethanol intoxication.

It has been suggested[27] that there is a time course for these effects, beginning
with an almost immediate period of emotional release and excitation that can be euphoric and last up to an hour. This is followed by a period of visual distortions and other
hallucinatory effects commonly attributed to LSD use which may last for an additional
two hours. The last phase is one that may be marked by emotional swings, which may
be adverse. This temporal scheme of events is not invariant and will of course depend
on the individual's expectations and environment (i.e., the user's set and setting).

Regardless of the sequence, the duration of the LSD experience can be as short as six hours[28] or as long as twelve hours.[27]

Mescaline and psilocin.   The hallucinations produced by mescaline are somewhat different than those of LSD. Perhaps the most distinctive differences are the prominence of color in the hallucinations and that the hallucinations are consistent with actual experiences.[28] They are typically intensifications of the stimulus properties of objects and sounds. For example, ordinary colors of objects appear brilliant and intense. Unlike LSD, mescaline does not induce distortions of form or kaleidoscopic experiences. However, like LSD, mescaline can induce auditory stimuli to be perceived as color, and like LSD, the duration of mescaline's effects can last as long as twelve hours.[27]

The general characteristics of the hallucinations induced by psilocin are virtually identical to those induced by mescaline, however, the duration of its effects are comparatively short-lasting, approximately four hours.[15]

TOLERANCE AND WITHDRAWAL

Tolerance develops so rapidly to LSD that within a few days of repeated doses, the initial dose is ineffective.[15] However, tolerance will disappear as quickly as it takes to develop, and a few days of abstinence will return the effectiveness of the initial dose.[27] While it is not certain that mescaline and psilocin share this characteristic with LSD, there is a robust cross-tolerance among these three hallucinogens that does not extend to other hallucinogens, which further argues the point that they should be classified in the same category.

There is virtually no withdrawal syndrome seen when chronic use of any of these drugs is abruptly ceased.[27] As we have discussed in previous chapters, the absence of a withdrawal syndrome should not be taken as an indication that dependency cannot develop to any of these substances. However, in the case of these hallucinogens, dependency is not frequently a problem.

DIMETHYLTRYPTAMINE (DMT) AND BUFOTENIN

Aboriginal snuffs used by South and Central American natives contain a variety of components. Among the more important, in terms of inducing hallucinations, are dimethyltryptamine (DMT) and bufotenin (5-hydroxy-dimethyltryptamine). Although the plants used for these snuffs vary, they share some common features. One is an extremely rapid onset of intoxication, producing the following symptoms: increased perspiration, running nose, increased salivation, headache, vomiting, swelling and reddening of the face and limbs, excitation, tremors and ataxia, possible convulsions, and then stupor, in which the person experiences communication with supernatural forces like deceased relatives or spirits of animals, then a period of unconsciousness.[11,15] The latter communication with the supernatural has not always been experienced by Western researchers,[25] and it has been questioned whether true hallucinations actually are induced by these snuffs.[28] Another interesting feature of the snuffs is its short duration of effects. In addition, there appears to be little risk of dependency with these substances. One report indicates that although hallucinogenic snuffs can be used often, the tribe people can just as easily refrain from its use for weeks, without experiencing any symptoms of withdrawal or any cravings for the substances, which was not true for this particular tribe's experience with tobacco, which did elicit cravings and withdrawal symptoms.[40] When DMT and bufotenin are examined separately some further important characteristics emerge.

Dimethyltryptamine is not effective when taken orally, thus it must be administered parenterally. A moderately high dose of DMT, 50 mg to 100 mg, does induce hallucinations, euphoria, and uncontrolled compulsive motor behaviors, the entire syndrome lasting only one hour.[41] Oral doses of the same dose are not effective.[41] Some of the important differences between DMT and LSD are: 1. The rapid onset and short duration of the effects from DMT compared to LSD; 2. The unusual motor behavior seen with DMT, not seen with LSD; and 3. The hallucinations induced with DMT seems to be restricted to visual events, not the case with LSD.[28] Furthermore, there has been a provocative literature that reports DMT can be detected in the urine of schizophrenic patients when their symptoms become worse.[42] This suggests that there may be some inappropriate biotransformation of tryptamine in this population that perhaps may contribute to this pathology. In other words, schizophrenics may produce their own hallucinogenic substance. It should be remembered that this study did not find urinary DMT when there was a rapid worsening of behavior.[42]

Bufotenin is 5-hydroxy DMT and while structurally similar to DMT, it also is different from DMT, and all of the other hallucinogens in a very peculiar way. Bufotenin is the only hallucinogen that is also found in animals. It has been detected in the skin glands of certain frogs, *bufo marinus* and *bufo alvarius*.[11] When examined directly, parenteral IV bufotenin, at doses of 16 mg, has been shown to produce intense emotional and visual effects that have been described as "color visions."[43,44] There have been significant side effects reported as well, including nausea and vomiting.[43] It is not clear that oral administrations of bufotenin are ineffective, as is the case with DMT. There is evidence that the ancient use of toad skin secretions probably included potions and preparations that were orally ingested.[26,11] Furthermore, the relatively recent rediscovery of the presence of bufotenin in frog skin led to the practice of "toad licking" in the late 1980s,[45] which some contend can introduce enough bufotenin to cause hallucinations.[46] However, it seems clear from the parenteral administration accounts that the use of frog secretions, which in addition to containing bufotenin also are poisonous, leads to a different type of experience marked by severe toxicity, compared to snuffs that contain bufotenin.[11]

SPECIAL ISSUES

Flashbacks

The occurrence of flashbacks, that is, hallucinations experienced a long time after a dose of LSD, has been difficult to explain. It is clearly not the case that LSD is somehow accumulating in some body compartment and later released. Perhaps a more workable hypothesis is that a flashback may be similar to some aspects of post traumatic shock disorder (PTSD), in which an intense situation experienced in the past may be reexperienced years later. So similar is this symptom between LSD users and PTSD patients that some Vietnam returnees with flashback experiences have been misdiagnosed as LSD users, even though they had not taken LSD.[47] Perhaps the experiences while under the influence of LSD can be so emotional and intense, and even stressful, that LSD-induced flashbacks should be considered a type of PTSD. Subsequent research may help explain this commonly experienced LSD effect.

Phencyclidine—"Angel Dust"—Facts and Media Hype

Phencyclidine was initially developed as an anesthetic in the mid 1950s and was tested on humans in 1957.[48] The type of anesthesia produced by phencyclidine is termed a "dissociative anesthesia" and is quite different from the more traditional anesthetics. Essentially, the person experiences an intense detachment or dissociation from the immediate environment. In addition, phencyclidine often induces confusion, delirium, and, in some cases, a peculiar type of hallucination that makes it unacceptable for human use. Shortly after its introduction in the medical community, phencyclidine became a drug of abuse. In the mid 1960s, it was available only in tablet or capsule form, making it more difficult to avoid accidental overdoses. The introduction of phencyclidine in powder form in the 1970s allowed a more controlled dosing, and its popularity as an illicit drug grew.[49]

The issues surrounding phencyclidine have been hopelessly complicated by the campaign waged to control its illegal use. The strategy of "villainizing" a drug by reporting unsubstantiated anecdotes, while ignoring controlled scientific studies, is essentially the same one that produced the "reefer madness" mentality of the 1930s. Although motivated by a positive goal to prevent the illegal use of this drug, these scare tactics usually are of limited usefulness and often are actually counterproductive in the long run. The responsibility for this campaign must be shared by the Drug Enforcement Agency, and the subsequent, often inaccurate, media coverage of phencyclidine-intoxicated individuals. To better understand the behavioral pharmacology of phencyclidine, we should examine the scientific literature concerning phencyclidine prior to the "phencyclidine madness"-"angel death" hype with which we are all too familiar.

Phencyclidine can be administered parenterally, either IV or IM, for inducing surgical anesthesia, intranasally, or smoked, when it is sprinkled on tobacco (or a marijuana cigarette). It also can be taken enterally as a tablet or capsule. For all of these routes of administration, phencyclidine is readily absorbed into the circulation. As seen with smoking cocaine, smoking phencyclidine causes a quick absorption of the drug. The latency for effects after smoking phencyclidine is approximately two to five minutes.[50] The half-life of phencyclidine can be as short as 45 minutes at low doses[51] or as long as three weeks in overdose cases.[27]

The behavioral effects following phencyclidine use vary according to the dose. Small doses produce an intoxication and numbness in the extremities, moderate doses will clearly produce anesthesia and analgesia, and high doses will induce convulsions.[52,48] A moderate dose is typical in abusing populations and can range from 50 mg to 100 mg, intranasally, to 1 to 2 mg/kg IM or IV.[53] It was observed early in the history of phencyclidine use that its behavioral outcome was influenced by the setting in which the drug was taken, the personality of the user, and the presence of other drugs.[54] Following a phencyclidine-induced anesthetic state, the post-operative patient had been initially characterized as confused, disoriented, euphoric, and exhibiting behavior similar to an ethanol-induced intoxication.[48] One of the early studies specifically examined the phencyclidine-intoxicated driver. The studies found that the most common symptoms of phencyclidine intoxication were staggering, an unsteady gait, slurred speech, bloodshot eyes, a glassy stare, and nystagmus (i.e., a rapid flicking of the eyes from one side to the other).[55] Most of the 50 phencyclidine-intoxicated drivers were cooperative, and only one was combative. An earlier study also did not report hostility or combativeness in phencyclidine intoxication.[54] The peculiar psychological effects following phencyclidine use were initially described as severe changes in body image, loss of ego boundaries, and depersonalization,[56] an ability to focus on one object and "see" intense beauty in it, religious thoughts, and experiences of death.[49] Rarely did these subjects actually report visual hallucinations.[49] The change in body image was a sense of feeling like ones limbs were longer than they were and that their bodies were floating, walking in space,[57] or in a void. A later study of 300 recreational users of phencyclidine reported the following subjective experiences during phencyclidine intoxication: increased sensitivity to stimuli (94 percent), increased stimulation (94 percent), dissociation (88 percent), mood elevation (61 percent), relaxation (53 percent), hallucinations (30 percent), increased cognitive activity (11 percent), and euphoria (8 percent).[53] This recent survey raises several interesting issues. Since only 8 percent report euphoria, what then is the reinforcement for taking this drug? Why do some people find phencyclidine stimulating while others find it relaxing? How is it that some people find an increase in cognitive abilities, while most find phencyclidine to be dissociative? Why is phencyclidine listed as a hallucinogen if it only rarely induces true hallucinations?

Notably absent from these accounts is the association of phencyclidine with violence. Phencyclidine does not *cause* aggression or criminal behavior. The link between its use and violent behavior is not pharmacologically induced, but rather the result of a confluence of several factors, which merits attention on many levels. Dealing with any kind of intoxicated individual is complex enough, in terms of reasoning with them and using physical restraint, if needed, to contain them. Phencyclidine intoxication poses an especially difficult problem. Pharmacologically, recall that it does produce analgesia (a lack of pain perception) at levels that are commonly used to induce intoxication, as well as a heightened sensitivity to stimuli. This greatly complicates the way one should deal with a phencyclidine-intoxicated individual. Normal routine police procedures which, under most circumstances, are entirely appropriate and effective may not be effective or appropriate for the phencyclidine-intoxicated suspect. This should in no way be considered an indictment of police protocol. Consider that police officers provide one of the most dangerous services to a community, at great personal risk. Officers must routinely detain and interrogate suspicious individuals, as well as arrest and take into custody criminals who are quite often dangerous. When involved in such a situation, it is the officer who must evaluate and determine, on a moment-by-moment basis, the amount of force that will be necessary to accomplish a particular goal. The reactions of the suspect during the process is critical in the officer's decision to increase or decrease the force used. This system works fine in most situations, but phencyclidine intoxication complicates it. Since the typical phencyclidine-intoxicated person is anesthetized, the person will not respond to painful arrest techniques. For example, baton hits by an officer may not accomplish its goal and in fact may instigate a violent counterresponse by the suspect. Thus, the so-called violence induced by phencyclidine is not a true pharmacological property of the drug, but rather, is due to many factors.

Regardless of the precise causes, phencyclidine has acquired a reputation for directly inducing aggression, which addresses the issue of user expectation. We have seen in previous chapters how set (i.e., expectation) and setting (i.e., the environment in which the drug is taken) are two of the most important factors in the expression of behavior following ingestion of a drug. A societal expectation can be formed and also can be an important factor in how a community deals with drug users. The societal expectation that phencyclidine will induce both aggression and superhuman strength has not been substantiated by controlled and careful scientific studies. The initial studies in humans did not report aggressive reactions to phencyclidine or increased strength.[58,55] In fact, the study in which the Sheriff's Office of Santa Ana, California, participated, examined phencyclidine-intoxicated drivers and found aggressive behavior in only one of fifty cases presented.[55] In that report, one driver was pulled over and found to be foaming at the mouth, clenching and unclenching his fists, and totally unresponsive to verbal commands. The officer summoned the paramedics instead of attempting to take the suspect into custody himself, and the result was a nonviolent arrest. However, the *expectation* of encountering violence when approaching a phencyclidine-intoxicated individual has now become so established in our society that some law enforcement officials have determined ahead of time that maximal force will be necessary in such situations. Take, for example, the infamous Rodney King incident in Los Angeles, in which the officers at the scene testified that they thought Mr. King was "dusted," that is, he had consumed phencyclidine, which should justify the force that was used to subdue him. In another (in)famous case, also in Los Angeles, an officer shot six times at point blank range and killed an unarmed (actually totally naked) individual, who had no arrest history and was described as a nonviolent, peaceful man, but who was suspected of being under the influence of phencyclidine.[59] A police officer must use deadly force in certain situations that rely on his or her judgment. The misinformation generated by those public officials determined to stem the use of phencyclidine by scare tactics and the misinformation propagated by the media is in part responsible for the information that an officer has available to him or her in the immediate life-and-death decisions made in the field. In their attempts to paint the worst possible scenario of phencyclidine use, those officials and media involved have inadvertently given the officers whose lives are on the line every day the wrong information on which to base their decisions. Misinformation and the establishment of an inaccurate expectation is more than an academic exercise—it can mean someone's life.

Designer Drugs—Synthetic Analogs of the Hallucinogens

The practice of taking a well-known and well-used clinical drug and then altering its structure to develop a new drug is a not a new strategy in the development of medications. For example, the discovery of haloperidol (Haldol®) and Lomotil® was the accidental outcome of varying the structure of meperidine in an attempt to produce a better analgesic (see chapter 8). The search for newer illicit drugs also has employed this strategy. The term designer drugs has come to refer to those attempts at varying the molecular structure of certain legal drugs to produce similar and perhaps more intense effects as the original drug. There are certain variations of the norepinephrine molecule that have been termed designer drugs and categorized as hallucinogenic. The image of underground clandestine laboratories experimenting with various structures to produce the latest illegal drugs, however, is not the case for these particular designer drugs. These drugs were initially the products of legitimate research efforts that were later exploited by the street or recreational drug-using population. The principal drugs in question are 3,4 methylenedioxyamphetamine or MDA, 2,5-dimethoxy-4-methyl-amphetamine or DOM, and 3,4-methylene-dioxymethamphetamine or MDMA (also known as "ecstasy" or "Adam").

Since one of the distinguishing characteristics of these particular drugs is their structural similarity to existing drugs, let us first examine their molecular shapes. There are two drugs with molecular shapes similar to NE: amphetamines and mescaline (Figure 10–2). Designer drugs are considered by many to be variations or analogs of amphetamines. To the extent that these designer drugs are similar to amphetamines, they are also similar to NE and mescaline (Figure 10–2). This physical resemblance predicts that perhaps these designer drugs may have similar properties to both amphetamines and mescaline, and in fact they do.

DOM (2,5-dimethoxy-4-methyl-amphetamine).   Introduced in the 1960s, DOM was also known as "STP"* in the colorful street jargon. DOM is peculiar in that at lower doses, less than 2 mg, the effects induced are similar to amphetamines, without any hallucinatory properties. Higher doses, around 10 mg to 15 mg,

*The etiology of the street names for drugs is difficult at best. The name "STP" for DOM may have come from the popular gasoline additive STP, which stood for "scientifically treated petroleum," or as some have suggested, "STP" stood for "serenity, tranquility, and peace." Remember, DOM was introduced during the 1960s, a time when antiwar activity was high and a time of "hippies" and "flower children."

induce effects similar to mescaline, with the exception that the euphoria and stimulation experienced with DOM is more intense.[60] The duration of these effects is approximately seven to eight hours.[28]

The next two drugs, MDA and MDMA, are structurally related to one another and have been referred to as "entactogens," meaning a substance that produces empathy and sympathy and allows the user to "touch gently within."[61] While they share certain characteristics, for example, they both have similar half-lifes of around seven hours,[62] they are different from each other in certain critical aspects.

MDA (3,4 methylenedioxyamphetamine). MDA was first developed in the early 1900s as a legitimate sympathomimetic (a drug that induces a sympathetic response) for possible clinical use in humans but was not pursued by legitimate drug companies. Rediscovered in the 1960s and 1970s as a recreational street drug, MDA seems to induce a variety of effects. Among the effects observed are increased insight, heightened self-awareness, decreased anxiety, increased need for personal contact, increased tactile sensation, and no frank hallucinations.[63] MDA use has even been advocated in psychotherapy sessions as a "feeling enhancer" and as an aid to enable patients to better experience and deal with past events in their lives.[64] Many considered MDA to be a potentially useful tool in psychotherapy.[63]

However, the toxicity associated with MDA is significant and indicative of over-stimulation of the CNS. Symptoms of acute toxicity include: agitation, sweating, increased blood pressure, increased heart rate, dramatic increase in body temperature, and convulsions,[65] leading to death.[66] Death is usually the result of the cardiac effects and hemorrhaging in the brain.[67]

MDMA (3,4 methylenedioxymethamphetamine). Also known as "ecstasy" or "Adam," MDMA is perhaps the best known of these types of designer drugs. Developed in 1914 as an appetite suppressant, MDMA never was formally introduced into the legitimate market. It gained popularity in the 1970s because of the peculiar mental state it seemed to induce. Like MDA, MDMA is not a hallucinogen in the sense that it induces visual or auditory distortions like LSD or mescaline.[65] Instead, MDMA induces heightened sensual awareness, increased emotional energy, and even euphoria in some.[68] MDMA also has been reported to facilitate communication and intimacy between people involved in emotional situations.[69] It was this property of MDMA that was exploited by many therapists, which will be discussed later, and one of the main reasons for its soaring popularity as a recreational drug.

While MDA seems to have similar actions on neuronal activity as do the amphetamines, namely blocking reuptake of norepinephrine (NE) and enhancing release of NE,[63] the actions of MDMA are somewhat different. MDMA promotes serotonin release and can cause serotonin depletion.[70] It appears that MDMA may have a biphasic, serotonin-then-dopamine action.[71] The decreased dopamine-release effect is an indirect consequence of MDMA's direct effect on serotonin.[72] MDMA not only binds to serotonin reuptake sites, but also binds to the serotonin 5-HT2 receptor, as well as the alpha 2 adrenergic receptor and the acetylcholine M-1 muscarinic receptor.[73]

MDMA differs from MDA in its toxicity, in that it is clearly less toxic.[69] The adverse effects of MDMA include jaw clenching, headaches, and eye twitching.[68] There is no lethality associated with MDMA as there is with MDA, however, there does seem to be a clear sympathetic reaction to MDMA as evidenced by an increase in blood pressure, pulse rate, and pupil dilation.[68] However, there is no impaired consciousness, memory deficits, or loss of reality.[68,61] This profile has led many to consider MDMA to be reasonably safe, without evidence that it would be a drug of abuse and with little risk for even the naive user.[69] There has been some controversy, however, surrounding the issue of just how safe MDMA is. There has been a great deal of evidence that MDMA causes degeneration of serotonin neurons in the brain.[74,75] However, some of these same investigators caution that while ". . . the findings in animals are compelling, observations in humans are less clear."[74] It has yet to be determined if MDMA will cause serotonin neuronal damage in humans, which brings us to the controversial issue of government-controlled MDMA.

In the absence of direct toxicological data on MDMA, the Drug Enforcement Administration (DEA) relied on the similarity of MDMA to MDA, a substance with a well-known toxicity, to build its case against MDMA.[76] The fact that there is no cross-tolerance between MDA and MDMA suggests that the differences between these two drugs are significant, and they should not be considered as having the same effects. The high-profile proceedings by the DEA to control and ultimately ban MDMA in 1985 resulted in the creation of a forum for some of the difficult issues surrounding designer drugs. MDMA was used in a clinical manner as an adjunct to psychotherapy. Dr. George Greer published a study on the use of MDMA in his practice, in which he describes the positive effects MDMA can have in a therapeutic situation.[77] The many therapists who used MDMA in the context of their practices argued that MDMA did have medical usefulness and should be classified as a Schedule II substance, so physicians could prescribe it as they determined was necessary. One of the fundamental issues with designer drugs is government regulation and control of these substances. The risk of inducing significant toxicity is reason for the DEA to prevent the uncontrolled distribution of a substance. However, there are many such substances available to physicians and other professionals with prescription privileges to use in medicating situations. The classification of MDMA as a Schedule I substance: 1. Denies any bona fide medical usefulness of MDMA; 2. Indicates that it has a high potential for dependency; and 3. Makes it unavailable to medical professionals for use in treatment. It is unclear how the testimony of physicians who have used MDMA in their practices, data that indicates MDMA is not dangerous, and data that suggests MDMA has a low risk of forming a dependency leads to a Schedule I and not a Schedule II classification by the DEA.

The Hallucinogens Related to the Acetylcholine System in the Brain

Since recorded history and probably earlier, certain plants were known to be poisonous and also known to induce hallucinations. The prototypes of this class of hallucinogens are atropine (dl-hyoscyamine) and scopolamine (hyoscine), which are sometimes referred to as the "belladonna alkaloids." The plants that contain these compounds grow wild all over the world. The specific sources for these compounds include: *Datura stramonium* or jimsonweed, *Atropa belladonna,* or deadly night-shade, *Hyoscyamus niger* or henbane, *Scopolia carniolica,* and *Duboisia myoporoides,* to name a few. Both atropine and scopolamine block acetylcholine (ACh) receptors in the peripheral and central nervous systems. Because of the prominent role of ACh in the parasympathetic nervous system, both of these drugs, which are receptor blockers, induce a host of effects that are the opposite of a parasympathetic response.

The common peripheral effects of these drugs include increased heart rate (tachycardia), dry mouth, prolonged pupil dilation (mydriasis), and blurred vision. The common central effects include impaired memory, confusion, disorientation, a feeling of dysphoria, and, in some cases, hallucinations. At high doses coma may be induced, and despite the reputation of these drugs, death from overdose is rare.[28] There are some significant differences between the effects induced by atropine and those induced by scopolamine. At doses used in medicating situations, scopolamine causes drowsiness, euphoria, amnesia, a type of dreamlike sedation, decreased REM sleep, and occasionally excitement, delirium, and hallucinations, especially in the presence of pain.[78] Scopolamine is more potent as a CNS depressant[28] and more potent on secretory glands such as the salivary and bronchial secretory glands.[78] Atropine is more potent on heart muscle, intestines, and the bronchial muscles and has no CNS depressive effects. In addition, atropine is longer lasting than scopolamine and does not cross into the brain easily, so to induce hallucinations near-toxic doses are needed.[78]

There are several legitimate therapeutic uses for these drugs. The reduced secretions they produce in the respiratory tract is why these drugs are used in many over-the-counter cold medications such as Contact® cold capsules. The bronchial dilation induced by these drugs was the rationale for their use in treating asthma, however, more specific drugs like albuterol have replaced the belladonna alkaloids as the drug of choice for asthma. Perhaps the two most common medical uses of scopolamine are in the prevention of motion sickness and as a preparatory medication for surgical anesthesia. As a motion sickness medication, scopolamine needs to be given prophylactically, that is before symptoms appear, otherwise it is minimally effective.[78] Transdermal devices, that is, patches that are stuck onto the skin and from which scopolamine is slowly absorbed, have become quite popular. The use of scopolamine in surgery prior to anesthetic medications has multiple benefits. Scopolamine will inhibit excessive salivation and other respiratory secretions that might otherwise complicate a surgical procedure. The bronchial dilation is also helpful, and its sedative effects help calm patients before surgery.[78]

The actual induction of hallucinations is not a common outcome of the belladonna alkaloids, and it certainly does not appear without the aversive anticholinergic effects described earlier. One would think that this alone would discourage the abuse of these compounds to induce hallucinations. In fact, despite their easy availability, these drugs are not commonly abused. However, in the course of legitimate treatment, there is a toxic syndrome that may be exhibited with the use of these compounds, the central anticholinergic syndrome, or CAS. The cardinal signs of CAS are hallucinations, increased heart rate, fixed, dilated pupils, and dry mouth.[79] Other symptoms of CAS include difficulty in swallowing and talking, blurred vision, increased body temperature, heart palpitations, restlessness and excitation, motor incoordination, nausea and vomiting, and memory disturbances.[78] CAS has been reported in cases involving jimsonweed poisoning,[79] in post-operative cases,[80] with eyedropper applications of atropine,[81] and with transdermal scopolamine patches used to treat nausea.[82] The incidence of CAS has been reported to be from 1 percent to 40 percent of post-operative cases in which anticholinergics have been used as preparatory medications.[80]

Amanita Muscaria—The Ancient Hallucinogenic Mushroom of the "Old World"

This hallucinogenic mushroom has many interesting features. The intoxication by *Amanita muscaria* was characterized by reports written by investigators who had injected the substance, according to the accounts of Wasson.[83] There is a latency of approximately fifteen to twenty minutes from the time of ingestion to the first phase of intoxication, which is an odd type of sedation. This period can last two hours. The person experiences a sleep that Wasson called a "half-sleep," from which it is difficult to be roused and in which vivid images are seen. The next phase, which may last an additional three hours, is one of excitation, euphoria, and hallucinations. The person is not incapacitated, however, but rather is capable of "extraordinary physical efforts."[83]

The psychoactive components in *Amanita muscaria* include muscarine, choline, acetylcholine, atropine, hyoscyamine, bufotenin, muscimol, and ibotenic acid.[28] It appears that the ibotenic acid and muscimol are the psychoactive agents responsible for the intoxication profile just outlined.[84] Muscimol is one of the breakdown products of ibotenic acid.[85] All of the other components are present in amounts too small to affect behavior. Unlike all of the other hallucinogens, the brain system that seems to be affected directly by *Amanita muscaria* is the GABA neurotransmitter system. Muscimol is a powerful GABA agonist and since GABA mediates inhibition in the brain (see chapter 2), *Amanita muscaria* has the net result of inhibiting CNS neurons.[85] When muscimol itself is given to normal volunteers, it induces euphoria, hallucinations, a visual distortion in which visions are repeatedly experienced (sometimes referred to as "echo pictures"),[28] as well as a sympathetic response, that is, a dilation of pupils and a rise in body temperature, which may be secondary to the direct effects on GABA neurons.[85]

Perhaps the most distinctive characteristic of *Amanita muscaria*, which shocked the public and scientific circles when it was first described in the late eighteenth century, was drinking the urine of those who were intoxicated by *Amanita muscaria*. This ritual practice, performed by the Siberian Koryack tribespeople, was not universal to all of the tribal groups in Siberia but was nonetheless a common, well-established custom to many. Muscimol passes unchanged in the urine of the user in such high amounts that drinking the urine of a person intoxicated by *Amanita muscaria* will induce similar effects in the "second" user as in the first. Although not verified by any subsequent research, this ritual urine drinking, as described by Georg Heinrich von Langsdorf in the early 1800s,[86] has several curious characteristics. First, the urine of an intoxicated person seems to retain its hallucinogenic potency indefinitely across people. A person who becomes intoxicated by eating one or two *Amanita muscaria* mushrooms would produce urine that would induce a similar level of intoxication in a second person. The urine of the second person could induce a similar intoxication in a third, and the third person could do the same for the fourth, and so on. Second, the urine which contains active hallucinogens may actually be more potent than the *Amanita muscaria* mushrooms. Third, consuming the urine which contains active hallucinogens seems to have fewer negative effects, such as sweating and twitching,[28] than does consuming the actual mushrooms, which suggests that the initial user may act as a screening filter for the other components in the mushroom.

It has been reported that the consumption of *Amanita muscaria* mushrooms was preferred by the tribespeople over the consumption of the ethanol that was introduced by the Russians because *Amanita muscaria* consumption did not have the negative aspects of hangover, which is common with ethanol intoxication.[86] It leads one to wonder why the practice of eating *Amanita muscaria* did not continue and thrive in Siberia, or elsewhere, in the post–Russian Revolution era, as these tribes became more "modern" in their daily lives.

Lysergic Acid Amide Ololiuqui (Morning Glory Seeds)

The interest in ololiuqui stems from the initial reports of early Spanish explorers in South America and Mexico about a hallucinogen/intoxicant that was used by the Indians and the subsequent isolation of lysergic acid *amide* from these plant sources. The principal importance of ololiuqui then was the discovery of a lysergic acid derivative in an unaltered plant source.

Initially, there was considerable controversy in the attempt to describe precisely what the plant source for ololiuqui was. In the 1930s, the specific types of morning glory that seemed to be the bona fide source of ololiuqui were being identified, and in 1941 it was resolved that the sources were the seeds of *Rivea corymbosa* and *Ipomoea violacea* morning glory.[87] The isolation of lysergic acid derivatives, principally lysergic acid amide, was accomplished in the early 1960s.[88] However, whether administering the actual morning glory seeds or the isolated lysergic acid amides, studies have not demonstrated the hallucinogenic characteristics of ololiuqui. The initial studies in the mid 1950s and early 1960s in which the seeds, approximately 100 per dose, were ingested, resulted in sedation, apathy, and a feeling of well-being, but no hallucinations.[89,90] Studies with the isolated components also failed to induce frank hallucinations.[91,92] There, of course, remains the possibility that the reputation and accounts of the hallucinogenic capabilities of ololiuqui are due to other substances that may have been added to the morning glory seeds.

REVIEW EXAM

1. Name three hallucinogens that are structurally related to serotonin.
2. Name one hallucinogen that is structurally related to norepinephrine.
3. Name the three most potent hallucinogens.
4. What are the specific sources for psilocin and for mescaline?   ·
5. What are the two forms of ergotism?
6. Why is LSD considered a semisynthetic hallucinogen?
7. What are the sources for dimethyltryptamine (DMT) and bufotenin?
8. Compare the duration of action for LSD, psilocin, and mescaline.
9. Name four effects on the peripheral nervous system common to LSD, psilocin, and mescaline.
10. How does LSD and psilocin specifically alter the central nervous system?
11. Describe at least four general characteristics of the behavioral consequences following LSD use.
12. How are the hallucinations induced by mescaline and psilocin different from those induced by LSD?
13. Describe the tolerance and withdrawal associated with the use of LSD, mescaline, and psilocin.
14. Describe at least four general characteristics of the behavioral consequences following dimethyltryptamine (DMT) and/or bufotenin use.
15. What is the half-life of phencyclidine ("angel dust")?
16. Describe at least four behavioral characteristics following phencyclidine ("angel dust") use.
17. The designer drugs DOM, MDA, and MDMA are similar to what molecular structure(s)?
18. What are the common behavioral effects of MDA and MDMA?
19. Compare how MDA and MDMA alter brain functioning.
20. Name four effects on the peripheral nervous system of atropine and scopolamine.
21. Name three psychoactive agents in *Amanita muscaria*.
22. How does *Amanita muscaria* specifically alter the central nervous system?
23. What is the probable intoxicant in ololiuqui (morning glory seeds)?

REFERENCES

1. LABARRE, W. (1970). Old and new world narcotics: a statistical question and ethnological reply. *Economic Botany*, 24, 368–372.
2. FURST, P. (1976). *Hallucinogens and Culture* (pp. 1–18). Novato, CA: Chandler & Sharp Pub., Inc.
3. HERNANDEZ, F. (1651). *Nova Plantarum, Animalium et Mineralium Mexicanorum Historia*. B. Deuersini and Z. Masotti.
4. FURST, P. (1976). *Hallucinogens and Culture* (pp. 75–88). Novato, CA: Chandler & Sharp Pub., Inc.
5. DE BORHEGYI, S. (1961). Miniature mushroom stones from Guatemala. *American Antiquity*, 26, 498–504.

6. LOWY, B. (1971). New records of mushroom stones from Guatemala. *Mycologia,* 63(5), 983–993.
7. FURST, P. (1973). West Mexican art: secular or sacred. In *The Iconography of Middle American Sculpture* (pp. 98–103). New York: The Metropolitan Museum of Art.
8. SAPPER, C. (1898). Pilzformige Gotzenbilder aus Guatemala und San Salvador. *Globus,* 73, 327.
9. SCHULTES, R., & HOFMANN, A. (1973). *The Botany and Chemistry of Hallucinogens.* Springfield, IL: Charles C. Thomas.
10. SHARON, D. (1972). The San Pedro cactus in Peruvian folk healing. In P. Furst (Ed.), *Flesh of the Gods: the Ritual Use of Hallucinogens* (pp. 114–135). New York: Praeger.
11. FURST, P. (1976). *Hallucinogens and Culture* (pp. 109–119). Novato, CA: Chandler & Sharp Pub., Inc.
12. BULLIS, R. (1990). Swallowing the scroll: legal implications of the recent Supreme Court peyote cases. *Journal of Psychoactive Drugs,* 22(3), 325–332.
13. BOVE, F. (1970). *The Story of Ergot.* New York: S. Karger.
14. BARGER, G. (1931). *Ergot and Ergotism.* London: Gurney and Jackson.
15. FELDMAN, R., & QUENZER, L. (1984). *Fundamentals of Neuropsychopharmacology* (pp. 207–258). Sunderland, MA: Sinauer Assc., Inc.
16. CAPORAEL, L. (1976). Ergotism: the satan loose in Salem? *Science,* 192, 21–26.
17. MATOSSIAN, M. (1982). Ergot and the Salem witchcraft affair. *American Scientist,* 70(4), 355–357.
18. HOFMANN, A. (1970). Notes and documents concerning the discovery of LSD. *Agents and Actions,* 1(3), 148–150.
19. BUCKMAN, J. (1972). Brainwashing, LSD, and CIA: historical and ethical perspectives. *International Journal of Social Psychiatry,* 23(1), 8–19.
20. CLARK, W. (1985). Ethics and LSD. *Journal of Psychoactive Drugs,* 17(4), 229–234.
21. FURST, P. (1976). *Hallucinogens and Culture* (pp. 89–95). Novato, CA: Chandler & Sharp Pub., Inc.
22. WASSON, R. (1972). Soma, divine mushroom of immortality. In P. Furst (Ed.), *Flesh of the Gods: The Ritual Use of Hallucinogens* (pp. 185–200). New York: Praeger.
23. FURST, P. (1976). *Hallucinogens and Culture* (pp. 146–157). Novato, CA: Chandler & Sharp Pub., Inc.
24. WASSEN, S. (1967). Anthropological survey of the use of South American snuffs. In O. Efron (Ed.), *Ethnopharmacologic Search for Psychoactive Drugs* (pp. 233–289). Washington, DC: U.S. Health Service Publication No. 1645, U.S. Government Printing Office.
25. SCHULTES. R. (1972). An overview of hallucinogens in the Western hemisphere. In P. Furst (Ed.) *Flesh of the Gods: The Ritual Use of Hallucinogens* (pp. 3–54). New York: Praeger.
26. THOMPSON, J. (1970). *Maya History and Religion.* Norman, OK: University of Oklahoma Press.
27. JAFFE, J. (1980). Drug addiction and drug abuse. In G. Gilman, L. Goodman, & A. Gilman (Eds.), *The Pharmacological Basis of Therapeutics* (6th ed., pp. 535–584). New York: Macmillan Publishing Company, Inc.
28. LONGO, V. (1972). *Neuropharmacology and Behavior* (pp. 97–170). San Francisco, CA: W.H. Freeman and Co.
29. PAPAC, D., & FOLTZ, R. (1990). Measurement of lysergic acid diethylamide (LSD) in human plasma by gas chromatography/negative ion chemical ionization mass spectrometry. *Journal of Analytical Toxicology,* 14(3), 189–190.
30. SALMON, K., GABRIO, B., & THALE, T. (1949). A study on mescaline in human subjects. *Journal of Pharmacology and Experimental Therapeutics,* 95, 455–459.
31. MIRIN, S., & WEISS, R. (1983). Substance abuse. In E. Bassuk, S. Schoonover, & A. Gelenberg (Eds.), *The Practitioner's Guide to Psychoactive Drugs* (2nd ed., p. 266). New York: Plenum Medical Books.
32. FELTER, R., IZSAK, E., & LAWRENCE, S. (1987). Emergency department management of the intoxicated adolescent. *Pediatric Clinics of North America,* 34(2), 399–421.
33. STRASSMAN, R. (1992). Human hallucinogen interactions with drugs affecting serotonergic neurotransmission. *Neuropsychopharmacology,* 7(3), 241–243.
34. HOYER, D. (1991). The 5-HT receptor family: ligands, distribution, and receptor-effector coupling. In R. Rodgers & S. Cooper (Eds.), *5-HT$_{1A}$ Agonists, 5-HT$_3$ Antagonists and Benzodiazepines: Their Comparative Behavioral Pharmacology.* New York: John Wiley and Sons.
35. PIERCE, P., & PEROUTKA, S. (1990). Antagonist properties of d-LSD at 5-hydroxytryptamine2 receptors. *Neuropsychopharmacology,* 3(5–6), 503–508.
36. SADZOT, B., BARABAN, J., GLENNON, R., & LYON, R. (1989). Hallucinogenic drug interactions at human brain 5-HT-sub-2 receptors: implications for treating LSD-induced hallucinations. *Psychopharmacology,* 98(4), 495–499.

37. BUCKHOLTZ, N., ZHOU, D., FREEDMAN, D., & POTTER, W. (1990). Lysergic acid diethylamide (LSD) administration selectively downregulates serotonin2 receptors in rat brain. *Neuropsychopharmacology,* 3(2), 137–148.
38. JACOBS, B., & TRULSON, M. (1979). Mechanisms of action of LSD. *American Scientist,* 67(4), 396–404.
39. GHANSAH, E., KOPSOMBUT, P., MALLEQUE, M., & BROSSI, A. (1993). Effects of mescaline and some of its analogs on cholinergic neuromuscular transmission. *Neuropharmacology,* 32(2), 169–174.
40. CHAGNON, N., LAQUESNE, P., & COOK, J. (1971). Yanomamo hallucinogens: anthropological, botanical, and chemical findings. *Current Anthropology,* 12, 72–74.
41. SZARA, S. (1957). The comparison of the psychotic effect of tryptamine derivatives with the effects of mescaline and LSD-25 in self-experiments. In S. Garattini & V. Ghetti (Eds.), *Psychotropic Drugs* (pp. 460–467). Amsterdam: Elsevier.
42. CHECKLEY, S. (1980). A longitudinal study of urinary excretion on N,N-dimethyltryptamine in psychotic patients. *British Journal of Psychiatry,* 137, 236–239.
43. FABING, H., & HAWKINS, J. (1956). Intravenous bufotenin injection in the human being. *Science,* 123, 886–887.
44. MCLEOD, W., & SITARAM, B. (1985). Bufotenin reconsidered. *Acta Psychiatrica Scandinavica,* 72(5), 447–450.
45. LYTTLE, T. (1993). Misuse and legend in the "toad licking" phenomenon. *International Journal of Addictions,* 28(6), 521–538.
46. SIEGEL, D., & MCDANIEL, S. (1991). The frog prince: tale and toxicology. *American Journal of Orthopsychiatry,* 61(4), 558–562.
47. VAN PUTTEN, T. & EMORY-WARDEN, H. (1973). Traumatic neuroses in Vietnam returnees: A forgotten diagnosis? *Archives of General Psychiatry,* 29(5), 695–698.
48. GREIFENSTEIN, F., DE VAULT, M., YOSHITAKE, J., & GAJEWSKI, J. (1958). A study of l-aryl cyclohexamine for anesthesia. *Anesthesie et Analgesie,* 37, 283–294.
49. LERNER, S., & BURNS, R. (1978). Phencyclidine use among youth: history, epidemiology, and acute and chronic intoxication. In R. Peterson & R. Stillman (Eds.), *Phencyclidine (PCP) Abuse: An Appraisal, National Institute of Drug Abuse Research Monograph 21* (pp. 66–118). Washington, DC: U.S. Government Printing Office.
50. BURNS, R., & LERNER, S. (1976). Perspectives: acute phencyclidine intoxication. *Clinical Toxicology* 9(4), 477–501.
51. MIRIN, S., & WEISS, R. (1983). Substance abuse. In E. Bassuk, S. Schoonover, & A. Gelenberg (Eds.), *The Practitioner's Guide to Psychoactive Drugs* (2nd ed., p. 270). New York: Plenum Medical Books.
52. DOMINO, E. (1978). Neurobiology of phencyclidine—an update. In R. Peterson & R. Stillman (Eds.), *Phencyclidine (PCP) Abuse: An Appraisal, National Institute of Drug Abuse Research Monograph 21* (pp. 18–43). Washington, DC: U.S. Government Printing Office.
53. SEIGEL, R. (1978). Phencyclidine and ketamine intoxication: a study of four populations of recreational users. In R. Peterson & R. Stillman (Eds.), *Phencyclidine (PCP) Abuse: An Appraisal, National Institute of Drug Abuse Research Monograph 21* (pp. 119–147). Washington, DC: U.S. Government Printing Office.
54. GARVEY, R., WEISBERG, L., & HEATH, R. (1977). Phencyclidine: an overview. *Journal of Psychedelic Drugs,* 9, 280–285.
55. CLARDY, D., CRAVEY, R., MACDONALD, B., WIERSEMA, S., PEARCE, D., & RAGLE, J. (1979). The phencyclidine-intoxicated driver. *Journal of Analytical Toxicology* 3, 238–241.
56. LUBY, E., COHEN, B., ROSENBAUM, G., GOTTLIEB, J., & KELLY, R. (1959). Study of a new schizophrenomimetic drug—sernyl. *Archives of Neurological Psychiatry,* 81, 363–369.
57. SMITH, D., WESSON, D., BUXTON, M., SEYMOR, R., & KRAMER, H. (1978). The diagnosis and treatment of the PCP abuse syndrome. In R. Peterson & R. Stillman (Eds.), *Phencyclidine (PCP) Abuse: An Appraisal, National Institute of Drug Abuse Research Monograph 21* (pp. 229–240). Washington, DC: U.S. Government Printing Office.
58. DOMINO, E., & LUBY, E. (1972). Abnormal mental states induced by PCP as a model for schizophrenia. In J. Cole, A. Freedman, & A. Friedhoff (Eds.), *Psychopathology and Psychopharmacology* (pp. 37–50). Baltimore, MD: Johns Hopkins Press.
59. OVEREND, W. (1977, September 26). PCP: Death in the "dust." *Los Angeles Times,* p. 2.
60. JAFFE, J. (1975). Drug addiction and drug abuse. In L. Goodman & A. Gilman (Eds.), *The Pharmacological Basis of Therapeutics* (5th ed., pp. 284–324). New York: Macmillan Publishing Co., Inc.
61. LEVERANT, R. (1986). MDMA reconsidered. *Journal of Psychoactive Drugs,* 18(4), 373–379.

62. GARRETT, E., SEYDA, K., & MARROUM, P. (1991). High performance liquid chromatographic assays of the illicit designer drug ecstasy, a modified amphetamine, with applications to stability, partitioning, and plasma protein binding. *Acta Pharmaceutica Nordica*, 3(1), 9–14.
63. CLIMKO, R., ROERICH, H., SWEENEY, D., & AL-RAZI, J. (1986–87). Ecstasy: a review of MDMA and MDA. *International Journal of Psychiatry in Medicine*, 16(4), 359–372.
64. NARANJO, C. (1973). *The Healing Journey: New Approaches to Consciousness*. New York: Pantheon.
65. NICHOLS, D. (1990). Substituted amphetamine-controlled substance analogues. In K. Redda, C. Walker, & G. Barnett (Eds.), *Cocaine, Marijuana, Designer Drugs: Chemistry, Pharmacology, and Behavior* (pp. 175–185). Boca Raton, FL: CRC Press.
66. CIMBURA, G. (1972). 3,4 methylenedioxyamphetamine (MDA). Analytical and forensic aspects of fatal poisoning. *Journal of Forensic Science*, 18, 329.
67. BUCHMAN, J., & BROWN, C. (1988). Designer drugs. A problem in clinical toxicology. *Medical Toxicology and Adverse Drug Exposure*, 3(1), 1–17.
68. DOWNING, J. (1986). The psychological and physiological effects of MDMA on normal volunteers. *Journal of Psychoactive Drugs*, 18(4), 335–340.
69. SHULGIN, A. (1986). The background and chemistry of MDMA. *Journal of Psychoactive Drugs*, 18(4), 291–304.
70. MOLLIVER, M., BERGER, U., MAMOUNAS, L., MOLLIVER, D., O'HEARN, E., & WILSON, M. (1990). Neurotoxicity of MDMA and related compounds: anatomic studies. *Annals of the New York Academy of Science*, 600, 649–661.
71. SCHECHTER, M. (1988). Serotonergic-dopaminergic mediation of 3,4-methylenedioxymethamphetamine (MDMA, ecstasy). *Pharmacology, Biochemistry and Behavior*, 31(4), 817–824.
72. GAZZARA, R., TAKEDA, H., CHO, A., & HOWARD, S. (1989). Inhibition of dopamine release by methylenedioxymethamphetamine is mediated by serotonin. *European Journal of Pharmacology*, 168(2), 209–217.
73. BATTAGLIA, G., & DE SOUZA, E. (1989). Pharmacological profile of amphetamine derivatives at various brain recognition sites: selective effects on serotonergic systems. *National Institute of Drug Abuse Research Monographs*, 94, 240–258.
74. RICAURTE, G., &MCCANN, U. (1992). Neurotoxic amphetamine analogues: effects on monkeys and implications for humans. *Annals of the New York Academy of Science*, 648, 371–382.
75. DE SOUZA, E., & BATTAGLIA, G. (1989). Effects of MDMA and MDA on brain serotonin neurons: evidence from neurochemical and autoradiographic studies. *National Institute of Drug Abuse Research Monographs*, 94, 196–222.
76. ANDERSON, G., BRAUN, G., BRAUN, U., NICHOLS, D., & SHULGIN, A. (1978). Absolute configuration and psychotomimetic activity. In G. Barnett, M. Trsic, & R. Willette (Eds.), *QUASAR: Quantitative Structure Activity Relationships of Analgesics, Narcotic Antagonists, and Hallucinogens. National Institute of Drug Abuse Research Monographs*, 22.
77. GREER, G. (1983). *MDMA: A New Psychotropic Compound and Its Effects in Humans*. Santa Fe, NM.
78. WEINER, (1980). Atropine, scopolamine, and related antimuscarinic drugs. In A. Gilman, L. Goodman, & A. Gilman (Eds.), *The Pharmacological Basis of Therapeutics*, 6th ed. (pp. 120–137). New York: Macmillan Publishing Co., Inc.
79. RWIZA, H. (1991). Jimsonweed food poisoning. an epidemic at Usango rural government hospital. *Tropical and Geographical Medicine*, 43 (1–2), 85–90.
80. RUPREHT, J., & DWORACEK, B. (1990). Central anticholinergic syndrome during postoperative period. *Annales Francaises d'Anesthesie et de Reanimation*, 9(3), 295–304.
81. KORTABARRIA, R., DURAN, J., CHACON, J., DOMINGUEZ, F., & PINO, M. (1990). Toxic psychosis following cycloplegic eyedrops., *DICP*, 24(7–8), 708–709.
82. ZISKIND, A. (1988). Transdermal scopolamine-induced psychosis. *Postgraduate Medicine*, 84(3), 73–76.
83. WASSON, R. (1967). In D. Efron (Ed.), *Ethnopharmacologic Search for Psychoactive Drugs* (p. 419). Washington, DC: U.S. Dept. of Health, Education, and Welfare.
84. SCHULTES, R. (1970). The botanical and chemical distribution of hallucinogens. *Annual Review of Plant Physiology*, 21, 571–598.
85. FELDMAN, R., & QUENZER, L. (1984). *Fundamentals of Neuropsychopharmacology* (pp. 259–293). Sunderland, MA: Sinauer Associates Inc.
86. WASSON, R. (1968). *Soma, Divine Mushroom of Immortality. Ethno-Myco-Sabina and Her Mazatec Mushroom Velada*. New York: Harcourt Brace Jovanovich.
87. SCHULTES, R. (1941). *A Contribution to Our Knowledge of Rivea Corymbosa, the Narcotic Ololiuqui of the Aztecs*. Cambridge, MA: Botanical Museum of Harvard University.

88. HOFMAN, A., & TSCHERTER, A. (1960). Isolierung von Lysergsaure Alkaloiden aus der mexikanischen zauberdrage ololiuqui (*Rivea corymbosa*(L.) hall.F.). *Experientia*, 16, 414.
89. OSMOND, H. (1955). Ololiuqui: The ancient Aztec narcotic. *Journal of Mental Science*, 101, 526–527.
90. HOFMANN, A., & CERLETTI, A. (1961). Die wirkstoffe der dritten aztekischen zauberdrage. *Deutsche Medizinische Wochenschrift*, 86, 885–888.
91. SOLMS, H. (1956). Relationships between chemical structure and psychoses with the use of psychotoxic substances. *Journal of Clinical and Experimental Psychopathology*, 17, 429–433.
92. ISBELL, H., & GORODETSKI, C. (1966). Effects of alkaloids of ololiuqui in man. *Psychopharmacology*, 8(5), 331–339.

CHAPTER ELEVEN
DRUG INTAKE DURING PREGNANCY

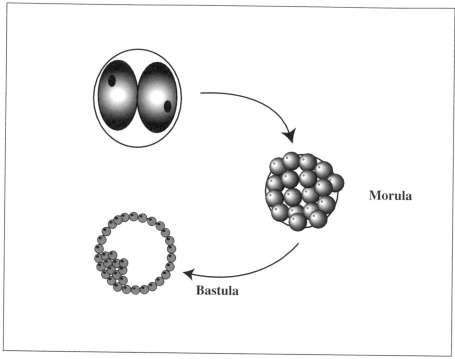

Morula

Bastula

FIGURE 11–1   The Early Changes in Development
Within the first five days following conception, the fertilized egg experiences intense cell divisions and soon becomes a solid ball of cells called the "morula." This solid ball of cells quickly becomes a fluid-filled ball of cells called the blastula (shown here in cross section), with a concentration of cells on one end.

during the first trimester may seriously jeopardize organogenesis and limb formation and ultimately cause malformations in the infant. Teratology is the study of those factors that may produce malformations by disrupting normal gestation, typically in the first trimester.

One of the most dramatic pharmacological interruptions of the growth program was the use of the sedative thalidomide. This drug, which is quite safe in every other facet of its physiology, specifically interferes with the development of limbs, so children who were exposed to thalidomide during the first trimester of their gestation were born with severely deformed arms and/or legs, or without limbs at all. No other body system was altered by thalidomide. For example, these children had normal brain development and normal motor coordination. This was an alarming example of how drugs could alter the developmental growth plan in very specific ways.

During the first eight weeks of gestation the organism is called an embryo; after that it is called a fetus.

The second and third trimesters. Once the organs have been formed during the first trimester, there are no new organs formed thereafter. What takes place in the second and third trimesters is the growth and development of the functional capacity of those organs. The organs begin to function as they would in the mature system.

Since clearly detectable malformations are likely to be caused in the first trimester, the risk of this anatomical chronological approach lies in considering that the first trimester is the only period critical to development. As we shall see, this is not the case.

The Functional Approach

An alternative to this chronological examination of the developmental process is to focus on the functional phases of development, regardless of when they occur relative to birth. In this type of approach, the general course of development is as follows:

1. Organogenesis is the general formation of the organs by the migration of cells to particular areas to form the mass of cells that will eventually become a particular body type.
2. Histogenesis next occurs, whereby the further specialization of cells to suit the tissue mass in the area in which it is located takes place; for example, kidney cells begin to exhibit the characteristic shape and size of specific kidney cells.
3. The final stage is the development of function, whereby cells, having massed in the appropriate numbers for a particular organ and having further specialized to look like the adult cells in the particular organ, now begin to perform the function of that organ. There is considerable variability between the organs in this final phase. For example, the heart begins to pump very early in the development of the organism, whereas liver cells that begin functioning in the third trimester are not yet functioning at adult levels at the time of birth.

The disruption of organogenesis during the first trimester is certainly a matter of vital concern and is the most apparent to evaluate. However, there are other events that occur later in development that are also critical for normal development. An organ that has successfully accomplished its organogenesis still must proceed through two additional phases—histogenesis and the development of function—before completing its growth program. Even though apparent malformations cannot be induced in the later stages of development, the growth program still can be seriously disrupted in the second and third trimesters by a variety of factors, including drugs. It is during this last phase of development that organs begin to exhibit adult functioning, thus the body's metabolic systems begin to express. For example, the insulin system begins to respond to circulating glucose by mid-gestation and continues to mature during the third trimester.[1]

Just as the development of structure can be disrupted, the normal development of metabolic systems also can be disrupted. Metabolic teratology refers to the study of factors that may disrupt the development of a metabolic system, so the adult system is functioning abnormally.[2] When one considers the importance of these later phases of development, one can appreciate how dangerous the common misconception is that the first trimester is the only period that requires care.

Since one of our main concerns is behavior, the development of the brain is especially important.

THE BRAIN GROWTH SPURT

Like all of the other organs, the brain is formed during organogenesis in the first trimester. However, the later phases of functional development also are critical for the growth program to produce a brain that functions normally. The critical stage of brain development that occurs later in gestation has been referred to as the brain growth spurt.

Two of the striking features of this particular phase of brain growth are the speed with which it occurs and the overwhelming increase in the size of the brain. The brain growth spurt is the period of time when the brain is growing at its absolute fastest rate.[3] In the human, the brain growth spurt begins around mid-gestation (that is, halfway through the second trimester) and continues through the fourth post-natal year.[4] This brain growth spurt occurs in all mammals, but the specific timing relative to the birth event varies considerably.

There are two types of cells in the brain: neurons, the cells that actually do the active processing of the CNS; and glial cells, which are not directly involved in the processing of information. Glial cells outnumber neuron cells by almost 10 to 1 in the CNS. We have seen one role of one type of glial cell, the astrocyte in the blood-brain barrier (see chapter 1). A role for another type of glial cell the oligodendrocyte, is to wrap myelin or fat around the axons of neurons, thereby causing the action potential to travel faster along the axon. The brain growth spurt occurs after most neurons have established their populations. Thus, the brain growth spurt is not primarily an effect of neuronal cell growth; the cells that are developing during this time are glial cells.

There are three main events that occur in the brain growth spurt:[3]

1. A rapid proliferation of glial cells, specifically of oligodendrocytes;
2. Rapid myelination—an accumulation of the glial material that wraps around the axons (myelin); and
3. A dramatic increase in the number of synapses.

The increase in the number of synapses is perhaps one of the most important events in the expression of behavior. Essentially the brain is wiring itself up during this brain growth spurt. The successful completion of this phase of development is critical for the proper functional organization of the adult brain. If we consider that the brain mediates behavior, then developing the proper functional organization of the brain becomes a critical factor in the behavioral patterns seen in the adult.

To disrupt the brain growth that occurs during the second and third trimesters is to risk malformed brain connections, which may result in abnormal or inappropriate behavioral patterns in the adult. Behavioral teratology refers to the study of factors that may disrupt normal brain development, so the individual may express abnormal behavioral patterns. Typically, there is much concern for the events of the first trimester. Pregnant women will take a great deal of care not to take inappropriate medications or other drugs. However, as much care should be taken for the second and third trimesters (and after birth) if the brain is to achieve normal functional development. Accomplishing a normal organogenesis of the brain simply ensures that the right number of cells have migrated and proliferated correctly. If these neurons are prevented from connecting properly to one another by disruptions that occur in the second and third trimesters, the outcome could be devastating, in terms of behavior.

Let us now consider the special issues of drug absorption, distribution, and excretion in the fetal compartment.

ABSORPTION AND EXCRETION IN THE FETAL COMPARTMENT

Although in general the gestating organism constitutes another compartment to which drugs will distribute, the relationship between the gestating organism and mother has some significant features that relate to the absorption and excretion of drugs.

First, the fetus has its own separate circulation. There is no direct connection between the mother's and the fetus' circulation. The fetus' circulation dangles in the mother's blood. Nutrients and waste products are exchanged by an elaborate diffusion system. This exchange occurs in an area of specialized tissue called the placenta. It was once believed that the placenta was a barrier that protected the fetus from harmful substances in the mother's circulation. This clearly is not the case with drugs, because the placenta offers no protection to the fetus and is simply another membrane for substances to cross. If a drug is lipid-soluble enough to cross membranes and distribute to the mother's various compartments, then that drug will distribute into the fetal compartment as well.

Second, the embryo and the early fetus is totally dependent on the mother's circulation for nutrients, waste removal, and for any biotransformation of drugs that must take place. Because its liver has yet to achieve mature functioning, the embryo and later the second-trimester fetus cannot biotransform drugs efficiently, depending on the mother not only to biotransform any drugs that are consumed but also to excrete the drug. Drugs that distribute to the early fetus remain there until the levels in mother's blood are low enough to set up the appropriate concentration gradients that will draw out the drug from the fetal compartment.

Third, the fetal compartment is not like any other body compartment in the mother. Whereas other compartments in the mother are fairly homogenous in their cell types, the fetal compartment is a microcosm or replica of the mother. When the mother takes a drug and it distributes to the fetal compartment, the drug will distribute not to one compartment but rather to the entire complement of the various fetal compartments, including the fetal brain. Furthermore, later in the third trimester the fetal liver and kidneys will begin to show some function. This older fetal liver will be capable of biotransforming some drug molecules, a portion of which the fetal kidneys will excrete. However, the fetus resides in a closed fluid-filled sac called the amnion. When the fetal kidneys excrete drug molecules, they excrete them out of the fetus but into the amniotic fluid. The fetus normally swallows much of the amniotic fluid, thus if it contains drug molecules that have passed unchanged or active metabolites of a drug, the fetus will dose itself again by this fetal enteral oral route of drug administration. A drug therefore has the capacity to reverberate in the fetal compartment through this process.

DRUG USE DURING PREGNANCY

The three drugs most frequently taken by pregnant women in the United States are nicotine, ethanol, and marijuana,[5,6] followed by opiates and cocaine.[51] The effects of these drugs taken during pregnancy on the later behavior of the infants will be reviewed. In addition, there are many women of childbearing age who have seizure disorders that require taking daily anticonvulsant medication. The behavioral effects of anticonvulsant medication taken during pregnancy also will be reviewed. We begin with ethanol use.

FETAL ALCOHOL SYNDROME (FAS)

As discussed in chapter 5, the use of ethanol; has an ancient history. It follows then that the use of ethanol by pregnant women probably would also have as long a history. There are some indications that the potential hazards of consuming ethanol during pregnancy were appreciated, even in biblical times[7] and during the time of Plato.[8]

Ethanol creates such a hostile environment for the process of development that one of the reliable effects of ethanol use during pregnancy is an increased risk of spontaneous abortion.[9] If the pregnancy does not result in abortion and progresses to term, the consequences of ingesting ethanol during the developmental process are staggering.

Despite this long history, the first specific descriptions of the effects of ethanol on the growth process were made in the late 1960s and early 1970s by two independent laboratories.[10,11] Since these initial descriptions the teratogenic effects of ethanol use during pregnancy have become the most studied insult to normal human development.[12] The question that immediately arises is, if drinking during pregnancy has been going on essentially for as long as ethanol has been used, why has it taken so long to describes its negative impact on gestation? The reasons for the relatively late detection of ethanol's effects on gestation are complex. One important reason is that the physical features are not as immediately apparent nor invariant as other syndromes, such as Down's. As we shall discuss later, there can be a variety of facial signs resulting from the mother's ethanol use during pregnancy. The other important reason is that ethanol is the accepted drug of Western culture, thus many of ethanol's clearly detrimental effects go unnoticed. For example, the carcinogenic effects of ethanol as well as its toxic effects on the brain are well-known but not well-publicized. In addition, any drug seeking government approval for human use that has similar negative effects to ethanol could not be approved by law, yet ethanol is not considered a "drug" and, as such, is not regulated like other "drugs."

Originally, in the United States, the effects on the offspring of maternal ethanol use during pregnancy were described in a population of heavy chronic ethanol users, that is, alcoholic women, and was termed fetal alcohol syndrome (FAS). FAS is a constellation of specific features that reflect disruptions of the growth program, seen in people who were exposed to ethanol during the gestation. These features can be classified into three general categories: 1. effects on the development of the central nervous system; 2. effects on growth in general; and 3. the resultant facial malformations seen in FAS children.

Central Nervous System Dysfunction

The most common outcome of ethanol use during pregnancy is mild-to-moderate mental retardation in offspring.[13] Drinking ethanol during pregnancy can be a major cause of what previously was considered an unexplained incidence of mental retardation. Furthermore, this cause of mental retardation is preventable. Another hallmark feature of FAS is an extremely small head circumference, which indicates microcephaly or a small brain. These two symptoms, the occurrence of mental retardation and microcephaly, occur in over 80 percent of FAS children.[13]

There are other ethanol-induced symptoms that suggest disruptions of CNS development. Irritability during infancy, which occurs in over 80 percent of FAS cases, may be the result of ethanol withdrawal these infants have to experience.[13] Infants born of chronic alcoholic mothers typically develop a dependency on ethanol just as an adult would, given a similar ethanol consumption history. Like an ethanol-dependent adult who stops drinking abruptly, these infants also experience ethanol withdrawal at birth. The symptoms of neonatal ethanol withdrawal include tremors, increased muscle tone, irritability, increased respiratory rates, hyperacusis, and, in some cases, seizures.[14] In addition to general irritability, infants experiencing ethanol withdrawal may have seizures and tremors and often will receive barbiturates or benzodiazepines to help them through this period.[14]

There is a more than 50 percent incidence of childhood hyperactivity seen in FAS children.[13,15] There may be so many circumstances involved in this particular behavior that in all likelihood ethanol may be one of the contributing factors in its occurrence but is not a direct causal factor.

There have been several clinical studies indicating that specifically third trimester ethanol exposure, a period when the brain growth spurt is beginning its acceleration, is critical in the brain-related effects of FAS. Women who abstained or reduced their drinking during the third trimester had infants with head circumferences that were normal and larger than women who continued to drink during this stage.[16,17] In another study, not only was head circumference correlated with maternal ethanol use during the third trimester, but it appears that there was a reduction of 5 mm of head circumference for each drink consumed per day by the mother.[18] These data indicate that for humans, as one would predict from the abundant literature concerning the brain growth spurt, brain development may be especially susceptible to disruption during the third trimester.

Growth Deficiency

There are two aspects of the overall growth of FAS children that are greatly disrupted. At birth, these FAS infants are quite small, and this is not due to prematurity. FAS infants are actually "small for gestational age," (SGA) which means they are still small when compared to infants who have developed in the same length of time. Over 80 percent of FAS infants are born approximately two standard deviations below the population mean, in both weight or length.[13] This decreased size at birth, observed in FAS infants, is called pre-natal growth deficiency because it seems to reflect some growth disruption that occurs in utero. It is important to note that there are two aspects of ethanol use that cause prenatal growth deficiency, as the following study illustrates. Alcoholic women who abstained from drinking ethanol during pregnancy still had infants that were significantly smaller than control infants but also significantly larger than alcoholic women who continued to drink ethanol during their pregnancies.[19] Thus, independent of ethanol use during pregnancy, maternal chronic heavy ethanol use prior to conception also had a significant negative impact on prenatal growth.

Once born, however, over 80 percent of FAS infants did not catch up on any measure and remained two standard deviations below population means.[13] Despite adequate post-natal nutrition and, in some cases, placement into foster homes, FAS infants do not show a rebound of any kind. This inability to catch up in terms of overall body size is called post-natal growth deficiency and reflects some change in the growth process in FAS infants.

In one of the original descriptions of FAS, the authors describe one case in which the FAS infant, which gestated for thirty-eight weeks, weighed 2,020 grams at birth, which was in the 50th percentile for an infant who had gestated thirty-two and one-half weeks.[20] At thirteen months, that same infant was still in the 50th percentile for an infant at three months. In a ten-year follow-up study of the original FAS children observed, Streissguth et al., report that ten years later these children remained growth-deficient.[21]

Facial Abnormalities

The distinctive face of the FAS infant and child has many individual components. There are three principal features of facial abnormalities that result from ethanol exposure during the developmental process: short eye slits, hypoplastic philtrum, and thin upper lip.

In many ways, the skin over our heads can be considered a type of mask, with several specialized entry and exit holes, namely the mouth, the nostrils, the ear holes, and the eyes. The slits in the "skin mask" for our eyes are called palpebral fissures and are remarkably shorter in FAS infants.[13] Just like the suppression of brain growth in microcephaly, discussed earlier, the shorter eye slits in FAS children probably reflect a direct effect of ethanol in the development of the eyes. The feature hypoplastic philtrum is not the result of growth retardation but rather the result of too many cells. The groove over the middle of the upper lip is called the philtrum. In FAS children, this groove in filled in or absent. In addition, the upper lip of FAS children is unusually thin.

Additional facial features of FAS include a flattened face profile and droopy eyelids. One can see that these facial abnormalities are somewhat subtle and are individually not diagnostic of FAS. However, collectively, they form a syndrome that some say is as easy to diagnose as Down syndrome.[13] The overall severity of the facial abnormalities observed in FAS seems to be correlated to the severity of mental retardation in these children, so the more severe the facial dysmorphology the more impaired their mental functioning.[22,23]

Describing the precise effects of ethanol use during pregnancy has been difficult since not many FAS children have been autopsied. However, two FAS fatalities did provide some information concerning brain damage as a result of ethanol

---

TABLE 11–1   A Summary of the Three General Classifications of FAS Effects

I. Central Nervous System Dysfunction
1. Mild-to-moderate mental retardation (seen in over 80 percent of cases)
2. Microcephaly—small brain (seen in over 80 percent of cases)
3. Poor coordination (seen in over 50 percent of cases)
4. Irritability in infancy, possibly due to withdrawal (seen in over 80 percent of cases)
5. Hyperactivity in childhood (seen in over 50 percent of cases)

II. Growth Deficiency
1. Prenatal growth deficiency (<2 standard deviations below the mean for body weight and body length at the time of birth), meaning these infants are born small for their gestational age.
2. Postnatal growth deficiency (<2 standard deviations below the mean for body weight and body length), meaning these infants remain small and do not catch up even when proper nutrition is provided.

III. Facial Abnormalities
1. Short eye slits
2. Hypoplastic philtrum—the groove under the nose is filled in
3. Thin upper lip
4. Flattened face
5. Droopy eyelids

consumption during pregnancy.[24] In this report, the mothers were heavy chronic ethanol users; in fact, one mother had a prenatal visit which revealed an extraordinary blood ethanol level of 175 mg/percent. Despite this level of blood ethanol, which would consider one legally intoxicated in all states, there was no charted entry of the mother seeming intoxicated, which suggested that the mother was showing robust tolerance and that maternal ethanol consumption was intense. At seven weeks of age, the baby died of respiratory suppression. The autopsy revealed a startling and unique neuropathology. Typically, the cerebral cortex is richly invaginated, giving it a "rolling hills" look, even in an infant. One entire side of the cerebral cortex of this FAS infant had a smooth surface, without convolutions.[24] The subsequent histological examination revealed that apparently there had been an abnormal migration of glial cells that moved in and filled up the convolutions.[24] The other FAS infant had such a small, malformed brain stem that life functions normally mediated in it could not be maintained. The aberrations of brain growth in these striking autopsy findings are so disruptive that it seems unlikely that surviving FAS infants have such neuropathologies. However, recent brain imaging data of FAS adolescents, using magnetic resonance imaging (MRI), indicated that these youngsters had a decrease in cerebral cortical tissue, not unlike that seen in Down syndrome, as well as decreased size of certain brain structures, specifically the thalamus and basal ganglia, which is not seen in Down syndrome.[25]

There are many critical issues surrounding FAS: What is the actual incidence of FAS? Is there recovery later in life or is FAS permanent? Is there a "safe" level of ethanol consumption during pregnancy or will moderate amounts of ethanol precipitate FAS? Are there behavioral effects in children born with FAS, in addition to the mental retardation? Initially, these issues were studied in already-diagnosed FAS children and thus were necessarily retrospective in nature. The major problem with retrospective studies is that they rely on the accuracy of the mothers' reports concerning what happened over a nine-month period. For example, can you recall what you ate for dinner each night for the last week? Now imagine asking subjects to recall how many ounces of ethanol they consumed on a daily basis during the full nine months of their pregnancies. However, these initial studies did provide provocative data from which more accurate studies were done. Since the description of FAS in the early 1970s, several prospective studies were launched in which women were followed prior to or early on in their pregnancies, and the progress of their children was also monitored. These studies best address the critical issues of FAS.

One of the fundamental issues concerning FAS is the fact that rarely is ethanol the sole drug taken in these cases. One study found that mothers who are heavy drinkers also are consuming many other drugs, in addition to ethanol.[26] Thus, the potential interactions of various licit and illicit drugs in these women make it difficult to attribute all of the symptoms of FAS to ethanol alone. In an attempt to resolve this problem, one study found that after sophisticated logistic regression analyses, FAS effects were related to absolute ethanol exposure and not to other drugs, like nicotine, caffeine, or marijuana, taken in addition to ethanol.[27]

The issue of incidence rates seems to depend on the size of the population that is examined. In a relatively small population of heavy chronic ethanol users, the incidence rate of FAS was estimated to be as high as 37 percent of that particular population studied.[20] More recent, and admittedly more conservative, estimates of the incidence of FAS in the overall population are at a rate of 0.29 per 1,000 in primarily white populations.[28] It is clear that ethnicity and socioeconomic status (SES) are important factors in FAS-incidence estimates. The Center for Disease Control (CDC) has reported that the incidence of FAS among Afro-American populations was seven times higher than that observed for white populations, and the incidence was thirty times higher for Native American populations.[29] In one specific study, the rate of FAS was 1 percent of the Caucasian upper-middle SES group, compared to 40.5 percent of the lower SES Afro-American and Hispanic groups.[30] It is important to note that these data are for the diagnosis of full FAS and not for those infants who may show only some of the symptoms of FAS. This issue will be further addressed later in this section.

The issue of the permanency of the FAS syndrome was first addressed in a ten-year follow-up of the original FAS children. This report indicated that fetal alcohol syndrome is permanent.[21] As mentioned earlier, the children remained growth-deficient and their facial abnormalities remained unchanged. When first described in 1963, their mean IQ was 56; ten years later it was 61, essentially the same.[21] None of these FAS children had a normal intellectual development. Moreover, home environment, even for those that were placed in better and more stable homes, did not alter the impact of the ethanol exposure in utero. However, there was improvement in the social and emotional development of those FAS children who were fostered into better homes and away from abusive, alcoholic parents.[21] In a subsequent study with an expanded subject population, the behavioral consequences of FAS were found to persist through adolescence and into adulthood.[31]

A question often raised about FAS deals with the level of ethanol consumption during pregnancy that is necessary to elicit FAS. One of the mothers, reported in the initial FAS study, had consumed over three quarts of red wine daily throughout her entire pregnancy.[20] The chronic heavy ethanol consumption of these "alcoholic" women is not typical of the population at large, so the issue of how much gestational ethanol exposure is necessary to produce FAS becomes important. An initial retrospective study focused on a population of white middle-class mothers who were moderate or social drinkers.[32] Consumption of one to two ounces of absolute ethanol per day was found to have a 10 percent risk of producing some ethanol effects in offspring, and two or more ounces of ethanol per day was found to have a 19 percent risk.[32] This suggests that the disruption of the growth program by ethanol is not an "all-or-none effect" but rather follows a dose-response relationship, namely the more ethanol one consumes during pregnancy, the greater the risk for abnormalities.

Over the years it has become apparent that some infants show some of the signs of FAS but not enough to be diagnosed as having FAS. To deal with this particular population, the diagnosis of FAE (fetal alcohol effects) has been used. In fact, the terms possible or probable FAE are not uncommon and underscore the ambiguity of some of the individual symptoms of FAS.[33] Because ethanol consumption is so much a part of Western culture, there would be a greater probability for moderate rather than heavy ethanol consumption to occur during pregnancy. In one prospective study of over 3,000 pregnancies in the Boston area, 2 percent of the women reported heavy ethanol use during their pregnancies, whereas 24 percent—almost twelve times as many—women reported moderate ethanol use.[34] This places many infants at risk for FAE. The incidence of FAE in the general population has been estimated to be as high as 90.1 per 1,000,[35] compared to the incidence of full FAS, cited earlier as 0.29 per 1,000.[28] Since most women do not consume enough ethanol to cause FAS, the question before them is not how much can I drink before running the risk of having an FAS infant? The better question is which FAE effects will my infant exhibit because of my drinking?

Since the focus of this book has been to show how drugs influence behavior, we should now turn our attention to the behavioral consequences of ethanol exposure during pregnancy. The diagnosis of FAS is usually done early in life and is based on symptoms that can be seen in infants. The mental retardation typically seen in FAS children was an immediately apparent, hallmark feature of FAS. However, as the initial infants diagnosed with FAS grew older and as more longitudinal prospective studies were launched, a more thorough picture of the behavioral effects caused by ethanol consumption during pregnancy emerged.

An early behavioral study examined fifteen children who experienced severe ethanol exposure during development but who were not mentally retarded.[15] Recall from our earlier discussion that even in a population of heavy chronic ethanol users the highest incidence rate of full FAS was only 40 percent,[30] meaning that even in the worst situation the majority of infants exposed to extremely high levels of ethanol during development did not show enough FAS symptoms to be diagnosed as such. Does this mean these infants are normal because they somehow avoided the detrimental effects of in utero ethanol exposure? This study attempted to address this question. Despite the fact that the IQ scores of this population were in the normal range (82–113), all of the children had major problems in school, from the onset of their education.[15] Thirteen of the fifteen subjects had been referred to special education programs by the time they reached first grade. All of the subjects had short attention spans and distractibility; all but one subject were diagnosed with hyperactivity. The authors conclude that the in utero ethanol exposure suffered by these children led to their persistent school-learning difficulties.

Subsequent longitudinal prospective studies have revealed much broader behavioral problems in adolescents and young adults whose mothers consumed ethanol, even in moderate amounts, during pregnancy. As we saw earlier, IQ estimates are typically low when tested early, and these low scores persist—58 percent of FAS and FAE subjects had IQs of 70 or below in one study,[31] and in another, 50 percent of subjects had borderline or retarded mental development.[36] In terms of academic functioning, deficits in arithmetic were the most common and most severe problem. These FAS/FAE adolescents and young adults, whose average age was seventeen years, were performing at a second-grade level in mathematics and at third- and fourth-grade levels for spelling and reading.[31] It is important to note that moderate ethanol consumption during pregnancy was found to result in deficits in arithmetic and reading skills in offspring at seven years of age.[37]

Behaviorally, there were severe problems in those FAS/FAE adolescents who were not classified as retarded, according to IQ scores. According to the behavioral adaptation inventory used in this study, the Vineland Adaptive Behavioral Scale (VABS), the characteristic problems of these FAS/FAE subjects were failure to consider the consequences of their actions, lack of initiative, and a lack of sensitivity to subtle social cues. As a group, these subjects had an average socialization skill level of a six-year-old and the average daily living skill (the ability to survive alone) of a nine-year-old.[31] In addition, 62 percent of these subjects had a significant level of maladaptive behaviors; the remaining 32 percent had an intermediate level of maladaptive behaviors. The maladaptive behaviors included stubbornness, social withdrawal, bullying, crying or laughing too easily, impulsivity, periods of high anxiety, lying and stealing, and lack of consideration for others.[31] The impulsivity and perseveration was also noted by another prospective study.[36]

The high incidence of maladaptive behaviors in FAS/FAE adolescents is more severe than the incidence levels seen in adolescents with other disorders like Down syndrome, in which there is a 15 percent to 32 percent incidence of maladaptive behaviors.[38] This may cause major problems in developing training programs to help FAS/FAE adolescents and adults live on their own successfully. It also raises the prospect that some FAS/FAE adults may need a great deal of custodial care for the rest of their lives.

To say that ethanol consumption during pregnancy influences the behavior of offspring is to understate the findings discussed above. Compared to any other drug, ethanol, the legal and accepted drug of Western culture, has the most profound and permanent effects on the behavior of offspring who are exposed to it during their development.

SMOKING DURING PREGNANCY

Exposure to cigarette smoking, whether directly through the mother or passively through the environment, may be one of the more frequent but avoidable dangers to the developing fetus.[39] There are at least two main causal factors that may be responsible for the detrimental effects of cigarette smoking during pregnancy: 1) the exposure to nicotine itself, and fetal hypoxia, which is a decrease in oxygen to the fetus because of a decrease in oxygen in the maternal blood supply to the fetus from cigarette smoke; and 2) decreased blood flow to the fetus. There may be other factors as well. Certainly there are other substances in the smoke from combusted tobacco, such as carbon monoxide and cyanide, but their roles in any of the effects observed in these children remain unknown.

The most common effect of smoking on development is intrauterine growth retardation, that is, babies are born smaller than those who are not exposed to smoking during pregnancy.[40] Relatively moderate smoke exposure can have major effects. Infants of mothers who smoked around six cigarettes a day or fathers who smoked more than twenty cigarettes (one pack) a day had birth weights that were 100 grams lighter than the control infants.[41] Another study found that mothers who smoked around five cigarettes a day had smaller infants.[42] Nicotine may play a direct role in the small birth weights of these exposed infants. One study found that mothers who smoked as many as thirteen low-nicotine cigarettes a day had infants with normal birth weights.[41]

Another common effect of smoke exposure during pregnancy is the higher incidence of respiratory problems in infants, increasing their risk for developing more lower-respiratory-tract infections with maternal use of five or less cigarettes a day.[42] Smoking around ten cigarettes a day is associated with higher rates of asthma and early-onset asthma in infants.[43] Prenatal maternal smoking also was associated with an increased frequency and length of obstructive apneas, periods in which the infant stops breathing. The risk was even higher if both parents smoked.[44] This raises an issue that arose in the intrauterine studies—that of passive smoking. Apparently it does not really matter whether the mother is actually drawing the cigarette smoke from a cigarette or breathing cigarette smoke in the environment. Passive exposure to one pack of cigarettes smoked at home is associated with a significant increase in lower respiratory problems in children ages seven to eleven.[45] Home is not the only environment in which cigarette smoke poses a hazard to the fetus. Smoke in the workplace is another potential problem. Depending on how much time a pregnant mother spends at work, exposure to cigarette smoke can be equivalent to the mother actually smoking five cigarettes a day. This has been associated with decreased birth weight.[46]

Somewhat related to the increased risk of respiratory problems, exposure to cigarette smoke during pregnancy leads to a higher risk for sudden infant death syndrome (SIDS). SIDS is the tragic disorder in which newborn infants, without warning and often without previously showing any symptoms of respiratory difficulties, will stop breathing in their sleep and often die. The general relationship between SIDS and smoking has been known for some time.[47,48] More recent studies have shown that even moderate exposure, such as a mother smoking six[49] to ten[50] cigarettes a day can significantly increase an infant's risk for SIDS. In addition, a father who smokes about a pack a day also increases an infant's risk for SIDS.[49] It appears that hypoxia during development may be the causal factor in the increased risk for SIDS, not smoking per se, since nonsmoking mothers who are anemic also have increased risks for having infants who develop SIDS.[50]

In addition to the effects reviewed preceding, it now appears that exposure to cigarette smoke during pregnancy leads to changes in behavior observed later in the lives of the exposed infants. When tested at three and four years of age, the children of mothers who smoked ten or more cigarettes a day during pregnancy had lower IQ scores than comparable control children.[51] Mothers who had a smoking habit of greater than ten cigarettes a day prior to their pregnancies but then quit smoking as soon as they were pregnant had children who performed significantly better in cognitive functioning than did the children of mothers who continued smoking ten cigarettes a day.[52] In addition to lower cognitive abilities, prenatal exposure to cigarette smoking also has been associated with poor language development when tested at four, five, and six years of age.[53] A fifteen-year longitudinal study of over 1,200 children found that the children of mothers who smoked over twenty cigarettes a day during pregnancy had increased rates of childhood behavior problems compared to control populations.[54] Furthermore, there appears to be a dose-response relationship between the amount of maternal smoking during pregnancy and later impulsive behavior.[55]

In summary, exposure to cigarette smoke during gestation appears to have a robust effect on intrauterine growth and the development of respiratory systems and a much less severe yet definitely negative effect on the later behavior of the child.

MARIJUANA USE DURING PREGNANCY

Cannabis is the most common illegal drug used during pregnancy[5] and is the third most frequently used drug during pregnancy, third only to alcohol and cigarettes.[56] The overall incidence of marijuana use during pregnancy has been estimated to be from 5 percent to 34 percent.[57] The effects of prenatal exposure to marijuana are not pronounced.[58] Certainly there are no apparent physical abnormalities like those seen in FAS/FAE.[59] There may be a small effect of cannabis exposure on overall body length at birth.[60] However, a longitudinal prospective study found that while exposure to cannabis in the first and second trimesters may lead to a decrease in body length at birth, exposure during the third trimester only was associated with an increase in body length.[61] One study found that infants exposed to cannabis during development had smaller head circumferences which persisted for two years.[62]

There are only minimal effects, if any, to cannabis use during pregnancy on the behavior of offspring. At birth, exposed infants seem to be more jittery, but this was a small effect.[63] Following infants from birth to five years of age whose Jamaican mothers used marijuana during their pregnancies, investigators found no effects in these infants compared to control infants.[64] There have been some provocative studies which have found that infants exposed to cannabis during development had deficits in attention,[55] and abstract reasoning and were more aggressive[65] when tested as children.

However, one study raised some critical issues regarding all of the drugs that may be taken during pregnancy, not only cannabis. In this study, school-aged children who were exposed to cannabis during their development were found to have behavioral problems, deficits in language comprehension, and increased distractibility, as the previous findings would have predicted.[66] When factors like maternal age at the time of delivery, the mother's personality, and the quality of the home environment were controlled for, the effects were no longer significantly different from the appropriate control groups.[66] Thus, it is important to have the correct control groups from which to draw comparisons.

Recall that the brain growth spurt continues after birth through the fourth postnatal year. This means that the neonatal period, in which infants are typically nursing, is also an important period of concern. Delta-9-tetrahydrocannabinol (Δ-9-THC), the principal psychoactive component in cannabis, has the unusual property of transferring to mother's milk at very high levels,[67] thus, for a nursing mother who is using marijuana, the infant is receiving a relatively high dose of Δ-9-THC. Infants who received Δ-9-THC in their mothers' milk during the first months of life were found to have impaired motor development when they were tested at age one.[57] This is one of the few clear demonstrations that even after birth drug exposure during the brain growth spurt can have a detrimental effect on development.

OPIATE USE DURING PREGNANCY

Although heroin has been referred to as the favored drug of abuse of the 1970s,[68] there has been a recent resurgence in its use. The topic of opiate use during pregnancy must address not only maternal use of heroin but also of methadone. Methadone maintenance programs may prevent individuals from using heroin, but in terms of a developing fetus, methadone poses a serious threat to normal development as does heroin. Thus, in the course of treating a drug addiction, the attending physician is introducing a pharmacological hazard to the normal development of the fetus. First let us review the effects of heroin use during pregnancy.

An infant who has been chronically exposed to heroin during gestation develops a dependency of sorts to heroin so that at birth their "supply" is abruptly terminated and they experience neonatal narcotic withdrawal syndrome. This neonatal withdrawal is characterized by central nervous system irritability, a persistent, high-pitch, shrill crying, tremors, an inability to sleep properly, hyperactive reflexes, frantic fist-sucking, not related to hunger since these infants feed poorly, vomiting and diarrhea, and, in extreme cases, convulsions.[69] The impact of this neonatal withdrawal syndrome can last as long as six months, at which time the infant begins to behave more normally.[70] Beside the occurrence of this neonatal withdrawal, a common effect of heroin exposure during pregnancy is intrauterine growth deficiency, which is typically seen in a decreased body weight.[71,72] Decreased head circumference also has been reported in heroin-exposed infants.[71] Later in life, children who were exposed to heroin during their gestation were not different than comparable controls in IQ tests, but they did have deficits in general cognitive abilities, like language, and showed many maladaptive behaviors such as uncontrollable temper, impulsiveness, and aggressiveness.[73] However, the high incidence of polydrug use in these initial subjects makes these data difficult to interpret,[73] which has prompted many investigators to more closely examine mothers who are participating in methadone maintenance programs.

At birth, infants of mothers who only took methadone during their pregnancies had significantly larger body weights compared to mothers who exclusively used heroin, but the methadone-exposed infants still were significantly lighter than non-drug exposed infant controls.[72] The methadone infants experienced a neonatal withdrawal syndrome that was moderate-to-mild in comparison to the heroin-exposed infants[74] and had similar symptoms like hypersensitivity to stimuli, irritability general, and sleep disturbances.[73] The methadone-exposed infants, like the heroin-exposed infants, had a high frequency of small head circumference which remained small for at least a year and a half.[74] At eighteen months, children exposed to methadone during development showed signs of developmental delays and deficits in motor and mental functioning.[74] Although at three years of age the methadone-exposed children were showing signs of poor learning behavior,[75] at school age, cognitive functioning did not appear to be different, but IQ scores were significantly lower; these children also were more aggressive and had higher anxiety levels than did the control populations.[76]

While these findings are collectively provocative, one must be cautious in interpreting the results. The lifestyle in the heroin- and/or methadone-dependent household can be a major factor in the behavioral development of drug-exposed infants. Just as we have seen in the marijuana literature discussed earlier, until the appropriate controls and statistical analyses are conducted, the long-term behavioral effects of opiate exposure during pregnancy remain an unresolved issue.

COCAINE USE DURING PREGNANCY

The recent near-epidemic use of cocaine in the United States has raised the concern that fetal drug exposure to cocaine may have serious long-lasting effects on brain development. The prevalence of cocaine use during pregnancy has been estimated to be from 8 percent to 17 percent.[77] In one urban hospital, 10 percent of newborns tested positive for cocaine.[78] Because this widespread use of cocaine during pregnancy is relatively recent, the immediate effects of cocaine use on pregnancy and the neonate have been well-described, whereas the long-term effects on behavior in particular are less clear. Let us first examine these immediate effects of cocaine on pregnancy and the newborn.

Recall from chapter 8 that cocaine is a stimulant that has powerful sympathomimetic effects. The consequences of having an intense sympathetic nervous system reaction, with an increased heart rate and blood pressure, have an immediate impact on pregnancy. The impact of cocaine use on pregnancy is primarily threefold. First, early pregnancy is threatened because cocaine produces effects that interfere with the course of development. Women who use cocaine during pregnancy have a higher incidence of first-trimester spontaneous abortions, perhaps a consequence of cocaine-induced decreased blood flow to the placenta.[78] Second, the use of cocaine in late pregnancy, during the third trimester, leads to serious complications. Shortly after taking cocaine, as soon as a few minutes or as late as a few hours, contractions may suddenly begin and send the mother into premature labor.[78] Fetal monitoring has indicated that a fetus will typically have a racing heart rate as a result of a mother's cocaine dose.[78] Third, in these cases of cocaine-induced premature labor, there is a high incidence of the placenta prematurely detaching, perhaps due to the increased blood pressure cocaine induces.[78]

Cocaine use during pregnancy also has direct effects on the infant. Prenatally, cocaine seems to induce an intrauterine growth retardation. Infants exposed to cocaine during development are smaller, have a lower birth weight, and are shorter than infants of mothers who did not take any drugs during their pregnancies.[79] One consistent effect of cocaine exposure during development is that infants have smaller head circumferences which seem to persist through the fourth year.[80] At birth, cocaine-exposed infants typically experience tremors and are extremely irritable. At three days of age, cocaine-exposed infants have been found to have a general deficit in their interactions with people; specifically they are are unable to respond to human voices or faces.[81] The combination of being difficult to console and extremely irritable not only creates a clinical problem at the hospital but also creates a situation at home in which the mother may have major difficulties bonding with and caring properly for the infant.

There has been a link made between cocaine use during pregnancy and a higher risk for sudden infant death syndrome (SIDS).[82] Although this increased risk is not as great as that observed following smoking during pregnancy, the increased risk is significant.[83] Cocaine alters the functioning of the locus coeruleus, a principal norepinephrine nucleus in the brain stem (see chapter 2) that may mediate arousal from sleep, and the increased risk for SIDS may be a direct result of this specific action of cocaine on brain development.[84]

Another immediate effect of cocaine exposure during pregnancy is an increased incidence of brain stroke associated with maternal cocaine use during the third trimester,[85] specifically with use just prior to labor and delivery.[86]

The studies examining the long-term behavioral effects of cocaine have been suggestive of learning and behavioral problems later in life but have basically been inconclusive.[87] Clearly there is no "fetal cocaine syndrome" that can be described,[88] and neurobehavioral consequences that can be attributed to cocaine use only during pregnancy are marginal and transitory.[89] For example, even though a smaller head circumference persists in children who were exposed to cocaine during development, they perform within normal ranges on mental tests, even though this condition in other situations is associated with poorer mental functioning.[90] Furthermore, it is not

TABLE 11–2   Effects of Cocaine on Pregnancy and On the Newborn

I. Effects on the Pregnancy
    1. Increased first-trimester spontaneous abortions
    2. Increased risk of sudden onset of contractions in the third trimester
    3. Increased risk of the placenta separating (abruptio placentae)
II. Effects on the Newborn
    1. Prenatal growth deficiency
    2. Microcephaly (small brain)
    3. Irritability and tremors
    4. Reduced ability of the infant to respond to faces or voices and interact with people in general, making them difficult to console
    5. Increased risk for SIDS

known if some of the short-term effects that are described are permanent or can be re-versed with time.[91] When infants who were exposed to cocaine during development were compared to infants exposed to other illicit drugs during development, few significant differences were found.[77]

In addition to all of these effects, cocaine apparently passes into maternal milk quite easily and may cause cocaine intoxication in breast-fed infants whose mothers used cocaine prior to breast-feeding.[92] In fact, there was a reported emergency room case of cocaine toxicity in an infant whose mother was breast-feeding while she was dosing with cocaine.[78] Cocaine can be present in the mother's milk for as long as two days after she takes it,[78] which strongly suggests that nursing mothers should refrain from cocaine use if they wish to breast-feed their infants.

ANTICONVULSANT MEDICATION USE DURING PREGNANCY

A major treatment dilemma in medicine today deals with seizure disorders in women of childbearing age. At the center of this dilemma is a host of successful medications that control seizure activity in adults and the concern of having development occur in the presence of powerful CNS depressants. Most of the children of epileptic mothers, approximately 89 percent,[93] were exposed to anticonvulsants during their development in utero, and overall, one in every 250 newborns were exposed to anticonvulsants during their development.[94]

The use of anticonvulsant medication throughout pregnancy may result in a syndrome that has been referred to as the fetal hydantoin syndrome (FHS). Although Dilantin®, diphenylhydantoin, is one of the more common anticonvulsants used to control seizures, it often is given in conjunction with other anticonvulsants like the barbiturates (phenobarbital, mephobarbital, etc.) and carbamazepine (Tegretol®). Thus, the name fetal hydantoin syndrome is somewhat misleading. Switching from Dilantin® and barbiturates to other anticonvulsants like carbamazepine or valproate sodium does not seem to change the risk of malformations in the infants.[95,96]

The fetal hydantoin syndrome is the name for the constellation of effects seen in children whose mothers were medicated with anticonvulsants throughout their pregnancies. In the initial reports[97,98] the observed effects fell into four general categories: deficiencies of growth, deficits in developmental performance, facial abnormalities, and limb malformations.

These FHS infants had prenatal and postnatal growth deficiencies, which means at birth they were smaller than comparable controls, and the FHS infants did not catch up to control levels and remained small.[98] An important feature of this growth deficiency is the significantly smaller head circumference, that is, microcephaly, seen in FHS infants.[98] Mental performance as measured by standard IQ testing in these children revealed that the FHS infants had a higher frequency of mild-to-moderate mental deficiency.[97] The facial abnormalities included a broad nasal ridge, droopy eyelids (i.e., ptosis), prominent low-set ears, and a wide mouth with prominent lips.[97] The most distinctive and almost diagnostic limb malformation was seen as a pathologically small last segment of the fingers and toes.[97]

Although certain features of the fetal hydantoin syndrome are common to FAS, namely the pre- and post-natal growth deficiencies and the smaller head circumference, FHS is decidedly different than FAS in all of its other features. In terms of behavior, the most significant difference between FHS and FAS/FAE is that of its severity. In FHS, the negative behavioral outcome is not as severe as a global mental retardation, which is seen often in FAS, but rather seen as a general deficit in cognitive abilities.[94] However, it is still not clear if these cognitive deficiencies in FHS children are directly due to the exposure of anticonvulsant medications during development. One study concludes that specific cognitive defects are associated with specific anticonvulsants,[99] whereas another, which also claims to have controlled for many variables, finds that the cognitive dysfunction found in FHS children is associated not with medication but rather with variables like maternal seizures during pregnancy and the parents' education.[93]

CAFFEINE USE DURING PREGNANCY

The popularity of coffee drinking in our culture has raised concern about its use during pregnancy. Moderate use of caffeine during pregnancy has no significant negative effect on fetal development, birth outcome, or neonatal behavior.[100,101] A small effect of caffeine-induced prenatal growth retardation has been reported,[102] but this effect was small and associated with greater than three cups of coffee per day.[103] This is not to say that caffeine does not have measurable effects on the fetus. Also reported was that high caffeine use, greater than 500 mg a day during the third trimester, caused the fetus to remain in an activated/arousal state longer than controls.[104] Moreover, caffeine has a longer half-life during the second and third trimesters compared to the first trimester or nonpregnant conditions, which means caffeine levels during these trimesters will be higher than in nonpregnant situations.[105] This may account for the caffeine withdrawal that has been observed in some infants during their first week of life.[105] Despite these immediate short-term effects, there appears to be no long-term effect of high caffeine use by mothers during their pregnancies.

REVIEW EXAM

1. What is the functional role of the placenta?
2. Define organogenesis.
3. What is "teratology"?
4. What occurs in the second and third trimesters?
5. What is "histogenesis"?
6. Define the "brain growth spurt."
7. Describe the three events of the brain growth spurt.

8. What is behavioral teratology?
9. How does the fetus obtain nutrients from maternal circulation?
10. Do drugs distribute to the fetus?
11. What is the effect of ethanol on the course of pregnancy?
12. What is the fetal alcohol syndrome (FAS)?
13. Why did it take so long to describe FAS?
14. Name the three general categories of FAS.
15. Name the specific features of central nervous system dysfunctions seen in FAS.
16. What specific growth deficiencies are seen in FAS?
17. Name the three prominent facial abnormalities seen in FAS.
18. What are some specific brain pathologies seen in FAS?
19. What is the incidence of FAS and of FAE?
20. Are the effects of FAS/FAE permanent?
21. What are some of the behavioral effects of FAS/FAE?
22. What are the causal factors in smoking during pregnancy?
23. What are the two most common effects of smoking during pregnancy on the infant?
24. What are the behavioral effects of smoking during pregnancy?
25. What are the general effects of marijuana use during pregnancy?
26. Describe the neonatal narcotic withdrawal syndrome.
27. What are the effects of opiate use during pregnancy?
28. What are the effects of cocaine use during pregnancy on the pregnancy itself?
29. What are the immediate effects of cocaine use during pregnancy on the infant?
30. What is the impact of cocaine in breast milk?
31. What is the fetal hydantoin syndrome (FHS)?
32. What are the major features of FHS?
33. What is the main behavioral effect of FHS?
34. What is the impact of caffeine use during pregnancy?

REFERENCES

1. OTONKOSKI, T., ANDERSSON, S., KNIP, M., & SIMELL, O. (1988). Maturation of insulin response to glucose during human fetal and neonatal development. *Diabetes, 37,* 286–291.
2. FREINKEL, N. (1980). Banting Lecture. Of pregnancy and progeny. *Diabetes, 29,* 1023–1035.
3. DOBBING, J. (1974). The later development of the brain and its vulnerability. In J. Davis (Ed.), *Scientific Foundations of Paediatrics* (pp. 565–577). London: Heinemann.
4. DOBBING. J., & SANDS, J. (1973). Quantitative growth and development of the human brain. *Archives of Disease in Childhood,* 48, 757–767.
5. BEHNKE, M., & EYLER, F. (1993). The consequences of prenatal substance use for the developing fetus, newborn, and young child. *International Journal of Addiction,* 28(13), 1341–1391.
6. SLOAN, L., GAY, J., SNYDER, S., & RALES, W. (1992). Substance abuse during pregnancy in a rural population. *Obstetrics and Gynecology,* 79(2), 245–248.
7. Book of Judges, 13:3–4.
8. ABEL, E. (1982). Consumption of alcohol during pregnancy: a review of effects on growth and development of offspring. *Human Biology,* 54(3), 421–453.
9. HARLAP, S., & SHIONO, P. (1980). Alcohol, smoking, and incidence of spontaneous abortions in the first and second trimester. *Lancet,* 2, 173–176.
10. LEMOINE, P., HARONSSEAU, H., BORTEYRU, J., & MENUET, J. (1967). Les enfants des parents alcooliques: anomalies observées à propos de 127 cases. *Archives of French Pediatrics,* 25, 830–832.

JONES, K., & SMITH, D. (1973). Recognition of the fetal alcohol syndrome in early infancy. *Lancet,* 2, 999–1001.

12. ABEL, E., & WELTE, J. (1986). Publication trends in fetal alcohol, tobacco, and narcotic effects. *Drug and Alcohol Dependence,* 18, 107–114.

13. CLARREN, S., & SMITH, D. (1978). The fetal alcohol syndrome. *New England Journal of Medicine,* 298, 1063–1067.

14. PIEROG, S., CHANDAVASU, O., & WEXLER, I. (1977). Withdrawal symptoms in infants with the fetal alcohol syndrome. *Journal of Pediatrics,* 90(4), 630–633.

15. SHAYWITZ, S., COHEN, D., & SHAYWITZ, B. (1980). Behavior and learning difficulties in children of normal intelligence born to alcoholic mothers. *Journal of Pediatrics,* 96(6), 978–982.

16. ROSETT, H., WEINER, L., LEE, A., ZUCKERMAN, B., DOOLING, E., & OPPENHEIMER, E. (1983). Patterns of alcohol consumption and fetal development. *Obstetrics and Gynecology,* 61(5), 539–546.

17. ROSETT, H., WEINER, L., ZUCKERMAN, B., MCKINLAY, S., & EDELIN, K. (1980). Reduction of alcohol consumption during pregnancy with benefits to the newborn. *Alcoholism, Clinical and Experimental Research,* 4(2), 178–184.

18. DAY, N., RICHARDSON, G., ROBLES, N., SAMBAMOORTHI, U., TAYLOR, P., SCHER, M., STOFFER, D., JASPERSE, D., & CORNELIUS, M. (1990). Effect of prenatal alcohol exposure on growth and morphology of offspring at 8 months of age. *Pediatrics,* 85(5), 748–752.

19. LITTLE, R., STREISSGUTH, A., BARR, H., & HERMAN, C. (1980). Decreased birth weight in infants of alcoholic women who abstained during pregnancy. *Journal of Pediatrics,* 96(6), 974–977.

20. JONES, K., & SMITH, D. (1975). The fetal alcohol syndrome. *Teratology,* 12, 1–10.

21. STREISSGUTH, A., CLARREN, S., & JONES, K. (1985). Natural history of the fetal alcohol syndrome: a 10-year follow-up of eleven patients. *Lancet,* 2, 85–92.

22. STREISSGUTH, A., HERMAN, C., & SMITH, D. (1978). Intelligence, behavior, and dysmorphogenesis in the fetal alcohol syndrome: a report on 20 patients. *Journal of Pediatrics,* 92(3), 363–367.

23. MAJEWSKI, F. (1981). Alcohol embryopathy: some facts and speculations about pathogenesis. *Neurobehavioral Toxicology and Teratology,* 3, 129–144.

24. CLARREN, S., ALVORD, E., SUMI, S., STREISSGUTH, A., & SMITH, D. (1978). Brain malformations related to prenatal exposure to ethanol. *Journal of Pediatrics,* 92(1), 64–67.

25. MATTSON, S., RILEY, E., JERIGAN, T., EHLERS, C., DELIS, D., JONES, K., STERN, C., JOHNSON, K., HESSELINK, J., & BELLUGI, U. (1992). Fetal alcohol syndrome: a case report of neuropsychological, MRI, and EEG assessment of two children. *Alcoholism, Clinical and Experimental Research,* 16(5), 1001–1003.

26. ALPERT, J., DAY, N., DOOLING, E., HINGSON, R., OPPENHEIMER, E., ROSETT, H., WEINER, L., & ZUCKERMAN, B. (1981). Maternal alcohol consumption and newborn assessment: methodology of the Boston City Hospital prospective study. *Neurobehavioral Toxicology and Teratology,* 3, 195–201.

27. GRAHAM, J., HANSON, J., DARBY, B., BARR, H., & STREISSGUTH, A. (1988). Independent dysmorphology evaluations at birth and 4 years of age for children exposed to varying amounts of alcohol in utero. *Pediatrics,* 81, 772–778.

28. ABEL, E., & SOKOI, R. (1991). A revised conservative estimate of the incidence of FAS and its economic impact. *Alcoholism, Clinical and Experimental Research,* 15(3), 514–524.

29. CHAVEZ, G., CORDER, J., & BECERRA, J. (1988). Leading major congenital malformations among minority groups in the United States. *MMWR-CDC SURVEILLANCE SUMMARIES,* 37, 17–24.

30. BINGOL, N., SCHUSTER, C., FUCHS, M., ISUB, S., TURNER, G., STONE, R., & GROMISCH, D. (1987). The influence of socioeconomic factors on the occurrence of fetal alcohol syndrome. *Advances in Alcohol and Substance Abuse,* 6, 105–118.

31. STREISSGUTH, A., AASE, J., CLARREN, S., RANDELS, S., LADUE, R., & SMITH, D. (1991). Fetal alcohol syndrome in adolescents and adults. *Journal of the American Medical Association,* 265(15), 1961–1967.

32. HANSON, J., STREISSGUTH, A., & SMITH, D. (1978). The effects of moderate alcohol consumption during pregnancy on fetal growth and morphogenesis. *Fetal and Neonatal Medicine,* 92(3), 457–460.

33. STREISSGUTH, A. (1992). Fetal alcohol syndrome and fetal alcohol effects: a clinical perspective of later developmental consequences. In I. Zagon & T. Slotkin (Eds.), *Maternal Substance Abuse and the Developing Nervous System* (pp. 5–24). San Diego, CA: Academic Press Inc.

34. ALPERT, J., DAY, N., DOOLING, E., HINGSON, R., OPPENHEIMER, E., ROSETT, H., WEINER, L., & ZUCKERMAN, B. (1981). Maternal alcohol consumption and newborn assessment: methodology of the Boston City Hospital prospective study. *Neurobehavioral Toxicology and Teratology,* 3, 195–201.
35. OUELLETTE, E., ROSETT, H., ROSMAN, N., & WEINER, L. (1977). Adverse effects on offspring of maternal alcohol abuse during pregnancy. *New England Journal of Medicine,* 297, 528–530.
36. ARONSON, M., SANDIN, B., SABEL, K., KYLLERMAN, M., & OLEGARD, R. (1984). Children of alcoholic mothers: outcome in relation to the social environment in which the children were brought up. *Reports Applied Psychology.,* 9(2), 3–7.
37. STREISSGUTH, A., SAMPSON, P., & BARR, H. (1989). Neurobehavioral dose-response effects of prenatal alcohol exposure in humans from infancy to adulthood. In D. Hutchings (Ed.), *Prenatal Abuse of Licit and Illicit Drugs.* Annals of the New York Academy of Science, 562, 145–158.
38. HARRIS, J. (1988). Psychological adaptation and psychiatric disorders in adolescents and young adults with Down's syndrome. In S. Pueschal (Ed.), *The Young Person with Down's Syndrome: Transition from Adolescence to Adulthood* (pp. 35–51). Baltimore, MD: Paul Brokes.
39. MAU, G. (1980). Smoking in pregnancy—effects on embryo and fetus. *Trends in Pharmacology,* 11, 345–346.
40. LANDESMAN-DWYER, S., & EMANUEL, I. (1979). Smoking during pregnancy. *Teratology,* 19, 119–125.
41. PEACOCK, J., BLAND, J., ANDERSON, H., & BROOKE, O. (1991). Cigarette smoking and birth weight: type of cigarette smoked and a possible threshold effect. *International Journal of Epidemiology,* 20(2), 404–412.
42. SCHULTE-HOBEIN, B., SCHWARTZ-BICKENBACH, D., ABT, S., PLUM, C., & NAU, H. (1992). Cigarette smoke exposure and development of infants throughout the first year of life: influence of passive smoking and nursing on cotinine levels in breast milk and infant urine. *Acta Paediatrica,* 81(6–7), 550–557.
43. WEITZMAN, M., GORTMAKER, S., WALKER, D., & SOBOL, A. (1990). Maternal smoking and childhood asthma., *Pediatrics,* 85(4), 505–511.
44. KAHN, A., GROSWASSER, J., SOTTIAUX, M., KELMANSON, I., REBUFFAT, E., FRANCO, P., DRAMAIX, M., & WAYENBERG, J. (1994). Prenatal exposure to cigarettes in infants with obstructive sleep apneas. *Pediatrics,* 93(5), 778–783.
45. NEAS, L., DOCKERY, D., WARE, J., SPENGLER, J., FERRIS, B., & SPEIZER, F. (1994). Concentration of indoor particulate matter as a determinant of respiratory health in children. *American Journal of Epidemiology,* 139(11), 1088–1099.
46. FORTIER, I., MARCOUX, S., & BRISSON, J. (1994). Passive smoking during pregnancy and the risk of delivering a small-for-gestational-age infant. *American Journal of Epidemiology,* 139(3), 294–301.
47. STELLE, R., & LANGWORTH, J. (1966). The relationship of antenatal and postnatal factors to sudden unexpected death in infancy. *Canadian Medical Association Journal,* 94, 1165–1171.
48. BERGMAN, A., & WIESNER, L. (1976). Relationship of passive cigarette smoking to SIDS. *Pediatrics,* 58, 665–668.
49. SAITO, R. (1991). The smoking habits of pregnant women and their husbands and the effect on their infants. *Nippon Koshu Eisei Zasshi,* 38(2), 124–131.
50. BULTERYS, M., GREENLAND, S., & KRAUS, J. (1990). Chronic fetal hypoxia and sudden infant death syndrome: interaction between maternal smoking and low hematocrit during pregnancy. *Pediatrics,* 86(4), 535–540.
51. OLDS, D., HENDERSON, C., & TATELBAUM, R. (1994). Intellectual impairment in children of women who smoke cigarettes during pregnancy. *Pediatrics,* 93(2), 221–227.
52. SEXTON, M., FOX, N., & HEBEL, J. (1990). Prenatal exposure to tobacco: II. effects on cognitive functioning at age three. *International Journal of Epidemiology,* 19(1), 72–77.
53. FRIED, P., O'CONNELL, C., & WATKINSON, B. (1992). 60- and 72-month follow up of children prenatally exposed to marijuana, cigarettes, and alcohol: cognitive and language assessment. *Journal of Developmental and Behavioral Pediatrics,* 13(6), 383–391.
54. FERGUSSON, D., HORWOOD, L., & LYNSKEY, M. (1993). Maternal smoking before and after pregnancy: effects on behavioral outcomes in middle childhood. *Pediatrics,* 92(6), 815–822.
55. FRIED, P., WATKINSON, B., & GRAY, R. (1992). A follow-up study of attentional behavior in 6-year-old children exposed prenatally to marijuana, cigarettes, and alcohol. *Neurotoxicology and Teratology,* 14(5), 299–311.

56. DAY, N., & RICHARDSON, G. (1991). Prenatal marijuana use: epidemiology, methodologic issues, and infant outcome. *Clinics in Perinatology,* 18(1), 77–91.
57. ASTLEY, S., & LITTLE, R. (1990). Maternal marijuana use during lactation and infant development at one year. *Neurotoxicology and Teratology,* 12(2), 161–168.
58. DREHER, M., NUGENT, K., & HUDGINS, R. (1994). Prenatal marijuana exposure and neonatal outcomes in Jamaica: an ethnographic study. *Pediatrics,* 93(2), 254–260.
59. ASTLEY, S., CLAREN, S., LITTLE, R., SAMPSON, P., & DALING, J. (1992). Analysis of facial shape in children gestationally exposed to marijuana, alcohol, and/or cocaine. *Pediatrics,* 89(1), 67–77.
60. DAY, N., CORNELIUS, M., GOLDSCHMIDT, L., RICHARDSON, G., ROBLES, N., & TAYLOR, P. (1992). The effects of prenatal tobacco and marijuana use on offspring growth from birth through 3 years of age. *Neurotoxicology and Teratology,* 14(6), 407–414.
61. DAY, N., SAMBAMOORTHI, U., TAYLOR, P., RICHARDSON, G., ROBLES, N., JHON, Y., SCHER, M., STOFFER, D., CORNELIUS, M., & JASPERSE, D. (1991). Prenatal marijuana use and neonatal outcome. *Neurotoxicology and Teratology,* 13(3), 329–334.
62. CHASNOFF, I., GRIFFITH, D., FREIER, C., & MURRAY, J. (1992). Cocaine/polydrug use in pregnancy: two-year follow up. *Pediatrics,* 89(2), 284–289.
63. PARKER, S., ZUCKERMAN, B., BAUCHNER, H., FRANK, D., VINCI, R., & CABRAL, H. (1990). Jitteriness in full-term neonates: prevalence and correlates. *Pediatrics,* 85(1), 17–23.
64. HAYES, J., LAMPART, R., DREHER, M., & MORGAN, L. (1991). Five-year follow up of rural Jamaican children whose mothers used marijuana during pregnancy. *West Indian Medical Journal,* 40(3), 120–123.
65. GRIFFITH, D., AZUMA, S., & CHASNOFF, I. (1994). Three-year outcome of children exposed prenatally to drugs. *Journal of the American Academy of Child and Adolescent Psychiatry,* 33(1), 20–27.
66. O'CONNELL, C., & FRIED, P. (1991). Prenatal exposure to cannabis: a preliminary report of postnatal consequences in school-age children. *Neurotoxicology and Teratology,* 13(6), 631–639.
67. PEREZ-REYES, M., & WALL, M. (1982). Presence of delta-9-tetrahydrocannabinol in human milk. *New England Journal of Medicine,* 307, 819–820.
68. PETERS, H., & THEORELL, C. (1991). Fetal and neonatal effects of maternal cocaine use. *Journal of Obstetric, Gynecologic and Neonatal Nursing,* 20(2), 121–6.
69. KRON, R., KAPLAN, S., FINNEGAN, L., LITT, M., & PHOENIX, M. (1975). The assessment of behavioral change in infants undergoing narcotic withdrawal: comparative data from clinical and objective methods. *Addictive Diseases, International Journal,* 2, 257–275.
70. CHASNOFF, I., HATCHER, R., & BURNS, W. (1980). Early growth patterns of methadone-addicted infants. *American Journal of Diseases of Children,* 134, 1049–1051.
71. LAM, S., TO, W., DUTHIE, S., & MA, H. (1992). Narcotic addiction in pregnancy with adverse maternal and perinatal outcome. *Australian and New Zealand in Journal of Obstetrics and Gynaecology,* 32(3), 216–221.
72. KANDALL, S., ALBIN, S., LOWINSON, J., BERLE, B., EIDELMAN, A., & GARTNER, L. (1976). Differential effects of maternal heroin and methadone use on birthweight. *Pediatrics,* 58, 681–685.
73. HUTCHINGS, D. (1982). Methadone and heroin during pregnancy: a review of behavioral effects in human and animal offspring. *Neurobehavioral Toxicology and Teratology,* 4, 429–434.
74. ROSEN, T., & JOHNSON, H. (1982). Children of methadone-maintained mothers: follow up to 18 months of age. *Journal of Pediatrics,* 101(2), 192–196.
75. JOHNSON, H., GLASSMAN, M., FIKS, K., & ROSEN, T. (1990). Resilient children: individual differences in developmental outcome of children born to drug abusers. *Journal of Genetic Psychology,* 151(4), 523–539.
76. DECUBAS, M., & FIELD, T. (1993). Children of methadone-dependent women: developmental outcomes. *American Orthopsychiatry,* 63(2), 266–276.
77. RICHARDSON, G., DAY, N., & MCGAUHEY, P. (1993). The impact of perinatal marijuana and cocaine use on the infant and child. *Clinical Obstetrics and Gynecology,* 36(2), 302–318.
78. CHASNOFF, I. (1987). Perinatal effects of cocaine. *Contemporary Obstetrics and Gynecology,* May, 163–179.
79. CHASNOFF, I., BURNS, K., & BURNS, W. (1987). Cocaine use in pregnancy: perinatal morbidity and mortality. *Neurotoxicology and Teratology,* 9(4), 291–293.
80. DAY, N., COTTREAU, C., & RICHARDSON, G. (1993). The epidemiology of alcohol, marijuana, and cocaine use among women of childbearing age and pregnant women. *Clinical Obstetrics and Gynecology,* 36(2), 267–278.
81. CHASNOFF, I., BURNS, W., SCHNOLL, S., & BURNS, K. (1985). Cocaine use in pregnancy. *New England Journal of Medicine,* 313(11), 666–669.

82. GINGRAS, J., & WEESE-MAYER, D. (1990). Maternal cocaine addiction. II. An animal mo͞ the study of brain stem mechanisms operative in sudden infant death syndrome. *Medical Hyp͞ses,* 33(4), 231–234.

83. KANDALL, S., & GAINES, J. (1991). Maternal substance use and subsequent sudden infant dea͞ syndrome (SIDS) in offspring. *Neurotoxicology and Teratology,* 13(2), 235–240.

84. GINGRAS, J., O'DONNELL, K., & HUME, R. (1990). Maternal cocaine addiction and fetal behavioral state. I. A human model for the study of sudden infant death syndrome. *Medical Hypotheses,* 33(4), 227–230.

85. HEIER, L., CARPANZANO, C., MAST, J., BRILL, P., WINCHESTER, P., & DECK, M. (1991). Maternal cocaine abuse: the spectrum of radiologic abnormalities in the neonatal CNS. *American Journal of Neuroradiology,* 12(5), 951–956.

86. CHASNOFF, I., BUSSEY, M., & SAVICH, R. (1986). Perinatal cerebral infarction and maternal cocaine abuse. *Journal of Pediatrics,* 108(3), 456–459.

87. SINGER, L., FARKAS, K., & KLIEGMAN, R. (1992). Childhood medical and behavioral consequences of maternal cocaine use. *Journal of Pediatric Psychology,* 17(4), 389-406.

88. PLESSINGER, M., & WOODS, J. (1993). Maternal, placental, and fetal pathophysiology of cocaine exposure during pregnancy. *Clinical Obstetrics and Gynecology,* 36(2), 267–278.

89. HUTCHINGS, D. (1993). The puzzle of cocaine's effects following maternal use during pregnancy: are there reconcilable differences? *Neurotoxicology and Teratology,* 15(5), 281–286.

90. BEHNKE, M., & EYLER, F. (1993). The consequences of prenatal substance use for the developing fetus, newborn, and young child. *International Journal of Addiction,* 28(13), 1341–1391.

91. GINGRAS, J., WEESE-MAYER, D., HUME, R., & O'DONNELL, K. (1992). Cocaine and development: mechanisms of fetal toxicity and neonatal consequences of perinatal cocaine exposure. *Early Human Development,* 31(1), 1–24.

92. YOUNG, S., VOSPER, H., & PHILLIPS, S. (1992). Cocaine: its effects on maternal and child health. *Pharmacotherapy,* 12(1), 2–17.

93. GAILY, E., KANTOLA-SORSA, E., & GRANSTROM, M. (1990). Specific cognitive dysfunction in children with epileptic mothers. *Developmental Medicine and Child Neurology,* 32(5), 403–414.

94. LINDHOUT, D., & OMTZIGT, J. (1994). Teratogenic effects of antiepileptic drugs: implications for the management of epilepsy in women of childbearing age. *Epilepsia,* 35 suppl.4, S19–S28.

95. MARTIN, P., & MILLAC, P. (1993). Pregnancy, epilepsy, management, and outcome: a 10-year perspective. *Seizure,* 2(4), 277–280.

96. BATTINO, D., BINELLI, S., CACCAMO, M., CANEVINI, M., CANGER, R., COMO, M., CROCI, D., DEGIAMBATTISTA, M., GRANATA, T., PARDI, G., ET AL. (1992). Malformations in offspring of 305 epileptic women: a prospective study. *Acta Neurological Scandinavien,* 85(3), 204–207.

97. HANSON, J., & SMITH, D. (1975). The fetal hydantoin syndrome. *Journal of Pediatrics,* 87(2), 285–290.

98. HANSON, J., MYRIANTHOPOULOS, N., HARVEY, M., & SMITH, D. (1976). Risks to the offspring of women treated with hydantoin anticonvulsants, with emphasis on the fetal hydantoin syndrome. *Journal of Pediatrics,* 89(4), 662–668.

99. LINDHOUT, D., & OMTZIGT, J. (1992). Pregnancy and the risk of teratogenicity. *Epilepsia,* 33 suppl.4, S41–S48.

100. SIVAK, A. (1994). Coteratogenic effects of caffeine. *Regulatory Toxicology and Pharmacology,* 19(1), 1–13.

101. NEHLIG, A., & DEBRY, G. (1994). Consequences on the newborn of chronic maternal consumption of coffee during gestation and lactation: a review. *Journal of the American College of Nutrition,* 13(1), 6–21.

102. FORTIER, I., MARCOUX, S., & BEAULAC-BAILLARGEON, L. (1993). Relation of caffeine intake during pregnancy to intrauterine growth retardation and pre-term birth. *American Journal of Epidemiology,* 137(9), 931–940.

103. NAROD, S., DESANJOS'E, S., & VICTORA, C. (1991). Coffee during pregnancy: a reproductive hazard? *American Journal of Obstetrics and Gynecology,* 164(4), 1109–1114.

104. DEVOE, L., MURRAY, C., YOUSSIF, A., & ARNAUD, M. (1993). Maternal caffeine consumption and fetal behavior in normal third-trimester pregnancy. *American Journal of Obstetrics and Gynecology,* 168(4), 1105–1111.

105. MCKIM, E. (1991). Caffeine and its effects on pregnancy and the neonate. *Journal of Nurse-Midwifery,* 36(4), 226–231.

GLOSSARY

absorption.   The time from the moment a drug is administered to its entry into the blood.

acetaldehyde.   The first metabolite in the biotransformation of ethanol, which is extremely toxic. Accumulation of acetaldehyde will lead to a toxic reaction.

acetyl group.   The radical CH_3CO.

acetylcholine (ACh).   One of the molecules used by certain neurons as a neurotransmitter.

active metabolites.   Those products produced in the process of biotransforming a drug which are psychoactive themselves.

albumin.   A type of protein found in blood and other body tissues such as muscle, as well as in egg whites, milk, and plant tissues.

alcohol dehydrogenase.   The first enzyme in one of the principal biotransformation processes that breaks down ethanol.

Amanita muscaria.   A class of hallucinogenic mushrooms that grows in the "Old World."

amotivational syndrome.   A persistent pattern of behavior in which a person does not feel motivated to accomplish anything.

anesthesia.   A reversible loss of sensation and pain perception.

angel dust.   The popular name for phencyclidine.

antiemetic.   Any agent that will alleviate nausea and prevent vomiting.

anxiolytic.   Any agent that will allay anxiety.

arrhythmia.   An irregular heart rate.

artery.   That part of the circulatory system that carries blood from the heart to the capillaries (as opposed to a vein).

ataxia.   Uncoordinated muscle activity.

autonomic nervous system (ANS).   The division of the peripheral nervous system that mediates the fight-or-flight sympathetic response and the rest-and-digest parasympathetic response.

axon.   When a neuron "fires," that part of the neuron through which the action potential, namely the output of the neuron, travels.

273

balanced placebo.   An experimental design that directly examines expectation and environment in drug-taking situations.

bhang.   A preparation of cannabis which is made up of the shoots as well as the leaves of the plant. (*See also* **marijuana, sinsemilla, ganja, hashish, hash, charas.**)

bile.   A fluid secreted by the liver into the small intestines which helps in the digestion of fats.

blood-brain barrier.   The combination of specialized capillaries and special cells in the brain that makes it extremely difficult for molecules to enter brain tissue.

borderline hypertensive.   A condition characterized by higher-than-normal blood pressure levels but not high enough to be classified as a threatening disease. (*See also* **hypertension.**)

bound drug molecules.   Drug molecules which bind to large proteins in the blood then are unable to move out of the blood. (*See also* **free drug molecules.**)

brain stem.   The lower portion of the brain from the spinal cord to the thalamus and hypothalamus (diencephalon).

butophanol (Stadol).   An anesthetic which is a synthetic opiate that has both agonistic and antagonistic properties. (*See also* **naltrexone—trexan; naloxone—narcan.**)

capillary.   The smallest diameter blood vessel and the functional point where the exchange of nutrients and waste products occurs between the cells and blood.

caudal.   A directional anatomical term that refers to the tail portion of an animal.

CBD (cannabinol).   One of the components found in marijuana that may have psychoactive properties.

central nervous system (CNS).   Consisting of the spinal cord and the brain, this tissue processes sensory input and sends out motor commands to muscle, and mediates the motivational, emotional, and cognitive functions of the animal.

cerebellum.   That portion of the brain which is located on the dorsal side of the metencephalon, important for coordination and precise motor behavior.

cerebral cortex.   Literally the bark, this is the outer or surface layer of the telencephalon, typically made up of six layers of cells. It is here that the highest form of neuronal processing occurs.

China white.   A designer drug, which is to say a variation of the drug fentanyl (Sublimaze®).

cirrhosis.   A disease characterized by a hardening of the liver, commonly caused by chronic excessive ethanol consumption.

clonidine (Catapres®).   A new antipsychotic medication that specifically blocks dopamine receptors in areas that mediate emotional behavior, without blocking those dopamine receptors in motor systems.

concordance.   The term that refers to the appearance of a characteristic in both siblings who are twins.

crack.   Cocaine that is freebased using a sodium bicarbonate procedure as opposed to an ether-extracting procedure.

cross-tolerance.   When tolerance develops to one drug, it also will develop to other drugs in that class.

dense bar.   The thickened portions of the presynaptic membrane that are involved in the process of neurotransmitter release.

diencephalon.   The portion of the central nervous system that is made up of the thalamus and hypothalamus.

disinhibition.   The process whereby normal inhibition is removed or prevented, resulting in excitation.

distillation.   The process of condensing products from the vapors of a heated compound.

dizogotic twin.   Fraternal twins (twins who are not identical). (*See also* **monozygotic twin.**)

dopamine (DA).   One of the molecules used by certain neurons as a neurotransmitter and classified in general as a monoamine (MA) and more specifically as a catecholamine (CA).

dose-response curve.   A way of expressing the relationship between the intensity of a drug effect and the dose of the drug needed to elicit that effect.

drug.   Any substance or compound not manufactured by the body that is ingested or somehow taken into the body.

drug receptor.   A specialized protein structure to which drug molecules bind and cause a physiological effect.

dynorphin.   One of the naturally occurring endogenous opiates used by some neurons as a neurotransmitter. It is found in high concentrations in the central gray region of the brain.

dysphoria.   A feeling of unease and discomfort.

ED.   effective dose, that is the dose of a drug needed to elicit a given behavior.

EEG (electroencephalograph).   The characteristic electrical activity of the brain that is typically recorded from surface electrodes placed on the scalp.

electrolyte.   A substance that becomes a charged particle when dissolved in a solvent like water, for example, when put into water, salt dissolves into the charged particles sodium and chloride.

encephalin. One of the naturally occurring endogenous opiates used by some neurons as a neuromitter. It is found throughout the brain in small interneurons.

endorphin. One of the naturally occurring endogenous opiates used by some neurons as a neurotramitter. It is made by the neurons in the hypothalamus.

enteral route of administration. Taking drugs through the alimentary canal, either by swallowing or rectally.

enzyme. A complex type of protein produced by the cell which will cause a biochemical reaction to occur.

epidural anesthesia. The process in which an analgesic agent is injected between the specialized tissue membranes that cover the spinal cord.

ERP (event-related potential). The electrical activity of a certain section of the brain which is provoked by some event.

ethanol (ethyl alcohol). That form of alcohol which is produced from the fermentation of various foods like grains or fruits.

exocytosis. The process whereby neurons release neurotransmitter molecules when an action potential reaches the axon terminal.

fermentation. In the case of ethanol, the process whereby the normal enzyme activity involved in respiration of yeast converts the complex sugars of fruits or grains into ethanol.

forebrain. That portion of the central nervous system consisting of the telencephalon and diencephalon.

free drug molecules. Drug molecules that are not bound to large proteins in the blood and are free to move out of the blood. (*See also* **bound drug molecules.)**

freebase. The process of removing the hydrochloride portion of the cocaine molecule which was added in the initial processing of cocaine.

fusion pore. The structure in the presynaptic membrane and in the membrane of the synaptic vesicles that forms the opening through which neurotransmitter molecules are released.

GABA (gamma-aminobutyric acid). A substance used by some neurons as a neurotransmitter, classified as an amino acid neurotransmitter and found throughout the brain in small inhibitory interneurons.

ganja. A preparation of cannabis which contains the resin-rich small leaves and flower brackets of the female and has relatively more psychoactive components than other preparations of cannabis. (*See also* **marijuana, sinsemilla, bhang, hashish, hash, charas.)**

gastric mucosa. Those skin layers that line the stomach which are rich in mucus glands.

glaucoma. A disease characterized by unusually high pressure within the eyeball that can lead to detachment of the retina and can ultimately result in blindness.

glia (glial cells). A type of cell in the nervous system which does not actively communicate with other cells and which may play a role in the blood-brain barrier or in wrapping the axons of neurons with a fatty sheath.

glutamate. A substance used by some neurons as a neurotransmitter, classified as an amino acid neurotransmitter and typically excitatory in nature.

half-life. The time it takes for half of an initial dose of a drug to be cleared from the blood.

hashish or hash. The concentrated resin of cannabis. (*See also* **marijuana, sinsemilla, ganja, bhang, charas.)**

heterogeneity. The state of being composed of differing or dissimilar components. (*See* homogeneity.)

hippocampus. A telencephalic limbic brain structure that lies below the cerebral cortex, which is critical in the formation of long-term memories.

homogeneity. The state of being composed of similar components. (*Compare with* **heterogeneity.)**

hypertension. A condition characterized by abnormal and often dangerously high blood pressure. (*See also* **borderline hypertensive.)**

hypnotic. Anything that will induce sleep ("hypnos") or a state of unconsciousness.

hypothalamus. A critical limbic structure made up of a collection of nuclei that forms the ventral part of the diencephalon and is involved with virtually all behavior.

intramuscular (IM) route of administration. That parenteral drug administration that involves injecting a drug directly into a mass of muscle, typically the forearm, thigh, or buttocks.

intranasal route of administration. That parenteral drug administration that involves inhaling a drug so it comes to lie on the nasal mucosa, where it is absorbed into the circulation.

knockout drops. *See* **Mickey Finn.**

Korsakoff's syndrome. An advanced form of Wernicke's encephalopathy syndrome, characterized by memory loss and profound apathy, typically caused by long-term excessive ethanol consumption.

LAAM (l-alpha acetyl methadyl). A long-acting synthetic opiate used to help break opiate dependencies.

~mation.   Tearing or crying.

(lethal dose).   The particular dose of a drug that will lead to death.

~nbic system.   The collection of various brain structures involved in the mediation of emotion.

~ipid.   Organic molecules which include fats, oils, and steroids which are not water-soluble.

lipid-solubility.   The ability of a drug to dissolve in fat.

locus coeruleus.   The brain nucleus located in the brain stem below the cerebellum which is the principal collection of neurons that use norepinephrine as a neurotransmitter and which is involved in various behaviors, including arousal, affect, and pleasure.

main effect.   The most robust of the many effects that a drug elicits or the particular effect of greatest interest.

marijuana.   The dried leaves and flowering tips of the cannabis plant, the form of cannabis most commonly smoked. (*See also* **sinsemilla, ganja, bhang, charas.**)

medial.   Refers to toward the midline.

medial forebrain bundle (MFB).   A collection of fibers from norepinephrine, serotonin, and dopamine neurons which courses through the brain, involved in the mediation of positive reinforcement, or pleasure.

membrane transport mechanism.   A specialized protein in a membrane that will recognize, bind, and transport into the cell certain structures such as a neurotransmitter or precursor substance for neurotransmitter synthesis.

MEOS (microsomal ethanol oxidizing system).   One of the two principal enzyme systems that metabolize ethanol.

meperidine (Demerol®).   A synthetic opiate that is used as a common medication to control pain.

mesencephalon (mid-brain).   One of the main divisions of the central nervous system which contains nuclei important in the processing of visual, auditory, and pain input, as well as areas involved in motor behavior.

mesocortical system.   A brain pathway originating in the mesencephalon and ending in the cerebral cortex. It plays a role in emotional behavior and is one of the principal targets of antipsychotic medication.

mesolimbic system.   A brain pathway originating in the mesencephalon and ending in a variety of limbic structures. It plays a role in emotional behavior and is one of the principal targets of antipsychotic medication.

metencephalon.   One of the main divisions of the central nervous system that consists of the cerebellum on the dorsal (back) side and the brain stem area on the front.

methadone (Dolophine®).   A synthetic opiate with a very long half-life, commonly used as a substitute opiate in treatment programs for people with heroin and/or morphine dependencies.

methanol (methyl alcohol).   A form of alcohol commonly referred to as wood alcohol.

Mickey Finn.   The literary name for a drink containing an additional sedative compound, historically ethanol combined with chloral hydrate, used to quickly induce unconsciousness in a person and enabling a kidnapping or another illegal activity; also referred to as knockout drops.

monozygotic twin.   Identical twins. (*Compare with* **dizygotic twin.**)

MPTP (l-methly-4-phenyl-1,2,3,6-tetrahydroperidine).   An illicit designer drug that causes lesions in the central nervous system similar to those seen in Parkinson's disease.

MRI (magnetic resonance imaging).   The process of imaging the central nervous system (CNS) in which the brain is placed in an intense magnetic field and in which manipulations of the field cause atoms in the CNS to produce a frequency that can be measured, resulting in precise pictures of the CNS.

myelencephalon (medulla).   One of the main divisions of the central nervous system which is the most caudal; it is the portion of the central nervous system that is an extension of the spinal cord.

naloxone (Narcan®).   One of the two pure opiate antagonists (i.e., a true opiate antidote) that is relatively long-lasting. (*See also* **naltrexone—Trexan®; butorphanol—Stadol®.**)

naltrexone (Trexan®).   One of the two pure opiate antagonists (i.e., a true opiate antidote) that is relatively short-lasting. (*See also* **naloxone—Narcan®; butorphanol—Stadol®.**)

neuron.   A type of cell in the nervous system that actively communicates and processes information.

neurotransmitter.   A molecule made in the neuron and released from the axon terminal when the neuron fires.

NMDA (N-methyl-D-aspartate).   An agonist of glutamate, which marks a unique class of glutamate receptors that may be involved in memory.

norepinephrine (NE).   One of the molecules used by certain neurons as a neurotransmitter and classified in general as a monoamine (MA) and more specifically as a catecholamine (CA).

nucleus (nuclei). When referring to a cell, that portion of the cell body which contains the DNA code and is responsible for the production of proteins and other activities essential for the survival of the cell; when referring to neuroanatomy, a cluster of neurons which performs a similar function.

nucleus accumbens. A nucleus in the telencephalon which is critical in the mediation of positive reinforcement (i.e., pleasure).

opium (opiate). Harvested from the seed pod of the opium poppy, this thick, milky substance contains a host of natural opiates, including morphine and codeine.

palpitation. Unusually strong and rapid heart beat.

parasympathetic nervous system. That division of the autonomic nervous system that mediates a rest-and-digest parasympathetic response. *(Compare with* **sympathetic nervous system.***)*

parenteral route of administration. Taking drugs by any route other than swallowing or rectally; parenteral routes include various injections, and pulmonary and topical routes.

peripheral nervous system (PNS). The collection of neurons and axons outside the central nervous system which consists of the somatic and autonomic nervous systems.

placebo. A substance (or procedure) that is inert and/or has no biological activity for a given condition. It often is used in experiments to determine the effectiveness of a drug which has biological activity.

pores. Small openings in a membrane.

proof. A common standard used to quantify the amount of ethanol in a beverage that is double the actual percent of ethanol in a beverage.

propanol (isopropyl alcohol). A form of alcohol which is not typically ingested, commonly referred to as rubbing alcohol.

protein. A class of biological compounds consisting of complex combinations of amino acids; proteins can be structural units in a cell and also can serve as enzymes that catalyze reactions.

pulmonary route of administration. That parenteral route of administration that occurs in the lungs.

pylorus sphincter. The ring of smooth muscle in the alimentary canal between the stomach and small intestine.

raphe nuclei. A collection of nuclei, primarily in the mesencephalon, which uses serotonin as a neurotransmitter and is involved with arousal, sleep, and affect.

redistribution. Occurs when drug molecules which have accumulated rapidly and preferentially into one compartment, usually highly lipid-soluble drugs distributing to fat stores, later are released into the bloodstream.

REM (rapid eye movement sleep). That stage of sleep for which mammals seem to have a biological need and in which dreaming occurs most frequently.

reverse tolerance. The situation in which a drug's effect becomes more intense following repeated doses.

rhinorrhea. A runny nose.

rostral. An anatomical term which refers to the direction toward the head portion of an animal.

serotonin (5-HT). One of the molecules used by certain neurons as a neurotransmitter, classified in general as a monoamine (MA) and more specifically as an indolamine.

side effect. When referring to the actions of a drug, those effects that are as intense or prominent as the so-called main effects, often used to describe those drug effects that are of little interest.

sinsemilla. A potent preparation of cannabis that is harvested before the plants have gone to seed. *(See also* **marijuana, ganja, bhang, hashish, hash, charas.***)*

skeletal muscle. Muscle tissue that is involved in moving bone (as opposed to muscle tissue in blood vessels and visceral organs).

somatic nervous system. The division of the peripheral nervous system that conveys sensory information from the various receptors in the body to the CNS and also conveys motor commands from the CNS to skeletal muscle tissues.

spinal anesthesia. The process in which an analgesic agent is injected directly onto a section of the spinal cord.

spleen. The visceral organ near the stomach which is involved in the storage of blood, as well as the destruction of blood cells.

subcutaneous (SQ) route of administration. That parenteral route of drug administration which involves placing a substance directly under the skin, usually accomplished by injection of the compound or placement of "spikes" that contain the drug (i.e., Norplant® spikes).

sublingual route of administration. That parenteral route of drug administration which involves placing a substance in the mouth, with absorption occurring at the mucosal lining of the mouth (i.e., nitro-glycerin capsules, chewing tobacco).

sympathetic nervous system.   The division of the autonomic nervous system which mediates the fight-or-flight sympathetic response. *(Compare with* **parasympathetic nervous system.)**

synapse.   The functional point of communication between neurons where neurotransmitter molecules are released from one neuron and then interact with receptor structures on the target surface, actually the gap between the axon terminal of one neuron (the presynaptic side) and the target surface (the postsynaptic side).

T-cell.   A cell made in the bone marrow and then modified by the thymus gland. It carries antibodies throughout the body and is one of the principal cell types in the immune system.

tachycardia.   A fast heart rate.

telencephalon.   The most rostral division of the central nervous system (CNS), consisting of the cerebral cortex and other structures under the surface; this is where the most complex processing in the CNS occurs.

THC (tetrahydrocannabinol).   One of the most significant psychoactive components of cannabis.

Therapeutic Index (TI).   An indicator of a drug's safety, this value reflects the difference in the dose for a given effect and the dose for lethal toxicity; it is calculated by dividing the effective dose$_{50}$ for a given outcome by the lethal dose$_{50}$.

thiamine.   One of the B-complex vitamins (vitamin B-1) which is important for normal brain functioning.

TIQ (tetrahydroquinoline).   A substance that is formed in the body by the combination of acetaldehyde, the toxic first breakdown product of ethanol metabolism, and naturally present catecholamines; it may stimulate brain opiate receptors.

transdermal route of administration (drug patch).   That parenteral route of drug administration which involves placing a substance directly onto the skin (i.e., scopolamine patch for seasickness).

vehicle.   The compound, usually inert and without active ingredients, in which a drug is dissolved and dispensed.

vein.   The part of the circulatory system that carries blood from the capillaries to the heart (as opposed to an artery).

ventral tegmental area (VTA).   The specific area in the telencephalon below the cerebral cortex that is involved in the mediation of pleasure and has a high density of opiate and dopamine receptors.

ventricle.   The caverns inside the central nervous system that are filled with cerebral spinal fluid.

vesicle.   The specialized protein structure in neurons in which neurotransmitter molecules are stored just prior to their release when the neuron fires.

viscera.   The organs that are located inside the body cavity (for example, the heart, kidneys, etc.).

Wernicke's encephalopathy.   A condition probably caused by general gastrointestinal malabsorption (often the result of chronic heavy alcohol consumption) and characterized by memory loss, confusion, and ataxia.

yen sleep.   A restless "sleep" which is often associated with opiate withdrawal.

INDEX